W0107376

Nadia Magnenat Thalmann
Daniel Thalmann (Eds.)

Computer Animation '91

With 164 Figures, Including 79 in Color

Springer Japan KK

Prof. Nadia Magnenat Thalmann
MIRALab, Centre Universitaire d'Informatique
University of Geneva
12, rue du Lac
CH-1207 Geneva
Switzerland

Prof. Daniel Thalmann
Computer Graphics Lab.
Swiss Federal Institute of Technology
CH-1015 Lausanne
Switzerland

Cover picture:
Design: Arghyro Paouri
Artistic and technical directors: Nadia Magnenat Thalmann and
    Daniel Thalmann
Copyright: MIRALab, University of Geneva and Computer Graphics Lab.,
    Swiss Federal Institute of Technology 1990

ISBN 978-4-431-66892-3   ISBN 978-4-431-66890-9 (eBook)
DOI 10.1007/978-4-431-66890-9

© Springer Japan 1991
Originally published by Springer-Verlag Tokyo in 1991
Softcover reprint of the hardcover 1st edition 1991

Preface

This book contains invited papers and a selection of research papers submitted to Computer Animation '91, the third international workshop on Computer Animation, which was held in Geneva on May 22-24. This workshop, now an annual event, has been organized by the Computer Graphics Society, the University of Geneva, and the Swiss Federal Institute of Technology in Lausanne. During the international workshop on Computer Animation '91, the fourth Computer-generated Film Festival of Geneva, was held.

The book presents original research results and applications experience of the various areas of computer animation. This year most papers are related to character animation, human animation, facial animation, and motion control.

NADIA MAGNENAT THALMANN
DANIEL THALMANN

Table of Contents

Part III: Systems and Languages for Motion Synthesis and Control

Part IV: Rendering Techniques for Animation

Part I

Facial Animation

Control Parameterization for Facial Animation

FREDERIC I. PARKE

Abstract

The control mechanisms currently used in facial animation are reviewed. It is argued that all currently used or anticipated facial animation control schemes should be viewed as parameterizations. The development of facial animation should be viewed as two independent activities; the development of "universal" control parameterizations and interfaces, and the development of optimal techniques to implement facial animation based on these parameterizations. The development of complete low level parameterizations enables the development of higher levels of control abstraction. Several possible directions for facial animation research are discussed.

Key Words: facial animation, animation control, parameterization

1. Introduction

In recent years there has been considerable renewed interest in computer based facial animation techniques. The initial efforts to represent and animate faces using computers go back almost 20 years (Chernoff 1971; Parke 1972; Gillenson 1974). The intent of this paper is to explore and develop a framework for the control aspects of facial animation. We will review, consolidate, and hopefully extend the approaches to control of facial animation.

From the animators view point, the important aspects of a facial animation system are the controllable features and characteristics, the range of control, and how control is accomplished. From the implementors point of view, the important aspects are the techniques and algorithms used to actually implement the controllable facial models.

2. Control Parameterization

The unifying theme proposed in this paper is that, from the animators view point, animation may be viewed as manipulating a set of control parameters. Animation then becomes the process of specifying and controlling parameter set values as functions of time.

Again from the animators point of view, the interesting questions are; (1) what are the parameters, (2) are the parameters adequate and appropriate, and (3) how are these parameters manipulated. The animator is not usually interested in the implementation algorithms or implementation details but only in the animation functionality provided. The animation system is viewed as a "black box" with (hopefully) a useful, predicatable interface that produces the desired results. The animator really does not care how the black box works, only that is does work and does provide appropriate functionality.

From the implementors point of view the interesting questions are; (1) what parameters should be provided, (2) what user interface to the the parameters should be provided, and (3) what techniques should be used to actually implement the facial animation system.

Most of the work in recent years has concentrated on on the latter of these; on the specific techniques for implementing facial animation. Relatively little work has been done on establishing what control functionality and what interfaces should be provided. Questions concerning useful, optimal, and "complete" control parameterizations remain mostly unanswered. The functionality provided by each implementation has been primarily influenced by the characteristics of the particular implementation technique rather than attempting to fulfill a well understood set of functionality and interface goals.

There are two major categories of specification or control parameters. The most often addressed of these concerns facial expression. The other concerns individual facial shape or conformation. Conformation control is used to select or specify a particular individual face from the universe of possible faces. Expression control is concerned with changes of facial expression. In the ideal case these two categories of control are orthogonal. Conformation should be independent of expression and expression independent of conformation.

3. Review of Facial Animation Techniques

In most facial animation systems to date, the visible surfaces of the face are modeled as networks of connected polygons as illustrated in Figure 3. The goal of the various animation techniques is to control the polygon vertex positions over time such that the rendered facial surfaces have the desired shapes in each frame of the animated sequence. A few implementations such as Waite (1989) have used curved surface techniques rather than polygon modeling techniques. However, the goal of controlling surface shape remains the same.

3.1 Key Expression Interpolation

Among the earlist and still most widely used schemes for implementing and controlling facial animation is the use of key expression poses and interpolation. Parke (1972) first demonstrated the use of this approach to produce viable facial animation. The basic idea and the control parameterization are very simple - and also limited. The idea is to collect by some means geometric data describing the face in at least two different expression poses. Then a single control parameter, the interpolation coefficient in the case of linear interpolation, is used as a function of time to change the face from one expression into the other. Figure 1 illustrates this approach. The two key expression poses are shown on the left and the right of the image. The middle image is an interpolation between the key poses.

This idea can be expanded in several ways. More than two expression poses may be used. If for example, four expressions are available then two interpolation parameters may be used to generate an expression which is a bi-linear blend of the four key poses. If eight key expressions are available then three interpolation parameters may be used to generate a tri-linear expression blend. Four interpolation parameters and 16 key expressions allow blending in a four dimensional interpolation space. Higher dimensionalities are also possible but probably not useful to the animator since this higher dimension expression interpolation is not very intuitive.

Another way of exploiting multiple expression poses is to allow pair-wise selection of the poses and use a single interpolation parameter to blend between the selected poses. This involves three parameters; starting pose, ending pose, and interpolation value.

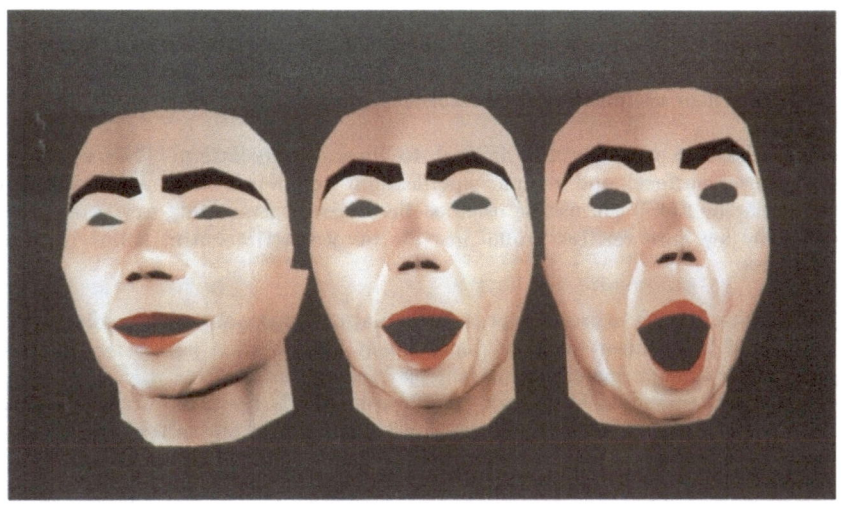

Figure 1 - Key expression interpolation. The middle face
is an interpolation of the left and right key poses.

Figure 2 - Bi-linear conformation interpolation. The
center face is an interpolated blend of the four corner faces.

Again, if many expression poses are available, they could be selected four at a time and used as the basis for bi-linear expression blending. Or, even selected eight at a time as the basis for tri-linear blending. The possible variations on these schemes seem quite open ended. However, their usefulness is not established.

These approaches are certainly not limited to linear interpolation. The vast array of parametric curve, surface, and volume specification techniques such as B-splines, beta-splines, etc. (Bartles 1987) can also be used as the basis for generating expression blends of key poses. The key pose vertices would provide the geometric control points required by these techniques.

A useful extension to the expression pose interpolation approach is to subdivide the face into a number of independent regions. Independent interpolation parameters are used for each region. This extends the control parameter space in an intuitive way. An example of this approach, first presented by Kleiser (1989), is to divide the face into an upper region and a lower region. The upper region is used primarily for emotional expression while the lower region is used primarily for speech expression. This allows some orthogonality between emotion and speech control. Special care must be exercised along the boundaries between the regions.

It should be pointed out that the use of key poses and interpolation is not limited just to expression animation. If poses for several different individuals are used, then animation of the face from one individual conformation into another is possible. Figure 2 illustrates bi-linear interpolation of four different individual faces. The central face is a blend of the four corner faces.

All of the key pose interpolation schemes outlined above have limitations. First, the range of expression control is directly related to the number and disparity of expression poses available. An expression which falls outside the bounds of the key pose set is unattainable except perhaps by extrapolation, an inherently risky approach. Also, each of the key poses requires an explicit geometric data collection or generation effort. For a large set of poses, this is a daunting task. If different individuals, as well as various expression poses, are to be included then the number of key poses may become very large. In all but the simplest cases, providing intuitive, orthogonal control parameters to the animator is difficult.

3.2 Ad-Hoc Parameterizations

Motivated by the difficulties associated with the key pose interpolation approach, Parke (1974, 1982) developed ad-hoc parameterized models. The desire was to create an encapsulated model which would generate a very wide range of faces based on a limited set of input parameter values. The goal was a model which allowed both facial expression and facial conformation to be controlled by the parameter set. The ideal would be a model that allowed any possible faces with any possible expressions to be specified by selecting the appropriate parameter value set. The ad-hoc models created to date are certainly less than ideal, but do allow a wide range of expressions for a fairly wide range of facial conformations. Example faces generated with this approach are shown in Figures 4, 5, and 6. As stated above, the challenge is to determine a "good" set of control parameters and then to implement a model that uses these parameters to generate the desired range of faces.

For the ad-hoc models developed to date, the parameter sets are fairly primitive and low level. The approach has been to apply operations such as rotation, scaling, positional offsets, and interpolation in combination to regions of the face. The control parameters provided include:

Expression	Conformation
eyelid opening	jaw width
eyebrow arch	forehead shape
eyebrow separation	nose length and width
jaw rotation	cheek shape
mouth width	chin shape
mouth expression	neck shape
upper lip position	eye size and separation
mouth corner position	face region proportions
eyes "look at"	overall face proportions

About ten expression parameters, as shown above, allow the animator to fairly easily specify and control a wide range of facial expressions. As implemented, about 20 parameters are used to control a limited range of facial conformation. Conformation parameterization is more open ended and less understood than expression parameterization.

These ad-hoc models were developed with little theoretical basis and without careful attention to facial anatomy. They were experimentally derived to represent the visible surface features of the face based on observation and a general knowledge of the underlying structures.

3.3 Muscle Action Models

The detailed anatomy of the head and face is a complex assembly of bones, cartilage, muscles, nerves, blood vessels, glands, fatty tissue, connective tissue, skin, and hair. To date, no facial animation models based on this complete detailed anatomy have been reported. However, several models have been developed which are based on simplified models of facial bone structure, muscles, connective tissue, and skin. A detailed look at the properties of human skin is presented in Pieper (1989). These models provide the ability to manipulate facial expression based primarily on simulating the characteristics of the facial muscles.

Platt and Badler (1981) developed a partial face model in which the vertices of the face surface (the skin) were interconnected elastically and also connected to the underlying bone structures by muscles modeled with elastic properties and contraction forces. The face expression was manipulated by applying forces to the elastically connected skin mesh via the underlying muscles. The muscle actions used were patterned after the Facial Action Coding System (FACS) described below.

3.4 The Facial Action Coding System

A widely used scheme for describing facial expressions was developed by Ekman and his colleagues (1977). Although not intended for use in computer animation, this descriptive scheme has been used as the basis for expression control in a number of facial animation models. This system describes the most basic facial muscle actions and their effect on facial expression. Ekman developed this system as a means of describing or encoding all possible facial expressions. It includes all muscle actions which can be independently controlled. Examples of the 46 Facial Action Coding units are listed below.

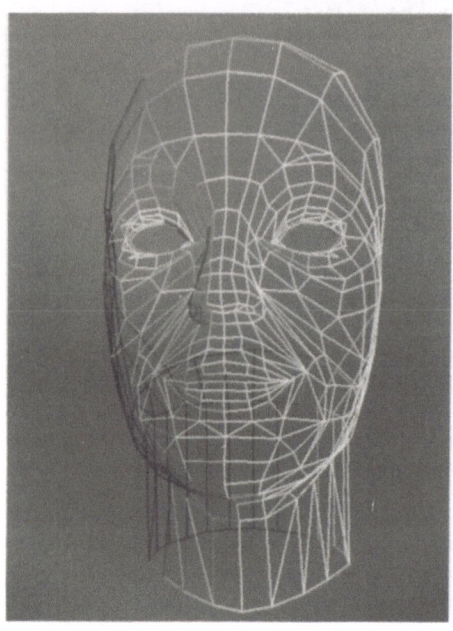

Figure 3 - Typical face model polygon structure.

Figure 4 - Parametric expression 1.

Figure 5 - Parametric expression 2.

Figure 6 - Parametric expression 3.

Action Unit	Muscular Basis
Lip Corner Puller	Zygomatic Major
Lower Lip Depressor	Depressor Labii
Lip Tightener	Orbicularis Oris
Chin Raiser	Mentalis
Upper Eyelid Raiser	Levator Palpebrae Superioris
Dimpler	Buccinnator
Wink	Orbicularis Oculi

3.5 Additional Muscle Models

Waters (1987) developed a face model which includes two types of muscles; linear muscles that pull, and sphincter muscles that squeeze. Like Platt and Badler, he uses a simple spring and mass model for the skin and muscles. However, his muscles have vector properties which are independent of the underlying bone structure. This makes the muscle model independent of specific face topology. Each muscle has a zone of influence. The influence of a particular muscle is reduced as a function of radial distance from the muscle vector point. Waters also uses control parameters based on FACS.

Magnenat-Thalmann, et. al. (1988) developed another muscle based model in which the control parameters are "Abstract Muscle Action" (AMA) procedures. These AMA procedures are similar to but not the same as the FACS action units. A partial list of the 30 AMA procedures is given below.

Vertical_Jaw	Close_Upper_Lip
Right_Eyelid	Close_Lower_Lip
Left_Eyelid	Compressed_Lip
Right_Zygomatic	Move_Right_Eyebrow
Left_Zygomatic	Move_Left_Eyebrow

Since these AMA procedures are not independent, ordering of the actions is important. This model allows facial control by manipulating the parameter values at the low-level AMA procedures and also at a higher "expressions" level. "Expressions" are formed by controlling the AMA procedures in groups. Two types of expression level control were developed; emotions and phonemes.

Extensions to the Waters model have recently been reported (Terzopoulos 1990). The same FACS based control parameterization is retained but the facial tissues are now modeled using a three layer deformable lattice structure. The three layers correspond to the skin, the subcutaneous fatty tissue, and the muscles. The bottom surface of the muscle layer is attached to the underlying bone.

3.6 "Performance" Driven Animation

Several authors have reported facial animation control techniques that rely on information derived from human performances. An early example of this is a technique used in making the short animated film "Tony De Peltrie." Bergeron (1985) reported on the use of expression mapping or expression slaving. A human face was photographically digitized for a large number of expressions. A technique was developed to map from the normal human face to the very exaggerated "Tony" caricature face. The human face shape change in the various digitized expressions was mapped to the caricature face. In this way a library of character expressions was developed and used to control the animation.

Parke at NYIT used more traditional rotoscoping techniques in conjunction with a parameterized facial model to animate the "hostess" character for the "3DV" animation. Video of a live action performance was manually analyzed on a frame by frame basis. This analysis was used to determine key frame parameter values. These parameter values were then smoothly interpolated to control the final facial animation.

At the SIGGRAPH 88 film show, Brad deGraf and Michael Wahrman demonstrated a real time facial animation system. This system (deGraf 1989) used a high performance graphics workstation to display a parameterized facial model controlled in real time. The real time control was achieved using special purpose interactive input devices called "waldos." The waldo is an multi-axis electromechanical device that allowed a "puppeteer" to control a number of facial parameters simultaneously in real time.

Recently Terzopoulos and Waters (1990) reported on the development of automated techniques for estimating face muscle contraction parameters from video sequences. These muscle contraction parameters can be used to drive a facial animation model or as input to further analysis such as automatic expression recognition.

Williams (1990) has also reported on techniques to automatically track information from video performances and to use that information to control facial animation. In his system, a number a fiducial points on the surface of a real face are automatically tracked. The locations of these points are used to control a texture map based technique which generates quite realistic facial animation.

4. Speech Synchronization

Speech synchronized animation is important in the context of this paper for two reasons. First, any control parameterization should certainly support speech animation. Second, as we shall see, speech animation control is often a good example of second level parameterized control. In many cases, speech animation is controlled using a higher level parameterization built on top of a lower level basic parameterization. The idea of building more abstract, higher level parameterizations on top of lower level, more detailed parameterizations can be very powerful.

The second level parameterization used in speech animation is usually in terms of speech phonemes. A fairly small number of phonemes are needed to produce convincing animation. The required phonemes are specified in terms of the lower level basic parameters. The higher level control is defined in terms of phoneme transitions which are in turn transformed by the system into the lower level parameter transitions. It is important that the speech parameterization be orthogonal to the emotional parameters. The same words may be spoken with a number of different emotional overlays. A phrase may be said with joy, with sadness, with anger, or with no emotion at all.

The second level phoneme parameterization approach has been used by Bergeron and Lachapelle (1985), Lewis and Parke (1987), Hill et. al. (1988), and Magnenat-Thalmann et. al. (1988) to produce successful speech animation. Parke (1974) produced the first speech animation using only basic low level parameters.

Speech animation points to a deficiency in most facial models. Few models include the interior of the mouth as part of the model. High quality speech animation requires that at least some parts of the mouth interior be included. At least the most visible part of the tongue and the more visible teeth should be included. Control of the tongue should be included in the low level parameter set and reflected in the higher level phoneme parameterization.

Efforts to automate the production of speech animation have been reported by Hill et. al. (1988) and Lewis and Parke (1987). These two approaches are quite different. The approach reported by Hill was to start with text for the desired speech and transform it into a phoneme sequence. The phoneme sequence is then used to control speech generation algorithms or hardware and also to control a parameterized facial animation system. The synthetic speech and the facial image sequence are merged to form the final speech animation. In the approach reported by Lewis, the desired speech is spoken and recorded. This recording is then sampled and algorithmically analyzed to produce a timed sequence of pauses and phonemes. This timed sequence is then used to control a facial animation model using second level phoneme parameterization. The generated facial image sequence is merged with the original spoken soundtrack to form the final speech animation.

5. Ideal Parameterizations

The ideal parameterization and interface is one which allows the animator to "easily" specify any individual face with any speech and/or expression sequence. This is in fact is the definition for a "universal" parameterization. One which enables all possible individual faces and which enables all possible expressions and expression transitions.

No implemented facial parameterization to date is even close to being universal. As was outlined above, most of the implementations have focused on expression control. Only the early work by Parke (1974, 1982) included control of conformation as part of the parameterization. The FACS seems the best current basis for expression parameterization, but is probably not ideal from the animators viewpoint. None of the existing facial animation systems appears to implement the complete set of FACS action units.

The available bases for conformation parameterizations are much more tenuous. Sources of conformation information include facial anatomy, physical anthropology, and the art disciplines concerned with human representation. Principles from sculpture and portraiture may be useful. The notions of distortion and exaggeration from conventional animation also play a role.

Input and guidance from animators is certainly needed in the development of good, useful parameterizations. The focus should be on developing powerful control parameter sets that are motivated by the needs of the facial animator, NOT based on the characteristics of a particular implementation scheme.

5.2 Quality of Control Parameterizations

Assuming that truly universal parameterizations are not possible, at least in the near term, what are the metrics for judging the quality of a control parameterization? Attributes such as control range, complexity, number of parameters, intuitive, natural, and interfaces immediately come to mind. Certainly an important measure is the range of possible faces and expressions that can be specified. How much of the universe of faces and facial expression is covered by the parameterization? Judgement in this aspect is somewhat application dependent. For example, if the application only requires animation of one specific character then conformation control is not a big issue.

Complexity, number of parameters, intuitive, and natural are all directly related attributes. The number of parameters provided and the overall complexity of the parameterization should be just sufficient. Unnecessary parameters or parameter complexity should be avoided. Ease of use will be strongly coupled to how natural and intuitive are the parameters and the interface to the parameters.

Subtlety and orthogonality are also measures of parameterization quality. Subtle variations in expression and conformation are often needed. The ability of a parameterization to support these subtle variations is highly desired. Mutual independence of the parameters is an issue. The change in one parameter value should have minimal and predictable interaction with other parameters. Change in one parameter should not require reworking other parameter values. This is particularly true for the interactions between expression and conformation parameters and between speech and expression parameters.

Another measure of an effective parameterization is its capability to serve as the basis for higher levels of control abstraction. As in the case of speech animation, the construction of control parameters at the phoneme or higher levels of abstraction, built on top of the basic parameterization should be possible.

6. Future Directions

A major focus of future efforts should be on development of the effective general parameterizations discussed above. The availability of such control mechanisms would greatly facilitate development of very capable interactive facial animation systems. It would also support the developments outlined below.

6.1 Behavior Driven Systems

An area of much current interest in the computer animation community is the development of animation techniques that operate at the behavior level. That is, the animator/director expresses the desired actions in terms of high level behaviors rather than in detailed low level motions. This work to date has concentrated on high level activities such as legged locomotion and grasping objects. The underlying detailed control parameters for these activities are very well defined.

The ability of the animator to specify facial actions in terms of high level behaviors is certainly desired. The availability of complete, well defined low level control parameters for the face would greatly facilitate development of behavior level animation capabilities.

6.2 Story Driven Animation

Takashima, et. al. (1987) outlined the development of a story driven animation system. This is an example of animation control at a very high level of abstraction. Their system was limited to simple childrens stories. However, it did demonstrate a useful framework for such systems. Their system is based on three major activities; story understanding, stage direction, and action generation. One can envision future story driven systems which would include facial animation. Story understanding and stage direction are largely knowledge based AI activities. Behavior driven facial animation systems as discussed above would be a part of the action generation activity.

7. Summary

A number of facial animation implementations have been reviewed. Each of these has an associated animation control parameterization. In most cases, the control paradigm for each implementation is intimately related to the technique. The central thesis of this paper has been that control for facial animation should be viewed as a parameterization and interface issue. Furthermore, parameterization development and implementation development should be decoupled. Parameterization research should focus on developing high quality parameterizations and interfaces while implementation research should focus on developing optimum techniques for generating faces and facial expressions based on these parameterizations.

Developing a truly "universal" parameterization appears very difficult and may not be possible. However, developing useful, broadly applicable parameterizations seems quite feasible and very worthwhile. Such low level parameterizations would support the development of higher level, more abstract levels of control including behavior driven and story driven animation.

References

Bartles R, Beatty J, Barsky B (1987) An Introduction to Splines for use in Computer Graphics and Geometric Modeling. Morgan Kaufmann, Los Altos CA

Bergeron P, Lachapelle P (1985) Techniques for Animating Characters. SIGGRAPH '85 Tutorial: Advanced Computer Graphics Animation 2

Chernoff H, (1971) The Use of Faces to Represent Points in N-Dimensional Space Graphically. Technical Report 71, Project NR-042-993, Office of Naval Research

deGraf B, (1989) in State of the Art in Facial Animation. SIGGRAPH '89 Course Notes 22: 10-11

Ekman P, Friensen WV (1977) Manual for the Facial Action Coding System. Consulting Psychologists Press, Palo Alto CA

Gillenson, ML (1974) The Interactive Generation of Facial Images on a CRT Using a Heuristic Strategy. Ph.D. Dissertation, Ohio State University, Columbus, Ohio

Hill DR, Pearce A, Wyvill B (1988) Animating Speech: An Automated Approach Using Speech Synthesis by Rules," Visual Computer 3: 277-289

Kleiser J, (1989) in State of the Art in Facial Animation. SIGGRAPH '89 Course Notes 22: 37-40

Lewis JP, Parke FI (1987) Automated Lipsynch and Speech Synthesis for Character Animation. Proc. CHI+CG '87, Toronto, pp 143-147

Magnenat-Thalmann N, Primeau E, Thalmann D (1988) Abstract Muscle Action Procedures for Human Face Animation. Visual Computer 3: 290-297.

Parke FI (1982) Parameterized Models for Facial Animation. IEEE CG&A 2(9): 61-68

Parke FI (1974) A Parametric Model for Human Faces. Ph.D. Dissertation, Technical Report UTEC-CSc-75-047, University of Utah, Salt Lake City, Utah

Parke FI (1972) Computer Generated Animation of Faces. Proc. ACM Nat'l Conf., 1:451-457 also M.S. Thesis, Technical Report UTEC-Csc-72-120, University of Utah, Salt Lake City, Utah

Pieper S (1989) More than Skin Deep: Physical Modeling of Facial Tissue. M. S. Thesis, MIT Media Lab, Cambridge MA

Platt SM, Badler NI (1981) Animating Facial Expressions. Computer Graphics 15(3): 245-252.

Takashima Y, Shimazu H, Tomono M (1987) Story Driven Animation. Proc. CHI+GI'87 Conf, Toronto, pp 149-153.

Terzopoulos D, Waters K (1990) Physically Based Facial Modeling, Analysis, and Animation. Visualization and Computer Animation, 1(2): 73-80

Waite C (1989) The Facial Action Control Editor, Face: A Parametric Facial Expression Editor for Computer Generated Animation. M. S. Thesis, MIT, Cambridge MA

Waters K (1987) A Muscle Model for Animating Three-Dimensional Facial Expression. Computer Graphics 21(3): 17-24

Williams L, (1990) Performance Driven Facial Animation. Computer Graphics 24(3): 235-242

Frederic I. Parke is a Professor of Computer Science at NYIT and Director of the NYIT Computer Graphics Laboratory from 1981 until 1989. Dr. Parke has been involved in the development of facial animation since 1971 and received his Ph.D. in 1974 from the University of Utah. He is the author of a number of technical papers on facial animation and has lectured widely on this subject. He chaired the SIGGRAPH "Introduction to Computer Animation" tutorials in 1983, 1984, and 1985 and the SIGGRAPH "State of the Art in Facial Animation" tutorials in 1989 and 1990.

Address: NYIT Computer Graphics Laboratory, Wheatley Road, Old Westbury, New York, 11568.

Linguistic Issues in Facial Animation

CATHERINE PELACHAUD, NORMAN I. BADLER, and MARK STEEDMAN

ABSTRACT

Our goal is to build a system of 3D animation of facial expressions of emotion correlated with the intonation of the voice. Up till now, the existing systems did not take into account the link between these two features. We will look at the rules that control these relations (*intonation/emotions* and *facial expressions/emotions*) as well as the coordination of these various modes of expressions. Given an utterance, we consider how the messages (what is *new/old* information in the given context) transmitted through the choice of accents and their placement, are conveyed through the face. The facial model integrates the action of each muscle or group of muscles as well as the propagation of the muscles' movement. Our first step will be to enumerate and to differentiate facial movements linked to emotions as opposed to those linked to conversation. Then, we will examine what the rules are that drive them and how their different functions interact.

Key words: facial animation, emotion, intonation, coarticulation, conversational signals

1   INTRODUCTION

The face is an important and complex communication channel. While talking, a person is rarely still. The face changes expressions constantly. Emotions are part of our daily life. They are one of the most important human motivations. They are mainly expressed with the face and the voice. Faces have their own language where each expression is not only related to emotions, but is also linked to the intonation and the content of speech, following the flow of speech. Many linguists and psychologists have noted the importance of spoken intonation for conveying different emotions associated with speakers' messages. Moreover, some psychologists have found some universal facial expressions linked to emotions and attitudes. Thus, in order to improve facial animation systems, understanding such a language and its interaction with intonation is one of the most important steps.

There already exist some facial animation systems which incorporate speech and facial expression. F. Parke (1982, 1990; Lewis 1987) was the first one to propose a facial model whose animation was based on parameters which effect not only the structure of the model but also its expressions (opening the mouth, raising the eyebrows). N. Magnenat-Thalmann and D. Thalmann, for their movie "Rendez-vous à Montreal" (1987) differentiated two levels of facial expressions (one for the shape of the mouth for phonemes and the second for emotions), and they control their model through parameters. The separation between conformation parameters and expression parameters imply the independence of the production of an expression and the considered face. But, the use of a limited set of parameters enhances a limited set of facial expressions. Various animations such as "Tony de Peltrie" (Bergeron 1985) and "Sextone for President" (Kleiser 1988) were made from a library of digitized expressions. Such systems are very tedious to manipulate and are valid for one particular facial model only.

M. Nahas, H. Huitric and M. Saintourens defined a B-spline model (1988) where the animation is done using given control points. K. Waters (1987, 1990) simulated muscle motion with a 2-D deformation function. Lip shapes for each visible vowel and consonant were defined in the same way. He recorded real actors and manually matched lip positions and phonemes. But, collecting this type of data for these last two models is very difficult. On the other hand, point-to-point control has the advantage of more realistically producing the facial tissue.

D. Hill, A. Pearce, and B. Wyvill, using F. Parke's parametric model (Pearce 1986; Hill 1988; Wyvill 1990) presented an automatic process for synchronizing speech and lip movements. They approach expressions through a set of rules where every element (of the sound and of the face) can be modified interactively through the use of parameters, however this model would be enhanced if the control was based on the properties of facial muscles (Hill 1988).

No system up to now has considered the link between intonation and emotion to drive their system.

Our work will resolve the difficulty of manipulating the action of each muscle by offering to the user a higher level of animation by lip synchronization and automatic computation of the facial expressions related to the patterns of the voice. We will differentiate facial expressions linked to emotion from nonexpressive ones. We will elaborate a repertory of such movements.

Our facial model integrates the action of each muscle or group of muscles as well as the propagation of the muscles' movement. It is also adapted to the **FACS** notation (Facial Action Coding System) created by P. Ekman and W. Friesen (Ekman 1978) to describe facial expressions. The computation of the facial expressions linked to one particular utterance with its intonation and emotion is done independently of the facial model. Contrary to the technique of using a stored library of expressions (Bergeron 1985; Kleiser 1988) which computes facial expressions for one model only, this method used the decomposition of the facial model into two levels: the physical level (described in previous sections) and the expression level. The facial expressions may be applied to any other facial model (having the same underlying structure).

After defining what *emotion* is for present purposes, we introduce our facial model. We also present the intonational system we are using and the characteristics of the voice for each of the emotions we are looking at.

Finally, we will characterize one by one the various types of facial expressions. Specifically, we will look at how we solve lip synchronization and coarticulation problems.

2 EMOTION

An emotion is generated not only by the perception of an action but also by its signifigance to us. It is a function of our memories, our present and future motivations. Emotion is described as a process (Scherer 1988; Ekman 1989), with various components such as physiological responses (visceral and muscular states), autonomic nervous system and brain responses, verbal responses (vocalizations), memories, feelings and facial expressions. For example, anger can be characterized by muscle tension, decrease of salivation, lowered brow, tense lips, increase of the heart rate. Each emotion modifies in a particular way the physiology of a being. The variations of physical organs affect the vocal track while the variations of muscle actions affect the facial expressions.

Six emotions (anger, disgust, fear, happiness, sadness and surprise) were found to have universal facial expressions (Ekman 1975). We have chosen to study these. There are three main areas in the face where changes occur: the upper part of the face with the brows and forehead, the eyes, and the lower part of the face with the mouth (Ekman 1975). Each emotion is characterized by specific facial changes: fear is recognized by the raised and drawn together eyebrows and lips stretched tense; sadness is characterized by the inner side of the brows drawn up, the upper eyelid inner corner raised and the corners of the lips down (Figure 1).

3 OTHER FACIAL EXPRESSIONS AND THEIR RULES

Animating the face by specifying every action manually is a very tedious task and often does not yield every subtle facial expression. While talking, a person not only uses his lips to talk, but his eyebrows may raise, his eyes may move, his head may turn, he may blink...

3.1 Clustering of the Facial Expressions

All facial expressions do not necessarily correspond to emotion. Some facial movements are used to delineate items in a sequence as punctuation marks do in a written text. The raising eyebrows can punctuate a discourse and not be a signal of surprise. P. Ekman (1989) characterizes facial expressions into the following groups:

emblems correspond to movements whose meaning is very well-known and culturally dependent. They are produced to replace common verbal expressions. For example, instead of saying 'sure' or 'I agree' one can nod.

emotional emblems (also called referential expressions or mock expressions) are made to convey signals about emotions. A person uses them to mention an emotion: he does not feel the emotion at the time of the facial action. He only refers to them. It is quite common, when talking about a disgusting thing, to wrinkle one's nose. Such movements are part of the emotional state (wrinkling the nose is part of the facial expression of disgust).

conversational signals (also called illustrators) are made to punctuate a speech, to emphasize it. Raising the eyebrows often accompanies an accented vowel.

punctuators are movements occurring at pauses.

regulators are movements that help the interaction between speaker/listener. They control the speaking turn in a conversation.

manipulators correspond to the biological needs of the face, like blinking the eyes to keep them wet, and wetting the lips.

affect displays are the facial expressions of emotion.

We have to include all these movements to obtain a more complete facial animation. A face can make many more movements such as grimacing, contorting, lip-biting, twitching, and so on, but we are not considering them. They are not related, a priori, to emotion or speech. Also, the consideration of emblems and emotional emblems is out of scope of this study since they imply the voluntary participation of the speaker. They are given by the semantic of the utterance and not (at least directly) by the intonation of the voice.

3.2 Organization of the Rules

The computation of facial expressions corresponding to each item listed above, is done by a set of rules. Two parameters are used to define an action: its type and its time of occurrence. Our rationale is to allow the user to modify one of the parameters for one action without touching any other variable in the system. It is a very useful scheme since the type of actions performed by a person while talking is still not very well-known by researchers. Most of the people show eyebrow movements to accentuate a word but other facial action may be chosen such as nose wrinkling or eye flashes (Ekman 1979). The user just needs to modify the rule which describes the action and need not alter the rules of occurrence. Another unknown parameter is the effective occurrence of an action. Indeed, a paralanguage feature is not always accompanied by a facial movement. The function of the last one is established (focus one word, etc) but their effective existence is uncertain. Thus we need to have access to the timing of the occurrence of an action. Moreover, the attitude of the speaker (what he wants to convey) and his personality are important factors in his facial behavior. But such points are not yet incorporated in the present study. Offering a tool to compute separately each of the above groups of facial expressions offers a better grasp and control over the final animation.

3.3 Synchronism

An important property linking intonation and facial expression (in fact, it is extended to body movement) is the existence of synchrony between them (Condon 1971). Synchrony implies that changes occurring in speech and in body movements should appear at the same time.

Synchrony occurs at all levels of speech. That is, it occurs at the level of phoneme, syllable (these two are defined by how their patterns are articulated), word, phrase or long utterance. Some body and facial motions are isomorphic to these groups. Some of them are more adapted to the phoneme level (like an eye blink), some others at the word level (like a frown) or even at the phrase level (like an hand gesture).

The main point is that there is no part of speech or body motion that is not grouped together in some sort of cluster. This is the basic rule we are using to compute animation in relation to speech.

4 FACIAL MODEL

We present here the descriptive notational system and the facial model we are using.

4.1 Facial Action Coding System

Facial Action Coding System or **FACS** is a notational system developed by P. Ekman and W. Friesen (Ekman 1978). It describes all visible facial movements that are either emotional signals or conversational signals. **FACS** is derived from an analysis of the anatomical basis of facial movements. Because every facial movement is the result of muscular action, a system could be obtained based on how each muscle of the face acts to change visible appearance.

One of the constraints of **FACS** is, by its descriptive functionality, that it deals only with movements and what is visible on the face (no other perturbations, like blushing or tears, are considered). They also introduce what they call an Action Unit (**AU**). It is an action produced by one or more muscles.

4.2 Structural Model

Our model of the face was developed by Steve Platt (Figure 1); it is a hierarchically structured, regionally defined object (Platt 1985). The face is decomposed into regions and subregions. A particular region corresponds to one muscle or group of muscles. Each of them is simulated by specifying the precise location of their attachment to the surface structure. These regions can, under the action of a muscle, either contract or be affected by a propagated movement of an adjacent region. A region can contain 3 types of information:

- physical information (what is displayed on the screen): a set of 3D points.

- functional information (where it is now): how an **AU** will modify the region.

- connective information: to which regions its movements should be propagated in order to bring secondary movement.

We use **FACS** here to encode any basic action. Concurrent actions can occur. In such a case the final position of a region is the summation of movements (or propagation) of all applied **AUs**. The hierarchy of description of the model allows us to modify its physical shape (i.e. the geometrical position of the points) without affecting the functional information (how an action is performed) and vice versa, where no change on the underlying structural definition (connection of the regions) is made. Both types of information are, thus, independent of each other. This model uses **FACS** and simulates the muscle propagation, taking into account secondary motions. It integrates the elasticity of the muscle and the skin. We choose this model for its muscle structures, movement simulation, its hierarchical definition of the face and its decompostion between physical and functional parameters.

5   INTONATION

Intonation is defined as the melodic feature of an utterance and can be decomposed into three components linked to: the syntax of an utterance (such as interrogative, declarative), the attitudes of the speaker (what the speaker wants to explicitly show to the listener: for example, politeness, irony) and finally the emotions (involuntary aspects of the speaker's speech) (Scherer 1984). In our current research, we are not considering the second feature. The third feature, also called *paralanguage* (Crystal 1975), is differentiated mainly by the pitch (while frequency is a physical property of sound, pitch is a subjective one), loudness (the perceived intensity of a sound), pitch contour (the global envelope of the pitch), tempo (rate of speech) and pause. For example, anger is characterized by a high pitch level, wide pitch range and large pitch variations. Its intensity has a very high mean, a high range and also high fluctuations. Its articulation is precise and its speech rate fast. Sadness, however, is characterized by a low pitch level, a narrow pitch range and very small pitch variations. Its intensity is soft, its mean low, its range narrow and its fluctuations small. Its speech rate is slow with the highest number of pauses of the longest duration (Cahn 1989; Ladd 1985; Williams 1981).

To define the syntactic structure of intonation, we are using Janet Pierrehumbert's notation (Hirschberg 1986). Under this definition, intonation consists of a linear sequence of accents. Utterances are decomposed into *intonational* and *intermediate* phrases. Both of them consist of *pitch accent(s)*, a *phrase accent*; intonational phrases are terminated by a *boundary tone*. Different intonational "tunes" composed of these elements are used to convey various discourse-related distinctions of "focus". That is givenness or newness of information, contrast and propositional attitude. Thus they serve to indicate the status of the current phrase related to the next one, for example, the continuation of the same topic or the introduction of a new one.

We can represent the decomposition of an utterance into intonational (or intermediate) phrases by brackets (see below). The appropriate use of intonational bracketing is determined by the context in which the utterance is produced and by the meaning of the utterance (i.e. what the speaker wants to focus on, what he considers as new information versus old). This bracketing is (partially) reflected in intonation.

Consider the sentence *"Julia prefers popcorn"* (the example is related to one discussed in (Steedman 1990)). The possible intonational bracketings reflect the distinction between an utterance which is about *Who prefers popcorn* or about *What Julia prefers*:

- (Julia)(prefers popcorn)

- (Julia prefers)(popcorn)

These bracketings can be imposed by intonational tones.

For example, in the following context, we will have the following tune:

```
Question: Well, what about JUlia? What does SHE prefer?
Answer: (JUlia prefers) (pOpcorn).
Accent: (L+H*      LH%) ( H*  LL%)
```

(**H** and **L** denote high and low tones which combine in the various pitch accents and boundary tones. **L+H*** and **H*** are different kinds of pitch accent, and **LH%**, **LL%** and **L** below are boundaries.)

By contrast, in the following context, we will have a different bracketing, imposed by a different set of intonational tunes:

```
Question: Well, what about the pOpcorn? Who prefers IT?
Answer: (JUlia) (prefers pOpcorn).
Accent: (H*  L) (         L+H* LH%)
```

These two examples show different intonational patterns. They emphasize different information (in the first context, the new message is *'popcorn'* versus *'Julia'* in the second one). The bracketing of the sentence, the placement of pauses and the type of accents vary also. Consequently the facial conversational signals and punctuators related to the first utterance will differ from those of the second one.

We assume that the input is an utterance already decomposed and written in its phonetic representation with its accents marked in its bracketed elements. For the moment, we are using recorded natural speech to guide our animation. After recording a sentence, we extract from its spectrogram the timing of each phoneme and pause. We would like later on to use analysis-and-resynthesis methods to automate the determination of paralanguage parameters and phoneme timing (Charpentier 1989; Hamon 1989) driven by a representation like the above.

6   STEPS FOR COMPUTING FACIAL EXPRESSIONS

Each facial expression is expressed as a set of **AUs**. The sentence is scanned at various levels. The lip shapes and blinks are computed at the phoneme level while the conversational and punctuator signals are obtained by its intonational pattern at the word level. First, we compute the list of **AUs** for the given emotion. We add to this list the **AUs** needed for the mouth shape synchronized with each phoneme. Finally, using a set of rules, we compute the conversational signals, the punctuators, head and eye movements, and eyeblinks.

Emotion does not modify the shape of the contour of an utterance, i.e. it does not affect either the type or the placement of the accents (which are defined, indeed, by the context of the utterance, what is new/old information to the speaker). This property allows us to compute every facial action corresponding to the given intonational pattern. Nevertheless, their final occurrence and their type is emotion dependent. The emotion will affect in an overall manner the first computation. In further sections, we will explain how we derive this set of rules.

Our first step for the animation is lip synchronization. Speechreading techniques offer the possibility to define a lip shape for each cluster of phonemes.

6.1   Speechreading

J. Jeffers and M. Barley (1971) define speechreading as "the gross process of looking at, perceiving, and interpreting spoken symbols". This method is designed for hearing-impaired. These people learn to read speech from lip movements and facial expressions. Unfortunately, there exists a lot of homophonous words; that is, words that look alike on the face, even if they differ in spelling and meaning. These words cannot be differentiated by their lip, jaw or tongue movements. For example, 'b', 'p', and 'm' involve the same facial movements. Moreover, most of the speech sounds are highly, if not completely invisible (they might involve only an obscure tongue movement, for example).

In our case, we are only interested in visible movements. Vowels and consonants are divided into clusters corresponding to their lip shapes. Each of these groups are ranked from the highest to the lowest visible movements (for example, the phonemes 'f', 'v' are part of the top group, the least deformable one, while 's', 'n' are very context dependent). We should notice that such clustering depends on the speech rate and visual conditions. These are defined by the visual accuracy the listener has of the speaker (such as light on the speaker, and physical distance between speaker and hearer). A person who articulates each word carefully shows more speech movements, of course. The faster a person speaks, the less effort he makes and fewer movements will be produced. With a fast speech rate or under poor visual conditions, the number of clusters diminishes. In addition, the lip shapes of most groups lose their well pronounced characteristics (lips drawn backward for the 'i', lips puckered for the 'o') and tend to have a more neutral position (moderate opening of the mouth).

Intonation of an utterance is the enunciation of a sequence of accented and non-accented phonemes. An accented vowel is differentiated acoustically from the remaining part of the utterance by its longer duration and increased loudness; visually, the jaw dropping motion is a characteristic of accented or emphasized segments.

This phonemic notation, however, does not tell us how to deal with the difficult problem of coarticulation. In the next section, we introduce a first attempt to solve this problem.

6.2   Coarticulation

Coarticulation means "articulatory movements associated with one phonetic segment overlap with the movements for surrounding segments" (Kent 1977). If one does not consider the problem of coarticulation, incorrect mouth positions can occur.

Speech has been decomposed into a sequence of discrete units such as syllables and phonemes. However, speech production does not follow such constructions. There is an overlap between units during their production, thus the boundaries among them are blurred.

A simple solution to the problem of coarticulation will be to look at the previous, the present, and the next phonemes to determine the mouth positions (Waters 1987). But in some cases this is not enough, since the correct position can depend on a phoneme up to five positions before or after the current one (Kent 1977).

Forward coarticulation is defined when "an articulatory adjustment for one phonetic segment is anticipated during an earlier segment in the phonetic string" (Kent 1977) while backward coarticulation is defined when "an articulatory adjustment for one segment appears to have been carried over to a later segment in the phonetic string" (Kent 1977). For example, forward coarticulation arises in a sequence of consonants (not belonging to the highly visible clusters such as 'f', 'v', ...) followed by a vowel, since the lips show the influence of the vowel on the first consonant of the sequence. In the sequence of phonemes *'istrstry'* (example cited in (Kent 77)) the influence of the 'y' is shown on the first 's' (forward rule). We have implemented these two coarticulation rules.

A complete set of such rules does not exist. To solve particular problems which cannot be solved by these two rules, we consider a three-step algorithm. On the first step, coarticulation rules are applied to all clusters which have been defined as context-dependent. The next pass is to consider relaxation and contraction time of a muscle (Bourne 1973) and finally to look at the way two consecutive actions are performed. Therefore, the speech context is considered.

After the first computation, we check that each action (**AU**) has time to contract after the previous phoneme (or, respectively, to relax before the next one). If the time between two consecutive phonemes is smaller than the contraction time of a muscle, the previous phoneme is influenced by the contraction of the current phoneme. Similarly, if the time between two consecutive phonemes is smaller than the relaxation time, the current phoneme will influence the next phoneme when relaxing.

Finally, we take into account the geometric relationship between successive actions. Indeed, the closure of the lips is more easily performed from a slightly parted position than from a puckered position. The intensity of an action is rescaled depending on its surrounding context.

At the end of these steps, we obtain a list of **AUs** for each phoneme.

These constraints between adjacent **AUs** are defined by a constant and are easily changed as is relaxation/contraction simulation. Moreover, lip shapes associated with each phoneme are determined by rules and are also easily modified. This provides a tool for phoneticians to study coarticulation problems.

7 CONVERSATIONAL SIGNALS

A stressed segment is often accompanied not by a particular movement but by an accumulation of rapid movements (such as more pronounced mouth motion, blinks, or rapid head movements).

Conversational signals may occur on an accented item within a word, or, it may stretch out over a syntactic portion of the sentence (corresponding to an emphatic movement).

Most of the time these signals involve actions of the eyebrows. P. Ekman (1989) found that **AU1+2** (the eyebrows raised of surprise) and **AU4** (the frown of anger) are commonly used. Raised eyebrows can occur to signal a question, especially when it is not syntactically defined. Head and eye motions can illustrate a word; an accented word is often accompanied by a rapid head movement (Hadar 1984; Bull 1985). A blink can also occur on a stressed vowel (Condon 1971).

Each emotion does not activate the same number of facial movements. An angry or happy person will have more facial motions than a sad person. Also, emotion intensity affects the amount and type of facial movements (Collier 1985). Thus we will select the occurrence of conversational signals depending on the emotion and intensity.

8 PUNCTUATORS

Punctuators can appear at a pause (due to hesitation) or to signal punctuation marks (such as a comma or exclamation marks) (Dittman 1974). The number of pauses affect the speech rate: a sad person has a slow speech rate due in part to a large number of long pauses, while a frightened person's speech shows very few pauses of short duration (Cahn 1989). Thus the occurrence of punctuators and their type (i.e. their corresponding facial expressions) are emotion-dependent: a happy person has the tendency to punctuate his speech by smiling. Certain types of head movements occur during pauses. A boundary point (between intermediate phrases, for example) will be underlined by slow movement and a final pause will coincide with stillness (Hadar 1984). Eyeblinks can occur also during pauses (Condon 1971).

9 REGULATORS

Regulators correspond to how people take turns speaking in a conversation, or any ritual meeting. We are still in the process of implementing this section. Much study has been given to speaking-turn system. S. Duncan (1974) enumerates them:

- Speaker-Turn-Signal: is emitted when the speaker wants to give his turn of speaking to the auditor. It is composed of several clues in his intonation, paralanguage, body movements and syntax.

- Speaker-State-Signal: is displayed at the beginning of a speaking turn. It is composed, at the least, of the speaker turning his head away from the listener and the starting of a

- Speaker-Within-Turn: is used when the speaker wants to keep his speaking turn, and assures himself that the listener is following. It occurs at the completion of a grammatical clause; the speaker turns his head toward the listener.

- Speaker-Continuation-Signal: frequently follows a Speaker-Within-Turn. In such case, the speaker turns his head (and eyes) away from the listener.

10 MANIPULATORS

Blinking is the only phenomena we are taking into account in this category. The eye blinks occur quite frequently. They serve not only to accentuate speech but also to address a physical need (to keep the eyes wet). There is at least one eye blink per utterance.

The internal structure of an eye blink, i.e., when it is closed and when it opens, is synchronized with the articulation (Condon 1971). The eye in blinking might close over one syllable and start opening again over another word/syllable. Blink occurrence is also emotion dependent. During fear, tension, and anger, excitement and lying, the amount of blinking increases; it decreases during concentrated thought (Collier 1985).

We first compute all the blinks occurring as conversational signals or punctuators. Then, since eyeblinks should occur periodically we add any necessary ones. The period of occurrence is emotion-dependent. This time will be shorter for fear and longer for sadness.

11 PUPIL SIZE

The pupil constricts in bright light, while it dilates in weak light. Moreover, a person with light eye color will have the tendency to have larger pupils and will show larger pupil dilation. Pupil changes also occur during emotional experiences. Pupil dilation is followed by pupil constriction during happiness and anger and remains dilated during fear and sadness (Hess 1975).

12 ANIMATION

We should note that every facial action (except those involved in the lip synchronization since they are already taking into account by the three-step algorithm) will have three parameters: onset, apex, and offset. Apex corresponds to the time the action is occurring. Onset and offset define the manner of appearance and disappearance of the action;they are emotion dependent. For example, surprise has the shortest onset time while sadness has the longest offset (Ekman 1984).

Having computed the list of **AUs** for each phoneme, the animation can then be performed. We apply the heuristic that quick abrupt changes for a particular portion of the face cannot occur in too short a time. The regions of the face are organized into three sets: one with high movement (like the lips, the brows), one with medium movement (forehead, cheeks), and one with low movement (outer part of the face). We compute the rate of displacement between each consecutive key-frame. That is, the average displacement of all the points inside each region of the face divided by the time separating the two frames. Each point of every frame is then modified by this *"weight"*. The in-between frames are obtained by computing the B-spline going through the weighted points (Farin 1990). This is the way to handle any brusque movement and some coarticulation problems which the proposed algorithm does not take care of.

13 EXAMPLE

Let us consider the example introduced in a previous section: *'Julia prefers popcorn'* with the emotion *disgust*. We record this utterance; we find its intonational pattern; we decompose it into a sequence of phonemes (we use Dectalk's notation); and we extract from its spectrogram the timing of each phoneme.

We consider first the computation of the lip shapes. For every phoneme, we find the group (as defined in (Jeffers 1971)) in which it belongs. Figure 3 depicts the lip shapes for the word *'popcorn'* in the case of fast and slow speech rate. The value of the speech rate modifies the clustering of phonemes; lips tend to correspond to a moderate opening of the mouth for fast speech rate. To highly malleable phonemes (such as 'n', 't'), we apply the forward and backward coarticulation rules. In Figure 2, the phoneme /LL/ in the word *'Julia'* receives the same list of **AUs** with lower intensity as its preceding vowel (/UW/ belongs to a less malleable cluster than /YY/; therefore the backward rule is applied for /LL/). Our next step is to consider the environment of each phoneme and its relaxation and contraction times. For the phoneme /YY/ in *'Julia'*, we can notice the apparition of some pucker effect from the phonemes /UW/ and /LL/. The lip shapes for /LL/ do not have enough time to relax completely from their puckered position to their extended lip shapes: Some puckered effect remains, so we have applied a control over time. On the other hand, the pucker position of the item /AO/ from the syllable *'pop'* is altered due to its surrounding lip closures for the two /PP/s, so we applied a control over space.

The emotion gives the overall orientation of the head. For the emotion *disgust*, the head has globally a backward and upward direction. The utterance is a statement: a Speaker-State-Signal (speaker looks away from listener) is emitted and the head is positioned to look down as the speaker reaches the end of the sentence.

Conversational signals appear in this example, on pitch accents under various forms. Eyebrow movements start, for both actions, at the beginning of the considered syllable. Rapid movements around the actual position of the head or a sharp repositionment of small amplitude caracterizes the head motion on the pitch accent. Moreover, blinks acting as conversational signals start at the beginning of the accented syllables and are synchronized at the phoneme level.

Disgust is characterized by few pauses, therefore no pause is found between the two intonational phrases and only the juncture pause at the end of the utterance is considered. Nose wrinkling and a blink occur then. They begin and finish at the same time as the juncture pause. The sentence finishes with slow movement followed by stillness of the head motion.

The last step is to look if more blinks are needed (called periodic blink). In our case, none is needed since already computed blinks occur at a sufficient rate. The Figure 4 summarizes in a table this sequence of coordinated expressions.

14 SUMMARY

We have presented here a tool which enhances facial animation. Our method is based on finding the link between the spoken intonation, the transmitted information in the given context, and the facial movements. First, we presented our facial model. We also enumerated and differentiated facial movements due to emotion or due to conversation. We look more particularly on the coarticulation problem where we examine how the action of a muscle is affected by temporal and spatial context. Currently we are working on the rules that coordinate these various facial motions with the intonation. Indeed, while a substantial number of these relations have been studied and described, many more remain to be investigated. We offer a tool to analyze, manipulate and integrate these different channels of communication and to facilitate the further research of human communicative faculties via animation.

15 ACKNOWLEDGEMENTS

We would like to thank Steve Platt for his facial model and for very useful comments. We would like to thank also Soetjianto and Khairol Yussof who have improved the facial model. We are also very grateful to Jean Griffin and Mike Edwards who developed the B-spline program for the animation software, and more particularly to Francisco Azuola who has included the weight parameter in this software. Finally, we would like to thank all the members of the graphics laboratory.

This research is partially supported by Lockheed Engineering and Management Services (NASA Johnson Space Center), NASA Ames Grant NAG-2-426, NASA Goddard through University of Iowa UICR, FMC Corporation, Martin-Marietta Denver Aerospace, Deere and Company, Siemens Research, NSF CISE Grant CDA88-22719, and ARO Grant DAAL03-89-C-0031 including participation by the U.S. Army Human Engineering Laboratory and the U.S. Army Natick Laboratory.

16 BIBLIOGRAPHY

M. Argyle, M. Cook (1976) Gaze and Mutual Gaze. Cambridge University Press

P. Bergeron, P. Lachapelle (1985) Controlling Facial Expressions and Body Movements in the Computer Generated Animated Short "Tony de Peltrie". ACM SIGGRAPH'85 Tutorial Notes, Advanced Computer Animation Course

G.H. Bourne (1973) The Structure and Function of Muscle. vol. III, Physiology and Biochemistry, Academic Press, Second Edition

P. Bull, G. Connelly (1985) Body Movement and Emphasis in Speech. Journal of Nonverbal Behavior, vol. 9, n. 3: 169-186

J. Cahn (1989) Generating expression in synthesized speech. Masters Thesis, M.I.T.

F. Charpentier, E. Moulines (1989) Pitch-synchronous waveform processing techniques for text-to-speech synthesis using diphones. Proceedings EUROSPEECH' 89, vol. 2

G. Collier (1985) Emotional expression. Lawrence Erlbaum Associates.

W.S. Condon, W.D. Ogston (1971) Speech and body motion synchrony of the speaker-hearer. in The perception of Language, D.H. Horton, J.J. Jenkins ed.: 150-185

D. Crystal (1975) Paralinguistics. in The body as a medium of expression, J. Benthall, T. Polhemus ed.: 163-174

A.T. Dittman (1974) The body movement-speech rhythm relationship as a cue to speech encoding. in Nonverbal Communication, Weitz ed.: 169-181

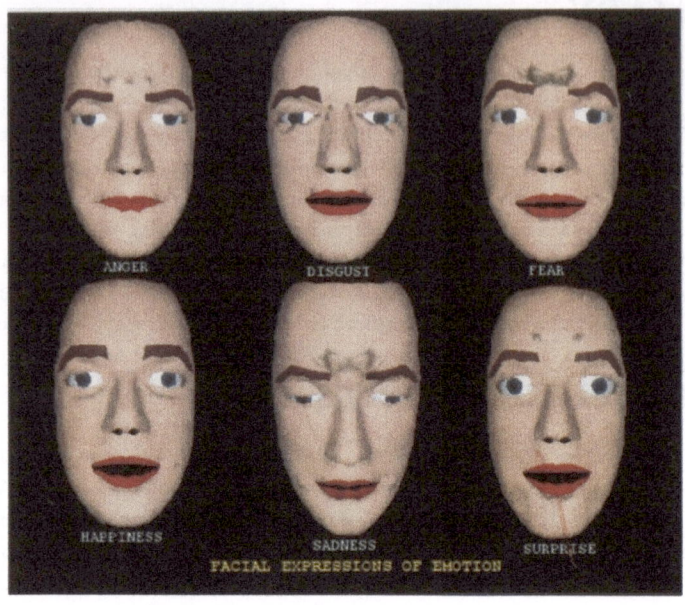

Figure 1 "Facial Expressions of Emotion"

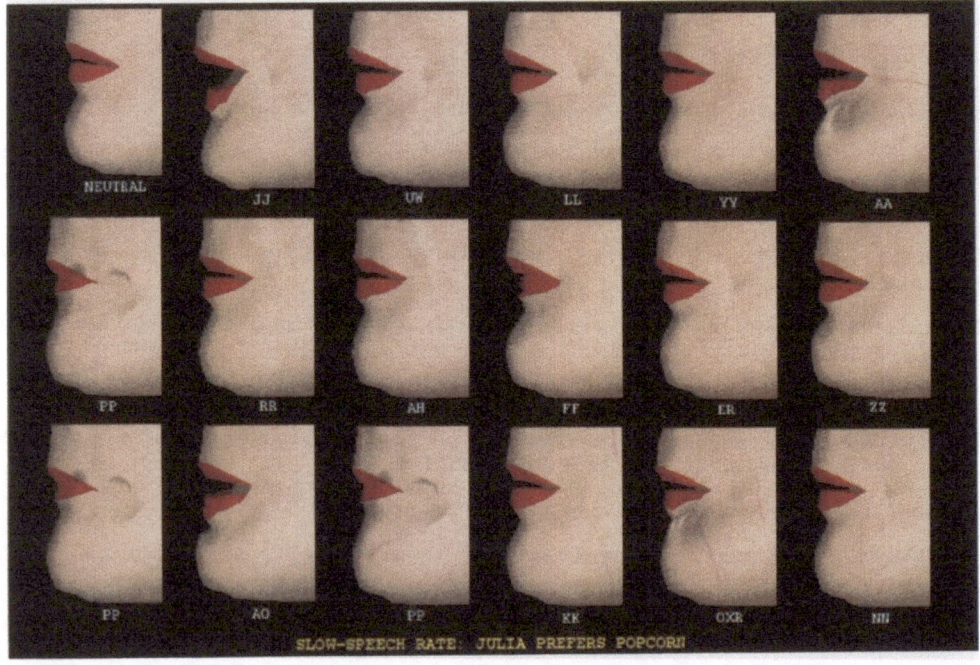

Figure 2 "Julia prefers popcorn."

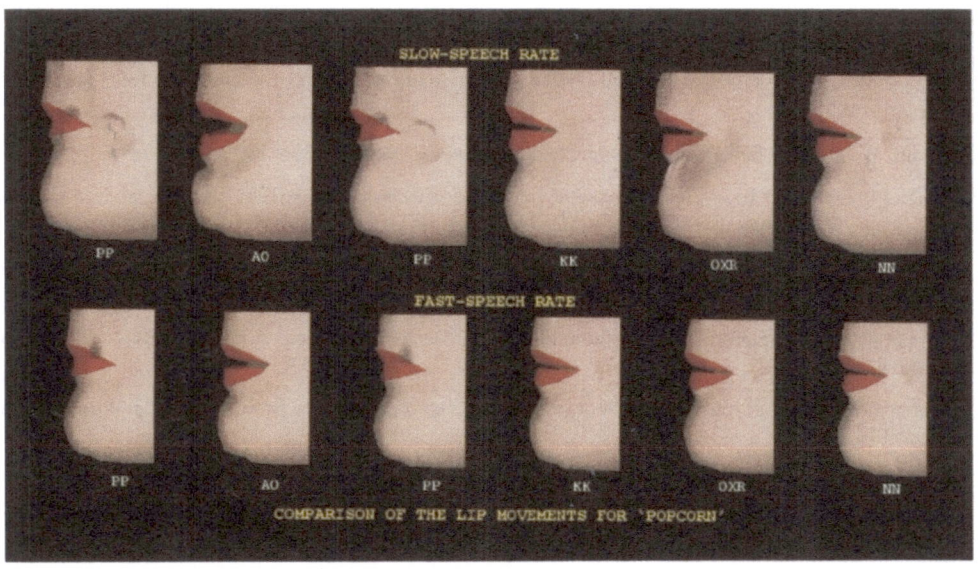

Figure 3 "Comparison for the Lip Movements for 'popcorn'"

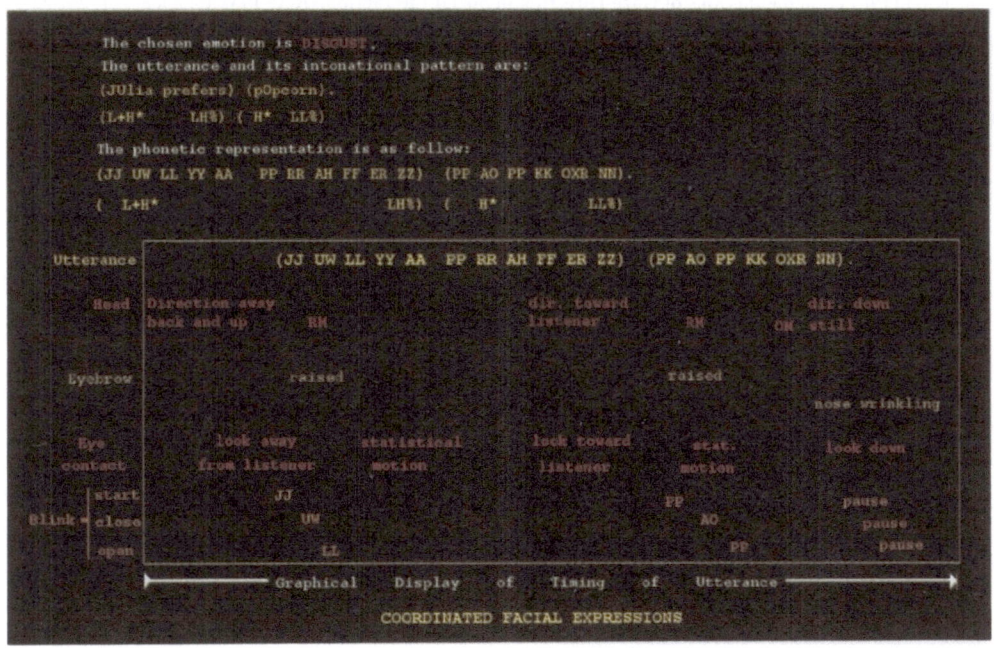

Figure 4 "Coordinated Facial Expressions"

S. Duncan (1974) On the structure of speaker-auditor interaction during speaking turns. Language in Society, v. 3: 161-180

P. Ekman, W. Friesen (1975) Unmasking the Face: A guide to recognizing emotions from facial clues. Prentice-Hall

P. Ekman, W. Friesen (1978) Facial Action Coding System. Consulting Psychologists Press

P. Ekman (1979) About brows: emotional and conversational signals. in Human ethology, M. von Cranach, K. Foppa, W. Lepenies, D. Ploog ed.: 169-249

P. Ekman (1984) Expression and the nature of emotion. in Approaches to emotion, K. Scherer, P. Ekman ed.

G. Farin (1990) Curves and Surfaces for Computed Aided Geometric Design. A Practical Guide, 2nd edition, Academic Press.

C. Hamon et al. (1969) A diphone synthesis system based on time-domain prosodic modifications of speech. ICASSP' 89.

E.H. Hess (1975) The role of the pupil size in communication. Scientific American, November: 113-119

D.R. Hill, A. Pearce, B. Wyvill (1988) Animating speech: an automated approach using speech synthesised by rules. The Visual Computer, v. 3: 277-289

J. Hirschberg, J. Pierrehumbert (1986) The intonational structuring of discourse. 24th Annual Meeting of the Association for Computational Linguistics: 136-144

J. Jeffers, M. Barley (1971) Speechreading (lipreading C. C. Thomas

A. Kendon (1967) Some Functions of Gaze-Direction in Social Interaction. Acta Psychologica, vol. 26: 22-63

A. Kendon (1972) Some Relationships Between Body Motion and Speech. Studies in Dyadic Communication, ed. A.W. Siegman, B. Pope: 177-210

R.D. Kent, F.D. Minifie (1977) Coarticulation in recent speech production models. Journal of Phonetics, n. 5: 115-133

Kleiser-Walczak Construction Comp. (1988) Sextone for President. ACM SIGGRAPH' 88 Film and Video Show, issue 38/39

D.R. Ladd, K. Silverman, F. Tolkmitt, G. Bergmann, K. Scherer (1985) Evidence for the independent function of intonation, contour type, voice quality and F0 range in signaling speaker affect. Journal of Acoustical Society of America. n. 78: 435-444

J.P. Lewis. F.I. Parke (1987) Automated Lip-Synch and Speech Synthesis for Character Animation. CHI + GI: 143-147

N. Magnenat-Thalmann, D. Thalmann (1987) The direction of synthetic actors in the film Rendez-vous à Montrèal. IEEE Computer Graphics and Applications, December: 9-19

M. Nahas, H. Huitric, M. Saintourens (1988) Animation of B-spline figure. The Visual Computer, v. 3: 272-276

F. Parke (1982) Parameterized Models for Facial Animation. Computer Graphics and Applications, November: 61-68

F.I. Parke (1990) Parameterized facial animation - Revisited. ACM SIGGRAPH'90 Course Notes, State in the Art in Facial Animation: 44-75

A. Pearce, B. Wyvill, D.R. Hill (1986) Speech and expression: a computer solution to face animation. Graphics Interface'86, Vision Interface'86: 136-140

S.M. Platt, N.I. Badler (1981) Animating facial expressions. Computer Graphics, v. 15, n. 3: 245-252

S.M. Platt (1985) A Structural Model of the Human Face. Ph. D. thesis, Computer and Information Science Department, University of Pennsylvania

K. Scherer, D.R. Ladd, K. Silverman (1984) Vocal cues to speaker affect: testing two models. Journal of Acoustical Society of America, number 76, November: 1346-1356

K. Scherer (1988) Facets of emotion: recent research. Lawrence Erlbaum Associates Publishers

M. Steedman (1990) Structure and intonation. Technical Report MS-CIS-90-45, LINC LAB 174, Computer and Information Science Department, University of Pennsylvania. To appear in Language 1991

K. Waters (1987) A muscle model for animating three-dimensional facial expression. Computer Graphics, v. 21, n. 4: 17-24

K. Waters (1990) Modeling 3D facial expressions. ACM SIGGRAPH'90 Course Notes, State in the Art in Facial Animation: 108-129

C. Williams, K. Stevens (1981) Vocal correlates of emotional states. Speech evaluation in psychiatry, ed. Darby: 221-240

B. Wyvill, D.R. Hill (1990) Expression control using synthetic speech. ACM SIGGRAPH'90 Course Notes, State in the Art in Facial Animation: 187-200

Catherine Pelachaud is a PhD student in the Departement of Computer and Information Science at the University of Pennsylvania since 1986. Her research interests include computer graphics and computer animation. She received maitrises in computer science from Paris VI, France, in 1984, in cinema-video and computer graphics from Paris VIII, France in 1986, and the MSE in Computer and Information Science in 1988 from the University of Pennsylvania. Pelachaud's address is Department of Computer and Information Science, University of Pennsylvania, Philadelphia, PA 19104-6389.

Dr. Norman I. Badler is the Cecilia Fitler Moore Professor and Chair of Computer and Information Science at the University of Pennsylvania and has been on that faculty since 1974. Active in computer graphics since 1968 with more than 80 technical papers, his research focuses on human figure modeling, manipulation, and animation. Badler received the BA degree in Creative Studies Mathematics from the University of California at Santa Barbara in 1970, the MSc in Mathematics in 1971, and the Ph.D. in Computer Science in 1975, both from the University of Toronto. He is a Senior Co-Editor of the new Journal "Graphical Models and Image Processing." He also directs the Computer Graphics Research Facility with two full time staff members and about 40 students. Badler's address is Department of Computer and Information Science, University of Pennsylvania, Philadelphia, PA 19104-6389.

Dr. Mark Steedman is an Associate Professor at Department of Computer and Information Science at the University of Pennsylvania since 1988. His research interests cover a range of issues in the areas of computational linguistics, artificial intelligence, computer science and cognitive science, including syntax and semantics of natural languages and programming languages, parsing and comprehension of natural language and discourse by humans and by machine, natural language generation, intonation in spoken discourse, and the formalisation of musical comprehension.Mark Steedman did his graduate study and research at the University of Edinburgh, receiving his Ph.D in Artificial Intelligence in 1973. He has held posts at the universities of Sussex, Warwick, and Texas at Austin, and was until recently a Reader in the Department of Artificial Intelligence and the Centre for Cognitive Science at the University of Edinburgh. Steedman's address is Department of Computer and Information Science, University of Pennsylvania, Philadelphia, PA 19104-6389.

Facial Animation by Spatial Mapping

ELIZABETH C. PATTERSON, PETER C. LITWINOWICZ, and NED GREENE

ABSTRACT

This paper describes a means for generating facial animation. Motion is captured on video from the actions of a live performer. Control points are obtained from the video, and this acquired motion is spatially mapped to conform to a synthetic actor's face. The mapping takes into account differences in proportions between the two faces. Animation is then generated by deforming the texture and geometry of the synthetic face around the control points. This technique was used in "The Audition" to animate a talking dog.

Keywords: facial animation, facial expression, spatial mapping, motion tracking, motion control

1. INTRODUCTION

This paper describes a means of animating faces which was demonstrated in "The Audition", a computer-generated animation first shown at Siggraph 1990. "The Audition" features a star-struck worm, auditioning for a position in a talking bulldog's circus. The ringmaster dog and his offscreen assistant Louie put the worm through a sequence of increasingly dangerous stunts, all of which he fails miserably, and then decide he has enough pluck to get the job anyway. One of the major technical accomplishments of this production is the performance-driven facial animation of the ringmaster. The dog talks, blinks, looks around, and shows expression. This paper describes how this animation was accomplished.

A human actor's facial expressions were captured on video as he performed the dog's dialog. Fluorescent spots on the actor's face were tracked as "motion control points". The acquired motion control points were spatially mapped to the face of the dog, giving new control points which were used to animate the dog's face. Section 2 puts this work in the context of other facial animation research. The following three sections discuss the details of generating the dog model, acquiring human motion, and applying that motion to the dog's face. The animation was produced using experimental software written in house, which is being developed as part of a more general interactive animation suite. A focus of our research is to enable the use of traditional media like video and painting in the design and control of computer animation. We are also investigating "clip" animation, in which motion from one character can be applied to many other characters. This facial animation technique illustrates our current progress toward both goals.

2. BACKGROUND

Facial animation has been studied for many years. Besides being of interest to animators, facial animation is important for other application areas such as low-bandwidth model-driven video telephony (Aizawa and Harashima 1989). Coupled with speech synthesis, facial animation provides another communications channel for education and aids for the hearing-impaired.

Some of the earliest facial animation research was done by Parke (1974). He digitized human faces, and devised a parametrically controllable face model, where geometric variables and local interpolations of facial subsections could be varied over time. Platt and Badler (1981) animated a facial mesh by propagating forces through "tension nets" representing muscle fibers connected to an outer layer of skin, and anchored to bone. This net could be controlled by "pulling" on various muscles in combination to approximate a desired expression.

To create the film "Tony de Peltrie", Bergeron (1986) digitized several human expressions, representing the range of desired facial movement. Once a correspondence was set up between the human data and the Tony model, the expressions could be mapped to the model's face. These pre-set expressions were combined and used as key frames, which were aligned to the sound by hand, and then inbetweens were interpolated.

Waters (1987, 1990) has developed a sophisticated physically-based facial model which includes muscles, bone, and a three-layer model of the skin and underlying soft tissue. Muscle forces displace the skin nodes, and neighboring areas are affected through spring equations and relaxation. He was able to obtain interesting skin motion, including wrinkles. The face of the baby in "Tin Toy" was animated using a muscle-based model similar to that of Waters (Reeves 1990).

Guenter (1989) also describes a system of applying muscle forces through a mesh to obtain facial expressions. With this system, a user can interactively specify muscle placement and wrinkle lines. Because muscle movements are calculated in 2D and then mapped onto the 3D face, the skin can be constrained to flow over the head shape.

Nahas, Huitric, Rioux and Domey (1990) acquired 3D head data using a rotating laser scanner. A subset of points were designated as controls, and were displaced to form different expressions.

Since animating a face is so complex, much of this work has concentrated on making the control manageable. It is extremely tedious for an animator to adjust every point on a facial model. The muscle models give one means of higher level control, the parametric solution of Parke is another, and using a finite set of pre-obtained expressions as keyframes in another. We take yet another approach by letting the human actor drive the motions of the synthetic face.

This work is a continuation of the work of Williams (1990-2). He also acquired motion from an actor, tracked it, and applied it to a model using warping. We describe several refinements on this work including interactive modeling of the 3D head, tracking color-discriminated dots in 3D, separating the rigid-body motion of the actor's head from his facial expression, and spatially mapping the actor's expressions to a face of greatly differing proportions.

What distinguishes this work is the three-dimensional representation of performance-driven facial expressions and the spatial mapping technique allowing us to apply the actor's facial movements to the dog's face. The current animation is not based on an underlying model of bones or skin, but is simply accomplished by local deformations of textures and geometry. An ideal performance-based system would allow us to capture all the nuances of expression of a real person. "Automatic rotoscoping" offers an alternative to keyframing facial positions by hand or driving a facial model with dynamics. The cross-mapping technique enables the application of motion obtained from one source to a wide range of target objects or characters of completely different proportions. As with Waters' (1987, 1990) method, this animation technique is independent of the animated face and its parameterization.

3. DOG MODEL ACQUISITION

The dog head was not obtained by using a 3D scanner, nor was it modelled using a traditional computer graphics modeler. It was created using off-the-shelf Macintosh™ painting programs coupled with a unique 3D display system (Williams, 1990-1) called "3D Paint", which allowed the intensities of the 2D painting to be seen as a relief map.

To create the texture for the dog, designer Bil Maher scanned in a black-and-white photograph of a chow. The three-quarter profile of the chow was reflected about a vertical axis through its nose to make a more bulldog-like face. The artist then remodeled and colored the image using standard Macintosh™ painting programs. The result became the texture of the front of the bulldog face used throughout the animation.

The 3D model based on the texture panting was created by designing a depth map on the 3D display system, which profiles intensities as depths. The display gives real-time feedback, enabling the artist to immediately see the result of his painting actions. He started with an initial depth map equal to the intensities in the texture, and modified it appropriately using standard painting tools like filter brushes and colormap modification. The final depth values as seen on the 3D display are shown in Fig. 1.

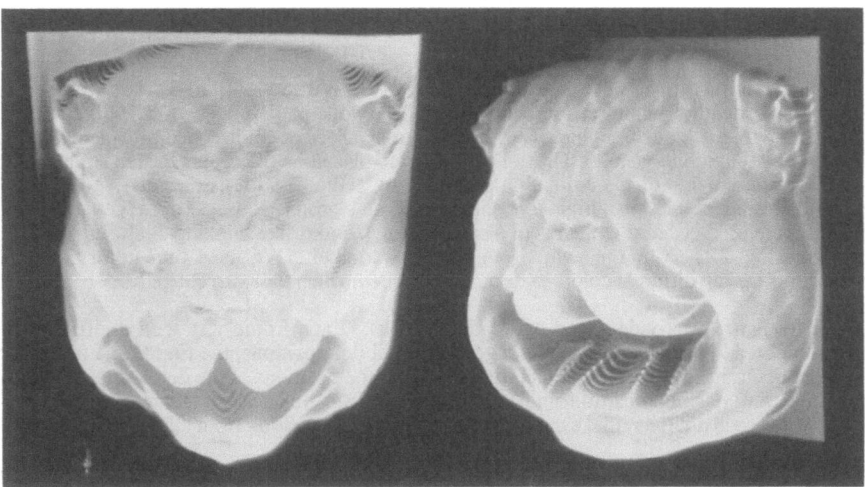

Fig 1. Dog face model, displayed on the 3D display, which profiles intensities as depths.

The depth and texture maps for the back of the dog's head were developed similarly. Although the face played the major role in the animation, an entire bulldog body was created to provide secondary motion and some background context. Fig. 2 is a frame from "The Audition" showing the entire dog.

4. MOTION ACQUISITION

The facial motion of the dog was obtained from video footage of a live actor reading a script and performing the corresponding actions. Motion acquired this way is much more realistic than that furnished by the current state of the art in dynamics, kinematics or keyframing. The actor was videotaped with special dots on his face, and the frames were analyzed to retrieve the control information necessary to animate the dog character.

4.1 Setup

The actor had fluorescent dots applied to his face. Then he stood with his head positioned between two mirrors, each at about a 45° angle from the plane of his face. This arrangement, shown in Fig. 3, allowed the video camera to simultaneously capture three views of his face, providing enough information for the recovery of the 3D position for each dot. To make this performance as realistic as possible, the actor was not constrained to keep his head stationary. Instead, he had a square placard attached to his forehead with a dot at each corner. This allowed the determination of rigid body motions of his head, which could later be "undone" so that the registered dots could be applied to the stationary dog. A video recording was made of the actor reading his lines, capturing sound as well as motion. Automatic lip-synching was accomplished by using this soundtrack as the voice of the dog after application of the actor's motion.

4.2 Dot Tracking

The idea of automatically tracking features from video and using them to offer some manner of control to a computer simulation is not new. DeWitt and Edelstein (1982) describe hardware they built to independently track up to 4 color markers in a frame. Applying this tracked motion to the motion of other video images is a process DeWitt dubbed "pantomation". Williams (1990-2) tracked dots on a performers face and used the information to control a synthetic face. More generally, similar technology is used to record human motion for research in sports and rehabilitative medicine, and for virtual-reality interactive games.

Our tracking is similar in purpose and method to that of Williams (1990-2), but we used colored fluorescent dots instead of white retroreflective dots. The dots, paper punched to 1/4 inch in diameter, glow under ultraviolet ("black") lights. They are sold to be used for color-coded price labelling, and can be purchased in any stationery store. Thirty-five dots were placed on the actor's face in strategic locations based on the requirements of the animation and tracking setup as well as the relative mobility of the features. (For instance, there is a high concentration of dots around the lips, but few on the forehead.) Colored dots were used because with dots of a single color, actions like blinking or closing the mouth can cause neighboring dots to merge, which confuses the tracker. We used four colors of dots, with neighboring dots having different colors to disambiguate them when they came together.

The live performance was videotaped under black lights. Each frame was then digitized into YUV components and read into the computer. To get the initial dot positions, the first frame of the sequence was displayed in our interactive animation program, where the positions of the dots were marked by hand. This specified the starting position and color of the dots. Successive frames were then tracked automatically; for each dot the initial estimate of position was the position from the previous frame.

The tracking algorithm is simple. Starting at the known positions and colors of the previous frame, the neighborhood around each old dot was searched for the new dot position. The size of the search areas is an estimate of the maximum distance a spot may move in 1/30th of a second; different search areas may be allotted to different spots. In the search area, a new dot center was calculated. For each pixel, if the Y (luminance) value was over a threshold, the UV color was examined. If it was close enough to the color of the spot being tracked, then the luminance value was used to weight the contribution of that pixel's x and y coordinates to a "center of mass" estimate of the dot's x,y center. To quickly determine color closeness a table was contructed. The 5 most significant bits of U and V indexed into this table, returning the label of the closest dot color. The outcome of tracking a sequence of frames is a sequence of dot positions, used to control the animation.

As machine vision technology progresses, it should be possible to automatically track expressions of the actor's face without requiring any special makeup or dots. One would expect such makeup to improve the accuracy of such tracking, however, especially in the smooth, relatively featureless areas of the face.

4.3 Recovery of 3D Dot Coordinates

This section describes recovery of 3D dot coordinates from the 2D video sequence. Reconstruction of 3D geometry from 2D projections is an involved topic that has been previously addressed in a variety of contexts (Ganapathy) (Fischler 1981). To simplify the problem, in our apparatus the mirrors are vertical, the camera is plumb, and the view angle of the camera is known. It is not necessary to know the distance from the camera to the performer, the location of the mirrors, or the angle between them.

Fig. 4 shows the relationship between the mirrors, the camera, and the virtual cameras associated with the mirrors. The mirror views contain the same information as views from independent cameras located in the virtual positions, except that the images are mirrored on x. Thus, views from the virtual cameras can be constructed from a video frame by reflecting 2D dot coordinates on x. In Fig. 4, for example, the camera sees dot A reflected in the left mirror at point A' in the image plane, and the corresponding point for the left virtual camera, labelled A", can be constructed by reflecting A' on the x-axis. Using this approach the dots in a video frame can be converted to three separate data sets of 2D dot coordinates, one for the camera and one for each of the virtual cameras.

Fig 2. A final frame from "The Audition", showing the rendered dog with a facial expression obtained from the performer.

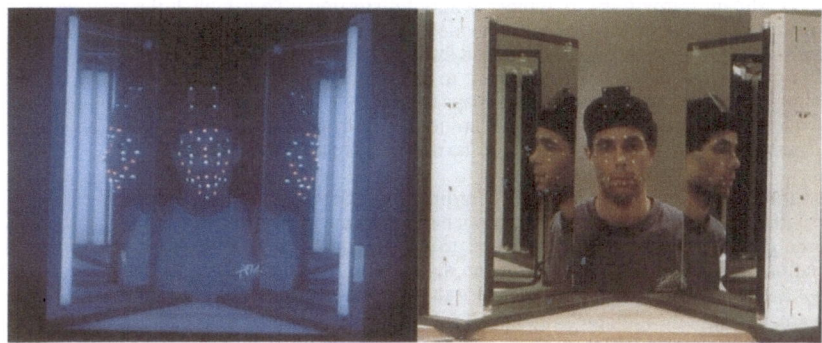

Fig 3. Three views of the performer's face as obtained from the mirror arrangement. The left picture shows the rotoscoping setup during video recording under fluorescent lights, and the right picture shows the setup under normal lighting.

Top View

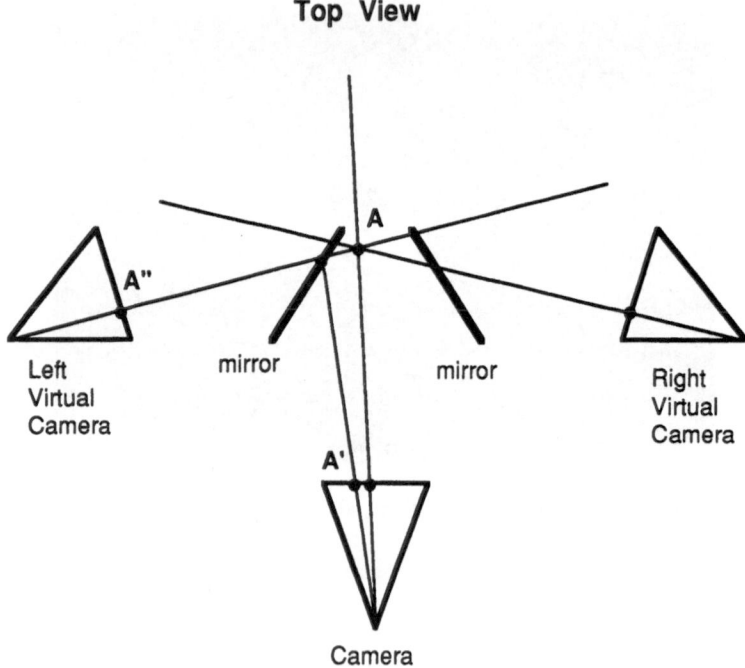

Fig 4. Locating dots in 3D by ray intersection.

By a rigid body transformation (RBT) we mean a translation followed by a rotation (or vice versa) that maps one coordinate frame (CF) to another without distortion. To establish the relative positions and orientations of the three cameras we choose a video frame (any frame will do) and find the RBTs from the CF of the placard in that frame to the CFs of the three cameras using the method of Appendix A. Then the RBT which maps from the CF of the camera to the CF of the left virtual camera can be obtained by concatenating the inverse of the RBT which maps from the CF of the placard to the CF of the camera with the RBT which maps from the CF of the placard to the CF of the left virtual camera. The transformation from the camera to the right virtual camera can be obtained analogously.

Once these transformations are known, 3D coordinates for dots in a given video frame can be established as follows. 2D dot coordinates extracted from the video frame are converted to separate data sets for each of the three cameras, and are then mapped to the image planes of the virtual cameras using the transformations described above (think of the data sets as being pasted onto the ends of the cameras' viewing pyramids). Then the direction of a dot in a camera CF can be established by constructing a ray from the camera origin through the projection of the dot, and the dot can be located in 3D by intersecting rays constructed in this manner.

For example, suppose dot A in Fig. 4 is visible to all three cameras. To determine A's 3D coordinates we construct a ray from each camera origin through the 2D projection of A in each view, and then find where the three rays intersect (in practice the rays won't intersect exactly due to measurement error). Note that two rays are necessary to locate a point, so any dot that is visible to at least two cameras can be located in this way.

This construction method yields 3D dot coordinates in the CF of the camera, but we really want them in a "canonical" CF registered with the performer's head such as the CF of the square placard. The RBT for mapping points from the CF of the camera to the CF of the placard is obtained for each video frame using the method of Appendix A.

To summarize, dots in video frame F are mapped to the canonical CF as follows:

1. Convert 2D dots in frame F to separate data sets for three independent views corresponding to the camera, the left virtual camera, and the right virtual camera.
2. Map 2D point sets to the image planes of the cameras and locate the corresponding 3D points in the CF of the camera by intersecting rays.
3. Map points from the CF of the camera to the canonical CF registered with the performer's head.

4.4 Mapping

Once the 3D positions have been obtained for each dot on the actor's face for every frame of the performance, this motion information must be mapped onto the dog. The sequence of dog dot positions will then control the animation by directing the spatial warping of the dog model. First a correspondence is set up between the dog's face and the actor's, by designating a position on the dog's face for each dot in the neutral position of the actor's. A straightforward way to implement the mapping of control dots would be to difference the actor's neutral face dots from successive frames of the actor's performance, and add these differences to the dog's dots. This was the technique used by Bergeron (1986) and Williams (1990-2). They also incorporated a scaling factor to the differences, allowing the motions to be caricatured or de-emphasized.

The problem with this technique is that using a uniform scale factor on the differences assumes that both faces are of the same proportions. However, the dog and the actor have very different faces. The dog has a wider mouth, a shorter mid-face, and closely-spaced eyes. A mapping that takes into account local differences in scale is needed. This mapping can be formulated as a random surface interpolation problem. Consider x and y destination surfaces to be defined as parametric functions of source space u and v. In this case, the u and v represent the x and y of the actor's face. For each known control point, the x and y of the destination face (the dog) is known and will become the coordinate at that u,v position. Constructing the mapping is then the problem of smoothly interpolating these coordinates to form a parametric surface.

There are several known ways of solving this problem. We use the thin-plate method of Terzopoulos (1984). The source space is discretized to a grid, and the solution is posed as fitting a thin plate over the known points, by minimizing the energy of the constrained plate. This gives an integral over the surface to be minimized. Discretizing the problem gives an update rule, in which each point on the source grid updated by computing a weighted average of its neighbors. The known points are not changed, but iterating over the grid causes the known values to propagate through the grid, eventually filling in the unknown values to converge to a surface. The resulting surface for the actor to dog mapping is shown in Fig 5, overlaid on the corresponding texture maps. If the two faces were similarly proportioned, the ruled lines across the surface would be uniformly spaced. The undulations show the local variations in scale.

To get an accurate solution, a grid of reasonable dimensions is needed. But the iterative nature of the algorithm makes the convergence time too long for large grids. To speed it up, a multi-grid approach was used. A surface was first found on a small grid, which converges rapidly. This result then used as the initial condition for a grid twice as large. This process is repeated until reaching a grid of the desired size. Multi-grid solutions are discussed by Terzopoulos (1984), but his technique is more complex, propagating information both up and down the hierarchy of grids. The multi-grid solution makes the mapping much faster, but it still takes over two hours on an SGI Personal Iris to solve a 256x256 grid. Note that the mapping could be done in three-space, mapping from x,y,z of the source space onto a volume, but this would greatly increase the computational requirements. For our animation, an x-y cross-mapping was sufficient, and z was calculated with scaled offsets as in (Bergeron 1986). We are currently investigating alternative methods of finding a surface based on pyramidal interpolation.

Once the mapping has been established for the neutral frames of the actor and the dog, the entire sequence of dots for the dog can be obtained simply by using the actor's dots as indices into the warped surface. This mapping capability is very general and useful for mapping any kind of motion from one character to another. This is an important element of a "clip motion" system.

Once the mapping capability exists, libraries of canonical dot positions for phonemes and expressions recorded from an actor can be created. Then the desired motion can be chosen, mapped to the desired face, and interpolated to produce animations.

5. APPLICATION OF MOTION TO MODEL

As described above, a correspondence is made between the neutral performer's face and the neutral dog's face. As the performer distorts from his neutral expression, the new positions of the dots on his face are then mapped to the dog's face. This section describes how the mapped positions of the dots are then used to create the facial animation for the dog.

5.1 Preparing the dog for animation

After the dog model is created, the resultant depth data is represented as a rectangular grid of height values. There are depth maps for both the front and the back of the head. This representation is cumbersome when dealing with disconnected parts of the face such as the lids of the eye. Therefore, the mesh is divided into bilinear Coons patches as shown in Fig. 6, where the eyes are not included.

As described above, points are designated on the dog's neutral face that correspond to the dots on the neutral performer's face. Each point describes the center of a cosine window basis function. As a point moves it pulls on geometry surrounding it proportional to the amplitude of the cosine window attached to it. The extent of each window, the affect region, is interactively designated as shown in Fig. 7. Currently affect regions must be circular. Each patch may be excluded from the influence of any of the window functions. In this way we can designate that the movement of a window on the upper lid of the eye has no affect on the lower lid patch, and similarly for the lips.

Now we have acquired 1) the geometry for the neutral position of the dog's face; 2) centers for the neutral position of each cosine window that will warp the face; and 3) affect regions for each cosine window and the patches that each window will affect.

5.2 Warping

For each frame in the animation the position of each dot on the performer's face is mapped to the dog's face. This position, along with a neutral position, describes a displacement for each dot as shown in Fig. 8. Geometry neighboring a displaced dot is moved by some fraction of the displacement depending on its distance from the dot. The general notion is to transform points according to a spatial vector field (Pintado 1988). Here the transformations are simply displacements and the basis functions with which the displacements are applied are 3D separable cosine windows.

c_i = center of the ith cosine window (corresponding to the ith dot)
e_i = extent of the ith cosine window (note: this is a scalar)
p = any point on the face
d_i = displacement for the point p as acted on by the ith cosine window

to calculate d_i:

    if (length(p - c_i) > e_i) or (p is on a patch not affected by the ith dot))
        the point is not part of the affect region for the
        given cosine window, so set the displacement to zero
        $d_i = 0$
   else {
        modify the displacement by a scalar based on distance
        from the center of the window
        $d_i = (p - c_i) * wf_i$; where wf_i is a weighting factor
                based on distance
   }

Because we are using a cosine (Hanning) window basis function the weighting factor has the formula:

$$wf_i = ((1 + \cos(\pi * \text{length}(p - c_i) / e_i)) / 2.0$$

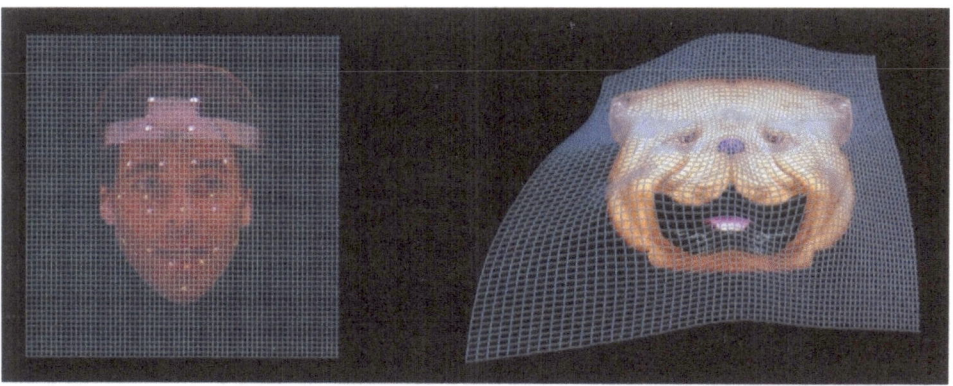

Fig 5. The grid on the right shows the surface resulting from mapping the performer's face to the dog's face. The corresponding textures are overlaid to highlight the local differences in scale.

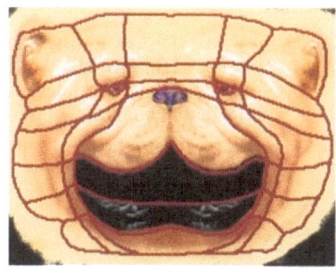

Fig 6 Dog color texture with Coons patch boundaries.

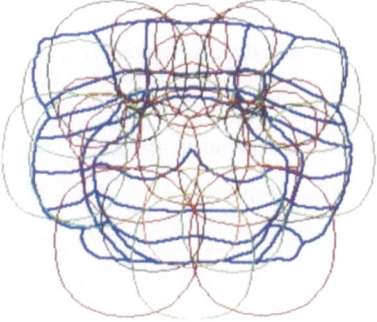

Fig 7. Cosine (Hanning) basis windows for the neutral position. The extent of each window is explicitly shown.

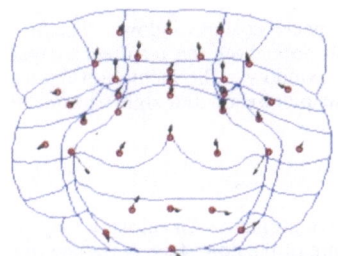

Fig 8. The centers of the cosine windows are shown, with a set of displacements for a frame in the animation.

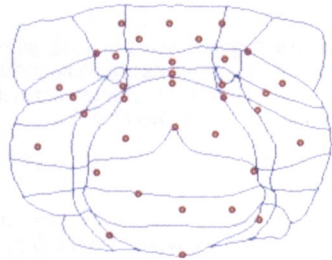

Fig 10. The displacements of figure 8 are used to warp the dog's face. Also shown are the new positions of the dots.

40

Each point on the face is then moved by the calculated d_i. Unfortunately, when two affect regions overlap, simply summing up the d_i's does not produce the intended effect. As shown in Fig. 9, if two cosine windows near each other move in the same direction, the points affected by both windows will move too far. To overcome this problem we introduce a normalization step in computing the displacement for a point (also shown in Fig. 9).

$$d_x = \text{Sum}(\ (p_x - c_{x_i}) * wf_i^2\ ) / \text{Sum}\ (\ (p_x - c_{x_i}) * wf_i\ ),$$
and similarly for the y and z components.

Note that in the case of a point affected by only one cosine window, the displacement for the point simply becomes $(p_x - c_{x_i}) * wf_i$, as desired.

See Fig. 10 for a warped frame of the animation using the technique just described.

This method differs considerably from that of Waters (1987, 1990). In these papers he describes methods to deform a face by activating muscles. The resulting facial expressions are thus completely synthetic. In our method we know nothing of the intention or mood in a created facial expression. We are told how points on a face are displaced (as acquired from a performer and then mapped to our character), and ours is a problem of interpolating displacements for points that lie in between the known ones. The portion of Waters' model which handles the surface, a three layer mesh with the capability to simulate wrinkles, could also be driven by our displacements. The more particular modeling of human facial musculature would be counter to our purposes, since we would like methods of animation which are not specific to human faces.

This technique also differs from the method described in Oka (1987) in which deformations are applied in an interactive mode to come up with a set of representative facial expressions. A particular expression in an animated sequence is simply a linear combination of the expressions in that set. Our technique is different in that we are calculating each expression from "scratch" by perturbing the neutral expression into the expression for a particular frame.

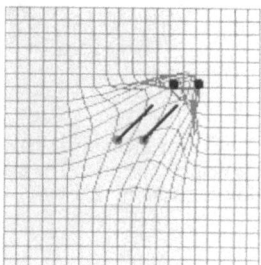 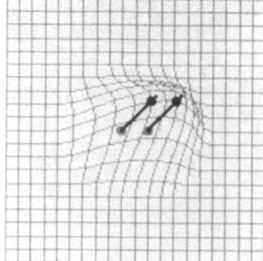

Fig 9. The gray dots show the centers of two closely spaced cosine windows. The lines show the displacement for each window. The black dots show the resultant warped positions of a point directly under the center of each window. The picture on the left shows the algorithm without normalization, and the picture on the right shows the algorithm with normalization.

Editing of the motion can be accomplished using a 2D interactive program. An animator may change the positions of the "warp windows" for the dog, and a line drawing of the dog's face is warped to show the effects of moving the windows. The animator can then insert this frame, blending the new positions into the surrounding frames so as to produce a smooth transition.

5.3 Facial Animation Miscellany

The eyes are simply texture mapped spheres that were keyframed by hand. The teeth model was created using the 3D display system already described. Teeth motion consisted solely of translations; the translations were automatically calculated as a linear combination of the displacements of the dots surrounding the mouth. The teeth and eyes were placed in the head model interactively, using a cut-away view of the head.

Most of the rigid body rotations for the head were also keyframed by hand. They could have been derived from the original head motion of the performer, but were animated by hand for improved staging.

6. CONCLUSION

We have described a facial animation technique that uses the expressions obtained from live performances to animate a computer-generated model. The performance motion data was acquired by automatically tracking color-discriminated dots in 3D, separating the rigid-body motion of the actor's head from his facial expression, and then spatially mapping the actor's expressions to a face of completely different proportions. The current animation was not based on an underlying model of bones or skin, but simply accomplished by local deformations of textures and geometry. This animation technique is demonstrated by the talking dog in "The Audition."

7. ACKNOWLEDGEMENTS

The authors would like to thank Lance Williams for his guidance and inspiration, Doug Turner for his riveting dog performance, designer Bil Maher for the dog model creation and artwork, and Kim Tempest for animation assistance.

8. REFERENCES

Aizawa K, Harashima H (1989) Model-based Analysis Synthesis Image Coding (MBASIC) System for a Person's Face. *Image Communication*, Vol 1, Number 2, Oct 1989, 139-152.

Bergeron P (1986) Controlling Facial Expressions and Body Movements in the Computer-Generated Short 'Tony de Peltrie'. Siggraph 86 Course Notes, Course 22: Advanced Computer Animation, 1986.

DeWitt T, Edelstein P (1982) Pantomation: A System for Position Tracking. *IEEE Proceedings of the Symposium on Small Computers in the Arts*, October 15-17, 1982, 61-69.

Fischler M and Bolles R (1981) Random Sample Consensus: A Paradigm for Model Fitting with Applications to Image Analysis and Automated Cartography. *Communications of the ACM,* Vol. 24, Number 6, June 1981, 381-395.

Ganapathy S (undated) Camera Location Determination Problem. Technical Memorandum, AT&T Bell Laboratories, Holmdel, New Jersey.

Guenter, B (1989) A System for Simulating Human Facial Expressions. *State-of-the-Art in Computer Animation*, edited by Nadia Magnetat-Thalman and Daniel Thalman. Springer-Verlag, 1989, 191-202.

Nahas M, Huitric H, Rioux M, Domey J (1990) Registered 3D Texture Imaging. *Computer Animation 90*, edited by Nadia Magnetat-Thalmann and Daniel Thalmann. Springer-Verlag, 1990, 81-90.

Oka M, Tsutsui K, Ohba A (1974) Real-Time Manipulation of Texture-Mapped Surfaces. *Computer Graphics*, Vol 21, Number 4, July 1987, 181-188.

Parke, FI (1974) A Parametric Model for Human Faces. PhD thesis, University of Utah Computer Science Department, 1974.

Pintado X, Fiume E (1988) Grafields: Filed-Directed Dynamic Splines for Interactive Motion Control. *Eurographics '88*, 1988, 43-54.

Platt SM, Badler NI (1981) Animating Facial Expressions. *Computer Graphics*, Vol 15, Number 3, August 1981, 245-252.

Reeves WT (1990) Simple and Complex Facial Animation: CaseStudies. Siggraph 90 Course Notes, Course 26: State of the Art in Facial Animation, 1990.

Terzopoulos, Demetri. "Multiresolution Algorithms in Computational Vision", Chapter 10 in *Image Understanding 1984*, edited by Shimon Ullman and Whitman Richards. Norwood, NJ: Ablex Publishing Corp, 1984.

Waters K (1987) A Muscle Model for Animating Three-Dimensional Facial Expression. *Computer Graphics*, Vol 21, Number 4, July 1987, 17-24.

Waters K, Terzopoulos D (1990) A Physical Model of Facial Tissue and Muscle Articulation. *Proceedings of the First Conference on Visualization in Biomedical Computing*, May 22-25, 1990, 77-82.

Williams L (1990-1) 3D Paint. *Computer Graphics*, Vol 24, Number 2, March 1990, 225-233.

Williams L (1990-2) Performance-Driven Facial Animation. *Computer Graphics*, Vol 24, Number 4, August 1990, 235-242.

9. APPENDIX A: Solving for Camera Transformations

The general problem of reconstructing a camera transformation from projections of points whose coordinates are known in some coordinate frame is called the camera location determination problem (Ganapathy) (Fischler 81). The problem has a variety of forms depending on what is known and what needs to be determined, but typically formulations are overconstrained and solution involves numerical methods. Our apparatus was designed to simplify locating the camera, allowing solution by simple analytic methods, but it is not as robust as some other methods. Our method assumes that the camera view angle is known.

The square placard defines a coordinate frame (CF) in 3D and we determine the rigid body transformation (RBT) from this CF to the CF of the camera as follows.

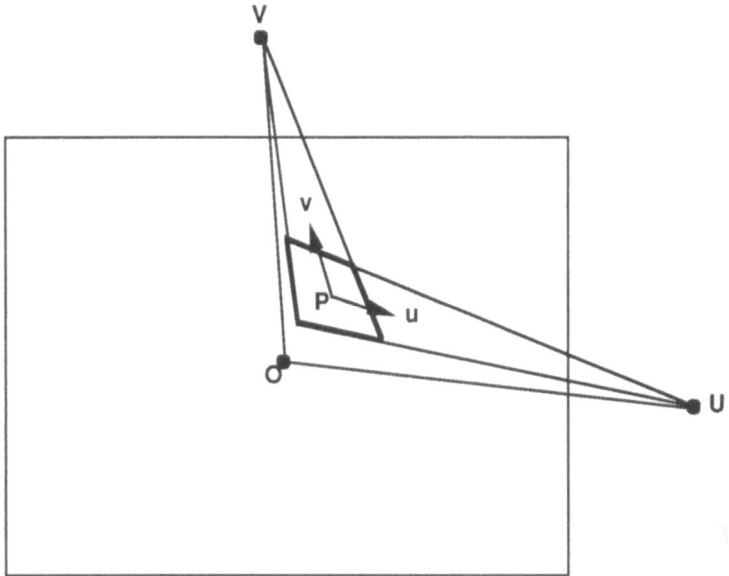

Fig 11. Solving for the camera transformation by constructing the vanishing points of the projected placard axes.

1. Construct vanishing points U and V in the image plane as shown in Fig. 11. This can't be done if opposite sides of the projected square are parallel, so we avoid straight-on viewing of the square by mounting it on the performer with a backward tilt. Actually, this method can still be used if opposite sides of the projected square are parallel by constructing vanishing points "at infinity." Projections of all lines that are parallel to the square's u-axis in 3D will pass through U and projections of all lines that are parallel to the square's v-axis in 3D will pass through V.

2. Camera origin O projects to the center of the frame. In 3D the square's u-axis is parallel to line OU from the camera origin through U and the square's v-axis is parallel to line OV from the camera origin through V. Camera origin O is on a line perpendicular to the screen and OU and OV are perpendicular to each other in 3D. This allows us to establish the z coordinate of O relative to the image plane, by "sliding" O out from the image plane (on a line perpendicular to the screen) until OU and OV are perpendicular.

3. Unitizing 3D vectors OU and OV yields unit length axes parallel to the square's axes in 3D. A 3x3 rotation matrix which rotates these axes to align with the camera CF's axes can be constructed by putting OU (unitized) in row 0, OV (unitized) in row 1, and their cross product in row2 (actually, this may be the transpose of the desired matrix depending on matrix conventions, whether points are represented as row matrices or column matrices, etc.). This rotation matrix is the rotational component of the desired RBT.

4. The square's center in the image plane, labeled P, can be constructed by intersecting diagonals of the projected square. To establish the translational component of the desired RBT we construct a square centered on the camera origin, rotated according to the matrix just derived and viewed in perspective with the known view angle. We then "slide" the square in the direction of 3D vector OP until its projection coincides with the observed projection, yielding the 3D translation vector from the camera origin to the square's center (and vice versa).

Thus we have the rotational and translational components of the RBT that maps from the CF of the square to the CF of the camera.

Elizabeth Patterson is a computer scientist in the Advanced Technologies Group at Apple Computer. As a member of the Graphics and Animation group, she develops animation algorithms, toolboxes, and user interfaces for potential use in future Apple products. Her research interests include computer animation, image processing, and neural networks. She received an BS in computer science and an MS in electrical engineering from MIT in 1986.

Address: libby.p@applelink.apple.com. Apple Computer, Inc. 20525 Mariani Dr, MS 60V, Cupertino, CA 95014, USA.

Pete Litwinowicz is a member of the Graphics Research Team in Apple's Advanced Technology Group, whose charter is to develop graphics algorithms, toolboxes and user interfaces for potential use in future Apple Products. Pete is an alumnus of UNC Chapel Hill, receiving his MS in Computer Science in 1987. At Apple his work entails developing animation algorithms and user interfaces, but his interests also includes modeling and rendering.

Address: litwinowicz@applelink.apple.com. Apple Computer, Inc. 20525 Mariani Dr, MS 60W, Cupertino, CA 95014, USA.

Ned Greene has worked in computer graphics research for ten years, beginning at the New York Institute of Technology where he learned computer animation as part of "The Works" group. He is currently with the graphics research group at Apple Computer and is finishing a PhD in computer science at the University of California at Santa Cruz. Recent research interests include modeling automata and realistic rendering.

Address: greene@applelink.apple.com. Apple Computer, Inc. 20525 Mariani Dr, MS 60W, Cupertino, CA 95014, USA.

A Transformation Method for Modeling and Animation of the Human Face from Photographs

TSUNEYA KURIHARA and KIYOSHI ARAI

ABSTRACT

This paper describes a new transformation method for modeling and animation of the human face. A 3-D canonical facial model is introduced which is transformed to a facial model that is consistent with photographs of an individual face. Facial expression is modified by transformation of the obtained facial model. By using the displacements of selected control points, the transformation determines the displacements of the remaining points by linear interpolation in a 2-D parameter space. To generate texture-mapped facial images, photographs are first projected onto a 2-D space using cylindrical coordinates and then combined, taking into account their positional certainty.

Keywords: computer facial animation, photograph, transformation, texture mapping.

1. INTRODUCTION

There are three steps in the computer animation of human faces: designing a facial model, modifying the facial expression, and generating the images.

Two techniques are generally used for entering the shape of the human face: 3-D digitizing (Magnenat-Thalmann and Thalmann 1987; Kleiser 1989) and 3-D reconstruction from 2-D images (Parke 1974). 3-D digitizing needs special hardware, while the reconstruction approach needs a mesh drawn on the face and is time-consuming.

Magnenat-Thalmann et al. (1989) introduced three approaches for the design of human faces: local deformation, interpolation between two faces, and composition of face parts. A new facial model is created by using a local transformation to modify and edit an existing facial model. This transformation method is based on a primitive operation that moves one vertex without altering the topology of the mesh, while arbitrary regions are modified according to a generalized "decay function" (Allan et al. 1989). In this technique, the control vertex, its displacement and decay function are specified in succession, but only one control vertex is allowed at each step. This is because it is difficult to blend the decay functions of multiple control vertices consistently. This may be a drawback for facial modeling and animation because it is convenient to specify multiple control vertices and their displacements simultaneously.

There are three fundamental approaches to facial animation: key framing, parameterization, and muscle-based modeling. Key framing requires complete specification of the model for each facial expression, and the key frame data for these expressions are different for the individual faces. In the parameterized model (Parke 1974), sets of parameters define the conformation and expression of the face. Since the transformation specified by the parameters is rather global, it is difficult to model complex expressions. In muscle-based modeling (Platt and Badler 1981; Waters 1987), muscles are geometric deformation operators. The deformation requires a sophisticated decay function which are specified by the vector contraction, the position of the head and tail of the vector and fall-off radius. Many muscle units and their parameter values must be specified to simulate natural expressions.

Because of the complex microstructure of the skin, the rendering of a human face is still a difficult problem. Texture mapping (Blinn and Newell 1976) is currently the most efficient technique, and has been used by Yau and Duffy (1987), Nahas et al. (1990), and Williams (1990). With this method, the texture of the face is mapped onto a 3-D structure obtained by a laser scanner. However, this technique requires special hardware as well as an actual human subject.

Another texture mapping approach has been proposed by Oka et al. (1987) in which a texture mapped plane is deformed interactively to make a facial model. Aizawa et al. (1987) proposed a technique, in which a universal facial model is modified interactively, and a photograph of the face is texture-mapped onto the modified model. Both these methods use only one photograph. Depth information is therefore specified interactively because it is not available from one frontal photograph. Komatsu (1990) proposed a method that uses biquartic Bézier patches. It therefore requires complex calculations to maintain a smooth connection of patches, and it is difficult to describe existing people because of the smoothness of the obtained model. Akimoto et al. (1990) proposed a method which uses multiple photographs; however, this method requires photographs taken directly from the front and side of the person.

This paper describes a efficient method, using photographs, to construct the shape of a human face and to animate it. Section 2 introduces a new transformation scheme to create and animate human faces. Section 3 discusses a way of constructing a facial model using this transformation scheme from multiple photographs, and Section 4 describes the rendering technique using composite texture mapping. Section 5 discusses a way of constructing a facial model using one photograph, while finally Section 6 describes a method for modifying facial expression.

2. TRANSFORMATION METHOD

Before describing the method for the creation and animation of the human face, we propose a transformation method for this purpose. The proposed transformation method utilizes the displacements of multiple control points to create and animate the facial model.

The model of the human face is defined by polygons. The transformation of this facial model is defined by the displacement of each vertex of these polygons. However, specifying all the displacements of the vertices is tedious and time-consuming. Control points to express the transformation are therefore selected from among all the vertices. The proposed method then interpolates the displacements of the remaining vertices as follows.

Let P_i $(1 \le i \le n_v)$ be the vertices of the polygons representing the face, and C_j and V_j $(1 \le j \le n_c)$ be the control points and their displacements, where n_v is the number of vertices and n_c is the number of control points (see Fig. 1(a)). Control points C_j are selected from vertices P_i. P_i, C_j, and V_j are 3-D vectors. The problem is to interpolate the displacement of each vertex P_i from the displacements V_j of the control points C_j.

This interpolation problem involves the difficulty in dealing with the points on a 3-D surface. When the surface is projected onto 2-D space, however, the interpolation problem is reduced into a 2-D case.

Many techniques can be used for projecting surfaces from 3-D to 2-D space. In the proposed method, cylindrical projection is used for simplicity (see Fig. 1(b)). The function that projects the point $A(x, y, z)$ into $A_s(\theta, H)$ in the cylindrical parameter space is defined as follows:

$$A_s (\theta, H) = (\tan^{-1}(z/x), y). \tag{1}$$

Let P_{si} and C_{sj} be the projection of vertex P_i and control point C_j onto 2-D space. The displacement W_i of each vertex is interpolated from displacement of the control points. For interpolation, the parameter space is triangulated by the control points C_{sj} using Delaunay triangulation (Sibson 1978) (see Fig. 1(b)).

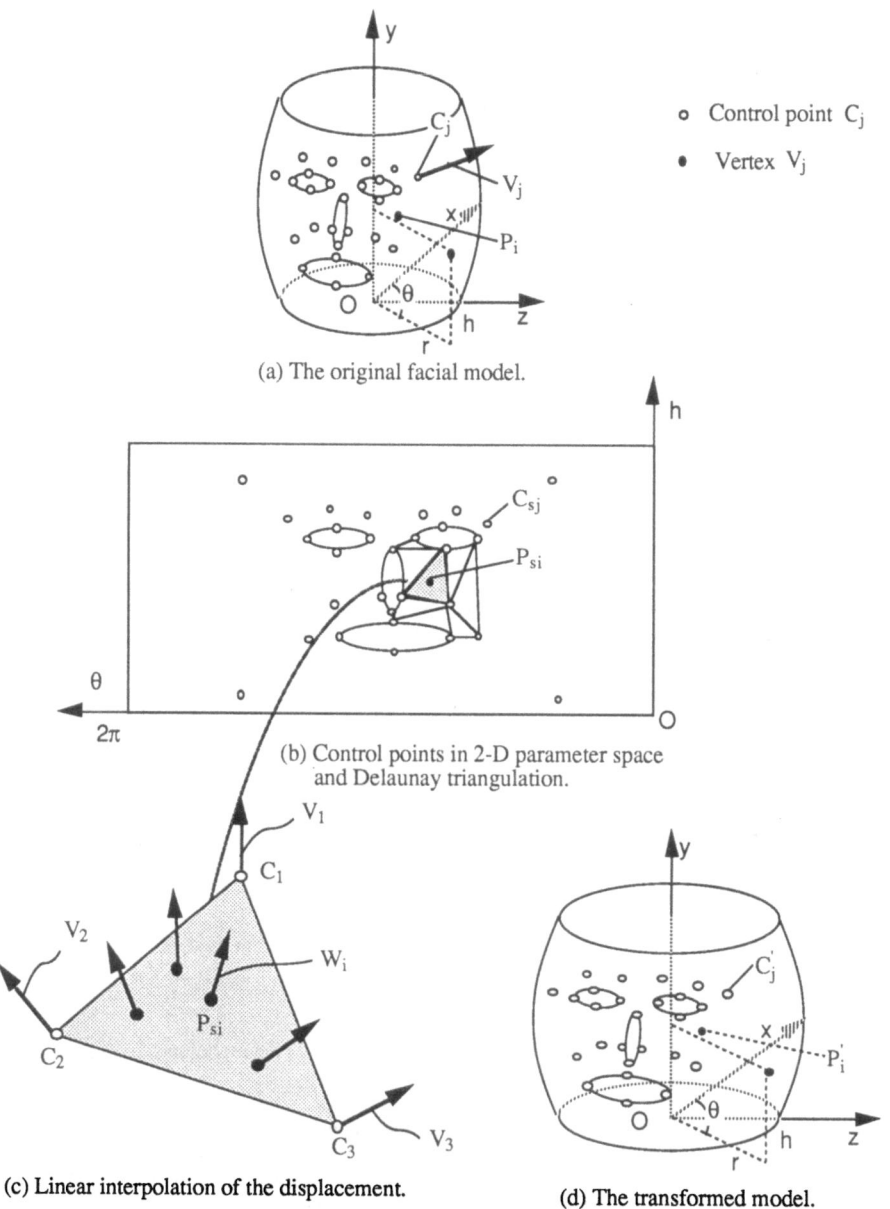

(a) The original facial model.

(b) Control points in 2-D parameter space
and Delaunay triangulation.

(c) Linear interpolation of the displacement.

(d) The transformed model.

Fig. 1 The Transformation Method.

The displacement W_i of the vertex P_{si} (θ, H) is interpolated as follows (see Fig. 1(c)):

1. Find the triangle that contains the vertex P_{si} (θ, H).
   Let $C_1(\theta_1, H_1)$, $C_2(\theta_2, H_2)$, $C_3(\theta_3, H_3)$ be the three vertices of this triangle, and V_1, V_2, V_3 be the displacements of each vertex.

2. Calculate weighting values k_1, k_2, k_3 ($k_1 + k_2 + k_3 = 1$) that satisfy the following equations:

$$\begin{aligned} \theta &= k_1 \cdot \theta_1 + k_2 \cdot \theta_2 + k_3 \cdot \theta_3 \\ H &= k_1 \cdot H_1 + k_2 \cdot H_2 + k_3 \cdot H_3 \end{aligned} \qquad (2)$$

3. Calculate the displacement $\mathbf{W}_i$ as follows:

$$\mathbf{W}_i = k_1 \cdot \mathbf{V}_1 + k_2 \cdot \mathbf{V}_2 + k_3 \cdot \mathbf{V}_3 \qquad (3)$$

This transformation is convenient because it requires only control points and their displacements, and nothing else, such as decay functions. In addition, this method specifies the displacements of multiple control points directly and simultaneously, is suitable for interactive use, and can describe a wide variety of transformations. The transformation can be applied when any part of all the control points is specified. We can interactively transform the model, specifying the control points successively, because the transformation is done quickly.

One disadvantage of the linear interpolation is that it may lead to first-derivative discontinuities. Although computationally expensive, one can use a more sophisticated interpolation method (Mallet 1989) if smoother interpolation is required.

The interpolation in 2-D cylindrical space causes one problem. It is difficult to transform features such as ears because a multi-valued function is required to describe these features in 2-D cylindrical space. One has to transform such features by using other methods. However, almost all other facial features can be described in 2-D cylindrical space, and can be transformed by the proposed method.

3. FACIAL MODELING

Every human face has the same structure and is similar in shape for every person. If a canonical model of the human face is prepared, it is therefore easy to construct the shape of an individual person's face by transforming the canonical model. Modeling human faces then consists of transforming the canonical facial model into an individual facial model.

A wide variety of faces can be generated using the transformation method described in Section 2. Interactive transformation can be used to create new faces. However, creation of a facial model from photographs is convenient because photographs are easily obtained.

Figure 2 shows the canonical facial model used for the experiments. This model has 2950 polygons which are obtained by digitizing a mannequin with a laser scanner.

The 3-D positions of the control points C_j and their displacements V_j have to be determined for the transformation (see Fig. 3). Let D_j be the destination points, which are the corresponding control points of the individual model ($D_j = C_j + V_j$), and let Q_{jk} be the projected points of D_j on photograph k ($1 \leq k \leq n_p$), where n_p is the number of photographs. We specify the 3-D coordinates of the control points C_j of the canonical model and the 2-D coordinates of the corresponding projected points Q_{jk} on the photographs, and estimate the 3-D coordinates of the destination points D_j of the individual model. We then transform the canonical model so that the coordinates of the control points on the transformed model coincide with those of the estimated destination points D_j.

Vertices that are important for transforming a facial model (such as the corners of the eyes and mouth) are specified as control points. Forty control points are registered for the experiments. Figure 4 shows four photographs of an individual face showing the front, right, left, and back views. There are no restrictions as to from what angles the photographs are taken, as long as all unique features are seen. Two photographs are used for the conformation, while the other two are used only for texture mapping. We

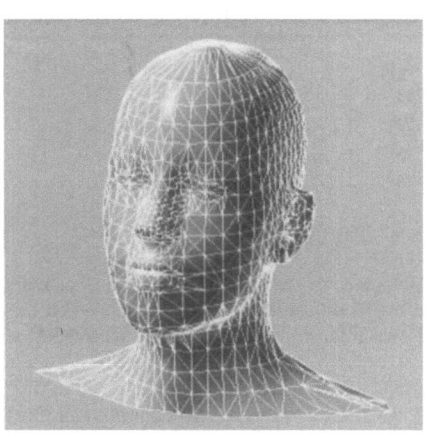

Fig. 2 The canonical model of the human face.

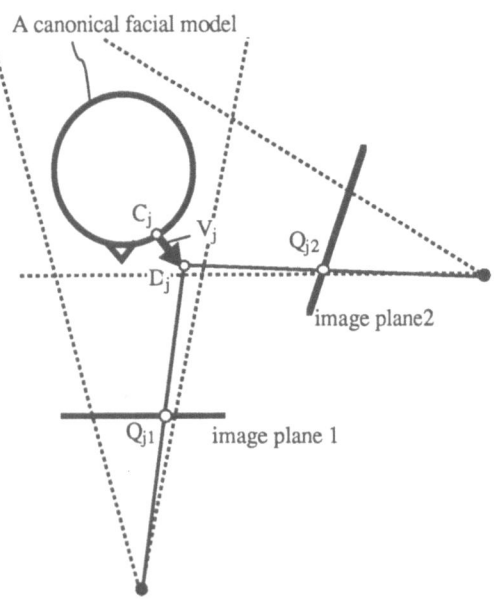

A canonical facial model

image plane2

image plane 1

Fig. 3 Estimation of the destination point D j (Top view).

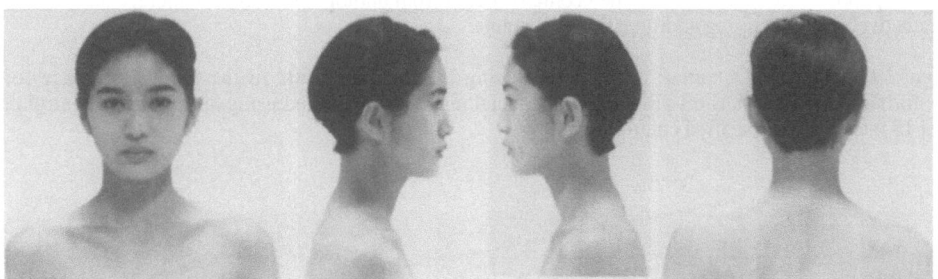

Fig. 4 Four photographs of an individual face showing the front, right, left, and back views.

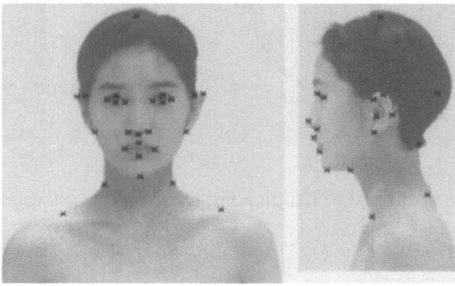

Fig. 5 Specified control points on the photographs.

then interactively specify 2-D coordinates of the projected points Q_{jk} of the destination points D_j on the photographs (see Fig. 5). To specify the coordinates automatically, more sophisticated techniques must be used for the recognition of the control points (Akimoto 1990).

The photograph is considered as a projected image from 3-D space, and the projection is described as follows:

$$[x\ y\ z\ 1] \begin{bmatrix} T_{11} & T_{12} & T_{13} \\ T_{21} & T_{22} & T_{23} \\ T_{31} & T_{32} & T_{33} \\ T_{41} & T_{42} & T_{43} \end{bmatrix} = [x\ y\ z\ 1]\ T$$

$$= [x'\ y'\ w]$$
$$= w[u\ v\ 1] \qquad (4)$$

where $u = x'/w$ and $v = y'/w$ are the coordinate values in the 2-D space of the photographs, and x, y, and z are the coordinate values in 3-D space. We assume that the projection matrix T is known. When this matrix T is unknown, it can be estimated if each photograph shows at least 6 reference points whose 3-D x, y, and z coordinates are known (Parke 1974).

If the projection matrix T and 2-D coordinates u and v are known, then we have two equations in three unknowns (x, y, z). If we have the u, v coordinates of a destination point D_j in at least two different photographs, it is therefore possible to solve for the position of the destination point D_j in 3-D space by using a least-squares method. If the destination point is shown on only one photograph, the 3-D coordinate value cannot be estimated. We therefore first transform the canonical model using only the destination points whose 3-D coordinates can be determined. This transformation moves the control points C_j to C_j'. We assume that this transformed model is a good approximation of the face to be modeled because many destination points are shown on at least two photographs. We estimate the 3-D coordinates of D_j shown on only one photograph as those of the point that satisfies Equation (4) and is nearest C_j' (see Fig. 6). The final model is obtained by transforming the approximated model using the estimated coordinates of all control points. If one can estimate the geometric detail from photographs, one can modify the facial model interactively, by specifying additional control points.

Figure 7 shows the Delaunay triangulation using the control points in the parameter space for the conformation. Figure 8 shows the individual facial model, transformed using 40 registered control points and 18 interactively specified control points.

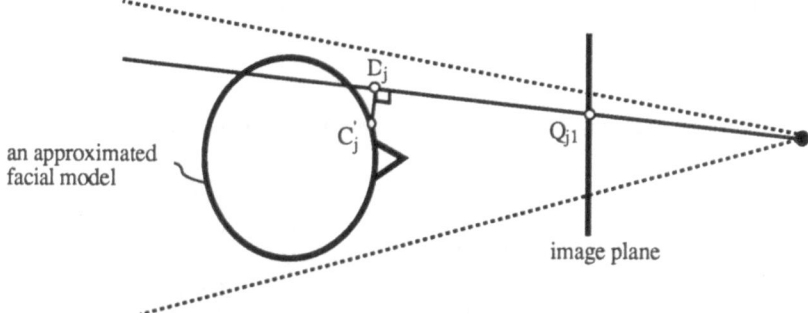

Fig. 6 Estimation of the destination point Dj from one photograph (Top view).

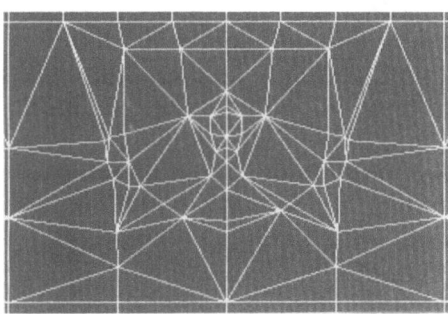

Fig. 7 Delaunay triangulation using the control
points in the parameter space for the
conformation of the face.

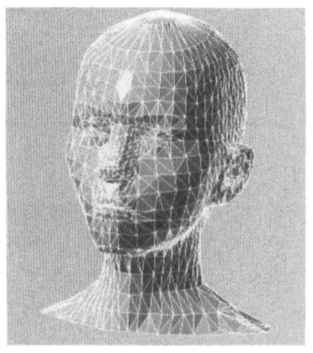

Fig. 8 The individual facial model.

4. COMPOSITE TEXTURE

Texture mapping is used for the rendering of the facial model. The photographs of the face have to be combined to make the model viewable from all directions.

The original photographs can be mapped on the model of the face. The positional certainty of the texture depends, however, on the angle between the viewing vector and the normal vector of the surface (see Fig. 9). It decreases as the angle increases. Positional certainty w is derived from an inner-product of the surface normal vector $\mathbf{N}$ and the viewing vector $\mathbf{V}$:

$$w = -\,\mathbf{N} \cdot \mathbf{V} \tag{5}$$

To combine all photographs, each photograph is projected onto cylindrical coordinates. The combined texture $\mathbf{I}(\theta,H)$ is the weighted average of all the projected textures $\mathbf{I}_j(\theta,H)$:

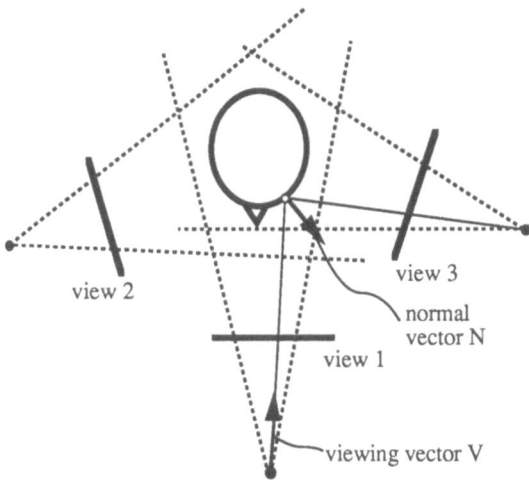

Fig. 9 Multiple textures and positional certainty.

$$I(\theta, H) = \frac{\sum_{j=1}^{n_p} I_j(\theta, H) \cdot f(w_j(\theta, H))}{\sum_{j=1}^{n_p} f(w_j(\theta, H))} \qquad (6)$$

where $I_j(\theta, H)$ and $w_j(\theta, H)$ are the intensity and positional certainty of texture j at pixel (θ, H), n_p is the number of photographs, and $f(w)$ is a function that ignores textures whose positional certainty is low. $f(w)$ is expressed by

$$f(w) = \begin{cases} \dfrac{(w - h)}{(1 - h)} & (w \geq h) \\[2ex] 0 & (w < h) \end{cases} \qquad (7)$$

where h is an arbitrary constant. If the positional certainty w is less than h, the texture is ignored. We used h = 0.5 for our experiments.

When the normal vector of the surface changes rapidly, the combined textures may be discontinuous. The normal vector is therefore smoothed to calculate the positional certainty. There may be "doubled" edges or features where the images misregister when combining textures. In this situation, one can suppress such artifacts using the interactive texture-warping method (Williams 1990).

Figure 10 shows the composite texture in cylindrical projection, and Plate 1 shows the texture-mapped images from different viewing directions. Hair is modeled only as texture-mapped polygons.

In Plate 1, one can see the neck shadows which appeared on the original photographs. To correctly generate variations in shade such as shadows, the reflection coefficient has to be determined from the photographs.

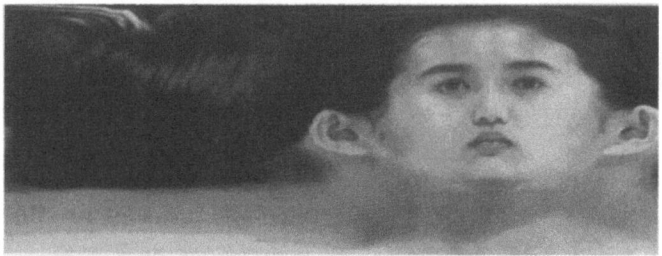

Fig. 10 The composite texture in cylindrical coordinates.

5. CREATION OF THE FACIAL MODEL USING ONE PHOTOGRAPH

In Section 3, we described the method for creating a facial model using multiple photographs. If we assume the face is right-left symmetrical, this method can be used to reconstruct a facial model from only one photograph. Because of the symmetry, the right-left mirror image of the photograph can be handled as another photograph taken from a different viewing direction. Therefore, we now have two photographs taken from different directions. These two photographs are used for the estimation of the 3-D coordinates

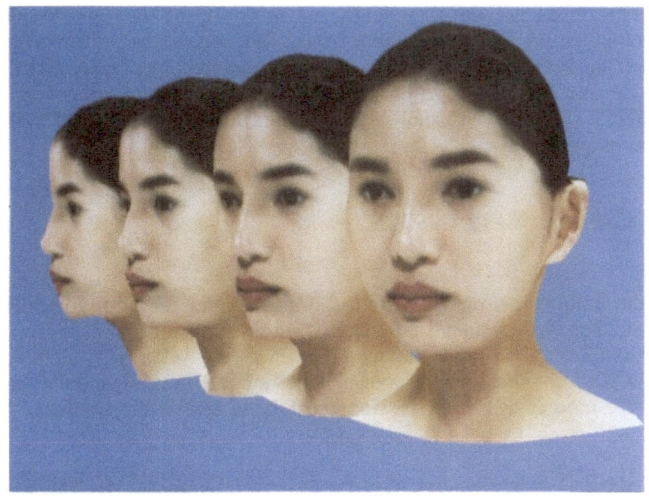

(a)

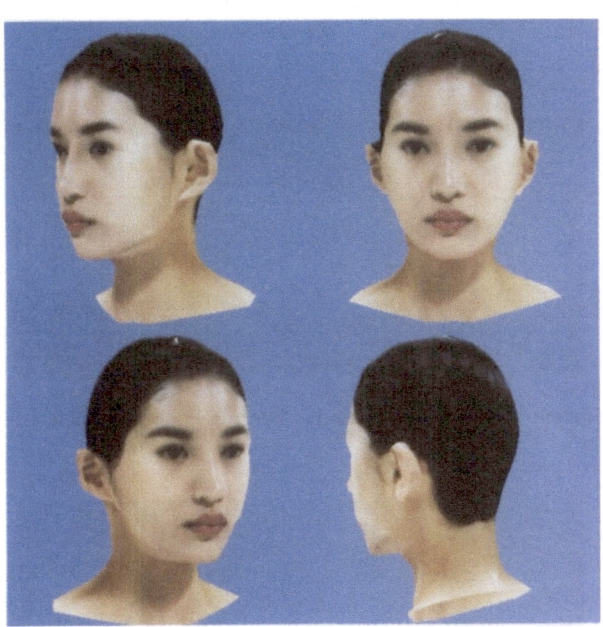

(b)

Plate 1: The synthesized images from different viewing directions.

of the destination points of the individual model (Komatsu 1990), and the reconstruction method can then be applied. The photograph should not be a direct frontal view, because its mirror image is identical, and it is difficult to estimate the 3-D coordinates of the destination points. The facial model is created from one photograph (Plate 2), and Plate 3 shows the resulting texture-mapped images in which the viewing directions are changed. Some parts (such as behind the left ear) look unnatural because only one photograph is texture-mapped.

6. MODIFYING FACIAL EXPRESSION

The transformation technique described in Section 2 is also applied for modifying facial expression. Only the control points and their displacements are required for this transformation of facial expression, though the muscle-based model requires more parameters such as the vector contraction and fall-off radius. Displacements of the vertices other than the control points are interpolated automatically. Figure 11 shows 105 control points for modifying the expression and Fig. 12 shows the Delaunay triangulation in 2-D parameter space.

One has to specify the 3-D displacements to change the facial expressions. This is not easy, however, because the computer display is only two-dimensional. In order to suppress this problem, we developed an interactive method to specify the 3-D displacement vector. With this method, the angular and height coordinates of the displacements are specified first, and then the radius coordinates are specified as follows:

1. Select the control point in the displayed 3-D facial model which you would like to move.
2. Interactively specify the destination position on the surface of the face where the control point is to be moved. Let (R_c, θ_c, H_c) and (R_d, θ_d, H_d) be the cylindrical coordinates of the control point and destination position respectively.

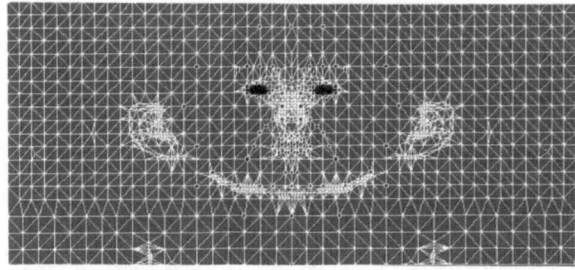

Fig. 11 The control points in the parameter space for modifying the facial expression.

Fig. 12 Delaunay triangulation using the control points.

3. Calculate the difference of the angular and height coordinates of the control points between destination points.

$$\theta_v = \theta_d - \theta_c$$
$$H_v = H_d - H_c \tag{8}$$

4. Specify the radius coordinates R_v of the displacement interactively.
5. Convert the displacement from cylindrical coordinates (R_v, θ_v, H_v) to Cartesian coordinates.

The radius coordinates R_v of the displacement is small for almost all facial expressions, and a wide variety of facial expressions can be generated by the displacement of only the angular and height coordinates θ_v and H_v. This specification method of the displacement vector is therefore a convenient method for specifying the facial expression.

6.1 Composition of Transformation

It is not convenient to specify the displacements of all the control points to modify the facial expression. One wishes to specify an expression by specifying sub-expressions of different parts of the face, each of which is defined by displacements of multiple control points. Therefore, the composition technique of transformation is developed. The transformation defined by the displacements of the shared control points is composed with weighting coefficients.

Let E_i $(1 \le i \le n)$ be the transformation elements, each of which is defined using shared control points C_j $(1 \le j \le m)$, and let V_{ij} be the displacements of control points C_j of the transformation element E_i, where n is the number of transformation elements and m is the number of shared control points. The composed transformation E_S is defined by the displacement V_j as follows:

$$V_j = \sum_{i=1}^{n} w_i \cdot V_{ij} \tag{9}$$

where V_j is the displacement of control point C_j for the composed transformation E_S, and w_i is the weighting coefficient. A new expression is thus obtained by this composed transformation.

6.2 Facial Expression by FACS

Facial Action Coding System (FACS) (Ekman 1977) describes the set of all possible basic actions (Action Units) performable on a human face. Some sample Action Units are Inner Brow Raiser, Outer Brow Raiser, and Lid Tightener. An Action Unit is a minimal action that cannot be broken up into smaller actions, and any facial expression can be described as the combination of Action Units. FACS is often used in facial animation because it is a high-level description for specifying facial expressions.

We have developed transformation elements for all FACS Action Units using the proposed transformation method. The combined expression of these Action Units is generated using the composition technique described above. One can use FACS as a high-level description, and then refine the expression by specifying the displacement interactively. Furthermore, control points can be added if subtle control is required to generate a complex expression. Plate 4 shows examples of the modified expressions using FACS.

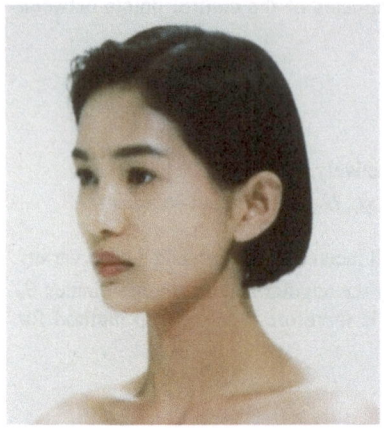

Plate 2: A photograph of the face.

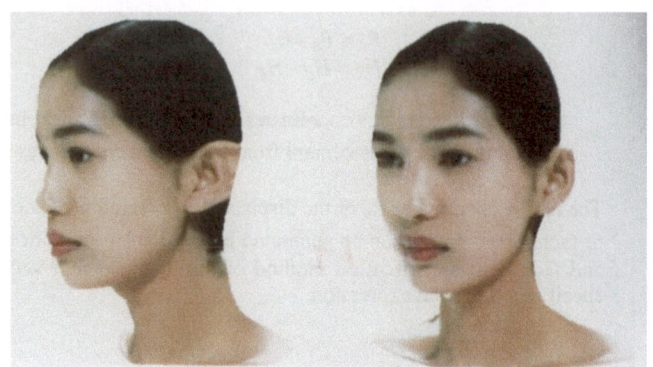

Plate 3: The created facial images from one photograph.

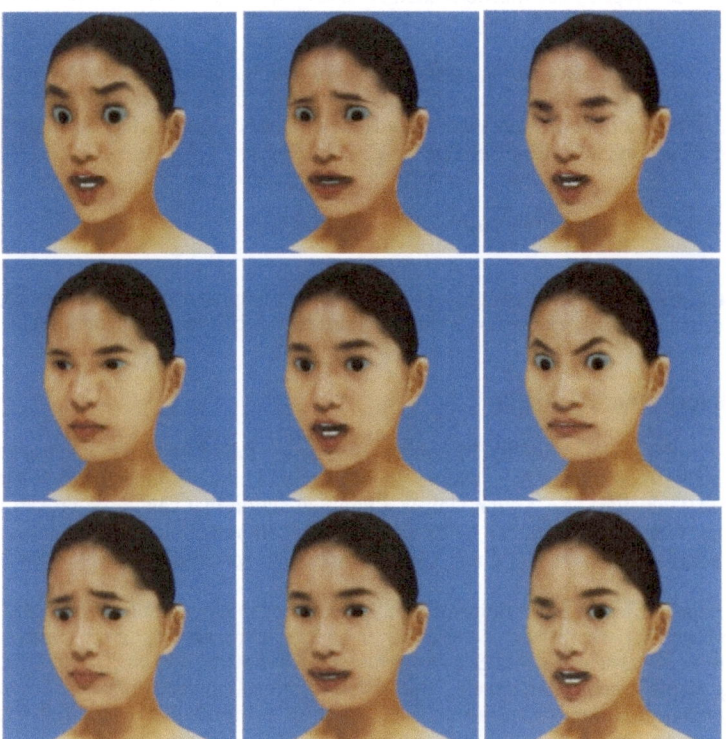

Plate 4: The modified facial expressions.

7. CONCLUSION

This paper has described a technique using photographs for facial modeling and animation. A new transformation method is presented for this purpose. The advantage of this transformation method is that multiple control points and their displacements can be specified directly and simultaneously. Using this transformation method, texture-mapped facial images of specific persons can be easily created and animated from photographs. In the future we would like to develop a method to determine the reflection coefficient from photographs so that shading can be accurately simulated. We are also currently working on a more realistic rendering method of hair. Nevertheless, we feel this approach is useful to create and animate the facial model.

ACKNOWLEDGMENTS

The authors are grateful to Akio Yajima and Ken-ichi Anjyo for many valuable discussions.

REFERENCES

Aizawa K, Yamada Y, Harashima H and Saito T (1987) Model-Based Synthesis Image Coding System - Modeling A Person's Face and Synthesis of Facial Expressions -, GLOBECOM '87 Conference Record, pp. 45-49.

Akimoto T, Wallace R and Suenaga Y (1990) Automatic creation of face model for human image generation from front and side views, Proceedings of Image' Com 90 (Bordeaux, France, 19-21 Nov. 1990), pp. 183-188.

Allan JB, Wyvill B and Witten IH (1989) A Methodology for Direct Manipulation of Polygon Meshes, Proceedings of CG International '89, pp. 451-469.

Blinn JF and Newell ME (1976) Texture and Reflection in Computer Generated Images, Comm. ACM, Vol. 19, No.10, pp.542-546.

Ekman P and Friesen W (1977) Facial Action Coding System, Consulting Psychologists Press, Palo Alto.

Kleiser J (1989) A Fast, Efficient, Accurate way to Represent the Human Face, SIGGRAPH '89, Course Notes on State of the Art in Facial Animation, pp. 35-40.

Komatsu K (1990) 3D Shape Reconstruction of Human Face from a 2D Facial Image and Change of the Expression, Trans. of IEICE Japan, Vol. J73-D-II, No. 5, pp. 707-716 (in Japanese).

Magnenat-Thalmann N and Thalmann D (1987) The Direction of Synthetic Actors in the Film Rendezvous a Montreal, IEEE Computer Graphics and Applications, Vol. 7, No. 12, pp. 9-12.

Magnenat-Thalmann N, Minh HT, de Angelis M and Thalmann D (1989) Design, Transformation and Animation of Human Faces, The Visual Computer, Vol. 5, No. 1, pp.32-39.

Mallet Jean-Laurent (1989) Direct Smooth Interpolation, ACM Transactions on Graphics, Vol. 8, No. 2, pp. 121-144.

Nahas M, Huitric H, Rioux M and Domey J (1990) Registered 3D-Texture Imaging, Computer Animation '90, pp. 81-91.

Oka M, Tsutsui K, Ohba A, Yoshida K, Kurauchi Y, and Tago T (1987) Real-Time Manipulation of Texture-mapped Surfaces, Computer Graphics, Vol. 21, No. 4, pp. 181-188.

Parke FI (1974) A Paramertic Model for Human Faces, PhD. dissertation, Department of Computer Science, University of Utah.

Platt SM and Badler NI (1981) Animating Facial Expressions, Computer Graphics, Vol. 15, No. 3, pp. 245-252.

Sibson R (1978) Locally Equiangular Triangulations, The Computer Journal, Vol. 21, No. 3, pp. 243-245.

Waters K (1987) A Muscle Model for Animating Three-Dimensional Facial Expression, Computer Graphics, Vol. 21, No. 4, pp. 17-24.

Williams L, (1990) Performance-Driven Facial Animation, Computer Graphics, Vol. 24, No. 4, pp. 235-242.

Yau JFS and Duffy ND (1988) A texture mapping approach to 3D facial image synthesis, Computer Graphics Forum, 7, pp. 129-134.

Tsuneya Kurihara is a researcher at the Central Research Laboratory, Hitachi, Ltd. He received the B.E. and M.E. degrees from the University of Tokyo, Tokyo, Japan, in 1981 and 1983. His research interests include computer animation and physically-based modeling. He is a member of ACM, IEEE CS and IPS of Japan.
Address: Central Research Laboratory, Hitachi, Ltd., Kokubunji, Tokyo 185 JAPAN.
E-mail: kurihara@hcrlgw.crl.hitachi.co.jp

Kiyoshi Arai is a researcher at the Central Research Laboratory, Hitachi, Ltd. He received the B.E. and M.E. degrees from Tokyo Institute of Technology, Tokyo, Japan, in 1987 and 1989. His research interests include geometric modeling and articulated figure animation. He is a member of IPS of Japan.
Address: Central Research Laboratory, Hitachi, Ltd., Kokubunji, Tokyo 185 JAPAN.
E-mail: arai @hcrlgw.crl.hitachi.co.jp

Techniques for Realistic Facial Modeling and Animation

Demetri Terzopoulos and Keith Waters

Abstract: This paper describes a methodology for constructing and animating realistic models of human faces. We present three physically-based techniques. The first, an adaptive meshing method, is able to create nonuniform facial meshes from high resolution data acquired by scanning a subject with a laser range sensor. Starting with a nonuniform mesh, the second method constructs a realistic model of the subject's face and head. The face model includes synthetic facial tissue and muscle actuators based on anatomical and biomechanical considerations. From video sequences of a subject performing expressive articulations, the third method estimates facial muscle contractions and inputs these as dynamic control parameters to the model in order to yield realistic, performance-controlled facial animation.

Keywords: facial modeling, facial animation, adaptive meshing, facial image analysis, deformable models, physically-based modeling, performance animation

1   Introduction

Physically-based graphics modeling in conjunction with image analysis, range sensor technology, and state-of-the-art rendering engines promises a dramatic improvement in our ability to animate synthetic human faces with very realistic results. Physically-based modeling is providing new approaches to acquire accurate facial geometries and textures, to synthesize expressive facial deformations, and to achieve natural, performance-controlled facial animation. In this paper we describe techniques that enable us to (1) extract essential geometric and photometric information from raw data acquired by scanning a person's head with a laser range sensor, (2) construct sophisticated yet parsimonious 3D models of subjects' heads, including synthetic facial tissue with embedded muscle actuators and high resolution photometric data texture mapped on the epidermis, and (3) realistically animate these models in real-time using information gleaned from video footage of (possibly different) subjects performing expressive facial articulations. The techniques make use of discrete deformable models (Terzopoulos and Fleischer, 1988) which are easy to formulate and compute. Let us consider the background of each of the above three areas of interest:

Modeling realistic facial geometries has been difficult and time consuming because the human face is highly curved and its intricate features captivate people's critical attention (Parke, 1986). The advent of high speed active range sensing provides a new wealth of accurate geometric and photometric data (Rioux and Cournoyer, 1988; Cyberware Laboratory, Inc., 1990). Facial maps containing 128K range and reflectance samples in registration can be readily captured in a few seconds to provide a very detailed database. From a practical standpoint, this much data is excessive, especially in flat or otherwise "uninteresting" regions of the head, and it must be reduced to a manageably sized polygonal mesh. A physically-based adaptive meshing technique has been developed in (Terzopoulos and Vasilescu, 1991) which is suitable for designing coarser, nonuniform meshes that capture the essential structure of the high resolution facial maps. These geometrically accurate facial meshes adapt to features of interest in the data, increasing polygon density over articulate facial areas, for instance. The illusion of detail can be restored on a well-designed coarse mesh by painting on it the high-resolution photometric map acquired by the sensor (Oka et al., 1987; Yau and Duffey, 1988; Williams, 1990; Nahas et al., 1990). Rendering hardware available in some high-end graphics workstations is able to perform the texture mapping in real time using the mesh polygon vertices as texture map coordinates. Section 2 presents the adaptive facial meshing method.

Prior work in facial animation has followed a road of development from keyframing to parameterized geometric models (see the survey (Parke, 1982)). Most recently, the focus has turned to physically-based techniques (Terzopoulos and Waters, 1990) because they clearly offer facial animators a significantly enhanced level of sophistication compared to purely geometric schemes. In particular, the realism of synthetic facial tissue which is subject to physically-based deformation through the action of contractile muscles may be exploited for no more manual effort than is required to animate the best geometric face models with anatomically motivated parameter sets, such as those described in (Waters, 1987), (Magnenat-Thalmann, Primeau and Thalmann, 1988), and (Reeves, 1990). The realistic deformations produced by the synthetic tissue, such as wrinkling, furrowing, and bulging, are highly desirable in animations because people can be very sensitive to subtle skin deformations when interpreting facial expressions. Section 3 describes our realistic face model which includes synthetic facial tissue and muscle actuators based on anatomical and biomechanical considerations.

Performance-controlled animation emerges as an important issue for animating realistic faces, especially as the sophistication of the facial model increases (deGraf, 1990; Williams, 1990; Terzopoulos and Waters, 1990). It is fairly easy to establish a correspondence between video footage of an actor and the model using intrusive schemes; for instance, by tracking markers placed on the actor's face which coincide with the positions of deformation control points distributed on the model (Williams, 1990). Despite the inherent quality of performance animation, however, geometrically distorting an infinitesimally thin surface with no underlying structure often produces spurious and unrealistic motions. The structure of our physically-based facial modeling suggests a more natural approach—to estimate the time-varying contractions of facial muscles from video footage of the performer's face. The estimates may then be input as animation control parameters to the facial model. This problem, first investigated in (Terzopoulos and Waters, 1990), is difficult because it requires the reliable estimation of quantitative information about the positions and shapes of extended facial features such as the eyebrows and mouth as they undergo nonrigid motion in the image plane. Section 4 describes our performance animation scheme, a technique that applies physically-based deformable contours or "snakes" (Kass, Witkin and Terzopoulos, 1987) to track facial features in video sequences.

2   Meshing Facial Geometries from Scanned Data

This section develops a technique for constructing nonuniformly meshed faces and heads from raw, high resolution range and photometric data. The technique makes use of a physically-based elastic model that we call an "adaptive mesh" (Terzopoulos and Vasilescu, 1991).

2.1 Adaptive Meshes

The nodes of the adaptive mesh are mobile observers or sampling sites and they distribute themselves over the data so as to represent the face with sufficient accuracy given the finite set of observations. Clearly, it is beneficial to concentrate the nodes of a facial mesh where they will do the most good—in highly curved areas of the facial surface, especially in articulate regions around the nose, eyes, and mouth. Each node of the adaptive mesh influences the other nodes, so that if one node moves to gain a better position, its neighbors will follow to some extent to maintain smooth coverage of the data.

An elastic mesh is constructed from nodes connected by springs. Let node i, where $i = 1, \ldots, N$, be a point mass m_i whose 3-space position is $x_i(t) = [x(t), y(t), z(t)]'$. The velocity of the node is $\mathbf{v}_i = d\mathbf{x}_i/dt$ and its acceleration is $\mathbf{a}_i = d^2\mathbf{x}_i/dt^2$. The equations of motion for the dynamic node/spring system is the system of coupled, second order ordinary differential equations

$$m_i \frac{d^2 \mathbf{x}_i}{dt^2} + \gamma_i \frac{d\mathbf{x}_i}{dt} + \mathbf{g}_i = \mathbf{f}_i; \qquad i = 1, \ldots, N, \tag{1}$$

where $\mathbf{g}_i(t)$ is the total internal force on node i due to springs connecting it to neighboring nodes $j \in \mathcal{N}_i$ and where $\mathbf{f}_i$ is a net external force acting on node i. The quantity γ_i is a velocity-dependent damping coefficient which dissipates the kinetic energy of the dynamic model through friction.

Let spring $k = ij$, which connects node i to node j, have natural length l_k and stiffness c_k.[1] The spring forces in (1) are

$$\mathbf{g}_i(t) = \sum_{j \in \mathcal{N}_i} \mathbf{s}_k, \tag{2}$$

where the force spring k exerts on node i is

$$\mathbf{s}_k = \frac{c_k e_k}{\|\mathbf{r}_k\|} \mathbf{r}_k, \tag{3}$$

with $\mathbf{r}_k = \mathbf{x}_j - \mathbf{x}_i$ being the vector separation of the nodes and $e_k = \|\mathbf{r}_k\| - l_k$ the deformation of the spring of actual length $\|\mathbf{r}_k\|$.

To simulate the dynamics of the mesh, we provide initial positions $\mathbf{x}_i^0$ and velocities $\mathbf{v}_i^0$ for each node i at $t = 0$, and numerically integrate the equations of motion forward though time using a simple and quick explicit (Euler) method. At each time step the integration method computes the forces and accelerations from the current positions and velocities at time t, and uses them to extrapolate the new velocities and positions at time $t + \Delta t$ as follows:

$$\begin{aligned} \mathbf{f}_i^{nt} &= \mathbf{f}_i^t - \gamma_i \mathbf{v}_i^t - \mathbf{g}_i; \\ \mathbf{a}_i^t &= \frac{\mathbf{B}_i \mathbf{f}_i^{nt}}{m_i}; \\ \mathbf{v}_i^{t+\Delta t} &= \mathbf{v}_i^t + \Delta t \, \mathbf{a}_i^t; \\ \mathbf{x}_i^{t+\Delta t} &= \mathbf{x}_i^t + \Delta t \, \mathbf{v}_i^{t+\Delta t}, \end{aligned} \tag{4}$$

where $\mathbf{f}_i^{nt}$ are the net nodal forces and $\mathbf{B}_i$ denotes an operator whose role is to enforce boundary conditions and constraints through a transformation of the nodal forces.

---

[1] The index k can be thought of as a multi-index $k = ij$. We employ the separate indices i and j or the multi-index k interchangeably as is convenient.

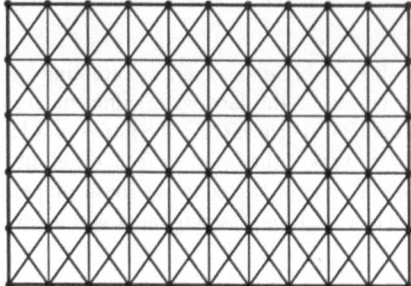

Fig. 1: A mesh of quadrilateral elements with cross springs. Interior nodes move freely in (x, y, z) space. Only z coordinates of boundary nodes are free, while x and y coordinates are constrained such that boundary nodes may slide along boundary (bold lines).

We construct adaptive meshes as shown in Fig. 1. Each quadrilateral in the mesh includes cross springs that provide resistance against shearing. The rectangular domain illustrated in the figure is covered by a mesh in its initial, regular configuration. The positions $\mathbf{x}_i$ of interior nodes are unconstrained, whereas boundary nodes are subject to boundary conditions. The operator $\mathbf{B}_i$ cancels the component of the net nodal force $\mathbf{f}_i^n$ which is parallel to the image plane and normal to the boundary. This ensures that the x_i and y_i components of boundary node positions $\mathbf{x}_i$ are constrained so as to remain on the boundary, while allowing them the freedom to slide like beads along the boundary.

2.2   Mesh Adaptation

The nodes of the adaptive mesh are able to make local observations about input data $\mathbf{d}(\boldsymbol{\xi})$, where $\boldsymbol{\xi}$ is the data coordinate system. In facial modeling applications, scanners provide surface range and RGB reflectance information. It is convenient to first transform this information into adaptation functions $a_{\mathbf{d}}(\boldsymbol{\xi})$ which determine how the mesh will adapt to the data.

Let $O_i(\mathbf{d})$ be a nodal observation; i.e., a measurement computed on $\mathbf{d}$ by node i through an adaptation function. We define an observation function

$$O_i(\mathbf{d}) = a_{\mathbf{d}}(\Pi \mathbf{x}_i), \tag{5}$$

where Π is an operator that projects the position $\mathbf{x}_i$ of node i into $\boldsymbol{\xi}$. We design the adaptation function so that larger values of O_i will indicate that from its vantage point $\mathbf{x}_i$, node i is observing "interesting" features in the data. Features of interest may include significant variations in surface shape and specific RGB reflectance patterns that occur around the nose and eyes.

The adaptive mesh is designed to increase its node density around interesting observations, at the expense of node density in regions where the data lack interesting features. This is done by automatically adjusting spring parameters c_{ij} according to the observations on the nodes to which the springs are attached. Assuming that the adaptation function has been scaled so that the values of observations fall in the range $[0, 1]$, a simple but effective relationship is

$$c_{ij} = (1 - \rho)c_{\min} - \rho c_{\max} \tag{6}$$

with

$$\rho = \frac{1}{2}(O_i + O_j), \tag{7}$$

where c_{min} and c_{max} are the minimum and maximum allowable values for the spring constant. Thus, the stiffness of spring ij is increased with increasing O_i and O_j, which indicates that the two associated nodes are observing interesting features in the data. Since the springs will repel nodes when they are compressed beyond their natural lengths l_{ij}, we can set these lengths to the minimum desired distance between nodes.

2.3 A Facial Meshing Example

Figures 2–6 illustrate an application of the adaptive meshing technique to the "Heidi" data set, acquired from a 360° scan of a woman's head and shoulders by the Cyberware, Inc., Color 3D Digitizer (the data set is included as part of the Cyberware demonstration system). The data set consists of a radial range map $R(\xi, \eta)$, which is displayed as a shaded terrain surface in Fig. 2, and a registered RGB photometric map $I(\xi, \eta)$ of the same resolution, shown in Fig. 3. The data is defined in cylindrical coordinates. The range and RGB maps are high-resolution 512×256 arrays, where ξ, running horizontally across the map, is the latitudinal angle around the head and η, running vertically, is the height up the head.

We have built a geometric model of the head by applying a 50×25 adaptive mesh to the data. Figures 4 and 5 show the initial unadapted mesh stretched over two of the adaptation functions obtained from the data. The mesh is constrained within the arrays by boundary conditions along the edges of the available data. An initialization procedure computes the starting configuration and boundary conditions automatically from the data. The constraints allow boundary nodes to slide along the vertical boundaries of the arrays and along the ragged upper and lower boundaries of the data.

Figure 4 shows a facial region adaptation function in which the face and hair regions have been manually segmented from the rest of the data. This function determines the maximum and minimum spring constants of the mesh as follows: Background (black) $c_{min} = 0.5$, $c_{max} = 10.0$; Hair (white): $c_{min} = 1.0$, $c_{max} = 10.0$; Face (grey): $c_{min} = 4.0$, $c_{max} = 20.0$. Figure 5 shows a second adaptation function computed as the magnitude of the gradient of the range map: $a_d = \|\nabla R\|$, where ∇ is the discrete gradient operator. We scale the result of the convolution to obtain an adaptation function whose values fall into the range $[0, 1]$. This function determines the value of ρ in (7) in order to increase the spring stiffness where the surface is undergoing rapid transitions. Both adaptation functions are accessed by projecting node positions $\mathbf{x}_i$ using the orthographic projection $(\xi_i, \eta_i) = \Pi \mathbf{x}_i = (x_i, y_i)$, the nodes compute the observations

$$O_i(d) = a_d(x_i, y_i), \tag{8}$$

where $a_d(x_i, y_i)$ is obtained by bilinearly interpolating $a_d(k, l)$. Figure 6 shows the adaptive mesh at equilibrium. Note the higher density of nodes in the facial area and around facial features. The parameters of the adaptive mesh simulation (4) were as follows: $m_i = 0.2$, $\gamma_i = 0.9$, $l_{ij} = 1.0$, $\Delta t = 0.02$, $\alpha = 10.0$.

The range map is sampled at the projected coordinates of the nodes of the adaptive mesh and the result $R(\xi_i, \eta_i)$ is used to convert the node to a point in space using the cylindrical transformation. Also, the projected coordinates serve as texture map coordinates for each polygon into the high-resolution RGB array of Fig. 3. With the photometric texture map painted on the nonuniform 50×25 polygonal surface (see Fig. 7), the visual quality of the head model is comparable to a 3D display of the original high resolution data, despite the significantly coarser geometry. Although deformed, the adapted mesh retains the simple topology of a rectangular mesh of quadrilateral elements such as that in Fig. 1, which facilitates the construction of physically-based face models.

3 Physically-Based Facial Modeling and Animation

The difficulty of devising a model of the face which is convenient for animators to use, physically realistic, and efficient enough to run at interactive rates suggests tackling the facial modeling task in hierarchical fashion. The model that we proposed in (Terzopoulos and Waters, 1990) spans six levels of abstraction. The most abstract is the *expression level* which interprets expression commands that enable the animator to think of facial actions in terms of meaningful moods such as happiness, sadness, anger, disgust, surprise, and fear. A muscle process at the *control level* translates expression commands into a coordinated activation of actuator groups. Each muscle at the *actuator level* consists of a bundle of contractile muscle fibers which displace their attachment points in the facial tissue (or jaw). At the *physics level* a numerical simulation computes large-scale tissue deformation by dynamically propagating through a synthetic facial tissue lattice the local stresses induced by activated muscle fibers. At the *geometry level* muscle-induced tissue deformations distort the neutral, nonuniform facial lattice into an expressive geometry. Finally, after each time step of the simulation procedure, standard rendering techniques, accelerated by graphics hardware, render the facial geometry and skin reflectance information to produce continuous output at the *image level*.

At the higher levels of abstraction, the face model offers the user a natural and semantically rich set of control parameters that reflect the constraints of real faces. The hierarchical structure of the model hides from the user the complexities of the underlying representations, invoking internal procedures that automatically handle the details in the lower level data structures.

3.1 Synthetic Facial Tissue

The main physically-based component of the face model is the synthetic tissue. Human facial tissue has a layered structure, including the epidermis, the dermis, and the muscle layer. The mechanical properties of tissue are due mostly to the dermis (Kenedi et al., 1975). Under low tensile stress, dermal tissue is relatively deformable, but under higher stress it becomes much more stretch resistant. The nonlinear stress strain curve is approximately biphasic, with two approximately linear regimes (Fig. 8). Consequently, we define a biphasic spring which is readily extensible at low strains, but exerts rapidly increasing restoring stresses after reaching a strain e^c. The biphasic spring exerts a force as in (3) with stiffness

$$c_k = \begin{cases} \alpha_k & \text{when } e_k \leq e_k^c; \\ \beta_k & \text{when } e_k > e_k^c; \end{cases} \tag{9}$$

where the small-strain stiffness α_k is smaller than than the large-strain stiffness β_k.

Considering spring $k = ij$ along with its attached nodes i and j as a uniaxial finite element, it is easy to assemble deformable structures with diverse topologies by allowing elements to share nodes. In particular, we construct a synthetic tissue model as a layer of tetrahedral elements (epidermis) and two layers of structurally stable hexahedral elements (dermis and muscle layer) with cross-strutted, shear-resisting faces, as shown in Fig. 9(b). The biphasic springs in each layer may have different stiffness parameters α_k and β_k in accordance with the layered inhomogeneities of real facial tissue. Elasticity aside, another important mechanical property of facial tissue stems from the incompressibility of the cutaneous ground substance and subcutaneous fatty tissues. Incompressibility is responsible for the bulging and dimpling of skin evident around the mouth and eyes as the facial muscles exert tractions. To model this behavior, we include a constraint into each element E that minimizes the deviation of the volume of the deformed element from its

Fig. 2: "Heidi" data set (range map).

Fig. 3: "Heidi" data set (RGB map).

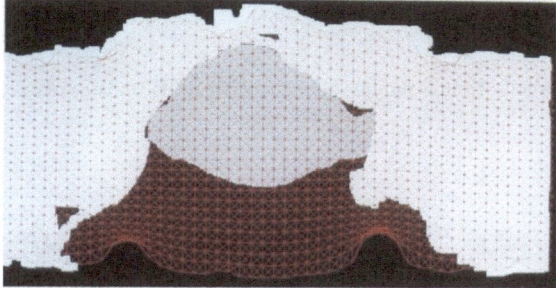

Fig. 4: Initial (unadapted) mesh overlayed on facial region adaptation function.

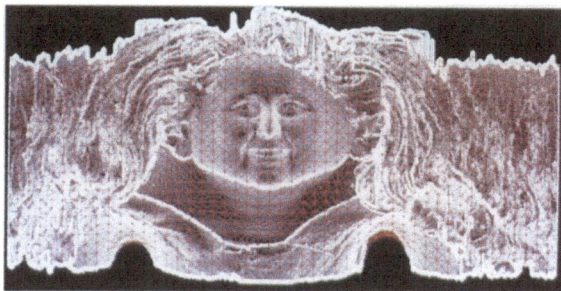

Fig. 5: Initial (unadapted) mesh overlayed on magnitude-of-range-gradient adaptation function.

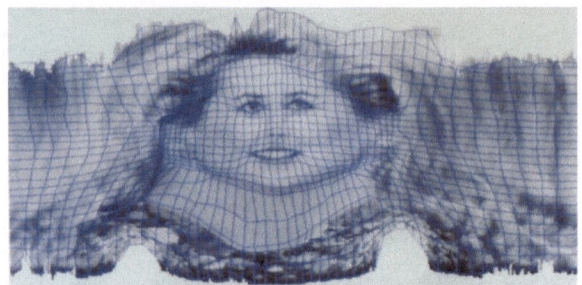

Fig. 6: Final (adapted) mesh overlayed on photometric map.

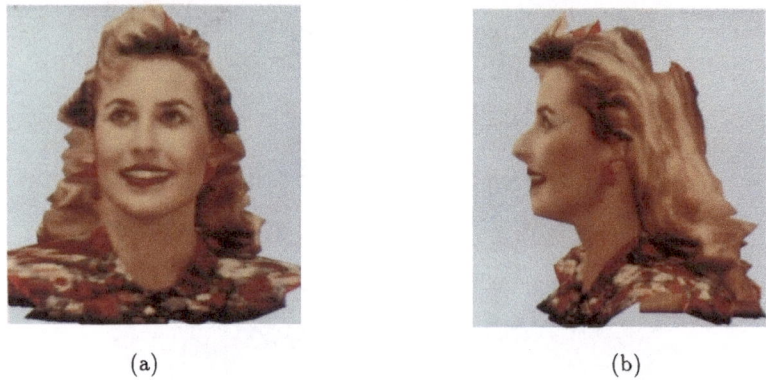

(a)   (b)

Fig. 7: Adaptively meshed "Heidi" model (50×25) with RGB texture map. (a) Frontal view. (b) Side view.

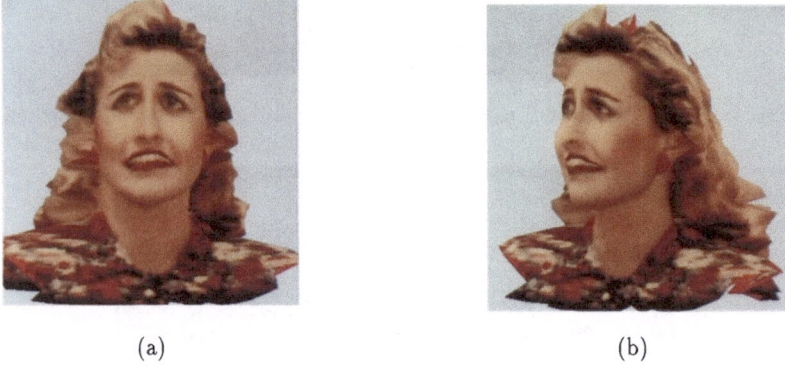

(a)   (b)

Fig. 11: Adaptively meshed "Heidi" model in a worried expression. (a) Frontal view. (b) Side view.

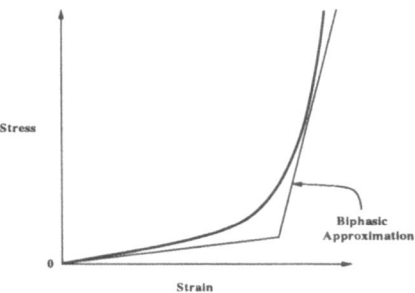

Fig. 8: Stress-strain curve of facial tissue and its biphasic approximation.

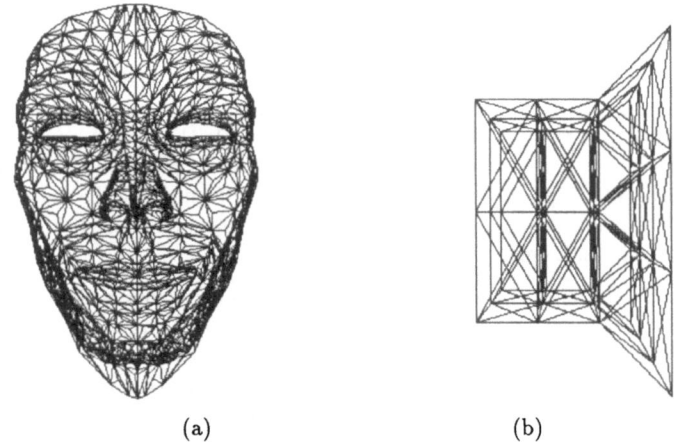

(a)   (b)

Fig. 9: Physically-based face model (a) containing approximately 6500 springs in the trilayer synthetic facial tissue. Enlarged portion of synthetic tissue (b).

natural volume V_E which is readily computed. This constraint yields a volume restoration force q_i at each node, so that the total internal force on the node in (1) is

$$g_i(t) = q_i + \sum_{j \in \mathcal{N}_i} s_k. \qquad (10)$$

The 3D facial model is constructed automatically starting from a nonuniform facial mesh. For example, starting with the manually-triangulated mesh used in (Waters, 1987), we obtain the 3D model illustrated in Fig. 9(a) (hexahedral layers are not drawn for clarity). After assembling the tetrahedral and hexahedral layers and immobilizing the bottommost layer of nodes in "bone" (by enforcing at these nodes the boundary conditions $B_i = 0$ in (4)), muscles are then automatically inserted through the muscle layer (see below).

3.2   Facial Muscle Control

The relevant anatomical details of facial muscles and the mathematical simulation of muscle actions in the face model are reviewed in (Waters, 1987; Terzopoulos and Waters, 1990). Briefly, the facial muscles are modeled as bundles of contractile muscle fibers. The muscle fibers are

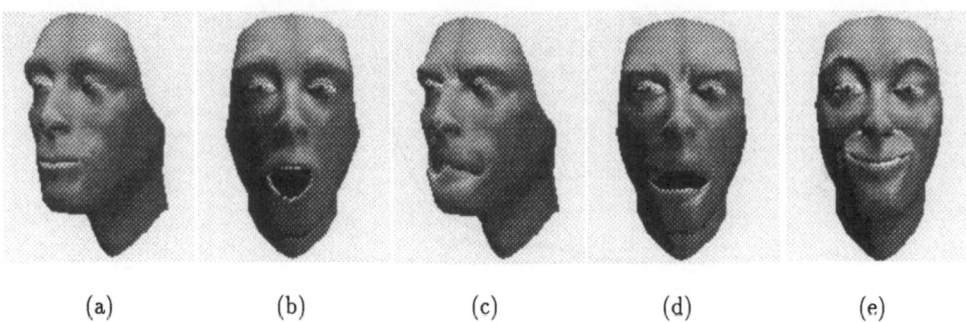

(a)   (b)   (c)   (d)   (e)

Fig. 10: Face model in relaxed condition (a) and expressions synthesized through muscle contractions (b)–(e).

inserted through the muscle layer from their emergence in bone to their nodes of attachment. When real facial muscles contract, they pull the facial soft tissue to which they attach towards the site where they emerge from the underlying skeletal framework. In the model, a muscle contraction displaces the muscle fiber attachment nodes situated at the bases of hexahedral elements of the first layer. As a result of the perturbation, those nodes not influenced by the muscle contraction are in an unstable state and unbalanced forces propagate through the tissue lattice to establish a new equilibrium position in a deformed state.

A facial expression is the result of a confluence of muscle contractions which together deform the neutral face into an expressive face. Ekman and Friesen have proposed the *Facial Action Coding System* (FACS), a quantitative abstraction of the actions of facial muscles, as a means of recording facial expressions independent of intercultural disparities (Ekman and Friesen, 1977). The FACS represents facial expressions in terms of 66 *action units* (AU) which involve one or more muscles and associated activation levels. The physically-based approach to facial modeling can incorporate the same FACS representation implemented as part of earlier geometric models, such as the one in (Waters, 1987). Through the FACS abstraction it is possible to suppress the low-level details of coordinated muscle actuation and provide a more convenient interface to the model in terms of the higher-level language of expressions.

Figure 10(a) illustrates the neutral (undeformed) face, along with several expressions synthesized by coordinated muscle contractions: (b) jaw rotated; (c) symmetric contraction of the anguli depressors, lateral corrugators, and labii superioris; (d) symmetric contraction of the anguli depressors, lateral corrugators, labii superioris, and jaw rotation yielding an expression of anger; (e) symmetric contraction of the zygomaticus major, frontalis, and labii superioris muscles yielding an expression of happiness. See (Terzopoulos and Waters, 1990) for the rendered color versions of these and other facial images synthesized by the physically-based model.

We have also constructed some preliminary physically-based face models with muscle actuators from adaptively meshed range sensor data. The assembly procedure is simpler when we construct a facial model starting from the adapted quadrilateral mesh, since the synthetic tissue can be constructed using layers of hexahedral elements exclusively. Figure 11 shows the physically-based "Heidi" model in a fearful expression with contracted anguli depressor and frontalis muscles.

4 Performance-Controlled Facial Animation

This section describes a performance facial animation technique which involves two steps: First, through (image) analysis of a performer's face in a video sequence, the technique estimates the dynamic contractions of the performer's facial muscles. Then, it inputs these contraction estimates as animation control parameters to the physically-based face model described in the previous section in order to produce realistic facial animation that imitates the performer's expressions.

Briefly, our image analysis method is as follows: Through straightforward image processing, we convert digitized image frames into 2D potential functions whose ravines (extended local minima) correspond to salient facial features such as the eyebrows, mouth, and chin. We employ a discrete variant of deformable contours (a.k.a. "snakes") first proposed in (Kass, Witkin and Terzopoulos, 1987). The discrete snakes lock onto the ravines, thereby tracking the nonrigidly moving facial features from frame to frame. Our method estimates dynamic muscle parameters for use by the physically-based face model by automatically interpreting the state variables of the snakes in successive image frames.

4.1 Discrete Snakes

A snake can be thought of as a dynamic deformable contour in the x-y image plane. We define a discrete deformable contour as a set of n nodes indexed by $i = 1, \ldots, n$, with time varying positions $\mathbf{x}_i(t) = [x_i(t), y_i(t)]'$. The nodes are coupled by internal forces

$$\mathbf{g}_i = \boldsymbol{\alpha}_i + \boldsymbol{\beta}_i, \tag{11}$$

where $\boldsymbol{\alpha}_i(t)$ are "compression" forces which make the contour act like a series of unilateral springs that resist compression and $\boldsymbol{\beta}_i(t)$ are "rigidity" forces which make the snake act like a thin wire that resists bending. To create an interactive discrete snake, we introduce (11) into (1), set the nodal masses $m_i = 0$, and simulate the resulting first-order dynamic system

$$\gamma_i \frac{d\mathbf{x}_i}{dt} + \boldsymbol{\alpha}_i + \boldsymbol{\beta}_i = \mathbf{f}_i; \qquad i = 1, \ldots, N, \tag{12}$$

where γ_i is a velocity-dependent damping constant and $\mathbf{f}_i$ are applied external forces (see below).

Following the formulation in (3), let l_i be given reference length of the spring connecting node i to node $i + 1$ and let $\mathbf{r}_i(t) = \mathbf{x}_{i+1} - \mathbf{x}_i$ be the separation of the nodes. Using the deformation $e_i(t) = \|\mathbf{r}_i\| - l_i$, we define

$$\boldsymbol{\alpha}_i = \frac{a_i e_i}{\|\mathbf{r}_i\|} \mathbf{r}_i - \frac{a_{i-1} e_{i-1}}{\|\mathbf{r}_{i-1}\|} \mathbf{r}_{i-1}. \tag{13}$$

To obtain contours that resist compression past a prespecified lower limit but that are able to stretch arbitrarily, we set

$$a_i(t) = \begin{cases} a & \text{if } e_i < 0, \\ 0 & \text{otherwise,} \end{cases} \tag{14}$$

so that each spring resists compression with stiffness a only when its actual length $\|\mathbf{r}_i\|$ is less than l_i. To also give the contours some rigidity, we introduce the variables b_i and define rigidity forces

$$\boldsymbol{\beta}_i = b_{i+1}(\mathbf{x}_{i+2} - 2\mathbf{x}_{i+1} + \mathbf{x}_i) - 2b_i(\mathbf{x}_{i+1} - 2\mathbf{x}_i + \mathbf{x}_{i-1}) + b_{i-1}(\mathbf{x}_i - 2\mathbf{x}_{i-1} + \mathbf{x}_{i-2}). \tag{15}$$

Note that in the absense of external forces, if the nodes are separated more than l_i, are equally spaced, and lie on a straight line, $\boldsymbol{\alpha}_i$ and $\boldsymbol{\beta}_i$ vanish and the contour will be at equilibrium.

Compression and rigidity are locally adjustable through the a_i and b_i variables. In particular, by setting $a_i = b_i = 0$, we are able to break a long deformable contour between nodes i and $i+1$ into two shorter contours (note that setting only $b_i = 0$ permits a tangent discontinuity to occur between these nodes).

To turn the deformable contour into a discrete snake, we make it responsive to a force field derived from the image. It is convenient to express the force field which influences the snake's shape and motion though a time-varying potential function $P(x, y, t)$. A user may also interact with the snake by applying forces $\mathbf{f}_i^u(t)$ using a mouse (see (Kass, Witkin and Terzopoulos, 1987) for details about user forces). We combine the image and user forces to define the external nodal forces on the right hand side of (12)

$$\mathbf{f}_i = p\nabla P(\mathbf{x}_i) + \mathbf{f}_i^u, \tag{16}$$

where p is the strength of the image forces and $\nabla = [\partial/\partial x, \partial/\partial y]'$ is the gradient operator in the image plane.

4.2 Facial Feature Tracking using Snakes

To apply discrete snakes to facial feature tracking, we first transform the image intensity function $I(x, y, t)$ at time t into a planar force field using simple image processing techniques. In the present application, we are concerned with extended image features such as the eyebrow and lip boundaries which are usually marked by high contrast edges in image intensity. To make intensity edges attract snakes, we create a 2D potential function $P(x, y, t)$ whose ravines correspond with intensity edges by simply computing the magnitude of the gradient of the image intensity

$$P(x, y, t) = - \|\nabla G_\sigma * I(x, y, t)\|,$$

where $G_\sigma *$ denotes convolution with a 2D Gaussian smoothing filter of width σ. The smoothing filter broadens the ravines so that they attract the snakes from a distance.

In a few simulation time steps the snakes slide downhill in $P(x, y, t)$ (for fixed t) and come to equilibrium at the bottoms of the nearest ravines, conforming to the shape of the associated facial feature. As soon as the snakes have settled into ravines associated with a particular image frame, we repeatedly replace it with the next frame in the video sequence. The snakes continue slide downhill into the perturbed ravines, and they are conveyed by the ravines, so long as the motion of the facial features of interest is small enough to retain the snakes on the slopes of the perturbed ravines along most of their lengths. Thus, the snakes track the nonrigid motions of extended image features. As the snakes evolve in successive frames, their dynamic state variables $\mathbf{x}_i^t$ provide quantitative information about the nonrigid shapes and motions of the facial features.

4.3 A Facial Image Analysis Example

We have applied our facial image analysis technique to a sample image sequence. One of the authors (DT) performed several facial expressions in frontal view before a video camera. A surprise expression was digitized as a sequence of 256x256x8-bit images and submitted to analysis using discrete snakes.

Figure 12(b) shows the (negative) potential function computed from the frame Fig. 12(a) which occurs near the start of the surprise sequence. To compute the potential, we apply a discrete smoothing filter $G(i, j)$ which consists of two applications of 4-neighbor local averaging of the

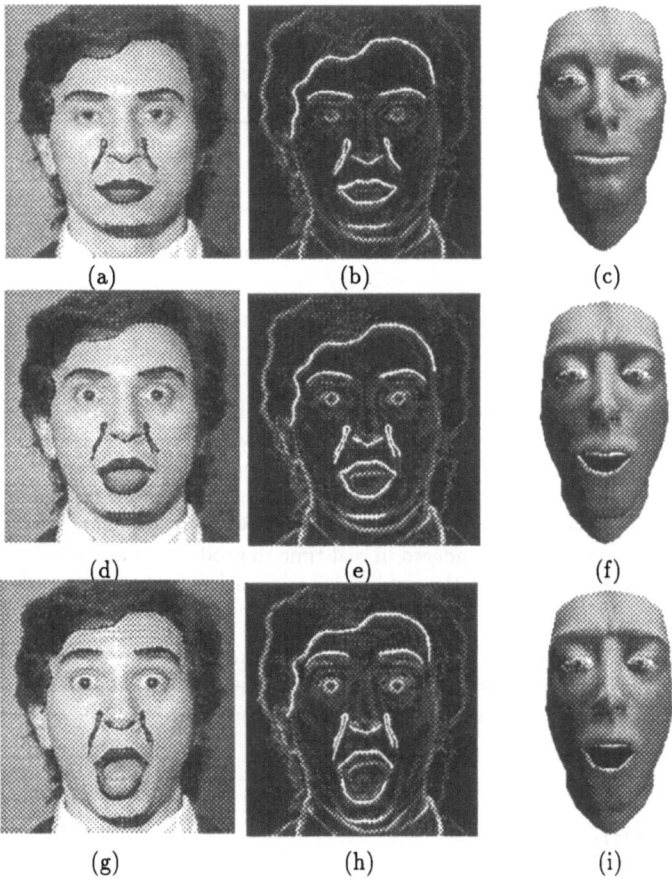

Fig. 12: Dynamic facial image analysis and muscle contraction estimation using snakes, and performance facial animation.

pixel intensities, followed by the application of a discrete approximation to the gradient operator: $\nabla v(i,j) = [(v(i+1,j) - v(i,j)), (v(i,j+1) - v(i,j))]'$. The outputs of the filters on the discrete array (i,j) are interpolated bilinearly between pixels to obtain the continuous potential $P(x,y,t)$.

Using the mouse, the user draws initial snakes along the hairline, the left and right eyebrows, the left and right naso-labial furrows, the tip of the nose, the upper and lower lips, and the chin boss. The initialization procedure places the snake nodes roughly 1 pixel apart and sets the rest lengths l_i in to the initial node separations. The parameter values of the snake simulation are $\gamma/\Delta t = 0.5$, $a_i = 1.0$ and $b_i = 0.5$ (except at the jump discontinuities between the snakes, where $a_i = b_i = 0.0$), and $p = 0.001$. The figures show the snakes at equilibrium locked onto the facial features (the snakes are displayed as black contours on Fig. 12(a) and as white contours on Fig. 12(b)).

From the position information stored in the state variable arrays of the snakes, calibrated estimates are computed of the following:

1. Contractions of the left and right zygomaticus major from the positions of the endpoints of the upper lip snake;

2. Contraction of the left and right levator labii superioris alaeque nasi from the positions of the uppermost points of the associated naso-labial furrow snakes;

3. Contractions of the left and right inner, major, and outer occipitofrontalis, respectively, from the positions of the innermost, center, and outermost points of the associated eyebrow snakes;

4. Jaw rotation from the average position of the chin boss snake;

5. Head reference frame from the average position of the hairline snake.

The positions of all facial feature points are computed relative to the head reference frame which, assuming a relatively stable hairline, will move with the performer's head in the image. The first frame in the sequence shows DT's face in a relaxed state. From this frame, the analysis procedure estimates the rest lengths of his facial muscles in the head reference frame and calibrates them against the rest lengths of the muscles in the face model. Figure 12(c) shows the rendered equilibrium position of the face model with the calibrated muscle rest lengths as inputs. The estimated muscle lengths from successive frames are scaled by the calibration factors and input to the physically-based model in sequence, the model quickly attains dynamic equilibrium on each frame, and the state variables are rendered in real-time to produce an animated sequence. Figure 12(d)–(f) illustrates the snakes and the rendered face model for a frame near the middle of the surprise sequence, and Fig. 12(g)–(i) show a later frame.

Our performance facial animation technique appears promising. The results demonstrate that snakes may be used to robustly estimate muscle contractions from images of a performer's face and that the estimates may be used to animate the expression in a physically-based face model with a different 3D geometry.

5 Conclusion

This paper has presented a physically-based approach to the realistic modeling of human heads and the animation of human faces. Three techniques are described: (1) an adaptive meshing method for creating nonuniform geometric meshes of the entire head from high resolution range sensor data with texture mapped color information; (2) a hierarchical method for modeling the face which includes deformable synthetic tissue with embedded muscle actuators; and (3) a performance-controlled animation technique which estimates dynamic muscle contractions from image sequences of an actor and uses them to animate the face model. The methods that we have developed make use of discrete deformable models that are assembled by interconnecting nodes with springs—deformable surfaces for the adaptive facial meshes, solids for the facial tissue, and curves for the discrete snakes. These models run at interactive rates on a Silicon Graphics 4D/340VGX workstation. Together, they form the basis of a promising new methodology for synthesising realistic animate human characters by making use of a wealth of information about the shape, structure, and behavior of real people.

References

Cyberware Laboratory, Inc. (1990). *4020/RGB 3D Scanner with Color Digitizer*. Monterey, CA.

deGraf, B. (1990). Performance facial animation notes. In Parke, F. I., editor, *State of the Art in Facial Animation*, pages 10–20. ACM Siggraph'90 Course 26 Notes, Dallas, TX.

Ekman, P. and Friesen, W. V. (1977). *Manual for the Facial Action Coding System*. Consulting Psychologist Press, Palo Alto, CA.

Kass, M., Witkin, A., and Terzopoulos, D. (1987). Snakes: Active contour models. *International Journal of Computer Vision*, 1(4):321–331.

Kenedi, R. M., Gibson, T., Evans, J. H., and Barbenel, J. C. (1975). Tissue mechanics. *Phys. Med. Biol.*, 20(5):699–717.

Magnenat-Thalmann, N., Primeau, E., and Thalmann, D. (1988). Abstract muscle action procedures for face animation. *The Visual Computer*, 3:290–297.

Nahas, M., Huitric, H., Rioux, M., and Domey, J. (1990). Facial image synthesis using skin texture recording. *The Visual Computer*, 6:337–343.

Oka, M., Tsutsui, K., Ohba, A., Kurauchi, Y., and Tago, T. (1987). Real-time manipulation of texture mapped surfaces. *Computer Graphics*, 21(4):181–188.

Parke, F. I. (1982). Parameterized models for facial animation. *IEEE Computer Graphics and Applications*, 2(9):61–68.

Parke, F. I. (1986). *A Parametric Model for Human Faces*. PhD thesis, Dept. of Computer Science, University of Utah, Salt Lake City, UT.

Reeves, W. T. (1990). Simple and complex facial animation: Case studies. In Parke, F. I., editor, *State of the Art in Facial Animation*, pages 90–106. ACM Siggraph'90 Course 26 Notes, Dallas, TX.

Rioux, M. and Cournoyer, L. (1988). The NRCC 3-dimensional image data files. Technical Report CNRC 29077, National Research Council of Canada, Ottawa, ON.

Terzopoulos, D. and Fleischer, K. (1988). Deformable models. *The Visual Computer*, 4(6):306–331.

Terzopoulos, D. and Vasilescu, M. (1991). Sampling and reconstruction with adaptive meshes. In *Proc. Computer Vision and Pattern Recognition Conf. (CVPR'91)*, Maui, HI. in press.

Terzopoulos, D. and Waters, K. (1990). Physically-based facial modelling, analysis, and animation. *Journal of Visualization and Computer Animation*, 1(2):73–80.

Waters, K. (1987). A muscle model for animating three-dimensional facial expression. *Computer Graphics*, 22(4):17–24.

Williams, L. (1990). Performance-driven facial animation. *Computer Graphics*, 24(4):235–242.

Yau, J. F. S. and Duffey, N. D. (1988). A texture mapping approach to 3-D facial image synthesis. *Computer Graphics Forum*, 7:129–134.

Demetri Terzopoulos is an associate professor of computer science at the University of Toronto and a fellow of the Canadian Institute for Advanced Research. For the past five years he has been affiliated with Schlumberger, Inc., serving as a program leader at the Laboratory for Computer Science, Austin, TX, and at the former Palo Alto Research Laboratory. Previously he was a research scientist at the MIT Artificial Intelligence Laboratory, Cambridge, MA. His areas of interest include computer vision, computer animation, visualization, and massively parallel computation. Terzopoulos received a PhD in artificial intelligence from MIT in 1984. He received an MEng in electrical engineering in 1980 and a BEng in honours electrical engineering in 1978, both from McGill University. He is a member of the editorial boards of *CVGIP: Graphical Models and Image Processing* and the *Journal of Visualization and Computer Animation* and is a member of the IEEE, AAAI, and Sigma Xi.
Address: Department of Computer Science, University of Toronto, 10 King's College Road, Toronto, ON, Canada M5S 1A4.

Keith Waters is a member of the technical staff at the Schlumberger Laboratory for Computer Science where he is responsible for visualization and interaction techniques for geophysical modeling and simulation. He received a PhD in computer graphics from Middlesex Polytechnic in 1988. Since then he has continued his research into expressive 3D facial modeling, animation, and control. He is a member of the editorial board of the *Journal of Visualization and Computer Animation* and is a member of IEEE.
Address: Schlumberger Laboratory for Computer Science, PO Box 200015, Austin, TX 78720, USA.

Part II
Human Modeling and Animation

Part II
Human Modeling and Animation

Generation of Human Motion with Emotion

MUNETOSHI UNUMA and RYOZO TAKEUCHI

Abstract

This paper describes a new functional generation method for human motion with emotion. In the method, the empirical data of the human joint angles in some typical motions with emotions are utilized. Based on the frequency analysis, the data are then classified into two groups, the basic factor and the additional factor. The former factor corresponds to a basic motion like "walking", whereas the latter means a descriptive part of the basic motion like "brisk" or "fast". Then, apart from the analysed emprical motion, more complex human motions with emotions are generated by interpolation and/or extrapolation of these factors in the frequency-phase domain. The sequences of the short animations obtained will illustrate the power of the method.

Keywords: human animation, human motion generation, joint movement, frequency analysis,
          functional motion generation

1. Introduction

Many human animations have been produced in recent years. But most of them are made by a traditional keyframe animation method, while a few are made by using a physically based method. In the keyframe animation method, it is neccessary to make a set of keyframes. Motion design is very difficult for computer users without professional animators. On the other hand, the physically based method gives human motion automatically. However this method is not efficient because of ambiguities in human behavior. Human motion has many degrees of freedom. Even if a starting position and final goal of the desired human motion are given, various solutions are possible.

Many motion generation methods have been already published, which include the Parameterized Keyframe[Hanrahan 85], Programming Method[Lundin 84], Scripting Animation[O'Donnell 81], Inverse Kinematics[Girard 85], Goal Directed System[Zeltzer 82], and Dynamics Simulation[Wilhelms 85]. Problems for future progress in this area have also been described[Sturman 87][Thalmann 89].

Other approaches for getting solutions to human motion generation seem necessary. Therefore we have tried to make a rule database for human motion description using a physical motion simulation method. In this research we have found a new functional method for human motion generation with emotion. This method can generate naturally looked human motions, but it cannot offer really simulated human motion. In this paper application of this method to walking and running is described.

2. Skeleton Model

Figure 1 shows a skeleton model for human motion generation. This model has nineteen joints marked as ⦿ in Fig. 1. These joints are selected for walking and running. So this model has no finger joints. The length of the bones between each joint is freely variable. Each joint is connected as a tree-like structure starting from the waist joint as shown in Fig.2. The waist joint is the root object of this model. Each joint has three degrees of freedom for rotation around X, Y and Z axes shown in Fig. 3. Only sets of a right-groin joint and a left-groin joint, and of a right-shoulder joint and a left-shoulder joint are described in a parallel state. Each joint has a conversion matrix from its own coordinates system to the previous object coordinates system toward the root object. Herein, Y-Axis of each joint is the same direction as the bone direction of the previous joint. Therefore each joint displacement can be described in the root coordinates system.

3. Analysis of Motion

When a human walks or runs, it seems that each joint moves in cycles of two steps. Therefore motion of each joint is analysed in one stable cycle.

3.1 Measurement of Human Motion

Real human motion is recorded in video images, in which the angle of each joint is measured in each frame. Fig.4 shows an angle measuring system of the human joint in motion. A real human subject, shown in Fig.5, has adhesive markers placed on each joint. Then the joint angle is measured based on these markers. In this paper "walk" and "run" are selected as sample human motions. The real human subject walks and runs on a line with various emotions. And the video images are taken from the front and side simultaneously. The angle of each joint is measured in each video frame.

Human motion changes slightly with conditions, such as emotion. There are differences in the joint angle movement for different emotional states. As an example, the measured angle movement of the left-knee joint is shown in Fig.6. There is clear difference between "walk" and "brisk walk". So, human motion seems to be composed of the basic factors and the additional factors. These differences are clarified by means of frequency analysis.

3.2 Frequency Analysis of Joint Movement

Using Fourier transformation, frequency analysis of joint angles is done. Fig.7 shows frequency analysis of "walking" and "brisk walking". Each angle shift of the joints is expressed as the following function of time $\Theta(t)$,

$$\Theta(t) = A_0 + \sum_{n=1}^{\infty} \{ A_n \cdot \sin(n \cdot t + \Psi_n) \} \qquad \cdots(1)$$

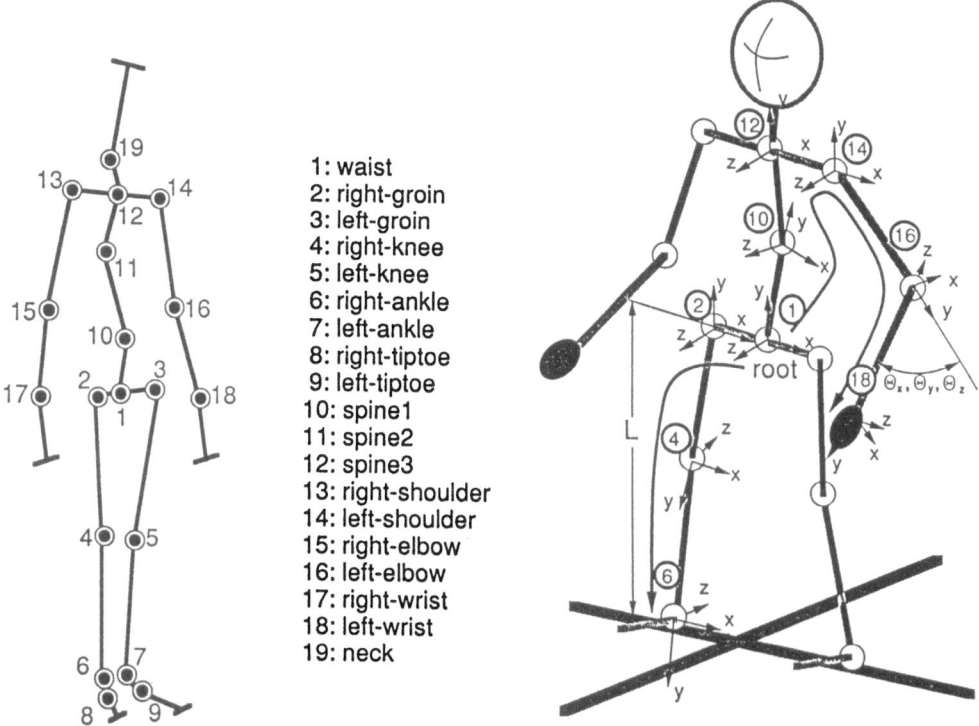

1: waist
2: right-groin
3: left-groin
4: right-knee
5: left-knee
6: right-ankle
7: left-ankle
8: right-tiptoe
9: left-tiptoe
10: spine1
11: spine2
12: spine3
13: right-shoulder
14: left-shoulder
15: right-elbow
16: left-elbow
17: right-wrist
18: left-wrist
19: neck

Fig.1 Skeleton model for human motion generation.

Fig.3 Coordinate system of each joint based on the root joint.

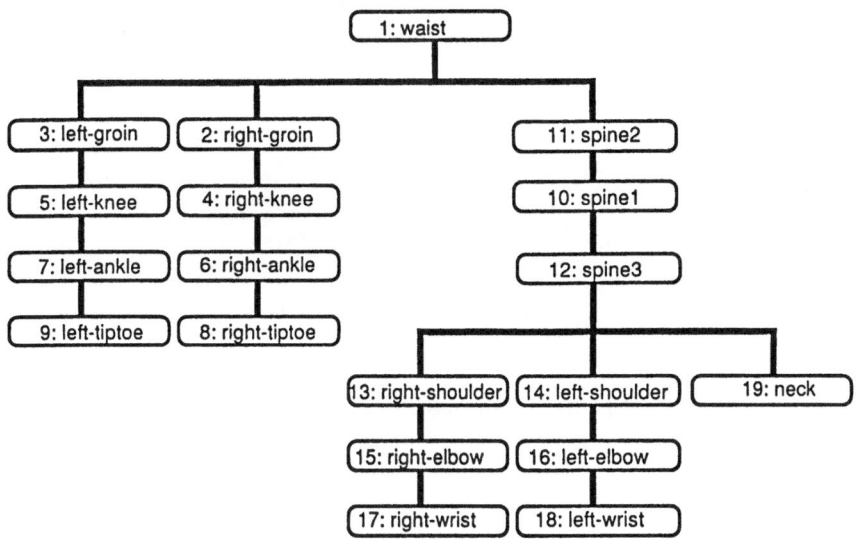

Fig.2 Connection of human joints.

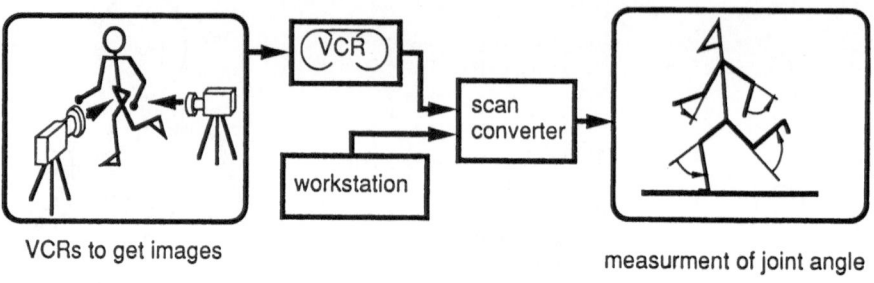

VCRs to get images   measurment of joint angle

VCR: Video Cassette Recorder

Fig.4 Angle measuring system of human joint in motion.

Fig.5 Real human subject for motion measurement.

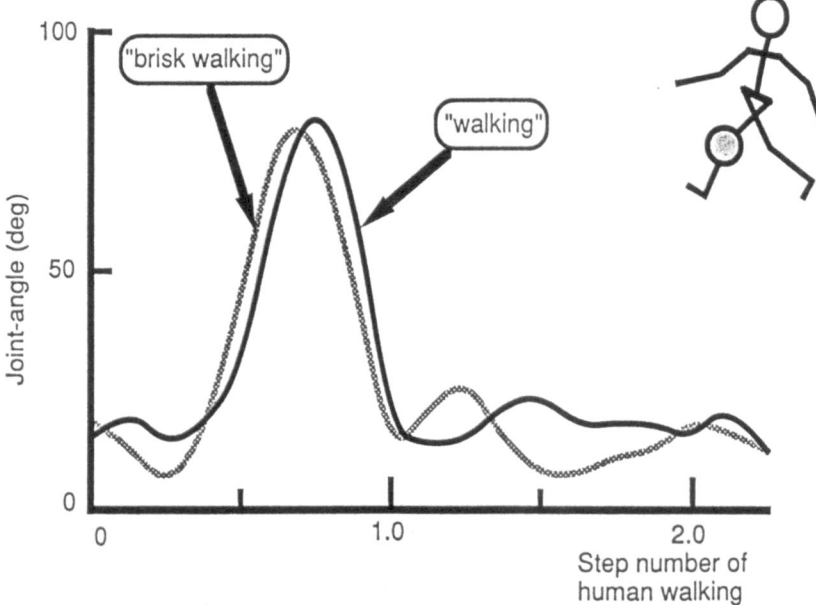

Fig.6 Flexing at the left-knee.

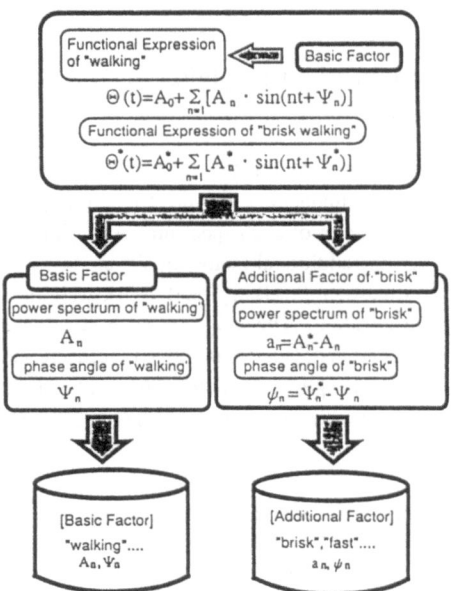

Fig.7 Basic factor and additional factor
of motion function.

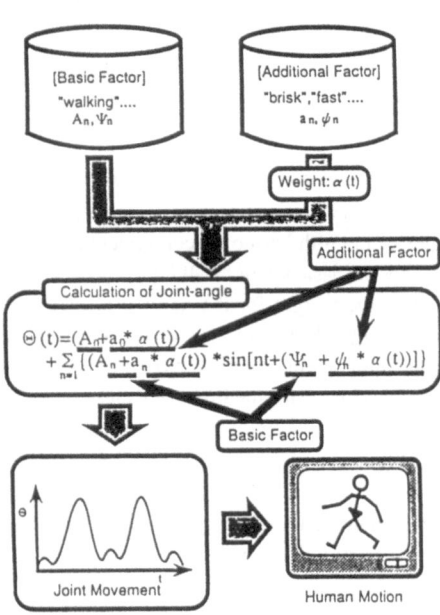

Fig.8 Generation of human motion.

where A_o is the power of the zero-th harmonic component, n is the order of each harmonic component, A_n is the power of the n-th harmonic component, and Ψ_n is the phase angle of the n-th harmonic component.

Characteristic values of motion after this transformation are the power spectra (A_o and A_n) and the phase angles (Ψ_n) of each motion. The difference of characteristic values between "walking" and "brisk walking" is compared. If the subtraction of the characteristic values of "walking" from those of "brisk walking" is "brisk", two factors of motion are separated. One is the basic factor which means the power spectra and the phase angles of "walking", the other is the additional factor which means the power spectra and the phase angles of "brisk". The basic factor and the additional factor are separately recorded in the motion database. This separation reduces the amount of motion data.

4. Generation of Human Motion

4.1 Approximate Function for Joint Movement

Human motion is generated by means of the inverse Fourier transformation using the basic factor and the additional factor of measured motion shown in Fig.8. Each joint angle is approximated as the following function of time $\Theta(t)$,

$$\Theta(t) = A_o + a_o \cdot \alpha(t) + \sum_{n=1}^{z} [(A_n + a_n \cdot \alpha(t))$$

$$\cdot \sin \{n \cdot t + (\Psi_n + \Phi_n \cdot \alpha(t) \}] \cdots (2)$$

where A_o and a_o are the powers of the zero-th harmonic component, n is the order of each harmonic component, A_n and a_n are the powers of the n-th harmonic component, Ψ_n and Φ_n are the phase angles of the n-th harmonic component and z is the maximum order of each spectrum. A_o, A_n and Ψ_n are the basic factor "walking". a_o, a_n and Φ_n are the additional factor "brisk" or "fast". And $\alpha(t)$ is the weight for the additional factor. Fine motion between "walking" and "brisk walking" is generated by selection of the weight value like "gradually brisk walking".The weight $\alpha(t)$ is effective for interpolation of emotion. It is difficult to measure every human motion. But it is possible to measure some typical motions. This method makes it possible to interpolate by changing the weight $\alpha(t)$ and using the basic factor and the additional factor between the typical motion without emotion and the typical motion with emotion.

Each joint motion is given by equation (2). But the phase angles of the 1-st harmonic component at the left groin is zero in this paper as shown in Fig.9. It is necessary for addition of the additional factor to the basic factor. Typical walking with various emotions is shown in Fig.10. These are measured data. And we can generate another motion with more complex emotion by equation (2).

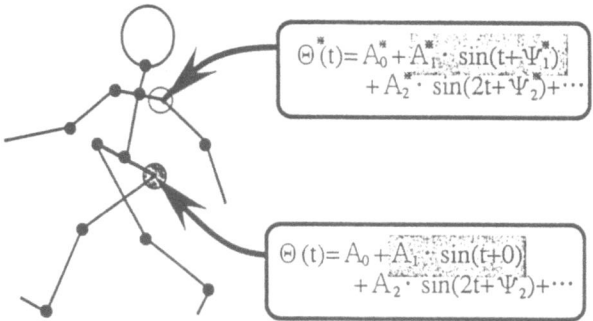

$$\Theta^{*}(t) = A_0^{*} + A_1^{*} \cdot \sin(t + \Psi_1^{*}) + A_2^{*} \cdot \sin(2t + \Psi_2^{*}) + \cdots$$

$$\Theta(t) = A_0 + A_1 \cdot \sin(t + 0) + A_2 \cdot \sin(2t + \Psi_2) + \cdots$$

Fig.9 Phase angles of each joint based on the left-groin.

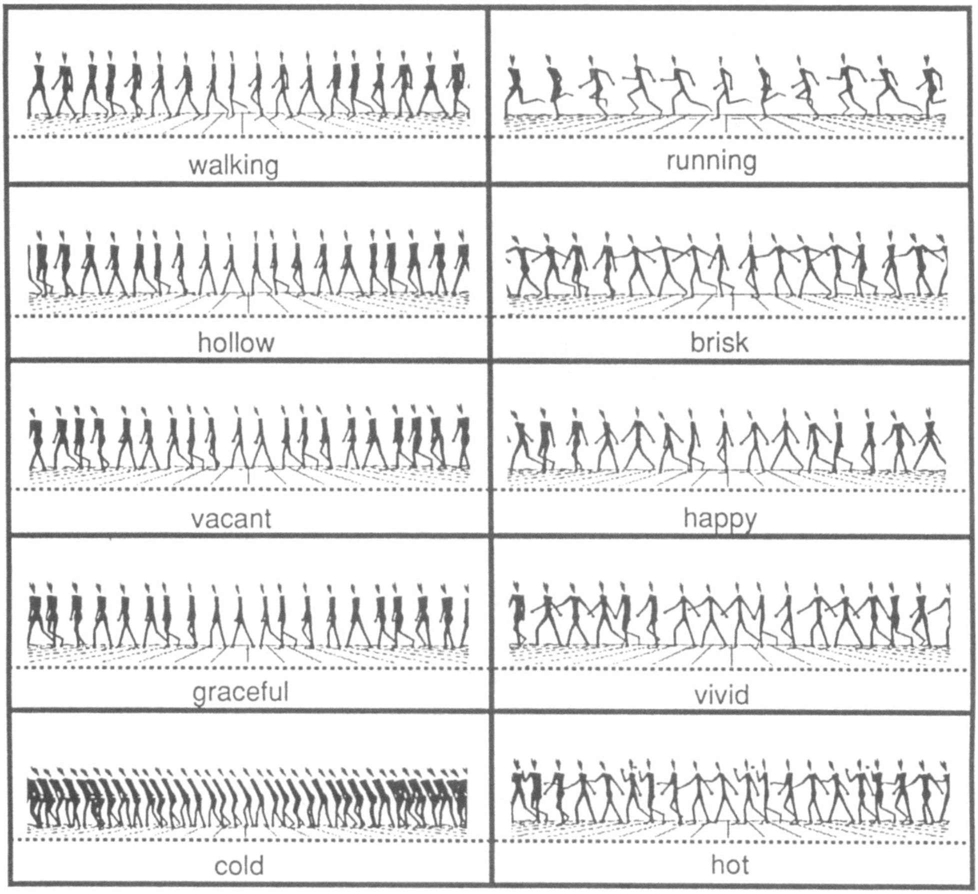

walking	running
hollow	brisk
vacant	happy
graceful	vivid
cold	hot

Fig.10 Generated walking with various emotion.

84

4.2 Samples of Generated Motion

At first the basic factor of "walking" and the additional factor of "brisk"is selected in the motion database. Each joint angle is calculated by using these data composed of the power spectra and the phase angles. Then each joint starts to move by the inverse Fourier transformation.

Fig.11 shows the influence of weight for "brisk walking". Generated motion is changed continuously from "walking" to "brisk walking" by increasing the weight α. Fig.12 shows the continuous sample image by changing the weight α from -1.0 to 1.0, where α =0 is "walking" and α =1.0 is "brisk walking". In this image, the generated human motion appears as "sadly walking" at weight α =-1.0.

The motion of "running" is composed of "walking" and "fast". So "running" is generated by using the basic factor "walking" and the additional factor "fast". Fig.13 shows continuous sample images from "walking" (α =0.0) to "running" (α =1.0). Generated human motion changes continuously. It is possible to select two additional factors. For example, "brisk running" is made by the basic factor "walking" and two of the additional factors "fast" and "brisk" shown in Fig.14.

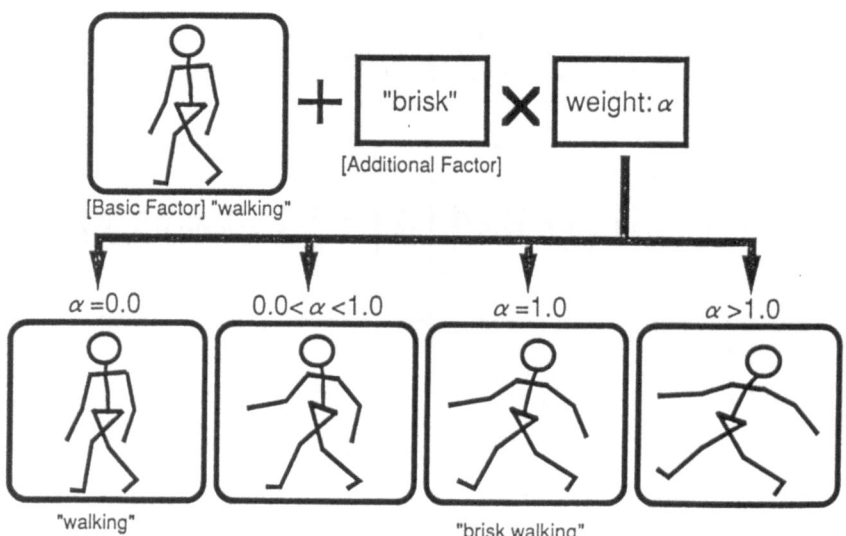

Fig.11 Influence of weight on walking motion.

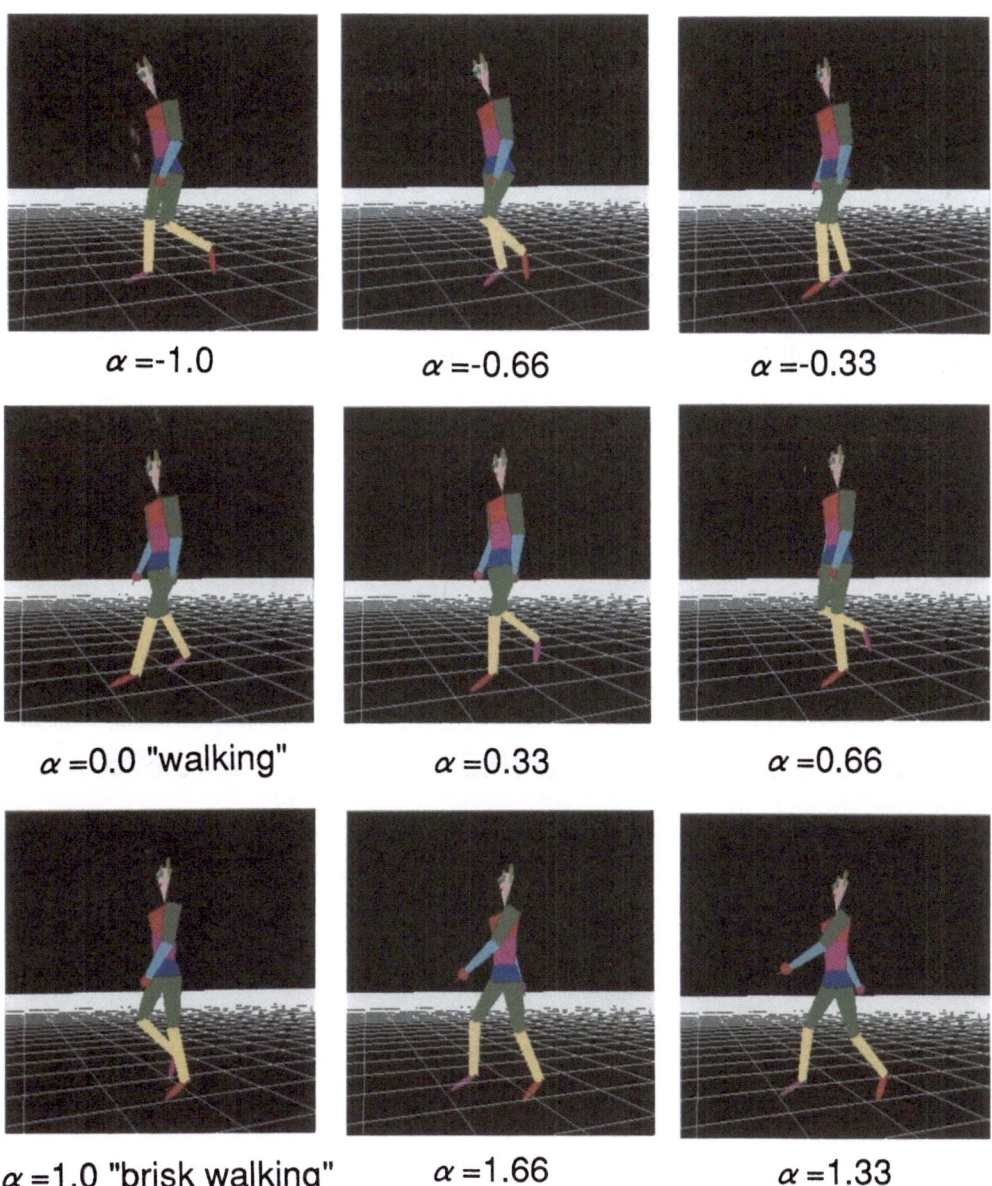

α =-1.0 $\qquad$ α =-0.66 $\qquad$ α =-0.33

α =0.0 "walking" $\qquad$ α =0.33 $\qquad$ α =0.66

α =1.0 "brisk walking" $\qquad$ α =1.66 $\qquad$ α =1.33

Fig.12 Generated continuous motion from "sadly walking"to "brisk walking".

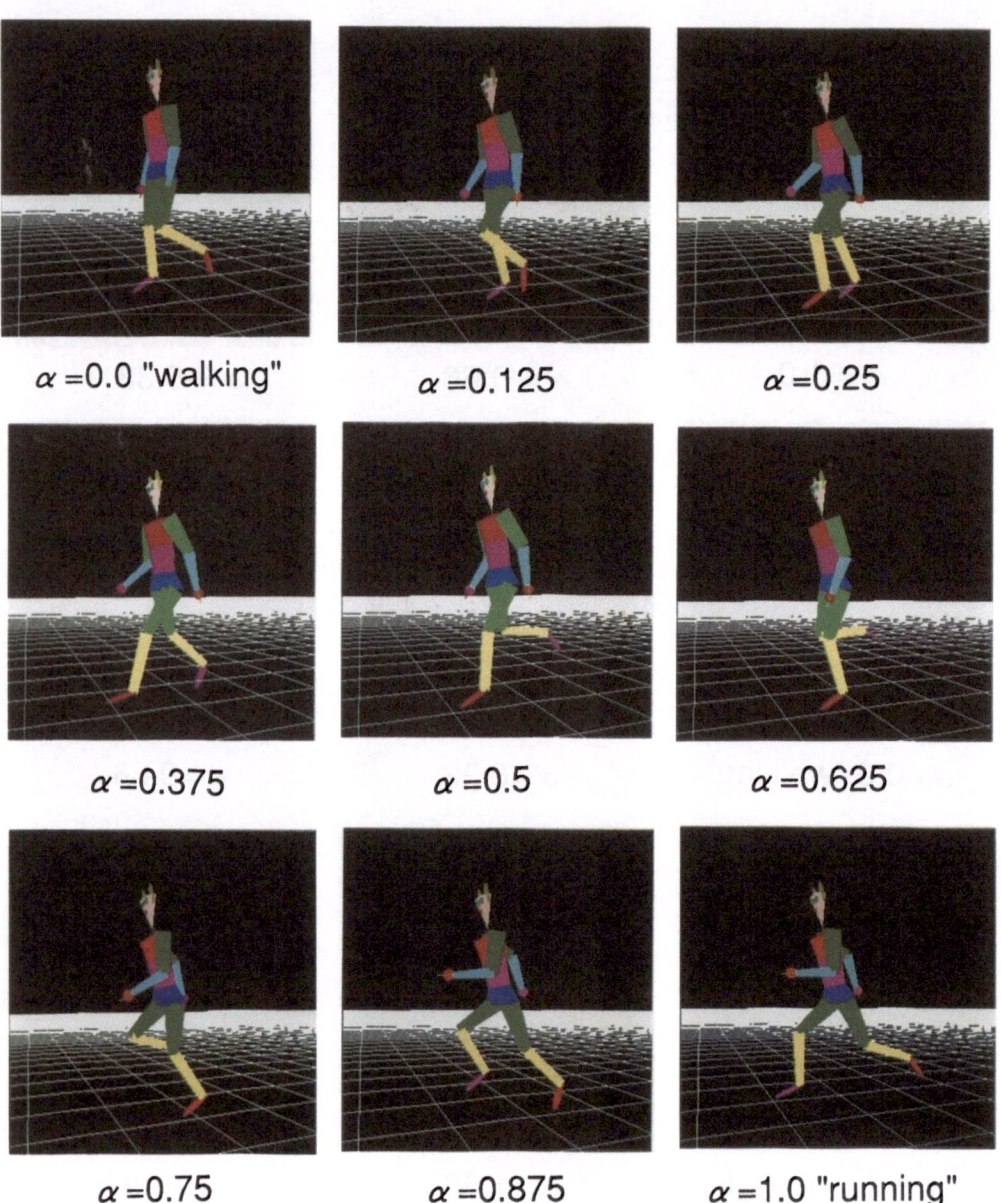

α =0.0 "walking" α =0.125 α =0.25

α =0.375 α =0.5 α =0.625

α =0.75 α =0.875 α =1.0 "running"

Fig.13 Generated continuous motion from "walking" to "running".

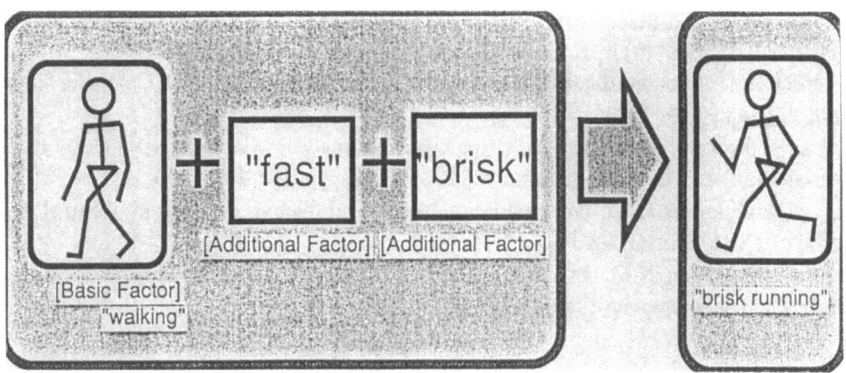

Fig. 14 Motion generation of "brisk running".

5. Conclusions

We have proposed a functional method for making computer animation of human motion with emotion. The method is based on the frequency analysis of the empirical data of joint angles from typical human motions. The heart of the method is to decompose the data into two parts, the basic factor and the additional factor in the frequency-phase domain, in stead of the 3D space-time domain. The simple interpolation and extrapolation techniques of these factors result in making more complex human motion with emotion. For example, the animation sequence from "brisk walking" to "sadly walking" is generated applying the techniques with the basic factor of "walking" and the additional factor of "brisk". The demonstrations containing other variations in this paper have shown the efficiency of the method.

Current developments include providing the theoretical foundation of the method and generalizing the method in order to get more realistic and more complex behavior of human motion.

6. Acknowledgments

The authors would like to thank Messers. Akio Yajima, Jyoji Nishiyama, Tsuneya Kurihara, Hiroaki Takatsuki, Ken-ichi Anjyo and Yoshiaki Usami for suggestions and discussions. They are also grateful to Dr. Kotaro Hirasawa, Messers. Masao Yanaka and Yoshio Kunitomo for their continuous encouragement.

7. References

[Hanrahan 85]Hanrahan P. and Sturman D.,"Interactive Animation of Parametric Models." The Visual Computer 1(4), pp.260-266, 1985

[Lundin 84]Lundin R.V.,"Motion Simulation.", NICOGRAPH'84 Conference Proceedings , pp.2-10, 1984

[O'Donnell 81]O'Donnell T.J. and Olson A.J.,"GRAMPS-A Graphical Language Interpreter for Real-time, Interactive, Three-dimensional Picture Editing and Animation .", SIGGRAPH'81 Conference Proceedings, pp.133-142, 1981

[Girard 85]Girard M. and Maciejewski A.,"Computational Modeling for the Computer Animation of Legged Figures.", SIGGRAPH'85 Conference Proceedings, pp.263-270, 1985

[Zeltzer 82]Zeltzer D.,"Motion Control Techniques for Figure Animation.", IEEE Computer Graphics and Application 2(9), pp.53-59, 1982

[Wilhelms 85]Wilhelms J. and Barksy B.,"Using Dynamic Analysis to Animate Articulated Bodies Such as Humans and Robots.", Graphics Interface '85 Proceedings, pp. 197-204, 1985

[Sturman 87]Sturman D.J.,"A Discussion on the Development of Motion Control Systems", SIGGRAPH'87 COURSE NOTES 10, pp.3-15, 1987

[Thalmann 89]Thalmann N.M. and Thalmann D.,"The Problematics of Human Prototyping and Animation.", Computer Graphics Forum 8, pp.115-123, 1989

Munetoshi Unuma received a BA in 1983 and a MA in 1985, both from Ibaraki University, Japan. Then he joined the Data Terminal Section in Hitachi Research Laboratory, Hitachi, Ltd., Japan, where he was engaged in the development of coder/decoder for facsimile based on the error diffusion method. He is currently a researcher in the Computer Graphics Section. His interest is human motion simulation.

Mr. Unuma is a member of the Institute of Electronics, Information and Communication Engineers of Japan.

address: The 3rd Department, Hitachi Research Laboratory, Hitachi, Ltd.,
          4026 Kuji-cho, Hitachi-shi, Ibaraki-ken 319-12 Japan

e-mail: unuma%hrl.hitachi.co.jp@uunet.uu.net

Ryozo Takeuchi received a BA in 1968 and a MA in 1970, both from Nagoya University, Japan. He first joined the Electrical Insulation Research Section in Hitachi Research Laboratory, Hitachi, Ltd., Japan in 1970, and later, in 1982 the Data Terminal Section where he was engaged in the development of full-color document scanners and full-color image printers. Then he has been a senior researcher in the Computer Graphics Section in 1987, where he is engaged in research on basic computer graphics technologies.

Mr. Takeuchi is a member of the Institute of Electrical and Electronics Engineers, and the Institute of Electronics, Information and Communication Engineers of Japan. He received an Outstanding Papers Award from the IEEE CES in 1977.

address: The 3rd Department, Hitachi Research Laboratory, Hitachi, Ltd.,
          4026 Kuji-cho, Hitachi-shi, Ibaraki-ken 319-12 Japan

e-mail: takeuchi%hrl.hitachi.co.jp@uunet.uu.net

Creating Realistic Three-Dimensional Human Shape Characters for Computer-Generated Films

ARGHYRO PAOURI, NADIA MAGNENAT THALMANN, and DANIEL THALMANN

ABSTRACT

In this paper, we discuss both the artistic and technical concerns involved in the construction of a computer-generated realistic human character. We investigate various methods for creating three-dimensional human shapes based on our experiences. The traditional approach consists in constructing the shapes from real human characters or plaster models. In the first part, we survey several methods that we have already used in the past: 3D reconstruction from 2D photos, 3D digitizing using a Polhemus digitizer, cross sections method and local deformations. Then, we show how a direct sculpting approach based on three-dimensional devices like the spaceball or the dataglove could considerably improve the situation. We have obtained a realistic human character with a method similar to the modelling of clay, work which essentially consists of adding or eliminating parts of the material, and turning around the object when the principal form has been set up.

1.INTRODUCTION

Through our understanding of modern science and technology, we are able to use the computer to simulate realistic environments, including human characters with animation.

The synthesis of realistic characters leads to obtain and include the specific features of the character of interest. For the universally known personalities (actors) such as Marilyn, Humphrey, and Elvis, there is a less scope to make mistakes as the deviations will be very easily detected by the spectator. In spite of this ambition to make realism, or better, imitation, this type of realism should not be confused with the photographic or the cinematographic realism.

Creating a human body for an actor is only the first step, his particular character depends on his body movements and his personality is defined by the subtle changes of his facial expressions and other gestures.

2. THE PROBLEM OF MODELING HUMAN SHAPES USING POLYGONAL MESHES

From a geometric modelling point-of-view, the most popular technique is still the polygonal mesh, because most of the latest superworkstations provide facilities to process them by hardware (fast rendering and matrix operations). Although often expensive in terms of CPU time, polygonal models of 3D objects are the most common ones. One of the reasons for using this kind of model is that the latest superworkstations provide facilities to process them by hardware (fast rendering and matrix operations). In these models, all objects are decomposed into polygonal faces. For objects such as cubes or regular polyhedra, this decomposition is very effective. But for objects such as spheres or revolution surfaces, approximations are required. Unfortunately, even if revolution surfaces are simple shapes, large numbers of polygons are often needed. Also, the essential character of some surfaces (e.g. spheres) is lost when they are approximated by collections of polygons.

A surface like a human face is irregular and composed of bossels and depressions. It is important to choose vertices on the top of bossels and the bottom of depressions. Important angle variations between adjacent facets should be avoided, because they cause undesirable variations in the shading, a physical phenomenon known as the Mach effect. The only solution consists of increasing the number of facets in regions where the curvature is important.

At this stage, the designer should be concerned with the animation:

1. First, the camera location must be considered: any curve (sequence of edges) which is shown from side-face must have numerous vertices. The more the camera eye near the vertices, the more the number of vertices should be increased, to make the surface smoother.

2. The actor motion also enters in consideration. A curve (sequence of edges) may vary in the animation. In this case the number of vertices should be increased for the maximum of curvature, to avoid any discontinuity of the surface during the motion.

3. METHODS USING A REAL HUMAN MODEL OR A PLASTER MODEL

Traditional methods to create irregular shapes like human shapes are based on digitizing. Three popular methods have been extensively used:

1. Three-dimensional reconstruction from two-dimensional photographs

Two or three projections (photos) are entered and the computer is used to derive the 3D coordinates. A photo of an object provides a perspective view of this object; the further the camera is from the object, the more parallel the view. Assume two parallel views at the same height; a fixed point will appear in two different locations. For example, consider a point on the shape to be digitized for a front view and a view at 60°. It is possible for the computer to determine the 3D location of the point from the two angles (0° and 60°) and the 2D location of the point on both views. The model to be digitized should be placed onto a turntable; this allows the object to turn and the camera to be made immovable. Photo angles should be chosen so that each point of the object is on at least two photos. It is now necessary to number facets and vertices on each photo. Once the photos are ready, we used our three-dimensional digitizing and reconstruction program DIGIT3D (Magnenat Thalmann and Thalmann 1990). With DIGIT3D, each vertex should be present on two photos. Once each vertex has been entered using two photos, the digitizing procedure is terminated and a file of three-dimensional vertices is created. The last stage consists of establishing a text file containing the list of vertex numbers for each facet. Finally, the complete object may be generated using the file of vertices and the file of facets. Synthetic Marilyn and Bogey in the film *Rendez-vous in Montreal* (Magnenat Thalmann and Thalmann 1987) were created using this approach. Plate 1 shows a ray-traced Marilyn's image.

2. Reconstruction from cross sections

This popular method consists of reconstructing an object from a set of serial cross sections, like tracing the contours from a topographic map. This method (Magnenat Thalmann and Thalmann 1990) has been used to create *Eglantine* , a computerized mannequin, who never existed before.

3. Three-dimensional digitizing

The technique is simply to enter the 3D coordinates using a 3D digitizer. Three types of devices are now available: devices based on three orthogonal magnetic fields transmitted to a wand, devices based on three sound captors, devices based on laser light. We used for example, the Polhemus 3D-digitizer (based on magnetic fields) to create various objects. The method is less time-consuming than the two other methods, because no photos are needed. However, there are limitations in the shapes, which can be digitized; cavities and small parts cannot be entered.

To indicate to the computer the character shape in the three methods, we need the real person herself or a reduced model; otherwise a plaster model similar to the person should be created. For the reconstitution of dead actors, it is necessary to find a person who has about the same dimensions or to create a plaster model from photos.

But, what to enter into the computer ? For the reconstruction from cross-sections, the cross sections have to be digitized. For the two other methods, it is necessary to digitize (in 2D or in 3D) a polygonal mesh as discussed in the first section. If a plaster model has to be digitized, it should be large enough to allow the drawing of facets and vertices on it. However, if photos have to be taken, the plaster model should be small enough to be easily photographed. Any material may be chosen for the object; however, the surface should be of a light color and non-reflective, to allow the drawing of lines and photos if necessary

Plaster models have to be created in order to be similar to the real persons to be displayed. To do that, photos of the persons have to be found at a certain age. The methodology generally differs according to the part of the person. For the heads, the teeths, the hands, the arms and the fingers, a sculptor creates the plasters from photos of the real persons. For the Marilyn's body, a person similar to Marilyn for the dimensions has to be found. Plaster is then flown onto the person body to create a plaster body.

Instead of drawing the polygonal mesh on the plaster model or the real person, a grid may be projected onto it. This method was used by Information International to enter the data of actor Peter Fonda's head into their computers for the movie *Futureworld* (Crow 1978).

4. TRANSFORMATIONS OF EXISTING SYNTHETIC ACTORS

As shown in the last section, the creation of new synthetic actors is a tedious and delicate task. The situation may be improved by introducing tools to model synthetic actors. Two approaches have been introduced by Magnenat-Thalmann et al. (1989) and will be briefly reviewed in the next sections:

1. A tool for generating a new synthetic actor obtained by interpolation between two existing actors
2. A tool for modifying and editing an existing synthetic actor using local transformations and sets

4.1 Shape Interpolation Between Human Faces

A shape interpolation consists in generating an inbetween human face from two given human faces. The main problem of this method is that both original faces may have different numbers of facets and vertices. The technique consists in extracting profiles of both human faces from selected planes and generating two grids which correspond to the original faces. Then a correspondence is establishing between the profiles, then the correspondence between the parallel sections is found using a similar method. Now the correspondence between points is straightforward. Finally an inbetween human face is just obtained by linear interpolation. The technique has been succesfully used in the film *Galaxy Sweetheart* to transform th synthetc actress Marilyn into the synthetic actor Bogey.

4.2 Introduction to local deformations

Local deformations are probably the best for the modification and even creation of human surfaces. Several authors have proposed methods to perform limited local deformations (Barr 1984; Sederberg and Parry 1986). Numerous methods based on parametric surfaces are extensively used in CAD and CAE. As these methods deal with control points, they are not suitable for human modeling except when no resemblance with existing people is required (Nahas et al. 1987; Komatsu 1988). Second, field functions (Wyvill and Wyvill 1989) model free-form surfaces and their local deformations, but the application of this for the creation of well-known personalities seems difficult.

Allan et al. (1989) proposed a general method for manipulating polygonal meshes. They introduced a basic operation "move-vertex", which specifies a new 3D position for a specific vertex called the current vertex. Their basic operation is extended in several ways: definition of a range of influence around the current vertex, decay function over the range of influence, binding and anchoring. Other operations include stretch, grow and randomize.

4.3 The use of sets and local deformations

An interactive editor based on local deformations has been developed using local deformations (Magnenat-Thalmann et al. 1989) and the concept of **sets**, which are non-ordered collections of elements. Sets are used to select regions of the surface to be processed. The main point is that manipulation commands work with sets and not with objects. There are several ways of building a set:

1. The set is built from the elements belonging to a given volume: e.g. an ellipsoid volume.
2. Vertices or polygons are selected by drawing a 2D region using the mouse.
3. Polygons in a color range are selected.
4. The set is obtained as a result of a set operation: union, intersection and difference.

Local transformations only affect sets. Three kinds of local transformations may be applied:

- *Individual transformations* only affect one vertex of the current figure.
- *Scaling operations* move all vertices of a set according to a type of scaling and a transformation function.
- In *Parallel transformations*, all vertices of a set are translated according to the transformation function.

Fig.1 shows how new faces may be obtained from Marilyn's face.

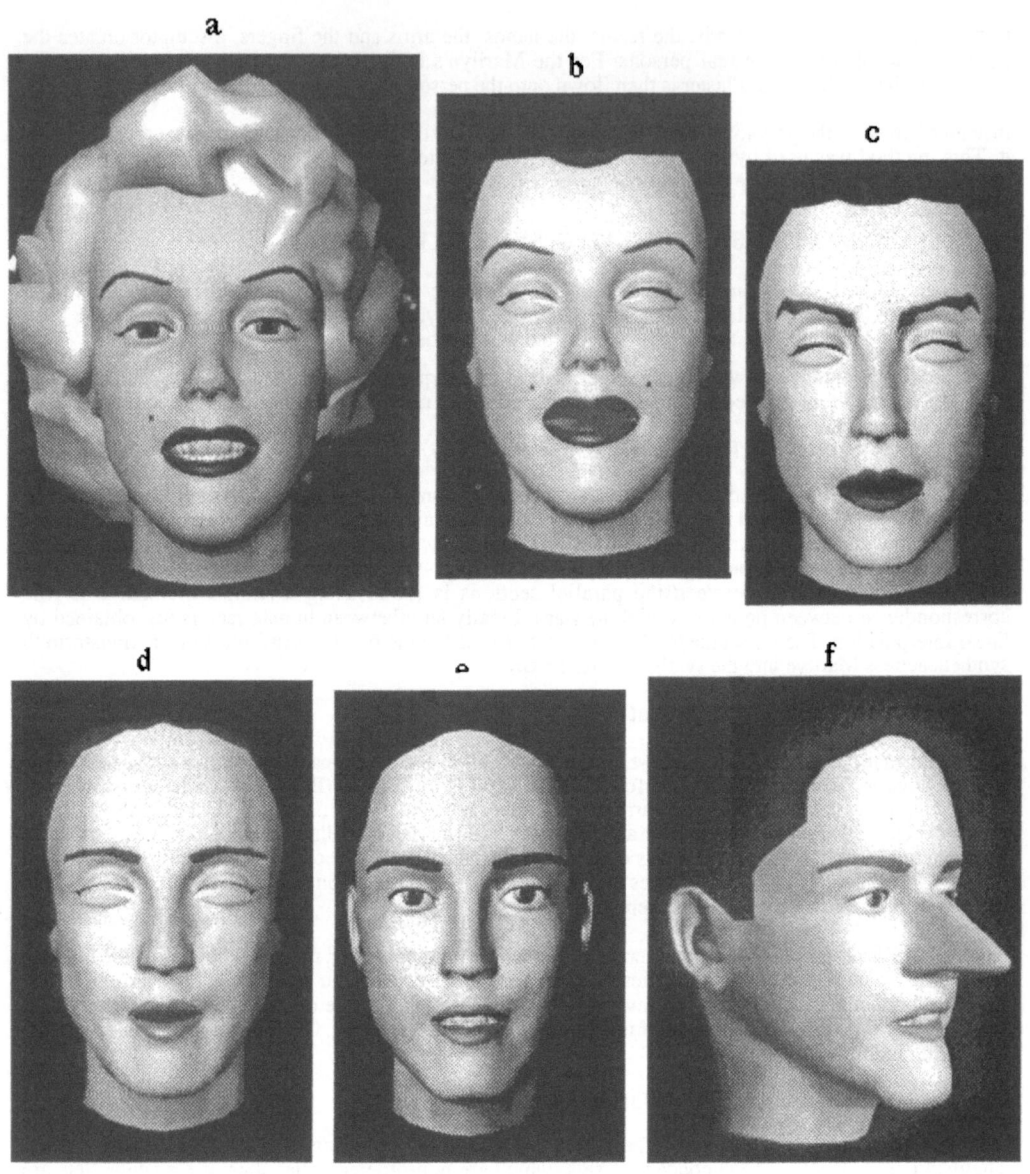

Fig.1 Transformation from Marilyn to Madonna
a) original Marilyn
b) Marilyn's face (without hair and teeth)
c) d) intermediate steps using local transformations
e) Madonna's face (without hair)
f) exaggerate face (based on Madonna's face)

5. THE SCULPTURE APPROACH

Methods based on local deformations are certainly the best for modeling human shapes. However, the designer-machine interface is essential. In this section, we show how a realistic human character may be produced with a method similar to the modelling of clay, work which essentially consists of adding or eliminating parts of the material, and turning around the object when the principal form has been set up.

5.1. Traditional sculpture

For sculpting an object, the sculptor selects a specific material corresponding to the type of the object wished. The chosen material constrains the type of treatment. We can consider the different actions involved for different types of materials:

Adding: (materials as the clay and wax)
The sculptor sets up a wooden or metal framework with the model's size, proportions and movement and then he adds matter in order to find the preliminary shape, and establish the volume of the model. His hands are dipping into the matter in order to describe the model's form, more and more in detail.

Removing: (materials such as stone, marble, wood...)
The sculptor is looking for the model's form in the interior of a mass. The form comes after eliminating parts.

Assembling: (principally materials such as metal, but also any other heterogeneous materials coming from the industry or the nature)
In this case, the sculptor creates a new sculpture joining the elements together and giving a very different form from the beginning.

5.2. Sculpting using computer

The operations conducted in a traditional sculpture can be performed by computer for computer generated objects. A sculpting software (Leblanc et al. 1991) which is based on an interactive input device called the Spaceball. This allows the user to create a polygon mesh surface. When used in conjunction with a common 2-D mouse such that the Spaceball is held in one hand and the mouse in the other, full three-dimensional user interaction is achieved.

The Spaceball device is used to move around the object being sculpted in order to examine it from various points of view, while the mouse carries out the picking and deformation work onto a magnifying image in order to see every small detail in real time (e.g. vertex creation, primitive selection and local surface deformations). In this way, the user not only sees the object from every angle but he can also apply and correct deformations from every angle interactively.

With this type of 3-dimensional interaction, the operations performed while sculpting an object closely resemble traditional sculpting. The major operations performed using this software include creation of primitives, selection, local surface deformations and global deformations. These are described briefly in the next sections.

5.2.1 Creation

Typically, the sculpting process may be initiated in two ways: by loading and altering an existing shape or by simply starting one from scratch. For example, we will use a sphere as a starting point for the head of a person and use cylinders for limbs.

We will then add or remove polygons according to the details needed and apply local deformations to alter the shape. When starting from scratch points are placed in 3D space and polygonized. However, it may be more tedious and time consuming.

5.2.2 Selection

To select parts of the objects, the mouse is used in conjunction with the Spaceball to quickly mark out the desired primitives in and around the object. This amounts to pressing the mouse button and sweeping the mouse cursor on the screen while moving the object with the Spaceball. All primitives (vertices, edges and polygons) can be selected. Mass picking may be done by moving the object away from the eye (assuming a perspective projection) and careful, minute picking may be done by bringing the object closer.

5.2.3 Local surface deformations.

These tools make it possible to produce local elevations or depressions on the surface and to even out unwanted bumps once the work is nearing completion.

Local deformations are applied while the Spaceball device is used to move the object and examine the progression of the deformation from different angles, mouse movements on the screen are used to produce vertex movements in 3D space from the current viewpoint.

The technique is intended to be a metaphor analogous to pinching, lifting and moving of a stretchable fabric material. Pushing the apex vertex inwards renders a believable effect of pressing a mould into clay.

5.2.4 The global deformations

These tools make it possible to produce global deformations on the whole object or some of the selected regions. For example, if the object has to grow in a certain direction, it can be obtained by scaling or shifting the object on the region of interest.

6. A CASE STUDY OF DESIGN PROCESS: ELVIS

In this section, we discuss a current project of creating a new synthetic actor Elvis. This project began by buying two books about Elvis life with several photographs. After getting familiar with the character, the design process involved breaking the human body into different logical anatomical parts.

Although Elvis' head (see Plate 2) had been modeled from a sphere, for the body we decided to do it neither from scratch, nor by digitalitalisation, but to take different parts of Marilyn's body such as legs, foot, arms as well as some other parts from Humphrey's figure such as hands and ears already available in the computer. They had been created using the 3D reconstruction from 2D photos, then improved using the LOCALTRANS software and we loaded them in the sculpting software as the starting point of the sculpting session.

In the modeling process, the following steps were used: extraction, composition, join, finding the preliminary figure, finishing process.

Extraction
Parts (such as arms, feet , etc.) were extracted from the other figures (see Plate 3) before adapting and joining them with the Elvis head. To do this we created another figure which contained the vertices, and corresponding polygons. In this manner we had a man's hands, a woman's torso,arms and legs as well as Elvis' original head. All these separate parts had different proportions and different colours.

Composition
This step involved the creation of one figure with positioning and assembling together the different parts, as exactly as possible according to the general proportions of the figure we want to create. Fig.2 shows the wire-frame composition of head and torso. This also required making the figure and his parts fit on the skeleton which will serve for the animation. This implied the use of elements common to both figures to allow them to be assembled as shown in Plate 4. The topology took into consideration the contours of the head and body and the position of the points necessary for animation.

The existing skeleton constrained us to :

1.The vertebral column should be as straight as possible
2. The arms should be perpendicular to the body.

Next we divide the body within a symmetry axis. Although we knew that a human face and body are not perfectly symmetric, we chose to work in the half figure because the manipulation is easier and the basic elements like facets and vertices are less. In particular, the display process is faster.

Join
In this step we had to create new polygons to join the parts, taking care to keep the continuity between the morphology of the existing figure and his new part. Plate 5 shows the process.

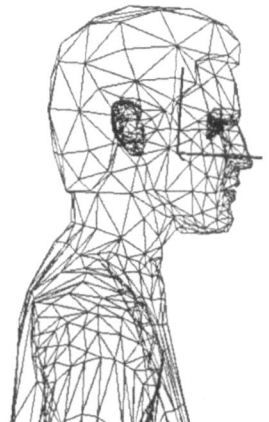

Fig.2 Composition of head and torso

Find the preliminary figure

Since the different parts of the body belonged to different characters, getting the proportioned figure of the desired character required some global and local deformations to be performed. For example, Plate 6 illustrates some global deformations applied to the selected regions. These deformations composed to the feedback obtained from the document in reference for the design process. At this moment we don't lose time to correct the imperfections in detail.

To eliminate problems appeared with scaling, we then use local deformations after selecting a vertex or a groupe of vertices. In this case deforming several vertices at the same time gave a more coherent result than deforming them with the same manner one by one.

We continue to work on the half of the figure but we frequently viewed the full figure in order to keep the whole volume in mind. In fact if we wanted to give the maximum of power and beauty we are forced to take in consideration the exterior contour .

Sometimes while working to find the preliminary shape we felt the need to give an accent to some characteristic details of the figure. At this point we would remove, exaggerate or soften different details .

The finishing process

The finishing process started when all the proportions had been found. Next we started to look at every part in detail and it was evident that this was the most delicate and difficult part of the work, which took much more time than the earlier parts. In this step we used the local surface deformations .

We divided the problems into two principal types:

1.defaults to eliminate
2.improvements wished

Examples of defaults to eliminate are details such as marks, black points, picks, etc. which had to simply be removed from the figure. The improvements were any changes required in order to make the figure acceptable.

In the construction of a certain category of figures like realistic human bodies, it is often preferable to keep certain irregularities on the surface. A very smooth skin, for example, does not necessarily guarantees a more realistic appearance. In very delicate parts like shoulders or cheeks the imperfections are visible and generally we have to get rid of them right away, but we can keep some others small irregularities in order to create a figure which seems less plastic and robotized and in order to attenuate the feeling we often feel in front of computer generated human bodies. This kind of imperfections in a realistic figure give the impression of a human figure which has not been conceived only in the "designer's" head but has really been observed from the reality.

Plate 1: Marilyn

Plate 2. Elvis' head (preliminary version)

Plate 3: Family photo

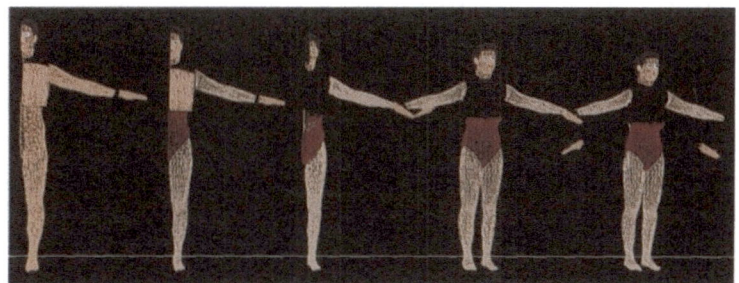

Plate 4. Bogey's hands, Marilyn's torso and arms, Elvis' head

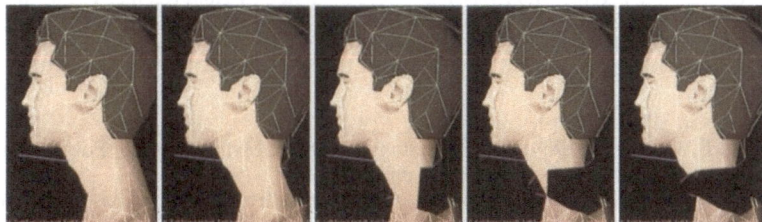

Plate 5. Adding polygons

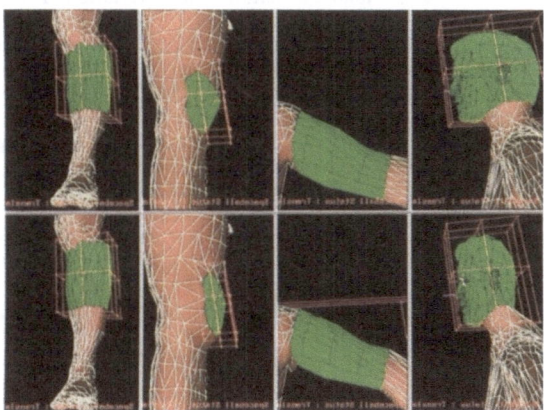

Plate 6. Sequence of images showing the selected parts for global deformations

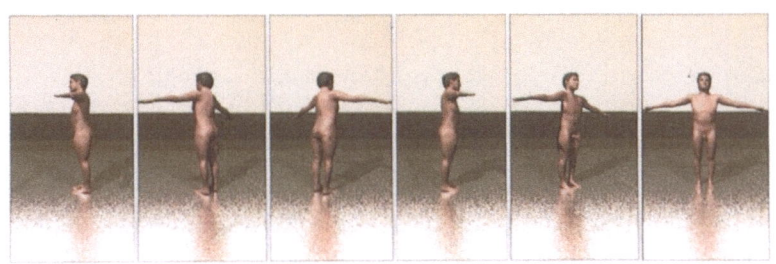

Figure 7 Several body views

These tools make it possible to produce local elevations or depressions on the surface and to even out unwanted bumps once the work is nearing completion.

Plate 7 shows several body's views.

7. CONCLUSION

As our understanding of reality and our tools become more sophisticated, we are beginning to simulate realistic environnements that even allow various degrees of physical interaction. We are able to make any character from the already existing characters in an intuitive way using natural gestures such as sculpting of different materials. This method of sculpting becomes more interesting and creative.

Acknowledgements
Sincere thanks to Prem Kalra and Russell Turner for their help in revising this text. The transformation from Marilyn to Madonna and the first Elvis' head were modelled by Ross Racine. The sculpting software has been implemented by André LeBlanc and Prem Kalra. The project has been partly sponsored by le Fonds National Suisse pour la Recherche Scientifique.

References

Allan JB, Wyvill B, Witten IA (1989) A Methodology for Direct Manipulation of Polygon Meshes, Proc. Computer Graphics International '89, Leeds, pp.451-469.

Barr AH (1984) Global and local deformations of solid primitives. Proc. SIGGRAPH '84, Computer Graphics 18(3):21-30

Crow FC (1978) Shaded Computer Graphics in the Entertainment Industry, Computer , Vol. 11, No3, pp.11-22

Komatsu, K (1988) Human skin model capable of natural shape variation, The Visual Computer, Vol.3, No5, pp.265-271

LeBlanc A, Kalra P, Magnenat-Thalmann N, Thalmann D (1991) Sculpting With the "Ball & Mouse" Metaphor - Proc. Graphics Interface '91, Calgary, Canada

Magnenat-Thalmann N, Thalmann D (1987) The Direction of Synthetic Actors in the Film Rendez-vous à Montréal, IEEE Computer Graphics and Applications , Vol. 7, No12

Magnenat-Thalmann N, Minh HT, de Angelis M, Thalmann D (1989) Design, Transformation and Animation of Human Faces, The Visual Computer, Vol.5, No3, pp.32-39

Magnenat Thalmann N, Thalmann D (1990), Synthetic Actors in Computer-Generated 3D Films, Springer-verlag, Tokyo

Nahas M, Huitric H, Rioux M, Domey J (1990) Proc. Computer Animation 90, Springer, Tokyo

Nahas M, Huitric H, Saintourens M (1987) Animation of a B-spline figure, The Visual Computer, Vol.3, No5,pp.272-276.

Sederberg TW, Parry SR (1986) Free-form deformation of solid geometric models. Proc. SIGGRAPH '86, Computer Graphics, Vol.20, No4, pp.151-160

Wyvill B, Wyvill G (1989) Field functions for iso-surfaces, The visual Computer, Vol.5, No3

Arghyro Paouri is assistant in the Computer Graphics Lab in the University of Geneva since 1989. She had studied "Arts and Technologies" in the University of Paris VIII as well as in the "Ecole Nationale Supérieure des Beaux Arts" in Paris.
Her interests are image synthesis and computer animation.

Nadia Magnenat Thalmann is currently full Professor of Computer Science at the University of Geneva, Switzerland and Adjunct Professor at HEC Montreal, Canada. She has served on a variety of government advisory boards and program committees in Canada. She has received several awards, including the 1985 Communications Award from the Government of Quebec. In May 1987, she was nominated woman of the year in sciences by the Montreal community. Dr. Magnenat Thalmann received a BS in psychology, an MS in biochemistry, and a Ph.D in quantum chemistry and computer graphics from the University of Geneva. She has written and edited several books and research papers in image synthesis and computer animation and was codirector of the computer-generated films *Dream Flight, Eglantine, Rendez-vous à Montréal, Galaxy Sweetheart, IAD and Flashback*. She served as chairperson of Graphics Interface '85, CGI '88, Computer Animation '89 and Computer Animation '90.
E-mail: thalmann@uni2a.unige.ch

Daniel Thalmann is currently full Professor and Director of the Computer Graphics Laboratory at the Swiss Federal Institute of Technology in Lausanne, Switzerland. Since 1977, he was Professor at the University of Montreal and codirector of the MIRALab research laboratory. He received his diploma in nuclear physics and Ph.D in Computer Science from the University of Geneva. He is coeditor-in-chief of the *Journal of Visualization and Computer Animation*, member of the editorial board of the *Visual Computer* and cochairs the EUROGRAPHICS Working Group on Computer Simulation and Animation. Daniel Thalmann's research interests include 3D computer animation, image synthesis, and scientific visualization. He has published more than 100 papers in these areas and is coauthor of several books including: *Computer Animation: Theory and Practice* and *Image Synthesis: Theory and Practice*. He is also codirector of several computer-generated films.
E-mail: thalmann@eldi.epfl.CH

The authors may be contacted at:

Computer Graphics Lab
Swiss Federal Institute of Technology
CH 1015 Lausanne
Switzerland

tel: ++ 41-21-693-5214
fax: ++ 41-21-693-3909

MIRALab, CUI
University of Geneva
12 rue du Lac
CH 1207 Geneva
Switzerland
tel: ++ 41-22-787-6581
fax: ++ 41-22-735-3905

Design of Realistic Gaits for the Purpose of Animation

NICKOS VASILONIKOLIDAKIS and GORDON J CLAPWORTHY

Abstract : The animation of articulated bodies and especially of human figures is a difficult task due to the number of articulations that they have. Many researchers have used dynamic analysis in order to allow easier control of the motion. However, only simple animation sequences have been designed for human models using dynamic analysis. The main reason is that using dynamics produces a model of great mathematical complexity. This paper presents a method for animating human walking. The method is based on careful study of the gait determinants and the co-ordination of the rest of the body to the motion of the legs. The motion control is based on inverse Lagrangian dynamics. The issue of ground reaction forces is addressed and solved using a reformulation of the Lagrangian algorithm. Finally, issues such as torque profiles and motion specification are discussed, together with possible extensions of the method to other types of motion.

Key words : Animation, Dynamic analysis, Lagrange equations, Gaits, Walking.

1. INTRODUCTION

The commonest forms of motion of humans and other articulated creatures, in general, are those of walking and running. An animation system for articulated bodies has, therefore, to offer to the animator, the facilities necessary to generate such motions. As they are performed very often, the objectives are to analyse the mechanics of locomotion and to identify the parameters of the problem. It is also important to minimize the number of parameters that the user has to specify. In order to accomplish this, the interrelationships between the various parameters of the problem have to be established. This has to be done, though, in such a way that the resultant walking model offers a large variety of motions and that fine details of the locomotion are preserved.

Work in animating human locomotion has been done by Boulic (1990) and Bruderlin (1989), and in biomechanics by McMahon (1984, 1987); Alexander (1983) and Dagg (1977) also give a detailed study of its gait determinants. Vubobratovic (1990) offers a large selection of research papers about the locomotion of anthropomorphic robots. Girard (1987) has produced some realistic animation sequences on human locomotion, and Zeltzer (1982/1, 1982/2) has animated moving human skeletons by using the synergic control approach. Useful work on directing motion has been produced by Thalmann (1987, 1990).

The way that human locomotion is approached by most researchers is to concentrate mostly on the motion of the legs, ignoring the problem of co-ordination with the rest of the body such as the torso and the arms. One way of solving the problem would be to use dynamics to control the motion of the legs, while using prescribed kinematics to define the movement of the rest of the body. However, the approach that is followed in this paper is to control the entire motion dynamically without involving any kinematic control. The dynamic analysis is based on the inverse Lagrangian formulation, which was developed originally by Hollerbach (1980, 1989) and modified by Vasilonikolidakis & Clapworthy (1990/1, 1990/2).

Another problem that is present in the animation of human locomotion is its motion specification. This is closely related to the way that parameters are defined and implemented internally in the animation system. For instance, one way of specifying parameters for a walking sequence is to provide some points on the path that the body has to follow and use inverse kinematics to find the target angles for the various links. On the other hand, motion can be specified as a sequence of simple commands such as "walk 30 metres" or "perform 10 steps".

Bipeds can move by using three different gaits. These gaits are hopping, walking and running. In hopping, the two lower limbs of the body are in phase, whereas in walking and running, they move in alternate phases. In walking, a lot of time is spent with both lower limbs on contact with the ground, as opposed to running where for most of the time, both limbs are off the ground. The gait determinants describe the movements of the individual limbs that are performed in order to make the body walk. When both legs are on contact with the ground, the body is in **double support state** and when one leg is off the ground, the body is in **single support state**. In single support state, the leg that is off the ground is called the **swing leg** and the leg in contact with the ground is called the **stance leg**.

2. GAIT DETERMINANTS FOR BIPEDAL WALKING

Although, there is no unique way of describing the gait determinants for walking, McMahon [87] defines them as a sequence of movements that depend on a single degree of freedom in one of the joints. This approach suits dynamic analysis particularly well, since it deals with individual degrees of freedom and the target angles can be found by establishing the relationships of these determinants. However, in the process of dynamic analysis, for reasons that will be explained later, a gait determinant, may involve quantities other than degrees of freedom. McMahon uses six gait determinants for walking, but only three of them are used here. The reason for this is that we aim to produce a fairly general motion, but try at the same time to keep the number of parameters minimal. The three gait determinants offer a great variety of motions and are described here :

i. Compass gait : This determinant refers to the motion of the pelvis through a series of arcs. The degree of freedom involved in compass gait is that of the trunk with respect to the world coordinate system as shown in Fig 1(a). This is true if the trunk is considered to be the root of the motion. However, because of the way rotations are performed in the hierarchy (additive effect of rotations from the root link to the end links), it was felt that the only way to perform realistic rotations is to use the ankle of one of the legs as the root of the model. This leg has to be the stance leg since it remains in contact with the ground during the dynamic analysis. This approach is used in the other gait determinants as well. As a result of this change, two degrees of freedom are involved, as shown in Fig1(b):

- A rotation of the root (ankle of the stance leg) w.r.t the world coordinate system which makes the body move in the direction of motion.

- A rotation of the pelvis w.r.t the upper limb (thigh) of the stance leg which extends the swing leg in the direction of motion.

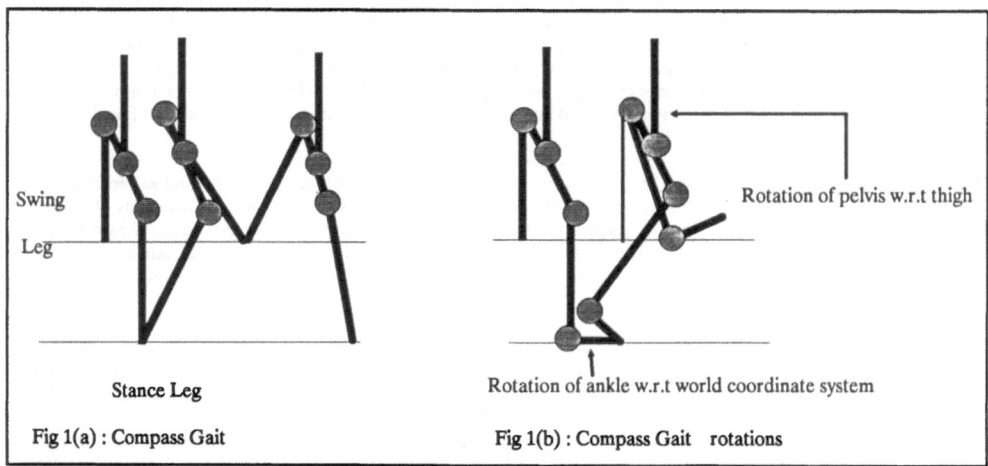

Swing

Leg

Rotation of pelvis w.r.t thigh

Rotation of ankle w.r.t world coordinate system

Stance Leg

Fig 1(a) : Compass Gait   Fig 1(b) : Compass Gait   rotations

ii. Pelvic tilt : Pelvic tilt involves the lowering of the swing leg at the pelvis as shown in Fig 2. This forces the knee of the swing leg to bend, thus introducing a flexion of the swing leg which is necessary to prevent the swing leg hitting the ground before it arrives at its end position. Again two degrees of freedom are involved here :

- A rotation of the pelvis w.r.t the top of the stance leg. The rotation is performed in the vertical direction and the effect it produces is to lower the pelvis from the side of the swing leg.

- A rotation of the upper limb of the swing leg w.r.t its lower limb. This is due to the vertical rotation of the pelvis and is necessary as the vertical height of the leg is now shorter.

iii. Stance leg flexion : This gait determinant is used by the body to flatten the arcs of the compass gait. It involves only one degree of freedom i.e a rotation of the lower limb of the stance leg w.r.t the thigh of the stance leg (Fig 3).

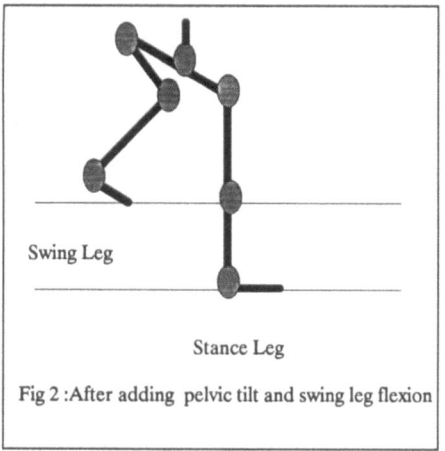

Swing Leg

Stance Leg

Fig 2 :After adding pelvic tilt and swing leg flexion

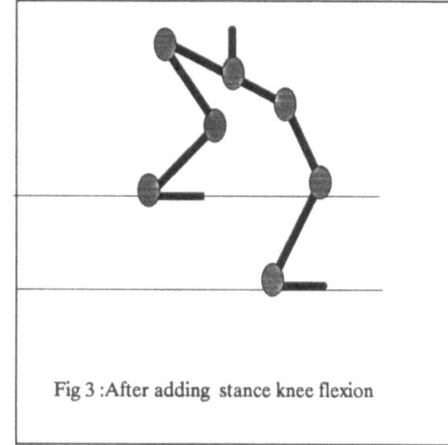

Fig 3 :After adding stance knee flexion

3. ANALYSIS OF BIPED WALKING

In order to analyse walking, three terms have to be defined. A **cycle** is the set of movements that the body performs in order to cover a stride as shown in Fig 4. A cycle will be related to the swing leg, and since walking occurs in alternate states, a typical sequence of events can be, left leg cycle followed by right leg cycle and so forth. It is obvious that after two successive cycles the body will start repeating the same sequence of movements. Two successive cycles form a **walking period** . Each cycle is divided into phases. A **phase** represents a proportion of time within a cycle. The number of phases is determined from the number of times that new target angles have to be achieved by some or all the limbs involved in the motion. In other words, there are as many phases as the number of times that dynamic analysis is performed within a cycle. It was proved that, by using the three gait determinants model, two phases are sufficient for each cycle. The following diagram shows how walking progresses.

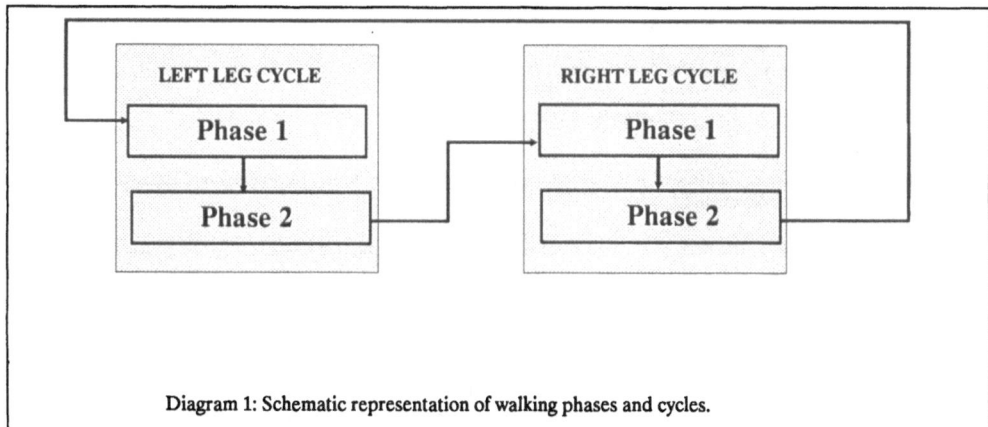

Diagram 1: Schematic representation of walking phases and cycles.

The two phases within a cycle are described in terms of the gait determinants as follows :

- Phase 1 : positive pelvic tilt and stance leg flexion which brings the swing leg to liftoff position

- Phase 2 : negative pelvic tilt and compass gait which moves the body in the direction of motion

Positive pelvic tilt occurs when swing leg lowers at the pelvis, while negative pelvic tilt refers to the opposite movement i.e elevation of the swing leg at the pelvis. The body is considered to start and finish its motion at rest, in which state both legs are in the same vertical plane. Therefore, for simplification, the cycles are classified into three categories, **starting**, **intermediate** and **finishing**. All these cycles have two phases, and the next task is to find the target angles for these phases.

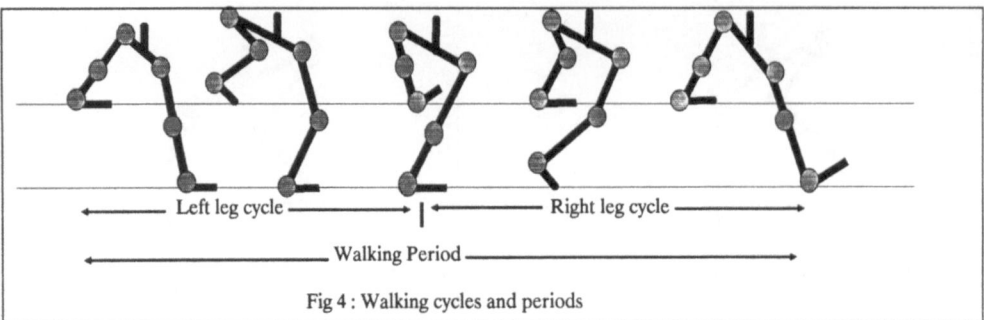

Left leg cycle ← | ← Right leg cycle →

← Walking Period →

Fig 4 : Walking cycles and periods

3.1 Starting Cycle

Phase 1 : Fig 5 shows how the body is positioned after phase 1. Two assumptions are made to simplify calculation:
- for the stance leg, the ankle joint and the hip joint are in the same vertical plane
- for the swing leg, the ankle joint remains at a right angle throughout this phase

There are five angles involved in the motion. The pelvic tilt is represented by an angle δ, and the stance leg flexion by angle χ. The other three angles (Fig 5) θ_1, θ_2 and θ_3, refer to the liftoff angles of the swing leg. L_1, L_2 and L_3 are the lengths of the thigh, lower-leg and foot respectively and L is the width of the pelvis. Some relationships between the angles can be established.

The original height of the stance leg was $L_1 + L_2$ and after the knee flexion this becomes M. Using $L_1 \sin\xi = L_2 \sin\chi$, M can be expressed as : $M = [L_{12} . L_2^2 \sin 2\chi]^{1/2} + L_2 \cos\chi$.

If the height of the swing leg is D, allowing for the descent owing to pelvic tilt

$$D = M - L\sin\delta = [L_1^2 . L_2^2 \sin 2\chi]^{1/2} + L_2 \cos\chi - L\sin\delta \qquad (1)$$

From the second assumption above we have $\theta_2 = \theta_3$ and hence :

$$A_1 + A_2 + A_3 = D \qquad (2)$$

where $A_3 = L_3 \sin\theta_3$, $A_2 = L_2 \cos\theta_2$ and $A_1 = L_1 \cos\theta_1$ (see Fig 5). Hence :

$$\cos\theta_1 = \frac{- L_2 \cos\theta_3 - L_3 \sin\theta_3 + D}{L_1} \qquad (3)$$

where D is given from eqn (1). Therefore, if the swing leg liftoff angle θ_3, the pelvic tilt angle δ and the stance leg flexion angle χ are given, θ_1 can be calculated.

Phase 2 : In Fig 6, the state of the body at the end of phase 2 is shown. During this phase a negative pelvic tilt rotation δ takes place and the legs stretch such that both knees are stiff. β is the angle that the stance leg makes with the horizontal at the end of phase 2, whereas α is the angle that the swing leg makes with the vertical plane. The heights of the two legs are equal which leads to the relationship :

$$\cos\alpha = \sin\beta \qquad (4)$$

The following table, shows the rotations of the degrees of freedom that are involved during the starting cycle. That is, if one direction is assigned arbitrary to be positive then the opposite direction will be negative. The angles indicated reflect the rotations which are passed through the hierarchy by successive rotations at the joint, starting at the root which is fixed at the stance leg.

Starting Cycle	Pelvic Rotation	Stance Leg		Swing Leg	
		Ankle	Knee	Hip	Knee
Phase 1	$+\delta$	χ	$\chi - \xi$	$-\theta_1$	$\theta_1 + \theta_3$
Phase 2	$-\delta$	$\alpha - \chi$	$\chi + \xi$	$-90 + \beta + \theta_1$	$-\theta_1 - \theta_3$

105

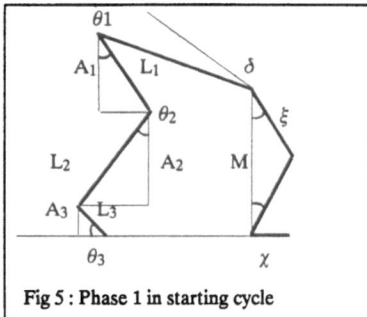

Fig 5 : Phase 1 in starting cycle

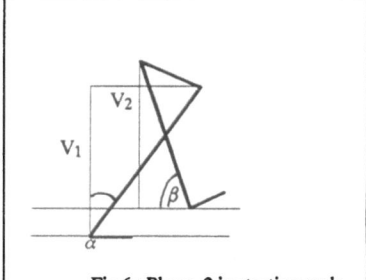

Fig 6 : Phase 2 in starting cycle

3.2 Intermediate Cycle

Phase 1: After the starting cycle, the motion is repeated in periods. The first phase of the intermediate cycle involves liftoff of the swing leg, stance knee flexion and positive pelvic tilt (Fig 7). The two assumptions that held for phase 1 of the starting cycle, are again adopted. Two new angles associated with the swing leg are introduced. ω is the angle that the upper leg makes with the vertical plane and φ is the angle that the lower limb of the swing leg makes with the upper limb. By using the vertical height in Fig 7 in a similar way to that used in Fig 5 for the starting cycle we obtain :

$$\cos\omega = \frac{-L_2\cos\varphi - L_3\sin\varphi + D}{L_1} \tag{5}$$

The similarity of (5) to (3) is obvious. If θ_3 is equal to φ, then ω is equal to θ_1 and eqns (3) and (5) are identical, but for generality, θ_3 and φ are assumed to be different.

Phase 2 : During phase 2, a negative pelvic tilt rotation takes place and both legs stretch so that there is no knee flexion at all (Fig 6). The direction of the pelvis is considered always to be perpendicular to the direction of motion so in this position each leg covers half a stride. Thus :

$$\sin\alpha = \cos\beta = \frac{S}{2(L_1 + L_2)} \tag{6}$$

The following table shows the rotations of the various joints which take place during the intermediate cycle.

Intermediate Cycle	Pelvic Rotation	Stance Leg		Swing Leg	
		Ankle	Knee	Hip	Knee
Phase 1	$+\delta$	$90 - \beta + \chi$	$-\chi - \xi$	$\omega - \alpha$	$\varphi - \omega$
Phase 2	$-\delta$	$\alpha - \chi$	$\chi + \xi$	$-90 + \beta - \omega$	$-\varphi + \omega$

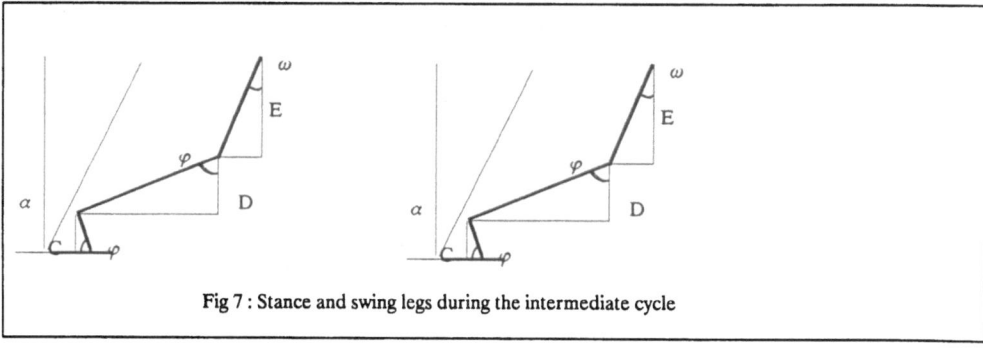

Fig 7 : Stance and swing legs during the intermediate cycle

3.3 Finishing Cycle

During the finishing cycle, no new relationships are derived. The following table shows the rotations of the joints which take place during the finishing cycle :

Intermediate Cycle	Pelvic Rotation	Stance Leg		Swing Leg	
		Ankle	Knee	Hip	Knee
Phase 1	$+\delta$	$90 - \beta$	0	$\omega - \alpha$	$\varphi - \omega$
Phase 2	$-\delta$	0	0	$-\omega$	$-\varphi + \omega$

3.4 Calculating The Unknown Parameters From The Gait Determinants

From the above analysis, the unknown parameters of the problem can be found by using relationships between the gait determinants. Given :

- θ_3, the swing leg liftoff angle in the starting cycle

- S, the stride length

- δ, the pelvic tilt angle

- χ, the stance knee flexion

- φ, the swing leg liftoff angle in the intermediate cycle,

the angle θ_1 can be found using (3) and ω can be found using (5). Angles α and β can be found using (6). In all calculations the lengths of the limbs are assumed known.

3.5 Eliminating Parameters By Using Motion Constraints

The number of input parameters can be decreased if the constraints of the motion are taken into account. There are four constraints which arise from the way the motion is prescribed :

Constraint i : $\alpha - \chi > 0$. This arises from phase 2 of the starting cycle, and with $\alpha, \chi < 90$, this implies that $\sin\alpha > \sin\chi$. The physical meaning of this constraint is that the stance leg inclines forward (with the ankle fixed on the ground) as the swing leg moves forward to hit the ground. From (6) :

$$\chi < \sin^{-1} [\frac{S}{2(L_1 + L_2)}]$$ (7)

Therefore an upper bound for χ is given by (7). On the other hand, (7) can be used to calculate χ, given the stride S of walking, by changing the inequality into equality, therefore assigning χ to its upper bound.

Constraint ii : $90 - \beta - \theta_1 > 0$. This also arises from phase 2 of the starting cycle and means that the thigh of the swing leg, rotates forward as the leg moves from liftoff to its next impact the ground. Therefore :

$\sin(90 - \beta) > \sin\theta_1 \Rightarrow \cos\theta_1 > (1 - \cos^2\beta)^{1/2}$, and from (3) $L_1\cos\theta_1 = -L_2\cos\theta_3 - L_3\sin\theta_3 + D$

These two expressions imply that $L_2\cos\theta_3 + L_3\sin\theta_3 < D - L_1 (1 - \cos^2\beta)^{1/2}$. By turning the inequality into equality and letting : $Q = D - L_1 (1 - \cos^2\beta)^{1/2}$,

$Q = L_2\cos\theta_3 + L_3\sin\theta_3 \Rightarrow L_{22} (1 - \sin^2\theta_3) = [Q - L_3\sin\theta_3]^2 \Rightarrow (L^2_2 + L^2_3)\sin^2\theta_3 - 2QL_3 \sin\theta_3 + (Q^2 - L^2_2) = 0$

By solving the quadratic :

$$\sin\theta_3 = \frac{QL_3 \pm L_2 [L_2^2 + L_3^2 - Q^2]^{1/2}}{(L_2^2 + L_3^2)} \tag{8}$$

For physical reasons, the positive root is taken as the value of θ_3. It can be seen that the solution of the quadratic is not necessarily real or even when it is , there is no assurance that one of the roots is positive.

Constraint iii : $\omega - \alpha > 0$. This arises from phase 1 of the intermediate cycle and means that the thigh of the swing leg, swings backwards, before liftoff. Therefore:

$$\omega > \sin^{-1} [\frac{S}{2(L_1 + L_2)}] \tag{9}$$

This is a lower bound for ω and can be used to check if the value of ω is acceptable.

Constraint iv : $\varphi - \omega > 0$. This also arises from phase 1 of the intermediate cycle and means that the knee joint of the swing leg, bends further during liftoff. Hence :

$$\cos\omega = \frac{-L_2\cos\varphi - L_3\sin\varphi + D}{L_1} > \cos\varphi \qquad \Rightarrow$$

$-L_2\cos\varphi - L_3\sin\varphi + D > L_1\cos\varphi$. By turning the inequality into equality :

$$(1 - \sin^2\varphi)^{1/2}(L_1 + L_2) = D - L_3\sin\varphi \qquad \Rightarrow$$

$$\sin^2\varphi [L_3^2 + (L_1 + L_2)^2] - 2DL_3\sin\varphi + [D^2 - (L_1 + L_2)^2] = 0 \qquad \Rightarrow$$

$$\sin\varphi = \frac{DL_3 \pm (L_1 + L_2)[L_3^2 + (L_1 + L_2)^2 - D^2]^{1/2}}{L_3^2 + (L_1 + L_2)^2} \tag{10}$$

Again the positive root is taken as the value of φ.

4. TIME DURATIONS

Each phase within a cycle occupies a fraction of the time that the cycle lasts. There are experimental results that relate the walking speed to the time that the body takes to perform a cycle. Bruderlin refers to some expressions that relate the various quantities. **Step frequency** (sf steps/min) is the quantity that gives the number of steps that the body performs per minute. Experimental results show that the **maximum step frequency** (sf_{max}) is :

$$sf_{max} = 182 \text{ steps/min} \tag{11}$$

This data refers to walking. There is also, a normalised relationship between step frequency and stride:

$$\frac{stride}{sf \times body\_height} = 0.004 \tag{12}$$

The height of the body is the quantity that normalises the relationship. If the forward velocity is V_f, then

$V_f = sf \times stride$, and from (12) :

$$sf^2 = \frac{V_f}{0.004 \times body\_height} \tag{13}$$

Two time periods are defined, $t_{double\_support}$ and t_{swing}. In the double support period, both feet are in contact with the ground, while, t_{swing} refers to the time during which the swing leg is off the ground. The time for a cycle is $t_{cycle} = 1/sf$ (14) . Experimental results have shown that :

$$t_{double\_support} = \frac{2(-0.16 \times sf + 29.08) \times t_{cycle}}{100} \tag{15}$$

108

Hence given the step frequency, t_{cycle} and $t_{double\_support}$ can be calculated from (14) and (15), and t_{swing} can be found as :

$$t_{swing} = t_{cycle} - t_{double\_support} \qquad (16)$$

which leads to the result that, given sf, all the times can be calculated. The following table shows the duration time for each walking cycle. In the starting cycle, phase 1, the duration is assumed to be equal to the double support period. This is not exactly correct as it spends approximately half of the double support period. The same happens at the end of the motion where in the finishing cycle, phase 2, the time duration will be half the swing time.

Cycle	Time for phase 1	Time for phase 2
Starting cycle	1/2 double support time	swing time
Intermediate cycle	double support time	swing time
Finishing cycle	double support time	1/2 swing time

5. ARM CO - ORDINATION

The previous sections described how to establish the target angles for the lower extremes of the body in each phase and cycle. This section investigates the motion of the arms during walking. It seems more difficult to find a way of describing the motion of the arms, mostly because their motion is less stereotyped. However, one can observe that the arms move in opposite phases with respect to the corresponding legs. This fact, coupled with the assumption that the target angles of the arms are related to the target angles of the legs, can be used to establish a correlation between the two set of angles. There are many ways of finding a relationship between them, but since they move in opposite phases, it is natural to relate the target angles of the left arm with the target angles of the right foot, and the target angles of the right leg with the target angles of the left leg. Figures 8,9 and 10 show the angles for each of the cycles : starting, intermediate and finishing.

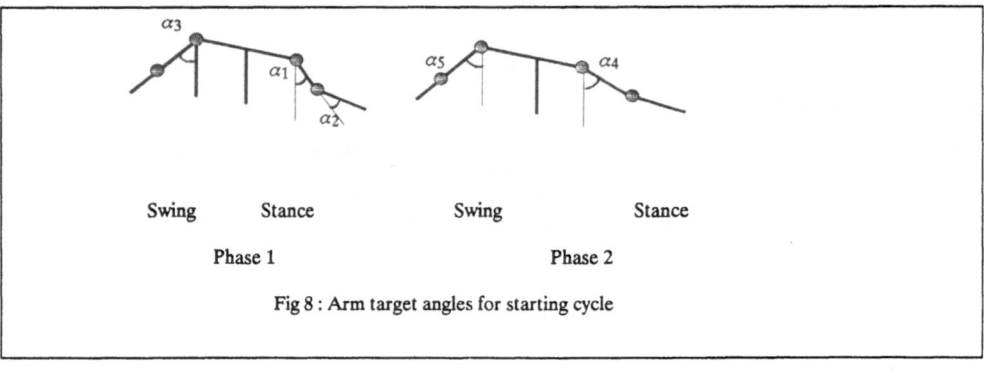

Fig 8 : Arm target angles for starting cycle

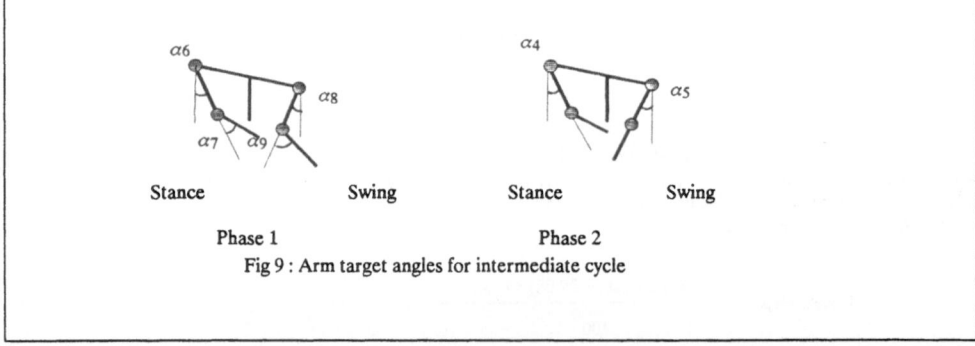

Fig 9 : Arm target angles for intermediate cycle

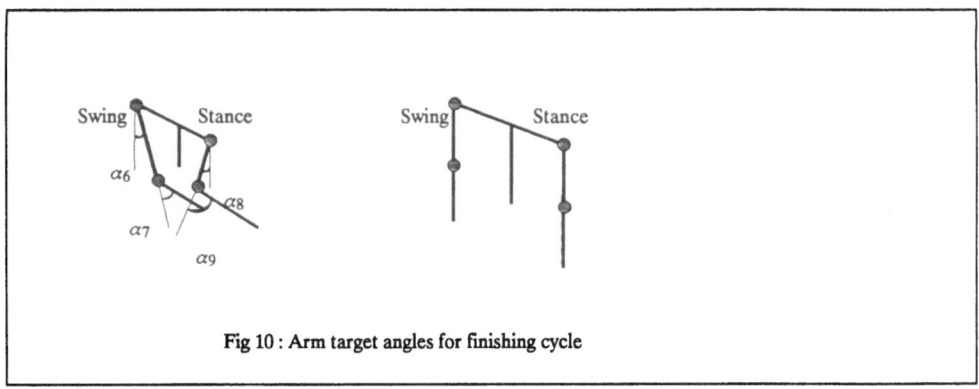

Fig 10 : Arm target angles for finishing cycle

According to this arrangement, there are nine angles involved, labelled α_1 to α_9. The following table gives the rotations which take place during each phase and cycle.

		Shoulder	Elbow
Starting Cycle - Phase1	Stance	$-\alpha_1$	$-\alpha_2$
	Swing	$-\alpha_3$	0
Starting Cycle - Phase 2	Stance	$-\alpha_4 + \alpha_1$	0
	Swing	$-\alpha_5 - \alpha_3$	0
Intermediate cycle - Phase 1	Stance	$-\alpha_5 + \alpha_6$	$-\alpha_7$
	Swing	$-\alpha_4 - \alpha_8$	$\alpha_2 - \alpha_9$
Intermediate cycle - Phase 2	Stance	$-\alpha_6 - \alpha_4$	$-\alpha_2 + \alpha_7$
	Swing	$\alpha_8 + \alpha_5$	α_9
Finishing cycle - Phase 1	Stance	$-\alpha_5 + \alpha_6$	$-\alpha_7$
	Swing	$\alpha_4 - \alpha_8$	$\alpha_2 - \alpha_9$
Finishing cycle - Phase 2	Stance	$-\alpha_6$	α_7
	Swing	α_8	α_9

These angles can be arbitrarily assigned by the user in order to generate a particular motion. However, this task can be extremely difficult as the angles that generate realistic motion are unknown. Hence, the next task is to associate these angles with the target angles for the legs. According to the assumption of relating the left arm with the right foot and the right arm with the left foot, α_1, α_2 and α_3 will relate to θ_1, θ_2, and χ. In this way, target angles for the arms can be expressed as ratios of the feet angles and this results to the following assignment :

$$\alpha_1 = k_1\theta_1 \qquad \alpha_2 = k_1\theta_3 \qquad \alpha_3 = k_1\chi$$
$$\alpha_4 = \alpha_1 + k_2\beta \qquad \alpha_5 = \alpha_3 + k_2\alpha$$
$$\alpha_6 = \alpha_5 - k_3\omega \qquad \alpha_7 = k_3\rho \qquad \alpha_8 = \alpha_4 - k_3\chi \qquad \alpha_9 = \alpha_2 - k_3\chi$$
$$\text{where } 0 \leq k_1, k_2, k_3 \leq 1$$

The three coefficients k_1, k_2 and k_3 are user-prescribed and allow a great variety of motions. Limiting them to lie between 0 and 1 is not a firm constraint, although, setting them to be greater than 1 might result in unnatural motion.

6. DYNAMIC ANALYSIS

The motion control of the current animation system is done by using solely dynamic analysis and although there is support for kinematic control, the objective is to avoid kinematics completely. The dynamic method originates in mechanics by Uicker [65], was modified for robotic mechanisms by Hollerbach [80 & 89], and is based on an inverse Lagrangian formulation. The original formulation by Uicker was of order $O(n^4)$, whereas Hollerbach's method is of linear order but with large coefficients. Chang-Jin-Li [89] suggested an alternative solution which speeded up the formulation and made its complexity to be equivalent of that of Newton-Euler dynamics. However, even earlier, Silver [81] had shown that such a method should exist, i.e the complexity of Lagrangian and Newton - Euler dynamics is equivalent. Vasilonikolidakis & Clapworthy [90/2] adapted the method to deal with multiple degree of freedom joints and branched kinematic chains, so that it could be applied to articulated body animation.

The central idea of **inverse Lagrangian dynamics** is to supply the accelerations, velocities and displacements for each degree of freedom of the body and the method then finds the forces that are necessary in order to generate such a motion. This is the opposite to the **direct method** which requires the specification of the forces acting on the body to be defined, in order to solve for accelerations, velocities and displacements.

The articulated body is represented as a hierarchical structure, where one of the links is considered to be the **root** of the motion. Most researchers consider the torso as being the root. However, as has been shown, for human walking the stance ankle is a more appropriate choice. The reason for this is that rotations should start from the ankle and not from the torso. If the torso is considered the root, then there is great difficulty in calculating the rotation angles and the motion looks unnatural. The idea of using the ankle as the root is natural because the translational effect of walking is a result of the rotational motion of the legs. This is the first time that such an arrangement has been reported. As a result of having the root at the ankle of the stance leg, the hierarchy of the model must be changed at the beginning of each cycle, as the stance leg changes from one foot to the other. The user should not have to worry about the modifications of the hierarchy of the model - the animation system must do this automatically.

The Lagrangian formulation is based on the principle of energy conservation, and solving for the forces gives :

$$F_i \; = \; \frac{d}{dt} \left(\frac{\partial L}{\partial \dot{a}_i} \right) - \frac{\partial L}{\partial a_i}$$

where $L = K - P$ is the Lagrangian, where K is the kinetic energy and P is the potential energy and a_i is the displacement of the ith link from its start position.

The solution is based on bi-directional recursive formulae, from the root to the end links (forward recursion) and from the end links to the root (backward recursion). The complexity of the method is linear, although the coefficients are high. If the body has N kinematic chains, where the ith chain has n_i degrees of freedom, the method requires :

$$\text{Multiplications} = \sum_{i=1}^{N} 888(n_i - 1) \quad \text{and Additions} = \sum_{i=1}^{N} 688(n_i - 1)$$

A complete description of the algorithm and the modifications that are necessary, can be found in Vasilonikolidakis & Clapworthy (1990/1 & 1990/2). Fig 11 illustrates the hierarchy of the body, if the root is the left ankle.

7. TORQUE - TIME PROFILES

Once the target angles have been calculated, they can be supplied to the dynamics formulation and the necessary forces can be calculated. From the forces the appropriate accelerations for each degree of freedom can be found. However, there must be a torque-time curve, to describe the behaviour of the link at the in-between positions. These profiles define the style of motion. It is important to try to preserve the physical properties of the model, i.e continuity of velocity and displacement, whenever possible.

i. Target oriented profile : This profile is constructed such that the link continues to move until the target angle for each link is achieved. It is impossible to know how many frames it will take for all links to achieve their target angles. The profile assumes constant acceleration :

$$\ddot{\omega}(t) = \gamma \qquad \dot{\omega}(t) = \gamma t + V_0 \qquad \omega(t) = \gamma t^2/2 + V_0 t$$

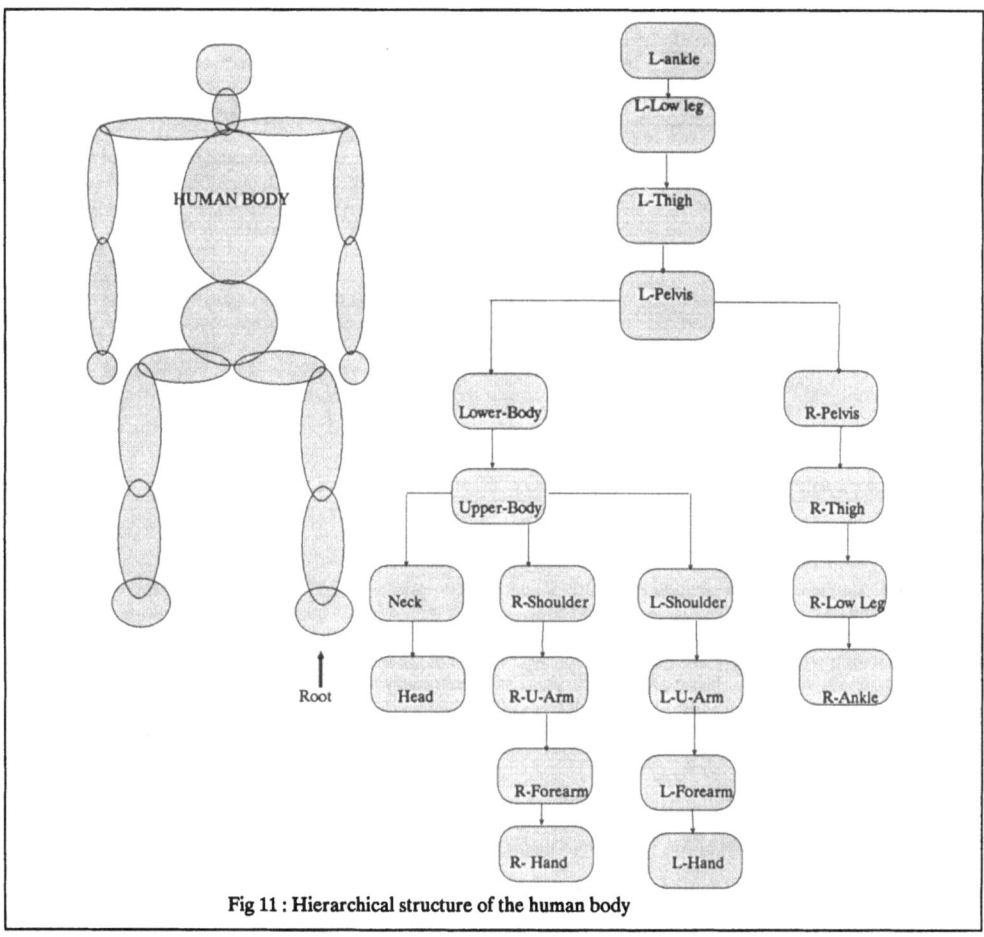

Fig 11 : Hierarchical structure of the human body

This construction ensures continuity of displacement and velocity. The model starts with initial velocity V_0 which should be the final velocity of the previous dynamic analysis and it also has zero start displacement. Once the target angles have been achieved, the new velocities and target angles are supplied into the dynamics, and the new set of accelerations is found.

ii. Time oriented profile : This profile is constructed such that the degrees of freedom arrive at their target angles at the end of the prescribed simulation time. The acceleration is again assumed to be constant :

$$\ddot{\omega}(t) = \gamma \qquad \dot{\omega}(t) = \gamma t + B \qquad \omega(t) = \gamma t^2/2 + Bt$$

If T is the simulation time and θ the target angle, then $\omega(T) = \theta \Rightarrow B = (2\theta - \gamma T^2)/2T$. This profile does not ensure continuity of velocity, only continuity of displacement. If the deviation of the actual initial velocity and the estimated one is small, then the resulting motion will still look natural.

8. GROUND REACTION FORCES

If the body is left under the control of gravity, the natural outcome will be for the body to collapse. Wilhelms (1985) proposed a model for applying ground reaction forces such that the body remains upright. Her model is based on a system of springs and dampers that are attached to the feet. Once the foot gets close to the ground the spring-damper system is activated such that it applies a force opposite to the direction of gravity. If the body continues to descend, additional forces can be applied. Although, the method is simple and easy to implement, it has the drawback that the forces may be applied after the body has descended below the ground surface. Hence, the method is heuristic and it may or may not work.

The approach that is used here is different, as the exact values of the accelerations are calculated so that the result of the external forces is off set. This approach requires re-formulation of the Lagrangian dynamics so that the direct problem is solved (solving for accelerations, given the forces). The method has been adapted successfully and the values of the required ground reaction forces (normal and tangential) can be found accurately. If the system of equations is solved such that the resultant external force is zero, then the body will always remain in contact with the ground. Although the method is exact, it introduces a computational overhead which results in doubling the time for simulating the motion. It has to be noted, however, that no optimization has been applied to the reformulation.

The method of calculating ground reaction forces, does not involve the introduction of extra degrees of freedom but operates as a hybrid-system, where the accelerations are provided and we solve for forces (inverse dynamics) and then these forces are supplied back to the system to solve for accelerations (direct dynamics). The direct problem is solved for the three translational degrees of freedom only. A full description of the solution can be found in Vasilonikolidakis & Clapworthy (1990/1).

9. IMPLEMENTATION

The animation system is implemented on a network of Sun 3/50-60 workstations, using C and Sunwindows. It is a window based system and totally interactive. The articulated body hierarchy is read from a file which includes information about the construction of local coordinate systems, inertia tensors, masses and order of rotations for each link. The user can change these quantities interactively from the interface of the system. One of the most important facilities that the system offers is that of changing the root of the hierarchy on-line. This can be extremely useful in implementing walking. The facility of assigning different time-torque profiles to various degrees of freedom is also offered. These profiles can be viewed by using cubic splines. Locking and unlocking degrees of freedom has been incorporated so that links can be excluded from the motion.

In walking, the user can either define all the angles for the legs, or define some of them and leave the system to calculate the rest by using the motion constraints. In the latter case, angles χ and δ must be prescribed together with the step frequency. In addition, the coefficients k_1, k_2 and k_3 have to be supplied by the user.

Motion is described in the form "walk 5 steps with step frequency 20 steps/min with time oriented profile". This means that the motion is defined as sequences of commands involving direction, speed and style. The system has been built upon this idea and future extensions such as controlling orientation, will be constructed using this approach.

The inclusion of ground reaction forces is optional. There are two reasons for this. The first is the computational overhead which it imposes, and the second is that there are types of motion, such as free fall, for which ground reaction forces are not applicable.

10. CONCLUSIONS

The analysis of walking parameters for the legs resulted in nine parameters, eight angles and the step frequency. By imposing the motion constraints, the number of parameters is restricted into three, the pelvic tilt angle, the stance knee flexion angle and the step frequency. The analysis of arm co-ordination resulted in relations between the angles of the arms and the angles of the legs. In these, the arm angles were expressed as ratios of the leg angles by introducing three coefficients k_1, k_2 and k_3. Hence walking, can be described by using six parameters.

At the beginning of each phase, the target angles are calculated and supplied into the dynamics component so that dynamic analysis can be performed. Once the forces have been found, the accelerations that apply to each degree of freedom of the body can be calculated. There are two options at this point, to include or exclude the calculation of ground reaction forces. Their inclusion will make the motion more realistic. An alternative way of preventing the body descending below the ground surface is to lock the translational degree of freedom associated with the vertical direction. This latter approach will not generate realistic motion but it is a useful technique for testing motion prototypes.

The system requires about 10 seconds CPU time for performing dynamic analysis on a model with 63 degrees of freedom on a Sun 3/60. The calculation of the ground reaction forces brings this time to 35 seconds. It is not only the calculation of ground reaction forces that increases the time but the fact that whenever these forces are included, dynamic analysis has to be performed twice for each frame.

The most important result is the ease of describing walking. The step frequency and the two angles (pelvic tilt and stance knee flexion) are easily comprehended by the user of the system. The effects on arm behaviour which will result from a particular choice of the three parameters are, as yet, not easy to predict, but research is being directed towards creating a database which will help the user to choose with confidence the parameter values which will create the required behaviour. Early results suggest that we can use only one parameter for controlling the arm without losing the generality of the motion.

Future research is directed towards the inclusion of more gait determinants and the investigation of other gaits such as running and half-stride walking.

ACKNOWLEDGEMENTS

This work has been funded by the National Advisory Board, and this help is gratefully acknowledged.

REFERENCES

Alexander (1983) Animal Mechanics. Blackwell Scientific Publications, London.

Armstrong W.W, Green M.W, Lake R (1987) Near Real Time Control of Human Figure Models. IEEE Computer Graphics and Applications, June 1987 : 52-61.

Armstrong W.W, Green M.W (1985) The Dynamics of Articulated Rigid Bodies for Purposes of Animation. The Visual Computer 1:231-240.

Boulic R, Thalmann N.M, Thalmann D (1990) Human Free-Walking Model for a Real-Time Interactive Design of Gaits. In : Computer Animation 90, Springer, Berlin Heidelberg New York Tokyo : pp 61-79.

Bruderlin A, Calvert T.W (1989) Goal Directed Dynamic Animation for Human Walking. Computer Graphics 23(3) : 233-241.

Chang-Jin-Li (1988) A Fast Computational Method of Lagrangian Dynamics for Robot Manipulators. International Journal of Robotics and Automation, 3(1) : 14-20.

Dagg A.I (1877) Running, Walking and Jumping : The Science of Locomotion. Wykeham Publications pp 29:47.

Girard M (1897) Interactive Design of 3D Computer Animated Legged Animal Motion. IEEE Computer Graphics and Applications, June 1987 : 39-51.

Hollerbach J (1980) A Recursive Lagrangian Formulation of Manipulator Dynamics and a Comparative Study Of Dynamics Formulation Complexity. IEEE Transactions on Systems Man and Cybernetics SMC10 (11) : 730-736.

Hollerbach J (1989) Kinematics and Dynamics for Control. In : Brady M (ed) Robotic Science. The MIT Press, pp 379-431.

McMahon T.A (1984) Mechanics of Locomotion. The International Journal of Robotics Research 3(2):4-28.

McMahon T.A (1987) Muscles, Reflexes and Locomotion. Princeton University Press.

Silver W (1981) On the Equivalence of Lagrangian and Newton-Euler Dynamics. Proc. 1981 Joint Automatic Conference, Green Valley Arizona, American Automatic Control Council, Paper No TA2A.

Thalmann N.M, Thalmann D (1987) The Direction of the Synthetic Actors In the Film : Rendezvous à Montréal. IEEE Computer Graphics and Applications, December 1987 : 9-19.

Thalmann N.M, Thalmann D (1990) Synthetic Actors In Computer-Generated 3D Films. In : Kunii T.I (ed) Computer Science Workbench. Springer, Berlin Heidelberg New York Tokyo.

Uicker J.J (1965) On the Dynamic Analysis of Spatial Linkages Using 4x4 Matrices. Ph.D Dissertation, Northwestern University, Aug 1965.

Wilhelms J (1985) Graphical Simulation of Articulated Bodies such as Human and Robots with Particular Emphasis on the Use of Dynamic Analysis. PhD Dissertation, University of California, Berkeley.

Vasilonikolidakis N, Clapworthy G.J (1990/1) Motion Control of Articulated Bodies using Dynamic Analysis. Journal of Visualisation and Computer Animation. (accepted for publication)

Vasilonikolidakis N, Clapworthy G.J (1990/2) Animating Human Walking Using Lagrangian Dynamics. Computer Graphics 90 : pp 189 - 203, On-Line Publications, London.

Vubobratovic M, Borovac B, Surla D, Stokic D (1990) Biped Locomotion. Springer, Berlin Heidelberg New York Tokyo.

Zeltzer D (1982/1) Motor Control Techniques for Figure Animation. IEEE Computer Graphics and Applications, November 1982 :53-59.

Zeltzer D (1982/2) Knowledge Based Animation. In : Badler N.I (ed) Motion : Representation and Perception. Elsevier Science, pp 318-323.

Nickos A. Vasilonikolidakis is currently a research assistant at the Polytechnic of North London. His main interest is computer graphics with special emphasis on the animation of human models using physical modelling. His research interest also include the use of parallelism for computer graphics applications.

Vasilonikolidakis is a member of the Computer Society of IEEE, Eurographics and the Institute of Mathematics and its Applications (IMA). He received his BSc degree in Computing from the Polytechnic of North London in 1987 and his MSc in Systems Analysis from the London School of Economics in 1988. He is currently enrolled for a PhD at the Polytechnic of North London.

Address : School of Computing, 2-16 Eden Grove, the Polytechnic of North London, London N7 8EA, U.K.

Gordon Clapworthy is currently a lecturer in Computing and Mathematics at the Polytechnic of North London. His research interests include computer graphics and computer animation, in particular figure animation. His publications include work on transonic aerodynamics in addition to computer graphics.

Clapworthy is a committee member of ACM (British Chapter) and a member of Eurographics. He received a BSc in Mathematics and a PhD in Aeronautical Engineering from the University of London and an MSc in Computer Science from the City University.

Address : School of Computing, 2-16 Eden Grove, the Polytechnic of North London, London N7 8EA, U.K.

Planning Human Movement Through Computer Animation

Olov Fahlander, Jonas Yngvesson, and Inge Wallin

ABSTRACT

This paper describes some of the results in real time 3-D animation done by the Retina 4 group at Linköping University. The scope of this research is to emphasis all three aspects of human motion synthesis, namely data capture from natural movements, motion editing and finally display, in real time as well as in slow motion high quality form. Much emphasis is put on the interaction task, i.e. the display dialogue where the movements can be edited in a form where angular paths are given by 2nd degree parabolics.

Keywords: Animation, Human movement design, Man/machine interface.

1 INTRODUCTION

As the discipline of computer graphics mature, the aspects of different applications become more important. For animation purposes we need efficient and easily comprehended man-machine interfaces that will allow us to handle very complex behaviors. In this report we will describe several issues, aimed mainly at human motion recording, editing and display. It may also be applicable to other linked structures such as industrial robots. The project was initially formulated out of the needs to prepare input data for ergonomic simulations.

For ergonomy purposes, efficient simulation of the human body can already be carried out by commercially available software. However, in dynamic situations such specification is extremely difficult, due to the complexity and diversity of human motions. We are developing both software and hardware for animated motion creation and editing. Among this is a computer interface to prepare input data for such simulation software. The human body is modeled as a 50-dimensional vector using the angles of the limbs as variables. The aim is to achieve a natural looking motion sequence specification and at the same time produce a computer animated "film" of such movements in real time, as well as in a high quality output form.

1.1 Some Paradigms for Motion Control

A number of different approaches to the control of complex motion has been formulated. From the cartoon world, computer graphics have inherited the concept of *key frames* which have a central importance. Another early concept was the P-curves, described by Baecker in [14].

Some of the concepts in use today are

- Dynamic simulations using forces, momentum etc
- Spring models using iterations for a steady state formulation.
- Inverse kinematic solutions from path specifications

- Notational systems used interactively on a workstation

- Goal-directedness

- Procedural declarative compilers

As an example, dynamic simulations have been used by several groups to produce motion sequences, more realistically than what is obtained by simple key frames. However, in these situations, the operator is still faced with the obstacle to correctly specify masses, forces, angular velocities etc. If properties like these are the "handles" left to specify for the user, such simulations can be very difficult indeed to implement correctly. The physical properties have very little relevance for the common user and are therefore unnatural as common grounds for an interactive language.

Clearly, what is needed is some concept which relates closely to our own sense of orientation within our environment. Goal-directedness[18] offers such a solution, but to simulate the smooth and curved trajectories found in real life, goal formulations can be expected to be very complex also.

We have tried a fairly different paradigm based on parameterized curve control with a hierarchical tree structure. This concept will be described next. The only similar approach we have found is the distance(time) graph editing scheme mentioned in [15] by Girard.

2 HIGHLEVEL ABSTRACTIONS FOR POSITIONING IN TIME AND SPACE

The main representation of the human figure is by skeleton "sticks". The skeleton is covered by a closed set of polygons forming the surface of the body. This is a rather standard type of representation, found in many similar systems. The position or "state" of this figure is given uniquely by the set of angles between neighboring limbs of the body. This then expresses the position with reference to the body itself. For the global position of the body relative to the surroundings on the other hand, only a single positioning vector is necessary. In our case the reference point is located at the center of the hips.

For the dynamic behavior of our model, each angle is represented as a function of time and/or phase. For trajectory movements such as general walking, the different angular curves may be expressed as a function of a common parameter. The parameter is then itself parameterized in time by a one-to-one mapping, which is not necessarily linear (figure 1) [15]. This hierarchical grouping of parameters reduces the number of free parameters left to specify. Modifications of a standard pattern of movement can be seen as controllable distortions of the set of angle-to-parameter mappings involved. As an example for walking curves, an increased walking speed may be expressed as an increased derivative for the parameter-to-time relationship, whereas an increased step length can be modified by a vertical magnification in Figure 1.

It may be noted that by using angles as the basis of representation, the problems associated with inverse kinematic calculations are avoided. Such calculations are performed in order to establish the angular position given some location path in space. In our case though, position may be evaluated from angles, which is a much simpler task. Goal fulfillment (such as in [18]) expressed as a location in space, can in our case preferably be determined interactively by the user through the procedures we are describing.

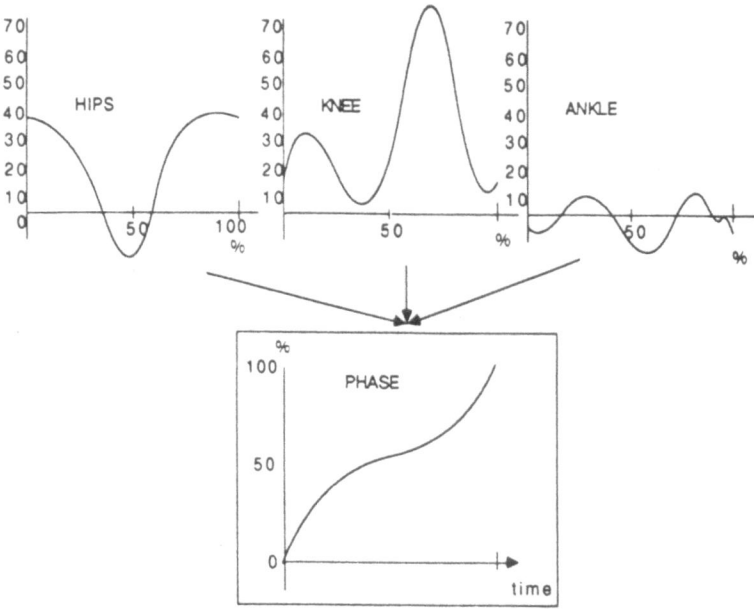

Figure 1: Angular curves with parametric grouping

3 MOVEMENT CAPTURE BY VIDEO DIGITIZATION

To set up the editing with reasonable starting values we are using a video digitizer to measure live human motions. A very simple and natural solution to this initial specification problem is to perform the intended movement using your own body and record it with a special purpose device. We are using the MacReflex system from Qualisys, a Swedish company specializing in laser and video measurements. With this system 2D data can be achieved very easily using a CCD video sensor.

The main idea is illustrated in figure 2, where the moving person is fitted with retro-reflective tape on measured points of the body. Centered around the camera lens is an internal LED flash for infrared illumination of the measured object. When the short flash light pulses illuminate the markers, they become the brightest shining objects in the field of view. The camera will automatically reduce its sensitivity so that only the markers will be visibile in the video image. This way an enormous data reduction is obtained. A special videoprocessor identifies these shining spots and performs a centroid calculation for each identified spot.

We are currently investigating a simple scheme of movement capture in cooperation with Qualisys Company. Using the setup in figure 2 two different views of the same scene can be obtained using the same camera. Through the method devised in [9] all three dimensions of the points can be calculated quite easily. The resulting 3D data is then interactively recalculated into corresponding angles and key frames are recognized heuristically. Finally data is sent to the angle editor as angle samples (see section 4), for further processing. For the Qualisys system, the spatial resolution is typically 0.005% of the field of view and sampling rate is 20 spots at 50 Hz.

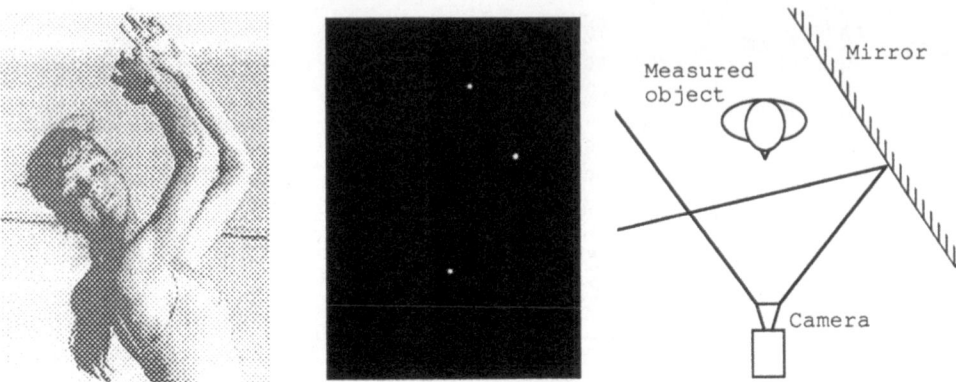

Figure 2: *Left*: A scene registered by a normal camera. *Middle*: Same scene registered by the MacReflex camera. *Right*: Movement Registration Setup.

4   AN ANGLE EDITOR

When a number of motions, or angle curves, have been entered into the system, e.g. through the means described in section 3, it is sometimes necessary to edit them before being able to use them. For the example of walking, initially the motions of the test person walking may not match perfectly the movements of the person we want to simulate, the path followed by the walking person may have to be altered, or we may want to introduce some walking defect.

Motion editing is a field few people have investigated. Some of the more well known examples are the dance and choreography editor done by Calvert [5] and Rajka's work with creating an editor for dance notation and animation [22]. Badler has also published some significant results in [18] and [13]. In [16], Girard and Maciejewski address the problem of modelling and animating the motion of legged bodies.

We have created a program, called M O S E S, (*MOtion Sequence Editor using Splines*), to edit such motions. M O S E S can be used both to enter new motion sequences given a skeleton description of a figure, and to edit old such sequences.

4.1   Curve Editing

In the Retina 4 system, and subsequently in M O S E S, each sequence of motions is represented as a number of key frames where the values of the angles of all joints in the figure are stored. Between the key frames, angles are interpolated using functional curves of second degree.

The reason for this representation is the direct correspondence to Newton's force law implying that the motions of stiff limbs tend to follow curves of second degree [19]. The method of joining second degree polynomial curves with continuous first derivatives is also described in here. Control points for the curves can be entered anywhere in between the key frames, and for different curves, control points may be located at different moments in time, i.e. control points of different curves are independent of each other.

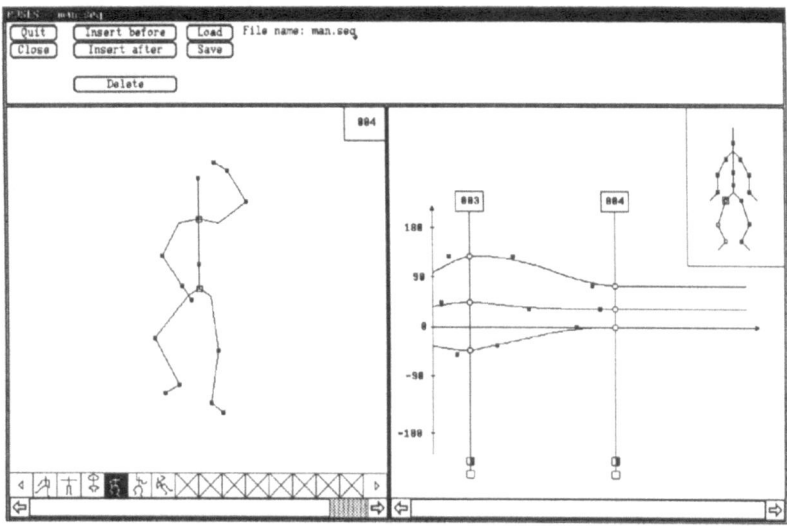

Figure 3: Layout of MOSES.

4.2   Window Layout of MOSES

The main window of MOSES is split into three sub windows (figure 3):

- A window in which the key frames are listed at the bottom. One of the key frames is the *current* key frame and this figure is currently being edited.

- A window where the angle curves are edited (to the right of the key frame window).

- A control window (above the two others).

4.2.1   The Key Frame Edit Window

The key frames represent static positions of selected instances in the motion sequence. This window is used to enter new key frames and to delete unwanted key frames. It is also possible to edit previously entered positions of the figure being animated.

Currently we have only implemented positioning of the 2-dimensional human figures shown in figure 3. To move a limb of the figure the mouse is clicked in one of the small squares at the end of each limb. We found this to be a reasonably simple way of positioning the limbs. However, it is not possible to alter more than one angle at a time, so it may be difficult to position the end point of a limb at a certain given spot. This limitation, though, is only temporary.

To remove this disadvantage, we have implemented another editing scheme based on a variant of *inverse kinematics* [18]. The end point which is to be moved is grabbed using the mouse pointer, and moved to its destination. All the limbs in the chain are automatically positioned so that the end point are moved as short a distance as possible. We are currently working to include the inverse kinematic editing model into MOSES.

Our approach to inverse kinematics differs somewhat from the more often used pseudo-inverse Jacobian which affects the whole chain simultaneously. [1]. In natural life, when a person reaches for an object, s/he tends to engage as small a number of limbs as possible. To model this behavior, our solution only changes the number of joints necessary to reach the goal state and as the end of the limbs is dragged further away, more central parts of the body chain is engaged by the inverse kinematics process. The time to engage one more link in the chain is when the previously used chain have all the joints stretched to zero angle. As a side effect, this also leads to a more simple mathematical solution.

4.2.2 The Curve Edit Window

The curve edit window gives the user ability to change the angle interpolation path between the key frames. Here, the user can also determine the time distance between key frames and permit key frames to be moved in relation to each other.

A typical animated figure (a human being) has about 50 degrees of freedom, i.e. joints whose angle paths can be edited. A selection must be done and some means have to be provided for the user to choose a subset to edit at a given moment. In $MOSES$, the user picks the curves he wants to edit by clicking at the joints in a stylized skeleton as shown in figure 3. The curves for the angles of the chosen joints appear in the curve edit window overlayed on top of each other. Optionally, the extension limits of each joint can also be shown in the window.

4.3 Extension to 3-D

The current version of $MOSES$ only offers editing of very simple 2-D figures. Our eventual goal is to provide simple editing of complex motions in 3 dimensions for 3-dimensional figures. Thus, a few parts of $MOSES$ will have to be enhanced. The skeleton model of the figures applies just as well to 3-D figures as to 2-D so nothing needs to be altered in the curve edit window. The key frame window is another matter, however. Editing motions in 3-D is substantially harder than editing 2-D motions, especially when using inherently 2-dimensional locators such as computer mice.

Other groups have done some work on editing 3-D figures using inherently 2-D control mechanisms [3], [5]. The approach taken by Calvert seems to be the most promising, but his solution lacks the advantages of the goal directed behaviour given by inverse kinematics.

5 CHARACTERISTICS OF THE SYNTHESIS

The animation synthesis provides real time interactive viewing or interactive display. By real time we mean that images are rendered at a speed of 25 frame/sec. Interactive viewing is a concept that we have developed during our work with Retina. It means that even if the motions in the animation sequence are precomputed, e.g. from a description in our editor or maybe from an advanced dynamic model, we still have some degree of interactive control at display time. Control is applied to the viewing and rendering parameters. Currently the system provides real time interactive camera positioning and full control of the timeflow. The speed of the animation can be set from very slow to very fast and the direction can be reversed, making it possible to view an animation backwards.

5.1 Interactive Camera Positioning

It is often convenient to have full control of the "camera" when watching an animation. Interesting parts of the sequence can easily be viewed from different angles and from different distances.

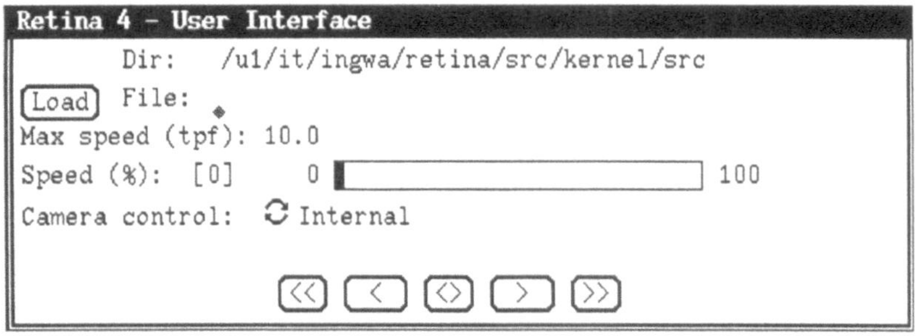

Figure 4: User interface to the kernel

Since Retina 4 calculates the viewing transformation from scratch for every frame, changing the camera position for every frame is no problem. The problem is rather how to provide a mechanism for the user to control the camera in an intuitive way. In [4], Ware describes three different metaphors for controlling a virtual camera using a Polhemus 3Space. Apart from these we have experimented with a few mechanisms using only an ordinary two dimensional mouse.

5.2 The Kernel Program

The final display of the animation is driven from a program called the *kernel*[11]. The kernel continuously scans the event lists produced by the motion editor, performs all necessary calculations in the "rendering pipeline" and finally send drawing commands to the display hardware. The calculations performed include the various transformations and deformations of objects, backface culling and clipping.

The user controls the behavior of the kernel through an interactive interface (see Figure 4). With buttons, similar to those on a tape recorder, the animation can be started, stopped or reversed. The speed of the animation is set with a slider.

The camera is normally controlled from within the event lists, but it is possible to override this and control it interactively at any time. The kernel then polls the device used for the control and adjust the viewpoint transformation accordingly.

6   ANIMATION USING STRUCTURED EVENT LISTS

To understand how it is possible to control all viewing parameters in real time and to control the time dimension it is necessary to understand some of the internals of the animation kernel. We will present three constructions - *Action Units*, *Structured Event Lists* and *Subsequences of Event Lists* that together form the core of the Retina 4 system.

6.1   Action Units

Deep down, all motions in Retina are described in terms of Action Units (AUs). The concept comes originally from FACS (Facial Action Coding System) by Ekman and Friesen[20]. In FACS an AU denotes a muscle or a group of muscles that is responsible for momentary changes in facial appearance. FACS defines a set of about 60 AUs like "Upper Lip Raiser", "Nose Wrinkler" etc. to denote a facial expression.

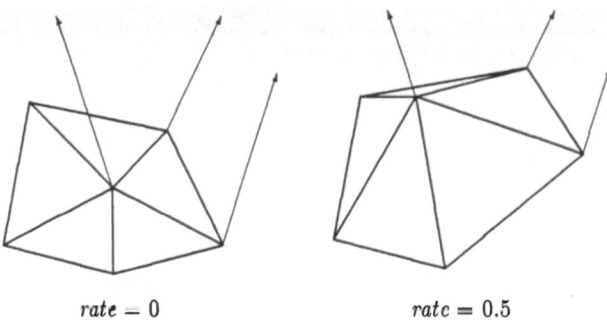

$rate = 0$ $rate = 0.5$

Figure 5: Application of a locally deforming AU

Our first use of AUs was to describe local deformations in a parametrized model of a human face, used in semantic image coding[21, 17]. In our implementations an AU is a collection of *AU-vectors*. In previous versions each AU-vector defines a direction in space and a unit amplitude that affects one vertex point in the triangular grid defining an object. When an AU is applied, a rate is given and all vertices affected by the AU-vectors in this AU will move along their direction the distance obtained when multiplying the rate with the unit distance (*Figure 1*). In this way AUs can describe local shape deformations only. A similar scheme is described in [10] and [8].

In Retina 4 we have generalized the concept of AUs, or rather AU-vectors. A vector is now able to affect entire objects in addition to vertices and have the ability to describe both rotational and translational motions. A rotational AU-vector defines an axis of rotation and a unit angle instead of a direction and unit distance. An AU often consists of an AU-vector rotating a limb, e.g. the lower leg around the knee joint, and several AU-vectors moving the vertices around the joint to achieve the necessary local deformations. This gives us a uniform way of handling both structural and shape deformations. Special AU-vectors are used to control movements of the viewpoint.

6.2 Event Lists

The intermediate format that we are using is lists of *events*. An event is a structure containing the following:

- A reference to an AU to activate.
- A start value (S_0).
- An interpolation speed factor (I_V).
- A starttime and a stoptime.

An event is *active* when the global time in the sequence is between the starttime and the stoptime of the event. Each active event are kept in a buffer together with it's *local time* (T_L). The local time is how far into the event we have gotten at the moment (global time - starttime). The local time is updated for each frame and the referenced AU is applied with the rate:

$$rate = S_0 + I_V T_L$$

The rates can not be calculated incrementally since the step in time between the frames is not always constant. The interpolation is only linear which means that we get discontinuous speed at the "edges"

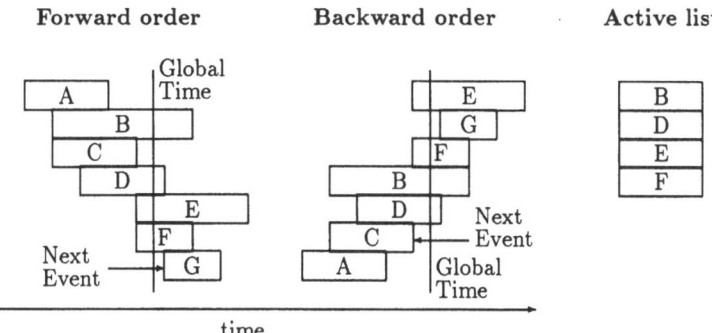

Figure 6: Eventlist organization at a certain point in time

of events. It would not present any difficulties to introduce another factor in an event description that regulated how the speed should change over time, and thus get second order interpolations. The effect of the discontinuities is hardly noticeable though, as long as the speed difference between adjoining events is "small enough".

There is a global reference in the program to the next event to be activated in the eventlist. The starttime of this event is checked against the global time before each new frame is calculated. If the event has become active it is inserted in the active list and the "next event" reference is moved forward in the eventlist.

The events are of different length in time, so to get a structure that is symmetrical in time we must sort the list in both directions as shown in figure 6. Note that when we change direction, the active list is not altered but the sorting order is completely different and the reference to the event to be activated next must be updated. In our implementation the eventlist is organized as a doubly linked list where each event has one reference to the event following when going forward in time, and one to the event following when going backwards. Then all we need to do when switching direction is to update the "next event" reference. This is done by following the references in the eventlist in the new direction until we reach an event that is not active.

The viewpoint is controlled by special AU-vectors as mentioned earlier, but there is also the possibility to take over and control it interactively at any time. The interactively defined parameters are then used instead of the parameters calculated from the eventlist. The viewing transformation is always performed for each frame so this offers no problem. During the interactive session, the viewing parameters from the eventlist are still calculated, so when we "give up" the interactive control we will be back in phase with the sequence.

To provide an intuitive method for the user to control the camera is a difficult problem in itself. Some experiences of doing this with a Polhemus 3Space is described in [4]. We have ourselves tried a number of methods using a normal two dimensional mouse since we believe this is a more familiar device for the user.

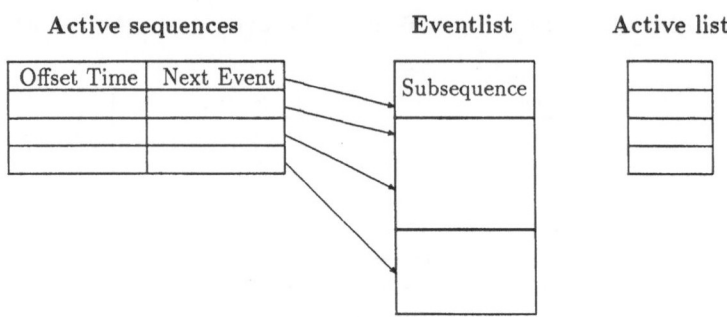

Figure 7: Extended structure to handle subsequences

6.3 Structured Event Lists

Motions of articulated figures, e.g. human bodies, are often cyclic in their nature, human walking being a typical example[7]. If such motions should be represented "as is" it would result in many repetitions of similar information. This can lead to very large amounts of data.

To avoid this problem we have introduced *subsequences* in the event lists. It is actually an event list in itself with its own local time. This subsequence can be activated from another sequence (which in its turn may be a subsequence, thus allowing nesting to an arbitrary level). A walking cycle need now only describe one single step cycle.

The subsequences introduces yet more problems in the timeflow control, especially when going from positive to negative increments or vice versa. Solutions to these problems are described in [12].

6.4 Subsequences

The scheme described above works quite well. We can move back and forth in a sequence with arbitrary steps in time, and since all the motions that are active at a certain time are quickly available in the active list, it is possible to calculate and display the frames quite rapidly. The problem is that the events are fixed in time. This means that if we want to perform a motion repeatedly, we must specify the same events several times but with different start- and stoptimes. If a motion is complex this can generate very large amounts of data.

The solution is to look form an analogy with programming. We notice that subroutine calls is supported on the machine language level as well as on the higher order levels. We therefore introduce the possibility to use *subsequences* in the eventlists. There is one major difference though, between usual program subroutines and subsequences. When a subroutine is called in a program, the calling routine is temporarily suspended and execution is continued in the subroutine. As the subroutine exits, program flow will continue at the same spot where the call was made. When activating a subsequence we do not wish the activating sequence to stop. The two sequences should both be active, and their motions should be performed in parallel.

We can achieve this if we extend the previous structure somewhat. The active list remains unchanged but we need another list of active subsequences. The eventlist is split up into several subsequences, each defined to start at time zero. When a subsequence is activated we store the actual starttime as an *offset time* which is then added to the various times in the events of the sequence. Instead of one global reference to the next event to activate, we keep one such reference for each active subsequence. The list of active sequences store this reference together with the offset time for the sequence. This scheme makes the subsequences reentrant, we can activate them more than once without waiting for them to finish inbetween. The extended structure is outlined in figure 7.

To activate a subsequence we need a new type of event. Instead of a reference to an AU, it has a reference to a subsequence. To be able to run the animation backwards and still activate subsequences at appropriate times we need a reference, not only to the first event in the subsequence, but also to the event that comes first when going backwards, i. e. the event that finishes last. The start- and stoptimes in the activating event must also correspond to the actual length of the subsequence.

Switching direction in the extended structure is not very different from before. Instead of updating one global "next event" reference, we must update all the references in the list of active sequences.

7   DISPLAY HARDWARE

The normal workstation displays are much too slow to allow a good quality display of 3D objects in real time. We are using a SUN Sparc station for the animated figure rendered as a b/w linedrawing with backfacing polygons omitted. However for solid areafilled surfaces, the speed would be too slow and a better solution is sought.

As a part of this project we have also constructed a special purpose hardware unit capable of the display of filled surfaces for a more solid look. The main basic principle behind this add-on unit is the Parity-Fill method which has been known for a long time[2], but since then very little is mentioned in the literature. To benefit from this elegant scheme however, the filling operation should be implemented in hardware. Also implemented in hardware is a surface priority scheme, which allows surfaces to overlap and still showing only the surface closest to the observer.

Images are created as 3D networks, which are dynamically transformed in such a way that each frame is shown only once, and thus the full interactivity to the synthesized image is maintained.

In all, this add-on unit occupies only the board space of one double-height EuroCard. The present configuration for the unit, is as a slave to a Sparc processor, which is then responsible for viewing transformations. Using a VME interface, we have currently connected the board to a SUN 4/110 computer. In the future, we plan to incorporate a DSP32C signal processor as an acceleration unit, thus relieving the Sparc from running the kernel.

8   FUTURE DEVELOPMENT

A general idea of a movement alphabet is very thrilling. Such an alphabet has already been formulated for the face[20], where symbols in this sense are called Action Units (AU's). For instance, for the case of the entire body, a movement symbol called "walk" would result in a repeating angular pattern as described earlier. Modifiers should be allowed, such as "jumping" or "leftlimp" and applied at varying degree. Motion is always controlled through the parametric bindings applicable for the selected type of motion and control could preferably be linked to the operator through a multidimensional sensing device such as the "Data glove" from VPL Research Labs.

The angle editor, MOSES, and the animation kernel will be merged so that it will be possible to view real time animations of the figures and the motions being edited inside the editor instead. This would remove the need of a separate program for the kernel. It will also be possible to define new skeletons of figures inside the editor.

The underlying data and program structure of the kernel could be enhanced in several ways. Conditional constructs in the event lists would provide powerful a control mechanism. To make such a construction time symmetric it would be necessary to use both pre- and postconditions. A way of formally represent action structures with pre-, post- and prevail conditions has been described by Sandewall[6].

Another deficiency of the current kernel is the lack of ability to control variations in speed within subsequences. Such control would make it substantially easier to create more varied animations without causing any particular increase in data size.

9 ACKNOWLEGEMENTS

This work was supported by CENIIT (Center of Industrial Information Technology) and STU (Swedish Board of Technical Development).

References

[1] Crotchow A. *Introduction to Robotics*. Macmillan Publishing Company, 1985.

[2] Ackland B. and Weste N. Real time animation playback on a frame store display. In *proceedings of the ACM SIGGRAPH*, 1980.

[3] Phillips C. Badler N. and Zhao J. Interactive real-time articulated figure manipulation using multiple kinematic constraints. *Computer Graphics*, 24(2), 1990.

[4] Ware C. and Osborne S. Exploration and virtual camera control in virtual three dimensional environments. *Computer Graphics*, 24(2), 1990.

[5] Gaudet S. Calvert T., Welman S. and Lee C. Composition of multiple figure sequences for dance and animation. In *"New Advances in Computer Graphics"*, *proceedings of Computer Graphics International*, 1989.

[6] Sandewall E. and Rönnquist R. A representation of action structures. Technical Report LiTH-IDA-R-86-13, Dept. of Comp. Sci., Linköping University, 1986.

[7] Bruderlin A. et al. Goal-directed, dynamic animation of human walking. In *proceedings of the ACM SIGGRAPH*, pages 233–242, 1989.

[8] Magnetat-Thalmann N. et al. Abstract muscle action procedures for human face animation. *The Visual Computer*, 3(6), 1987.

[9] Parke F. Measuring three-dimensional surfaces with a two-dimensional data tablet. *Computers & Graphics*, 1, 1975.

[10] Carl-Herman Hjortsjö. *Man's Face and Mimic Language*. Studentlitteratur, 1969.

[11] Yngvesson J. The retina 4 kernel. Technical Report LiTH-ISY-I-1026, Dept. of Elect. Eng., Linköping University, 1989.

[12] Yngvesson J. Interactive viewing through strucured eventlists. Technical Report LiTH-ISY-I-1112, Dept. of Elect. Eng., Linköping University, 1990.

[13] Wei S. Lee P. and Badler N. Zhao J. Strength guided motion. Technical Report MS-CIS-90-04, Dept. of Computer and Information Science, 1990.

[14] Baecker R. M. Picture driven animation. In *SJCC, AFIPS Conference*, volume 34, pages 273–288, 1969.

[15] Girard M. Interactive design of 3d computer-animated legged animal motion. *IEEE Computer Graphics & Applications*, 7(6):39–50, June 1987.

[16] Girard M. and Maciejewski A. A. Computational modeling for the computer animation of legged figures. In *proceedings of the ACM SIGGRAPH*, pages 263–270, 1985.

[17] Rydfalk M. Candide, a parameterized face. Technical Report LiTH-ISY-I-0866, Dept. of Elect. Eng., Linköping University, 1987.

[18] Badler N. Articulated figure positioning by multiple constraint. *IEEE Computer Graphics & Applications*, 7(6):28–38, 1987.

[19] Fahlander O. A practical scheme for continuous trajectory definition. Technical Report LiTH-ISY-I-1174, Dept. of Elec. Eng., 1991.

[20] Ekman P. and Friesen W.V. *Facial Action Coding System*. Consulting Psychologists Press, Calif., 1977.

[21] Forchheimer R. and Kronander T. Image coding - from waveforms to animation. *IEEE Transactions on acoustics, speech and signal processing*, 37(12), 1989.

[22] Rajka P. Ungvary and Waters. Nuntius - a computer system for the interactive composition and analysis of music and dance. Technical Report REP 189, 1989.

Part III

Systems and Languages for Motion Synthesis and Control

Part II

Toward an Integrated Motion-Synthesis Environment

SUSAN AMKRAUT and MICHAEL GIRARD

ABSTRACT

The problem of creating a flexible, integrated motion-synthesis environment that orchestrates the coordination of diverse motion control systems is discussed. An implemented prototype system, called *The Magic Theatre*, is described which attempts to factor out interactive and procedural functions common to many motion control schemas. A theoretical model is given in which diverse motion control systems may both interact with each other and operate in series on animated elements in a scene.

1. INTRODUCTION

In some general sense, photorealistic image-synthesis techniques are largely a matter of simulating the interplay of light in a 3D environment. Although there is a broad diversity of rendering approaches, it is nonetheless possible to base rendering on a single monolithic computational model that encompasses illumination, shape, and the inter-reflections of diffuse (radiosity) and specular (ray-tracing) reflections.

A difficulty with computational motion-synthesis is that, unlike the light/object elements of image-synthesis, motion phenomena are fundamentally more complex and heterogeneous in nature. For example, the physical models and computational techniques required for modelling the flexible deformations of objects [Platt 1988, Terzopolous 1988] are quite distinct from the fluid mechanical models we might use to animate the macroscopic behavior of flowing water [Kass and Miller 1990]. Furthermore, simulating motion governed by living organisms is enormously complicated by the need to model the specialized control systems animals use to manage their goal-directed behavior [Girard 1990].

Most computer animation professionals acknowledge that animation production is plagued by a lack of integrated techniques. While commercial animation systems are typically restricted to key-framed interpolation paradigms, research and development work is often also (understandably) isolated to an investigation of a single motion control system. Although there have been a number of excellent publications that classify motion control techniques[Zeltzer 1985] and describe animation systems that employ a number of different animation tools [Reeves 1990], the problem of designing animation systems that provide for the *interplay* of diverse motion control systems has not been rigorously addressed.

In this paper, we seek to formulate a general architecture for accommodating the software construction and user interface for an evolving set of harmoniously integrated motion control systems. In our view, the interface of an integrated animation system should ideally act to effectively link the high-level expressive controls of each motion control system with its corresponding visual effects in a conceptually direct and ergonomically effortless fashion. As such, we have eschewed programming approaches and command languages due to the low-level extraneous details and lack of interactivity associated with writing and compiling computer programming languages.

Instead we have opted for a visually-interactive approach that integrates user interaction with displayed objects and menu-based motion control systems through a uniformity of software-based virtual control devices (such as icons, sliders, graphs, keystrokes and mouse clicks). Each motion control module is highly specialized to enable ease of interaction in terms of its own structural and motion attributes. For example, facial expression systems must display and edit the design of muscle placement on the face [Waters 87, Wiiliams 90], whereas multi-legged locomotion systems must provide for menu-based specification of gait sequences or phase relations[Girard 87, Mckenna 90].

What is noteworthy is that a motion control system embodies more than a tool. It is not used to perform a single calculation on an object, rather it is a system of interactive design and control over ongoing functional behavior over time. The fundamental notion is one of designing a *dynamic process* rather than a static object. The temporal dimension substantially increases the complexity of the modelling problem, as now we must account for time-based controls of different processes that vary over time, objects that may be influenced (in some order) by several processes, and processes that may interact with each other through common variables (or procedure calls).

In summary, the desired properties of an integrated motion-synthesis environment are:
1. Diversity: Supportive of extensible, heterogeneous interacting motion control systems.
2. Interactivity: Design is through a visually interactive user-interface with virtual control devices, rather than programs.
3. Flexibility: Allows for runtime rearrangement of user defined connections between motion control systems and their associated visual influences.
4. Intelligibility: The behavior of the integrated systems must be understandable to the user.
5. Nonredundancy: Design functions that are common to multiple systems should be factored out.
6. Extensibility: Motion control systems may be easily added or removed from the environment.

It should be noted that while we have not yet succeeded in implementing a finished animation system that meets all of the above design criteria, our system Magic Theatre is well on its way toward achieving that aim. However, the primary goal of this paper is not to describe our particular system (except by way of example). Rather, it is our intent to attempt to lay the theoretical framework for the design of general-purpose motion-synthesis environments.

In section 2, we present an overview of the system architecture we prescribe for motion control synthesis. In order to properly motivate the kinds of integration problems one might encounter, in section 3 we describe examples of motion control systems we have recently developed. Section 4 outlines the organization of our implementation of an integrated motion-synthesis environment called Magic Theatre. Theoretical extensions to our current system are discussed in section 5. Finally, we make our concluding remarks in section 6.

2. SYSTEM ARCHITECTURE FOR MOTION SYNTHESIS

The components of a motion-synthesis environment are shown in figure 1. The *scene elements* comprise the set of information that is sent to the rendering program each frame: the 3D geometric objects in the scene, their world-space positions and reflectance properties; the positions and characteristics of the lights, and the position, aim, and view angle of the camera. Essentially, the *scene,* is what is represented at a single static moment in time.

The *motion control systems* are responsible for modifying the state of the scene elements as a function of time. These systems embody the tightly coupled specialized algorithmic techniques alluded to in the previous section, such as rigid-body dynamics, robot kinematics and fluid mechanics. Although each motion control system is assumed to have its own motion algorithms and internal logic, it is possible for several motion control systems to act on the same scene elements simultaneously. For example, the thigh of a character made out of water balloons would require the use of both articulated figure motion and flexible-body dynamics motion control systems.

For any motion control system, it is useful to distinguish the controls that are available to the designer. These may be conceived as the parametric inputs to a "black box" in which the motion control system resides. For example, in a rigid-body dynamics system, the parametric inputs might be the density of a object or the magnitude of gravitational acceleration. We define the *parametric controllers* as functions that are used to "animate" the input parameters of motion control systems over time in a general way. Examples of parametric controllers for real-number parameters(where $u = F(t)$) are sine-wave functions, one dimensional key-framing systems. These will be discussed in greater detail in section 4.10.

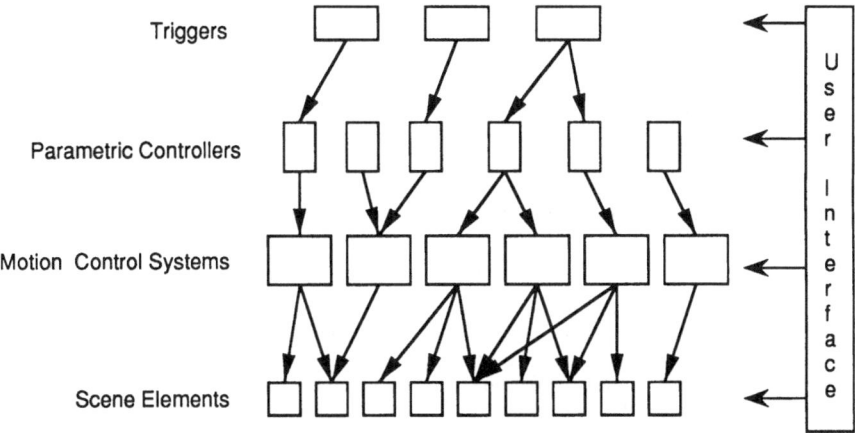

Figure 1: Overview of Integrated Motion-Synthesis Environment

Finally, events in the real world are rarely planned to occur at specific times. Instead they are caused by circumstances that are preconditions for their execution. For example, a hard rubber ball squishes when it hits the ground. Therefore, the application of flexible-body dynamics could be called with the precondition of ball/ground contact. In order to model state-based sychronization of motion control systems, we define *triggers* as conditional expressions evaluated at each time sample that may activate (or deactivate) the application of parametric controllers and their motion control systems. Behavioral systems [Reynolds 87], wherein motion control is conceptualized in terms of interaction between environmentally responsive state-based units, may be built up from rule-based triggers.

3. EXAMPLES OF MOTION CONTROL SYSTEMS

Our ongoing exploration and appreciation for diverse motion control systems has formed the basis for our thinking about how to design and integrate animation techniques. In this sense, our ideas are rooted in a "bottom-up" approach. This approach is perhaps the most logical in that the determination of common design parameters and control schemes for a motion-synthesis environment depends on the character of the motion modelling modules one wishes to integrate.In this section, we will give a brief survey of several motion control systems that we have been developing.

3.1 Key Frame Interpolation

Most commercially available computer animation systems are based on the traditional animation notion of setting key positions at "key-frames" that are then automatically interpolated to produce the frames in between. Our *Key* motion system [fig. 2A], like many of the commercial systems, allows us to smoothly interpolate the positions of objects along splined paths. The rotations of objects are splined using the quaternion formulation [Shoemake 85].The speed of motion may be decoupled from the path through the use of distance/time graphs [Girard 87], to be discussed in section 4.10.

The utility of key-framing is in its application to simple motion and the artificial smooth path generation which is required for camera movement. Moreover, key-framing is often suitable for any motion control parameter (such as gravity) or a rendering attribute (such as color) that must be informally manipulated over time in a smooth fashion, as we shall discuss in in section 4.10.

3.2 Rigid Body/Flexible Body Dynamics

In the last several years, physically-based modelling research in computer animation has focused on the problems associated with rigid body [Hahn 88, Baraff 90] and flexible-body dynamics[Platt 88]. The research at SCAN on modelling of rigid and flexible body dynamics is similar to the Terzopolous/Witkin algorithm [Terzopolous 1988] in which flexible body dynamics are decoupled in terms of deformations from a rigid shape [fig. 2B]. The rigid shape's motion may be computed according to newton's laws for translational motion and euler's equation of rotational motion of a rigid body in 3D space. The principal axes of rotation of an object may be computed as the eigenvectors of the body's inertial tensor [Hahn 1988]. The elasticity of deformation of material may be approximated using finite-element techniques, structural analysis, or simple mass-spring systems [Chadwick,Haumann 1989].

Given objects with moderate complexity, testing for collisions may become a primary computational bottleneck. The problem of efficiently detecting collisions between 3D polyhedral objects is another focus in our research program (see section 5.3). To date, publications on collision detection work only for convex polyhedra[Wilhelms 1988, Barr 1990, Gilbert 1988]. Recently, we have implemented an oct-tree based spatial decomposition algorithm that also works for concave polyhedra[Rijpkema 91], achieving $O(n \log n)$ time complexity.

Further research will incorporate the simulation of sliding and frictional contacts[Baraff 1989, Baraff 1990].

3.3 Articulated Limbs

Both animal limbs and robot manipulators are best described in terms of the mathematics of articulated systems, in which bodies are linked to form kinematic chains. The animation and simulation of intelligent goal-directed motion in *Limbs* requires the use of *inverse-kinematic* formulations, which compute the joint angles of a limb in terms of some desired hand (or foot) position. Our formulation for inverse-kinematics is based on a robotics technique called *resolved motion rate control*. This technique computes the pseudoinverse of the Jacobian transformation between joint rates and end-effector rates [Girard 1985]. An advantage of this approach is its ability to generalize to all limbs, including anthropomorphic limbs that are *redundant manipulators* having more the 6 joints (degrees-of-freedom), such as human arms, spines and legs.

The simulation of limb *dynamics* is needed if we wish to compute the Newtonian mechanical properties of a limb. Here, we are interested in the relationship between the limb forces applied at each of the joints, the mass and moments of the limb's links, environmental forces (such as gravity or the weight of objects being carried) and the resulting motion derivatives of the limb. Again, robot dynamics algorithms may be applied. In order to compute *inverse-dynamics*, which gives the joint torques required for a certain movement, we have implemented the efficient (linear time) Newton-Euler method. For *forward-dynamics*, which simulates the motion of a limb from a given set of joint torques, we have implemented the Walker-Orin Composite Rigid Body Method [Walker and Orin 1982].

Research from biodynamics and robotics has shown that the control of simulated natural limb motion is rooted in the global optimisation of performance of motion taken over a path, particularly with regard to minimum energy (for swinging motion) and minimization of jerk of the end of the limb (for goal-directed reaching motions). The robust computational framework for the optimization of multiple performance indices described in [Girard 1990] has been recently expanded to include obstacle avoidance [Stevens 1990].

The above techniques form the basis of the motion control system, *Limbs* [fig. 2C]. The user-interface is geared toward the task of designing trajectories of limbs defined in terms of inverse-kinematics, dynamics, and optimization criteria (such as minimum-jerk and minimum-energy speed distribution).

135

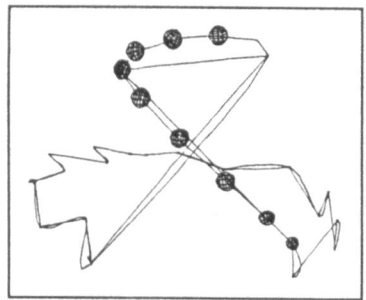

Figure 2A: Object Keyframed along Spline.

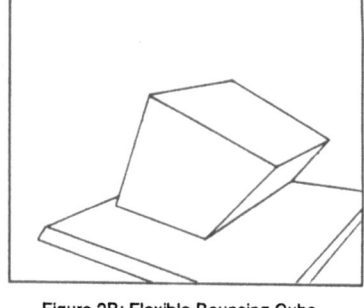

Figure 2B: Flexible Bouncing Cube.

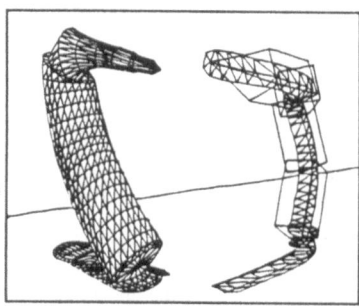

Figure 2C: Two Animated Limbs with Skin.

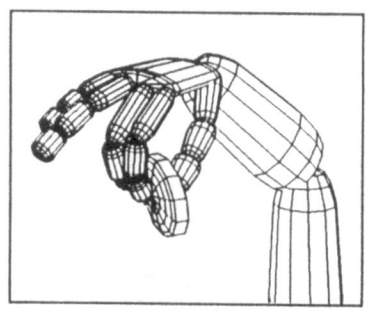

Figure 2D: Hand Grasping an Object.

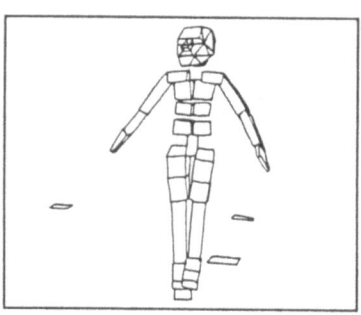

Figure 2E: Poda Human Figure Jumping.

Figure 2F: Flock of Birds.

Figure 2G: Free Form Deformations.

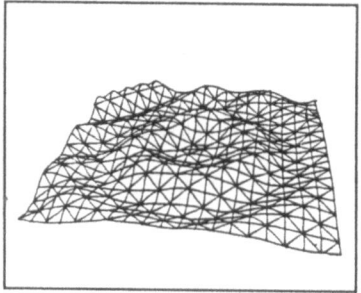

Figure 2H: Waves passing through Grid.

Figure 2: Motion Control Systems

3.4 Hand Grasping and Behavior

Recently, we have investigated the problem of modelling the intelligent grasping of objects [Brady 1989, Salisbury 1989]. A knowledge-based approach has been implemented that classifies objects according to their similarity to generic primitives such as blocks, cylinders, spheres, and rings [Rijpkema 1990, Tomovic 1989]. Once an object has been identified with a particular class, a corresponding grasping strategy (stored in the knowledge-base) belonging to that class is performed. Adaptive control techniques are then used to adjust to the object's deviation in form from its associated generic primitive's shape. In its current state, our implementation *Hands* works in concert with *Limbs* in order to automatically select an optimal grasp from a set of possible grasps associated with a polygonal object's class in the knowledge-base [fig. 2D]. Furthermore, higher-level control of hand behavior other the grasping, such as the pinching and spreading of selected groups of fingers, is provided by the *Hands* motion control system. A more detailed discussion may be found in [Rijpkema 1990].

3.5 Legged Animals: Poda

Animal motor skills as elementary as locomotion are not well understood and are the focus of research in biodynamics and the robotics of legged vehicles [Raibert 1989, Orin 1990]. However, complex motion systems are always hierarchical in nature, and operate through a precise coordination of lower-level motion behaviors. It seems clear that the *Limbs* control systems described in the previous section may be directed by higher-level strategies that take into account overall body motion, dynamic balance, and foothold planning. Indeed, our work in modelling legged locomotion is rooted in the formal models of gait developed for both engineering and analysis of legged systems[Girard 1987, McGhee 1980].

Of course, locomotion is only a small subset of animal motion behavior. Our research is primarily directed at the artistic expression of intelligent motion --- the domain of *dance*. The formulation of structure in dance has been a longstanding problem in the field of choreography. The Laba and Benesh systems of dance notation have attempted to formalize dance in an analogous fashion to music notation. However, due to complexity and range of gestural dynamics in human motion, notational systems are both inexact and extremely tedious to learn [Badler 1980, Calvert 1982].

The computer modelling and animation of human dance challenges us to address the problems of modelling coordination, grace, gesture and dynamics in a robust, expressive fashion. Our work in modelling human dance, the *Poda* system [fig. 2E], while still primitive, is among the most advanced systems for capturing the qualities of free-form movement in a physically credible way[Girard 1990].

3.6 Flocking: Vector Force Fields

Another domain of interest in modelling intelligent motion is in the study and synthesis of flocking, herding, and schooling behavior exhibited by groups of animals [Amkraut 1989, Reynolds 1987]. We have implemented a system that employs vector force fields as a means of both guiding the flow of individuals within a group, and insuring that collisions are avoided [Amkraut 1991][fig. 2F]. Aside from the creative possibilities of designing behavioral systems in which individuals are responsive to environmental rules, the standard key-frame based techniques available in commercial computer animation are incapable of managing the complexity which arises from interaction within large groups (such as bird flocks, fish schools, and cattle herds).

3.7 Other Motion Control Systems

Other useful methods of motion control are geometrically based. A hierarchical free-form deformation system similar to that used in P.D.I.'s "Locomotion" animation[Goldberg 1990] has been developed by Hans Rijpkema [fig. 2G]. The utility of integrating this system with other motion control techniques, such as mass-spring dynamics on the free-form deformation lattice [Chadwick and Haumann 1989], is clear.

Another motion control system (also designed by Hans Rijpkema) that has been added to our Magic Theatre environment is based on the notion of passing fourier-synthesized 2D waves through surfaces and 3D spatial waves through objects [fig. 2H]. The user may compose a series of waves to be added by frequency, amplitude and wave-type, each with an attack and decay envelope, thus insuring smooth transitions.

Of course, the motion control systems described above do not constitute a complete set of motion control schemes. Our philosophy is that a motion-synthesis environment is never complete. A good environment should provide for the seamless integration of new techniques as they are developed. These include, but are not limited to, already published techniques, such as facial expressions[Waters 87], particle-system dynamics[Reeves 84], fluid dynamics[Kass and Miller 90] and snake locomotion[Miller 88]. The problem is that each technique, aside from its internal algorithmic organization, embodies its own characteristic design parameters and interface.

4. IMPLEMENTATION: THE MAGIC THEATRE SYSTEM

There in little crazy letters that were scarcely legible was scrawled:
Tonight at the Magic Theatre
For Madmen Only
Price of Admission Your Mind
Not for Everybody
.... Herman Hesse's *Steppenwolf*

In this section, we describe our initial progress in the implementation of a flexible integrated motion-synthesis environment that accommodates many of the motion control systems described in the previous section. We begin by discussing the view of the environment of our implementation, Magic Theatre, as seen by the user, followed by an in-depth view of its internal organization and theoretically planned extensions.

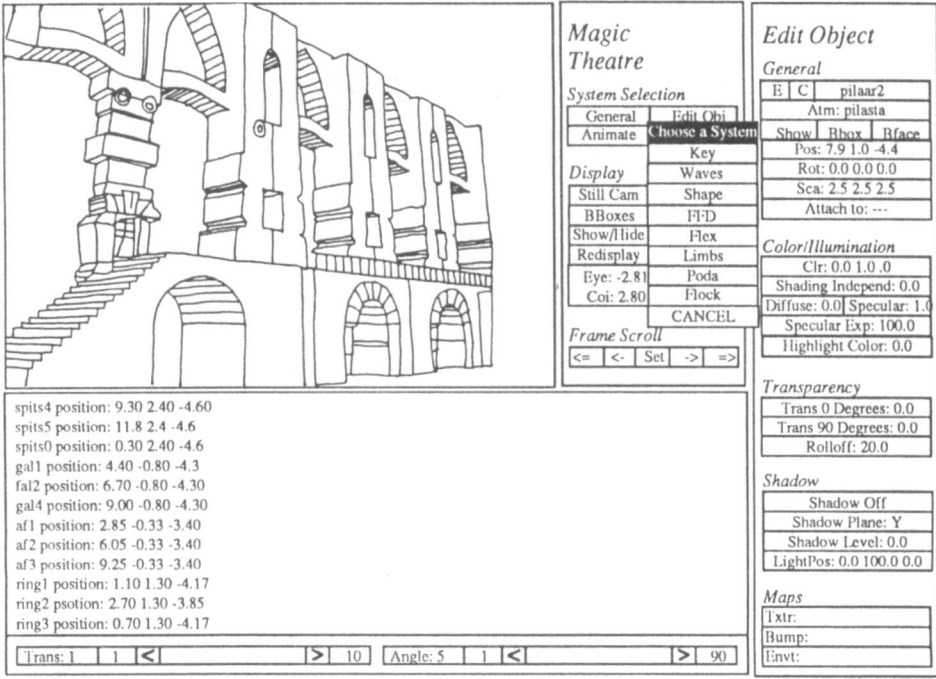

Figure 3: Magic Theatre User Interface

4.1 The User's View of Magic Theatre

When working with Magic Theatre, the user can select and switch between various menu interfaces. Menus which offer standard graphics and animation capabilities are a basic part of Magic Theatre. One such menu allows the user to edit the display parameters of a scene element. Another offers animation calculation and playback operations. Another lets the user create, delete, and show information about scene elements [fig. 3]. Each motion control system in Magic Theatre has its own menu interface, developed by the programmer of that system. To work with a particular motion control system, the user can select a system from a menu displaying the available motion control systems, thereby bringing up that system's menu interface. The user may switch between working within a particular motion control system, or working with the standard graphics and animation systems that are part of Magic Theatre. Regardless of what motion control systems are made available, these standard graphics and animation menu interfaces always exist as a basic foundation of Magic Theatre.

Separating motion control system menus and Magic Theatre standard operation menus simplifies the user interface of Magic Theatre. The user can start by learning the standard Magic Theatre menus, and gradually expand his or her knowledge of Magic Theatre by learning to work with different motion control systems. No matter what motion control system is acting upon a scene element, whether the element is being deformed or moving along a spline path, or both, the interface for altering its standard display parameters, or for computing animation, or for performing other standard operations on it always remains the same. So no matter how many new motion control systems the user learns, the methods for performing standard operations remain familiar.

4.2 Internal Organization of Magic Theatre

The interaction between Magic Theatre, scene elements, and motion control systems is depicted in figure 4. Magic Theatre maintains a list of all scene elements. Each motion control system contains pointers to the scene elements which it controls. Magic Theatre calls the motion control systems to perform functions upon the scene elements under their control. The motion control systems can in turn call Magic Theatre to perform general functions or get information about all scene elements.

4.2.1 Structure of Scene Elements

Scene elements contain information about the state of a particular displayable object or display element in the scene, at the current frame. No animation information is stored in a scene element. A scene element can be the camera, the center of interest, a depicted object, a light or a map. The camera, center of interest, lights and maps, although not renderable, can be displayed as 3d icons in wireframe for set-up purposes. Storing them in the form of scene elements makes it easy to perform standard display operations on them just as those operations are performed on all scene elements.

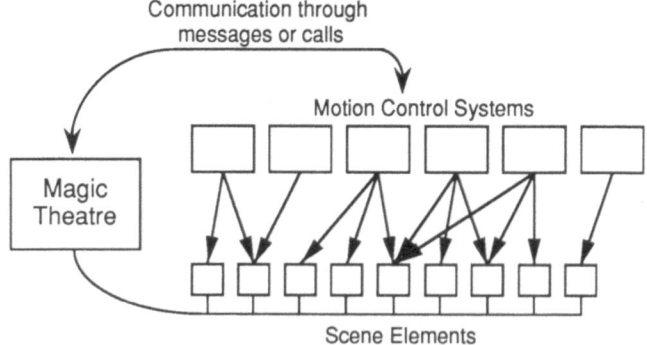

Figure 4: The Internal Structure of Magic Theatre

Scene element variables include position, rotation, scale and a transformation matrix. A pointer to a geometrical object structure is part of the scene element. A link to a parent scene element to form object hierarchies is also stored. The binary variables describing whether or not the object is displayed as a bounding box, whether its backfaces are visible, and whether it is hidden or shown are also part of the scene element structure. If the scene element is renderable, then a pointer to a structure containing color, illumination parameters, transparency values, shadow information, and applied texture, bump and environment maps is set. If the scene element itself is a map or a light, then a pointer to a structure containing the light or map parameters of that scene element is set.

4.2.2 Division of Tasks Between Magic Theatre and Motion Control Systems

Motion control systems alter the variables of the scene elements to which they point. They alter only those variables which they are animating. For instance, a free form deformation system will alter the points of a scene element's geometrical structure, while a rigid body dynamics system will alter only the position and rotation, and the transformation matrix of a scene element. Motion control systems make changes to the variables they animate only when called upon to do so by Magic Theatre (during animation calculation or frame update), or when the user is working with the motion control system's menu interface. Different motion control systems can point to the same scene element. In simple cases, this is functional, although problems of system conflict and ordering may result (see section 5).

Magic Theatre has direct access to the list of scene elements. Through user commands to Magic Theatre's menu interfaces, Magic Theatre acts directly upon the scene elements, creating and deleting them, altering their variables, displaying and rendering them. Magic Theatre does not act directly upon motion control system structures. It knows nothing about the structures of the motion control systems. Instead, it expects each motion control system to provide a set of standard functions, and it interfaces to the motion control systems through those functions. The motion control systems know nothing about the structure of Magic Theatre. However, they can communicate with Magic Theatre through a set of communication functions which Magic Theatre offers them.

This separation between Magic Theatre and the motion control systems simplifies the integration of motion control systems into Magic Theatre. The only requirement of the motion control system is to act upon scene elements and to provide certain Magic Theatre callable functions. The internal structures and workings of the motion control system are the decision of the programmer. Immediately upon integration, the programmer can take advantage of all of the standard graphics and animation capabilities available in Magic Theatre to visualize and perfect the motion control system. As new systems are added, Magic Theatre is altered and improved to accommodate them.

4.3 Channelling of User Input

Magic Theatre receives all input from the user. It decides whether to handle that input itself, or to send it on to a motion control system. Magic Theatre keeps track of what menu interface is active. If the user chooses a particular motion control system from the menu of available systems, then Magic Theatre tells that motion control system to bring up its menu interface and prepare for further commands. It then records the fact that that motion control system is active and all further mouse clicks made to that menu interface should be passed on to and handled exclusively by that motion control system.

If the user clicks on an icon in a Magic Theatre menu interface, or enters a keyboard command recognized by Magic Theatre, then Magic Theatre itself handles that request, either by acting upon scene elements or calling motion control systems, or performing some other task.

4.4 Selection of Scene Elements

In Magic Theatre as well as many motion control systems, the user often works with one scene element at a time, changing parameters which control that scene element. So Magic Theatre provides methods for selecting scene elements with which to work, thereby making those selection methods uniform within Magic Theatre and all motion control systems, simplifying the job of both the programmer and the user.

Every time a scene element is displayed, the center of the scene element on the screen is stored in the scene element structure. Magic Theatre lets the user select a scene element by clicking on its image in the display window. When a mouse click on the display window is detected, Magic Theatre processes the coordinates of that click to determine which scene element was chosen. Magic Theatre then works with that element, or calls the active motion control system to inform it that a new scene element has been selected by the user for consideration.

It is sometimes difficult to choose a scene element from the screen. The user may not know where the element is or what it looks like, or it may be off the screen, or so many elements may be displayed that it is impossible to point to a particular one. So Magic Theatre offers an alternative way of choosing a scene element. A function is available from Magic Theatre to all motion control systems for displaying a menu of the names of all scene elements and selecting one element.

Sometimes motion control systems do not work with individual scene elements, but with groups of scene elements. For instance, when working in the *Limbs* system, the user may be editing not only a link, but an entire limb, made up of many links. So when the user selects a scene element, a link, the *Limbs* system determines that not only was that link chosen for editing, but the limb of which that link is a part was also selected.

Some motion control systems request the user to select a point or polygon from a scene element's geometrical object. For instance, the *Waves* system can generate a wave from a desired point in a geometrical object. In the future, routines will be added to Magic Theatre for determining which point or polygon has been selected by the user from the screen, and sending that information to a motion control system which requests it.

4.5 Creation and Deletion of Scene Elements

Magic Theatre has menus which allow the user to create and delete scene elements. Typically, creation and deletion is performed on an element per element basis, and only by Magic Theatre. Instead of creating their own scene elements, most motion control systems add existing scene elements to their system by allowing the user to select the element to add, and then setting a pointer to that element.

However, some motion control systems work with a set of tightly coupled scene elements. For example, the *Limbs* systems works not on one scene element, but on a limb, consisting of a set of scene elements. So scene elements animated by the *Limbs* system must be created in the *Limbs* system. The *Limbs* system accomplishes this by calling Magic Theatre routines available for creating and adding scene elements to Magic Theatre.

When a user requests to delete a single scene element, all motion control systems must be polled to see if that element is deletable. For instance, a link from a limb is not deletable on its own. The entire limb must be deleted through the *Limbs* system. Whether a scene element is deleted through a Magic Theatre menu or through a motion control system menu, routines in Magic Theatre must be called to check whether the element is deletable, and if so, to extract the element from all motion control systems.

4.6 Alteration of Display Parameters

Magic Theatre provides menus for altering the static values of display parameters of scene elements. This includes most scene elements variables mentioned in section 4.1. Certain display parameters, such as bounding box display and showing and hiding scene elements, must be able to be altered quickly, often, and globally for all objects. These options are always easily accessible to the user. Also, controls for manipulation of the camera and center of interest position are always accessible.

Sometimes it is necessary to group and view a set of display parameters, such as all the current positions or lighting parameters of all the objects. This type of show capability is available in Magic Theatre.

4.7 Use of Script-Based Specification and Storage

Each motion control system can determine its own way of saving animation information. When creating a Magic Theatre script, Magic Theatre first stores information about scene elements and global values. It then calls each motion control system and tells it to add whatever information is necessary to the Magic Theatre script in order to store the system's animation. The system first writes an identifying string to the script, so that Magic Theatre can determine, upon loading of the script, which system should read which part of the script.

Magic Theatre is basically an interactive system, as opposed to a script based system. Although scripts are readable, they are not often directly altered by users or generated by separate programs. Users alter animation through interaction with Magic Theatre. Programmers write interactive systems to integrate their motion control systems into Magic Theatre.

4.8 Temporal Update, Animation and Display

In Magic Theatre, the user can easily update the display to a particular frame for viewing or altering purposes. An entire interface is also available to calculate and playback animation in wireframe with a hidden line option, or to compute rendered images. To display a frame, Magic Theatre calls each motion control system and tells it to update the variables of the scene elements under the system's control to a particular frame. Then Magic Theatre displays, or tells the renderer to render, each scene element, using the current values of the scene element variables.

Motion control systems may need to redisplay a frame or a particular scene element which has been altered by user interaction with the motion control system. The systems never directly display scene elements themselves. Instead, they call Magic Theatre routines for displaying a frame or redisplaying a single scene element. These routines take into account all the display variables of the scene elements, determining how and whether to display shadows, bounding boxes, backfaces, etc.

Sometimes a motion control system must display special objects which are not scene elements in Magic Theatre, for instance a spline path or a grid for describing an object deformation. These objects are called helper objects. They are displayed directly by the motion control system. When Magic Theatre displays a frame, it calls on all motion control systems to display their helper objects.

4.9: Frame Updating: Time-Based versus State-Based Motion Control Systems

Some motion control systems, such as *Flock*, base the computation of each frame upon the state of the system at the previous frame. We will call such a system a state-based system. A state-based system can easily compute consecutive frames, but has trouble updating to a random frame number. This is in contrast to a time-based system, such as *Key*, which can easily compute the state at any frame, regardless of what state it is currently in, because all values are a function of time.

To produce an accurate picture of a random frame, a state-based system must compute the animation sequentially from the first frame to the desired frame. This is much too time consuming, since the user often requests an update of the display to a random frame. So a state-based motion control system must develop a way to estimate the state at a random frame. One way of doing that is for the system to store its state during animation calculation, for instance every 50 frames. Then the system can linearly interpolate the values between the stored states to produce an estimated state at a random frame.

Still another problem exists for a state-based motion control system updating to a random frame. If the user has changed a system parameter, causing the animation to change, an update to a particular frame based on stored states which were computed using old system parameter values may be totally inaccurate. Perhaps the user can be trusted to be aware of the changes he or she has made, and to recompute the animation from the frame at which the change occurs. But the system could also be designed to be smart enough to keep track of the earliest frame at which a parameter change has been made. When update to a random frame is requested, the system could either warn the user of the need for recalculation from a particular frame, or simply perform the necessary recalculation.

For the sake of state-based motion control systems, Magic Theatre calls different frame update routines depending on the type of update requested. When the user requests to view a random frame, an update routine is called which updates the system and its scene elements to a random frame. In this routine, a state-based motion control system would compute an estimated state at that frame, using the techniques described above. A time-based motion control system would compute an accurate state at that frame.

The other type of update routine is one which occurs during animation calculation. Magic Theatre first calls a routine to tell the motion control systems to prepare for calculation, beginning at a particular frame. A state-based system would then update itself, accurately, to the state at that frame, by recomputing from the first frame of the animation if necessary. During animation calculation, Magic Theatre calls a sequential update routine which assumes that the state is being updated from the current state to the state at the next frame. In this way, a state-based motion control system can produce accurate frames in a reasonable period of time during animation calculation. A time-based motion control system performs the same type of update during animation as it does during an update to a random frame.

4.10 Parametric Controls

In a sense, a well designed motion control system should act as an instrument that transforms incoming design parameters into coherent motion behavior. Parametric controllers may be conceived as levers which act to expressively drive motion control system parameters. This is somewhat analogous to the way midi-controllers (such as keyboard, wind and guitar controllers)direct sound-generation modules (such as synthesizers, signal-processors, and samplers) in music technology .

The primary point here is that expressive control over systems may be codified according to data-streams or data-types that are then treated differently by different motion control systems. For example, a real number controller $F(t) = R$, such as a spline key-framed function, may be used to change an object's rigidity in a flexible-body dynamics system, the gravity in an animal locomotion system, and the strength of a vector-force field in a flocking system.

Many of our systems currently employ a double-interpolant key-based system as a parametric controller i.e. $R = Spline[u(t)]$ where $u[t]$ is a double-interpolant, or *timing graph* mapping time into the spline-parameter $u(t)$. The timing graph may be generalized to include both linear and eased interpolation between keys. Routines to access the timing graph parametric controller are available in Magic Theatre and callable by the motion control systems. In fact, this parametric controller forms the basis of the *Key* motion control system in Magic Theatre.

For control parameters that have metrics, such as path length or joint-space distance, it is appropriate to use distance/time parametric controllers,that compute $Dist(t)$ rather than $u(t)$. This approach allows the designer to directly visualize the speed of motion as the slope of the timing graph. Then the speed about specific positions (at given times) may be easily seen. However, the controller must reparameterize its motion trajectory by arc-length. We refer the reader to [Girard 1987] for a further discussion of these issues.

5. EXTENSIONS AND CONSIDERATIONS FOR THE FUTURE

5.1 Ordering of Operations Taken by Multiple Motion Control Systems

Computer graphics specialists are quite familiar with concept of ordering operations on objects: different permutations of rotation, scaling, translation, bending and twisting, free-form deformation, shape-interpolation produce different results. Furthermore, animation languages have been suggested that are based on a ordering of operators, such as pipeline of filters and data-flow connections.

Presently, Magic Theatre calls each motion control system once, and always in the same order, to update itself. However, the ability to handle more complex update ordering is necessary. In some cases, the user must have control over the order in which different motion control system update operations will occur, and this ordering must be specifiable per scene element. For instance, suppose the user alters the geometrical shape of a scene element using both a free form deformation motion control system, as well as the *Waves* motion control system. Then the user must have control over the order in which the systems will act upon the scene element.

In our theoretical framework, and a future implementation of Magic Theatre, the ordering of the motion system functions will be specifiable on an object by object basis, as follows:

For scene element $s_i \in S$ we define a permutation of operations:

$$\Phi_i = (f^1(s_i), f^2(s_i), \dots f^n(s_i))$$

where f^k are computed on s_i in order from $k = 1$ to n

However, some operations, such as n-body force-field dynamics, bird flocking or the simulation of colliding rigid objects, may be functions F of sets S_k composed of several scene elements, that is:

$$f^j = F^j(S_h) \text{ where } S_h \text{ is some subset of } S$$

This complicates matters since contradictions may now arise, such as:

For s_i: $F_i = (F_1(S_h), F_2(S_h))$
For s_k: $F_k = (F_2(S_h), F_1(S_h))$ with $S_h = \{s_i, s_k\}$

The contradiction is that for scene element s_i, the result of executing functions f_1 before f_2 will depend on the state of scene element s_k, but s_k should be updated by executing functions F_2 before F_1. Therefore we must add the following restriction that disallows set functions F_j of common elements S_h from being executed in different order. That is:

Ordering Theorem
If $f_1 = F_1(S_h)$ and $f_2 = F_2(S_m)$ and $S_h \wedge S_m$ is not empty then f_1 and f_2 must occur be in the same order in the permutations Φ_j for each $s_j \in S_h \wedge S_m$

In the absence of contradictions, we may fix the order of the motion control system operations that act on user-defined groups of scene elements S_h. For a given set S_h of scene elements there is a unique associated permutation of set functions:

$$\phi_h = (F^1(S_h), F^2(S_h), \dots F^n(S_h)).$$

We now present an algorithm that allows us to compute a permutation of functions on a given scene element s_i. This permutation may include both functions on itself $f(s_i)$ and functions on sets to which it belongs $F(S_k)$, $s_i \in S_k$.

For example, one such permutation might be:

$$\Phi_i = (f_3{}^1(s_i), F_2{}^2(S_h), f_1{}^3(s_i), F_1{}^4(s_i), F_3{}^5(S_h), f_4{}^6(s_i), f_2{}^7(s_i))$$
$$\text{with } s_i \in S_h$$

In this example, the element s_i is processed in the following order:
$$F_i = (f_3, F_2, f_1, F_1, F_3, f_4, f2)$$

where the f's act only on si
and the F's act on a set S_h containing s_i

In this example, the set S_h must have the order $\phi_h = (F_2, F_1, F_3)$

In general, we must process each scene element according to its specified permutation of motion control operations. Our algorithm executes set operations $F(S_h)$ only once, after insuring that all scene elements s_j in S_h are up to date. Each operation on single elements $f(s_j)$ that come before each $F(S_h)$ in Φ_j are executed and marked as follows:

Ordering Algorithm

For each subset $S_h \; \varepsilon \; S$, where S is the set of all scene elements
{
  For each operation $F^p(S_h)$ in order p=1 to n in ϕ_h
  {
    For each scene element $s_j \; \varepsilon \; S_h$

      For each $f_k(s_j)$ not executed in Φ_j before $F^p(S_n)$
        {execute $f_k(s_j)$ on scene element s_j

        mark $f_k(s_j)$ as executed in Φ_j}
    Execute $F^p(S_h)$ for set S_h
    For each scene element $s_j \; \varepsilon \; S_h$ mark $F^p(S_h)$ as executed in Φ_j
  }
  For each scene element $s_j \; \varepsilon \; S_h$

    For each $f_k(s_j)$ after $F^n(S_h)$ in Φ_j Execute $f_k(s_j)$
}

5.2 Grouping for Assignment and Stochastic Modelling

It is often appropriate to conceptually group scene elements or parametric controls, such as the initial positions of a school of fish, the color of sparks of fire, the size of stones placed on the ground, or the initial speed of a group of running dogs, etc. A *group* is defined as a set of elements having the same data type, for example: the set of scalars describing vertical speed, the set of vectors describing cartesian positions, the set of quaternions describing rotations, or the set of n-tuples describing joint-space positions of an n-degree-of-freedom robot manipulator.

The Magic Theatre system should allow the user to interactively form groups across different motion control systems, as long the elements of the group are of the same type. If we define an equality assignment operator for each user defined data-type, values may be then easily assigned to all members at once. For example, one may then quickly set the color of all fish to silver, or all the initial speeds of parked automobiles to zero.

In [Smith 84], Smith argues for the need for "database amplification". The essential notion is to compute variations in structure from a single elegant description. In [Reeves 85], Reeves uses particle systems as a method for controlling large numbers of elements in a controlled, but nondeterministic fashion. The use of stochastic assignment, in which variables are given values according to both a probability distribution and membership constraints drawn by the user may be generalized across all scalar and vector variables (i.e. compute a distribution of 50 vectors with magnitude less than 20.0 with minimum distance between any two vectors equal to and a mean of (1.0,2.0,1.5)). We plan to develop a general stochastic assignment modeller that may be applied to any group defined by the user. In this way we have:

1) A := B where A is a group of elements given the value of B.
2) A := stochastic(D,C) where A is a group of elements stochastically assigned according to distribution function D with Constraints C

5.3 Collision Detection

Since Magic Theatre keeps a list of all scene elements, it is possible to implement a *collision detector* at a higher-level that may serve all motion control systems during any animation and interactive positioning tasks. Our collision detector employs several hybrid spatial subdivision techniques to reduce both the $O(n^2)$ possible object-object tests and $O(n^2)$ possible polygon-polygon tests required for concave polyhedra A more detailed discussion will be found in [Rijpkema and Girard 1991]. In the case of motion control systems that must detect collisions with scene elements directed by other systems (i.e. rigid-body dynamics collisions of volleyballs kicked by a stampede of wild dogs), it becomes clear that the collision detector must operate at Magic Theatre's global level of control. We are planning to implement our collision detector at this level in the near future.

5.4 Conditional Triggering of Control

Although we have not yet implemented a means of specifying the conditional triggering of functions in the Magic Theatre system, we realize that triggers are a necessary and important means of describing causal motion and behavioral systems. The sychronization of events with preconditions allows for the timing of events based on state, rather than being fixed to a given frame. Examples of this include Zeltzer's finite-state control of walking[Zeltzer 85] and Raibert's state-based running vehicles[Raibert 86]. More obvious examples might be: "Let figure X kick any ball that his foot can reach." One difficulty with this extension is that we must probably resort to the design of these constructs by use of programming language specifications.

5.5 Interacting Motion Control Systems: Data Flow/Constraints

In our discussion, thus far, we have assumed that motion control systems operate solely on the scene elements, either one-to-one (bijectively) or many-to-one (injectively). However, it is also possible for motion control modules to act on each other. The notion of loosely-coupled modules that control each other is the basis for many domains of creative design activity, particularly with regard to electronic control systems.

One obvious example is in the design of sound with analogue synthesizers by means of connections between components. Due to its conceptual appeal, this method of design has been emulated in software-based sound synthesis systems as well as visually oriented *data-flow* networks of modular function icons. The application of data-flow between motion control modules is undoubtedly powerful in scope. For example, the direction vectors generated in the *Flock* vector force field system could be used to guide running legged animals in *Poda*. In this case a data-flow from would need to be directed from the position of the animal to the force field system, which would then return a data-flowed direction vector to a desired velocity variable in the *Poda* system.

A further elaboration is to provide bi-directional data-flow, or *constraints*, between variables belonging to different systems. In this case, relationships between variables of the same type are defined by the user, such as " the initial velocity and position of a ball at frame t = the velocity and position of animal Y's foot at frame t". In this case, the ball may be set according to where the animal is or vice-versa. Obviously, a difficulty here is to provide invertible functions so that constraints may be propagated in both directions [Borning 79]. Furthermore, a visual programming interface is probably necessary so that the behavior of the network may be intelligible to the user. In spite of these difficulties, we hope to provide both unidirectional and bidirectional dataflow capabilities to Magic Theatre in the future.

6. CONCLUSION

In its current state, The Magic Theatre environment we have built is designed in such a way that the programmer can concentrate on motion control, while taking advantage of all the interactive display capabilities that Magic Theatre offers. The environment's interface allows the user to coordinate all motion control systems at once. Scene elements that each motion control system controls can be displayed fully or turned into bounding boxes, viewed from various camera angles, updated at specific frames, animated and played back at different rates, viewed in combination with other animated objects, and operated on in other ways, with no effort from the programmer. Once the motion control system has been integrated into Magic Theatre, all of these operations become immediately available.

Some of the theoretical extensions to Magic Theatre which we have discussed are 1) the free ordering of serially chained motion control operations, 2) the introduction of data-flow connections between motion control parameters of different systems and 3) the use of conditional triggers to invoke the action of specific control systems at a given time or environmental state. Since these extensions will undoubtedly complicate the use of the motion-synthesis environment, the addition of visual programming aids to depict serial connections of operations, data-flow and constraint networks, and the activation of triggers must be carefully researched in the future. However, in spite of these complications, the combinatorial growth in overall system design afforded by a flexibility of interconnections between diverse motion control systems should challenge us to imagine new forms of computer animation.

REFERENCES

[Amkraut 1989] Amkraut S., "Flock: Computer Animation of Populations Using Vector Force Fields," Master Thesis, ACCAD, The Ohio State University 1989

[Amkraut 1991] Amkraut S., "Computer Animation with Vector Force Fields", in preparation

[Barr and Herzen 1990] "Geometric Collisions for Time-Dependent Parametric Surfaces", ACM Computer Graphics 24:39-48, Proc. Siggraph 1987

[Baraff 1990] "Curved Surfaces and Coherence for Non-penetrating Rigid body Simulation," ACM Computer Graphics 24:19-28, Proc. Siggraph 1990

[Barzel and Barr 1987], Barzel R. and Barr A.,"A Modelling system based on Dynamic Constraints", ACM Computer Graphics 22:179-188, Proc. Siggraph 1987

[Borning 1979], Borning A. "Thinglab: A Constraint-Oriented Simulation Laboratory," Stanford University Computer Science Department, Rep. 79-746, 1979

[Brady 1982] Robot Motion: Planning and Control, MIT Press 1982

[Chadwick and Haumann 1989], Chadwick J. and Haumann D., "Layered Construction of Deformable Animated Characters," ACM Computer Graphics 22: 179-252

[Gilbert 1988] "A fast procedure for computing the distance between complex objects in space," IEEE Journal of Robotics and Automation, vol 4., 1988

[Girard 1985] Girard M. "Computational Modelling for the Computer Animation of Legged Figures," ACM Computer Graphics 19:263-272, Proc. Siggraph 1985

[Girard 1987] Girard M. "Interactive Design of 3D Computer Animated Legged Animal Motion,", IEEE Computer Graphics and Applications, 7(6):39-51, 1987

[Girard 1990] "Constrained Optimization of Articulated Animal Motion in Computer animation," in Making Them Move: Mechanics,Control,and Animation of Articulated Figures ed. Badler, Barsky, and Zeltzer Morgan-Kaufmann Press 1990

[Hahn 1988] Hahn J., "Realistic Animation of Rigid Bodies," ACM Computer Graphics 22:299-308, Proc. Siggraph 1988

[Kass and Miller 1990] Kass M., and Miller G., "Rapid, Stable Fluid Dynamics for Computer Graphics," ACM Computer Graphics 24:49-58, Proc. Siggraph 1990

[Magnenat-Thalmann and Thalmann D. 1989] Magnenat-Thalmann N.and Thalmann D., "Simulation of Object and Human Skin Deformations in a Grasping Task," ACM Computer Graphics 23:21-29, Proc. Siggraph 1989

[Magnenat-Thalmann and Thalmann 1990] Magnenat-Thalmann N.and Thalmann D. "Human Body Deformations Using Joint-dependent Local Operators and Finite-Element Theory," in Making Them Move: Mechanics,Control,and Animation of Articulated Figures ed. Badler, Barsky, and Zeltzer Morgan-Kaufmann Press 1990

[Mckenna 1990] "Dynamic Simulation of Autonomous Legged Locomotion," ACM Computer Graphics 24:29-38, Proc. Siggraph 1990

[Miller 1988] Miller G. "The Motion Dynamics of Snakes and Worms,"ACM Computer Graphics 22:169-179, Proc. Siggraph 1988

[Orin 1981] "Efficient dynamic computer simulation of robotic mechanisms," IEEE Proceedings of Joint Automatic Control 1981

[Platt 1988], Platt J. and Barr A., "Constraint Methods for Flexible Models," ACM Computer Graphics 22:279-288, Proc. Siggraph 1988

[Raibert 1986] Legged Robots that Balance, MIT Press 1986

[Reynolds 1987] Reynolds C., "Flocks, Schools, and Herds: A Behavioral Model," ACM Computer Graphics 21, Proc. Siggraph 1987

[Reeves 1990] Reeves W., Ostby E., and Leffler S., "The Menv Modelling and Animation Environment", Journal of Visualization and Computer Animation, vol.1,no.1 Aug. 1990

[Rijpkema 1990] Rijpkema H. and M. Girard, "Computer Animation of Knowledge-Based Human Hand Grasping,", submitted for publication

[Rijpkema 1991] Rijpkema and Girard, "Efficient Collision Detection of Moving Concave Polyhedral Objects," (in preparation)

[Salisbury and Mason 1985] Robot hands and the Mechanics of Manipulation, MIT Press 1985

[Schoner and Zeltzer 1990] "The Virtual Erecter Set: Dynamic Simulation with Linear Recursive Constraint Propagation," Proc. 1990 Symposium on Interactive 3D Graphics, 1990

[Smith 1984] Smith A., "Plants, Fractals, and Formal Languages,"Computer Graphics 18:1-10, Proc. Siggraph 1984

[Stevens 1990] Stevens, Heidelmann,"Dynamics-Based Optimization of Articulated Figure Animation," Masters Thesis, Informatica, (RUG) Rijksuniversity Groningen 1990 (paper with Girard in preparation)

[Terzopoulos 1988], Terzopoulos D. and Witkin A. "Physically based models with rigid and deformable components," Proc. Graphics Interface, Canada 1988

[Wilhelms 1988] "Collision Detection and Response for Computer Animation", ACM Computer Graphics 22:289-299, Proc. Siggraph 1988

[Zeltzer 1985] Zeltzer D. "Toward an Integrated View of 3-D Computer Animation," The Visual Computer,1(4):249-259 1985

[Zeltzer and Sturman 1989] "An Integrated Graphical Simulation Platform," Proceedings Graphics Interface 1989

[Waters 1987] Waters, K., "A Muscle Model for Animating Three-Dimensional Facial Expressions", Computer Graphics 21:17-24, Proc. Siggraph 1987

[Williams 1990] Williams L., "Performance Driven Facial Animation," ACM Computer Graphics 24:235-242, Proc. Siggraph 1990

Michael Girard studied mathematics and computer science at the University of California and received Bachelor of Science degrees in each field. His desire to study and integrate the formal and expressive components of computer graphics and animation led him to join the Advanced Computing Center for the Arts and Design at the Ohio State University. As a graduate student in computer and information science, Girard's Ph.D. studies focused on the problem of the design, control, and simulation of legged animals. Other research interests include image-synthesis, geometric modelling and the integration of acoustical simulation with 3D computer-animated environments.

Susan Amkraut received a bachelor's degree in fine art from the University of California at Santa Cruz, where she focused on intaglio and lithographic printmaking. When her art studies were finished, she remained at the University of California to complete a bachelor's degree in computer and information science. Susan pursued her graduate studies in the computer art program at the Advanced Computing Center for the Arts and Design at the Ohio State University. There she developed techniques for flocking and schooling behavioral animation based on vector force fields. Besides motion-synthesis, current research interests include image-synthesis and object-oriented software methodologies.

Susan Amkraut and Michael Girard are currently associate professors at the National Institute for Computer Animation (Stichting Computeranimatie) in the Netherlands, an interdisciplinary center for the research, development and artistic expression of computer graphics and animation. Address: Stichting Computeranimatie, Westerhavenstraat 11-13, Postbus 1329, 9701 BH Groningen, The Netherlands

MacBounce:
A Dynamics-Based Modeler for Character Animation

GAVIN MILLER

Abstract

This paper describes MacBounce, an interactive system which uses dynamics for modeling and character animation. It covers the dynamics formulation used, and the user interface for creating and controlling simulations. The use of the system for the creation of a short film called "The Audition" is also discussed.

Keywords: Simulation, character animation, collision detection, interactive system.

1. INTRODUCTION

In recent years, dynamic simulation has begun to be used in computer animation. Dynamics has been used in a number of ways. One approach is to set up the initial conditions of a scene, involving the positions and velocities of objects, with the motion then being computed without further intervention from the user. If the simulation is very time-consuming, this approach may be the most convenient, and has been used to good effect when animating complex physical processes. An alternative is to use dynamics to produce secondary motion resulting from elements animated using key-frame interpolation. Also, key-framed motion may be used to compute the forces required to create that motion (Isaacs and Cohen '87).

Living tissue has been animated by changing the elastic properties of materials as a function of time. The worm in (Miller '88) moved convincingly along a straight path. It reacted physically to collisions, but did not have any behavior in response to external stimulus. By adding a homing mechanism to a dynamic snake, it became possible to make an animation in which the character had evident intention. "Her Majesty's Secret Serpent" (Miller and Kass '89) was produced in this way. The behavior of the snake was changed based on the proximity of its head to objects in the scene. The resultant animation was then purely a consequence of which behaviors were triggered by close-by objects as the animation proceeded. Once the simulation was begun, the motion was computed without further intervention from the user. The animation was also carefully contrived so that the snake did not collide with itself or its target. This meant that only collision detection with the terrain was required. A general purpose system should allow the user more control over the animation as it proceeds.

This paper describes an interactive dynamics-based animation system which was developed to answer the following questions:

a. Is it possible to build an interactive dynamics-based animation system with controls for the dynamic and time-dependent aspects of the simulation?

b. Can such a system be made to work at adequate speeds for interaction?

c. Can people use it to get the animations which they want ?

d. Is it any better than a more traditional key-frame approach?

In the Section 2 the dynamics formulation is described. In Section 3, the geometry for 3-D collision forces is explained. Section 4 describes the user-interface of the animation system. Section 5 introduces a dynamics-based character which has semi-autonomous behavior. Section 6 describes how this character was used to make segments of a film called "The Audition".

2. MASS-SPRING SYSTEM FORMULATION

A point mass was chosen as the canonical primitive of the system because:

a. Mass spring systems are easy to implement as a first animation system.

b. The formulation can be extended to include flexible and rigid bodies as well as particle systems.

A point mass in the system has mass, position and velocity variables as well as other variables which describe its state such as being selected, fixed and merged. (These states will be explained later in the paper). External forces act on the particle such as gravity and atmospheric drag.

$$\vec{f} = m\vec{g} + d\vec{v}$$

where

$\vec{f}$ is the force acting on the point.

$\vec{v}$ is the velocity of the point.

m is the mass of the point.

$\vec{g}$ is the gravity vector.

d is the atmospheric drag coefficient.

Other forces may be exerted on a point from the springs and restoring torques with which it is connected. Other unconnected springs may exert forces on a point due to close proximity collision effects.

Springs join two mass points and apply equal and opposite radial forces to each of them. Being equal, opposite and radial, the forces conserve both linear and angular momentum. Such a spring is illustrated in Fig.1.

Fig.1. A Spring Between Two Masses.

The force exerted by a connected spring is given by

$$\vec{f} = -k\left[\frac{|\vec{r}| - r_0}{r_0}\right]\frac{\vec{r}}{|\vec{r}|} - D\frac{[\vec{r} \cdot \vec{v}]}{\vec{r} \cdot \vec{r}}\vec{r}$$

where

$\vec{f}$ is the force acting on the point.

k is the spring stiffness.

D is the spring damping coefficient.

$\vec{r}$ is the displacement between the two mass points.

r_0 is the rest length of the spring.

A series of springs connected end to end form a chain which will resist stretching but will not resist bending forces.

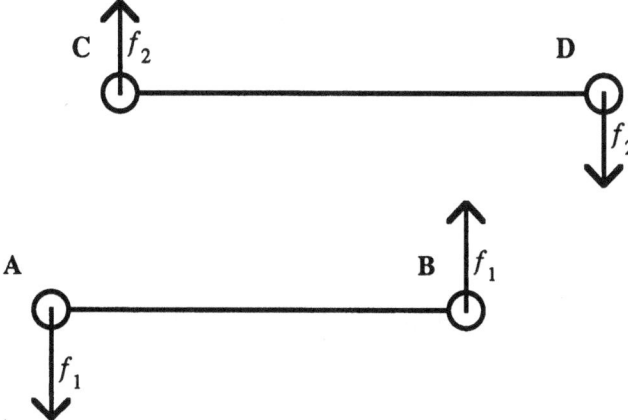

Fig.2. A Torque Between Two Mass Pairs

To resist bending, angular springs called "restoring torques" must be introduced. Restoring torques consist of two equal and opposite pairs of forces. These forces act at right angles to the line joining the masses together and perpendicular to the cross product of the two line segments. Figure 2 shows four mass points with a restoring torque acting on them. Because the forces are in equal and opposite pairs, they conserve linear momentum for the system. However, because they are not radial they do not necessarily conserve angular momentum. For the total angular momentum to be conserved it is required that

$$\vec{f_1} \times [\vec{B} - \vec{A}] + \vec{f_2} \times [\vec{D} - \vec{C}] = 0$$

A restoring torque uses such angular-momentum-conserving pairs of forces to try to keep two pairs of masses at the same angle to each other.

$$f_1 = \frac{-k\left[\theta_1 - \theta_2\right] - d\left[\dot{\theta}_1 - \dot{\theta}_2\right]}{|\vec{B} - \vec{A}|}$$

$$f_2 = \frac{k\left[\theta_1 - \theta_2\right] + d\left[\dot{\theta}_1 - \dot{\theta}_2\right]}{|\vec{D} - \vec{C}|}$$

where

f_1 is the magnitude of the force acting on A and B.

f_2 is the magnitude of the force acting on C and D.

$$\theta_1 = \tan^{-1}(B_y - A_y, B_x - A_x)$$

$$\theta_2 = \tan^{-1}(D_y - C_y, D_x - C_x)$$

$$\dot{\theta}_1 = \frac{\left[\vec{v}_B - \vec{v}_A\right] \times \left[\vec{B} - \vec{A}\right]}{|\vec{B} - \vec{A}|^2}$$

$$\dot{\theta}_2 = \frac{\left[\vec{v}_D - \vec{v}_C\right] \times \left[\vec{D} - \vec{C}\right]}{|\vec{D} - \vec{C}|^2}$$

and x and y refer to a coordinate frame in a plane which is parallel to both line segments.

A restoring torque is strictly speaking non-mechanical if it applies to two unconnected pairs of masses. The formulation described above is appropriate for constructing models in which angular constraints are part of the design, such as two lines being parallel or perpendicular.

If a mass point is shared between the two lines, the restoring torque does have a mechanical interpretation. The mass point will form a joint which resists bending. A chain of springs which have restoring torques at each of the intermediate mass points is called a "wire" and resists bending as well as stretching. In fact, if certain of the mass points are fixed in position, the wire will approximate a cubic spline. To take advantage of this effect in an interactive modeler, the wire may be "frozen" by setting the spring rest lengths and restoring torque rest angles to the current lengths and angles. This is a form of instantaneous plastic deformation. When the fixed points are released, the object will keep its deformed shape provided that there are no external forces. In this way, the user is not concerned with the manipulation of spline knot points as such, rather, the modeler has the feeling of being a forge in which the designer interacts with real materials.

A complex model is composed of many masses, springs and torques. If a number of existing objects need to be joined together, a short spring can be placed between mass points which need to be coincident. Unfortunately, forces which try to pull them apart will stretch the spring and the constraint will be violated. With a mass-spring system, this problem may be overcome by "merging" mass points. Mass points on the same merged list are used to compute the velocity and position of the center of mass of the list. They are then each given that velocity and position. This occurs for every iteration of the numerical integrator which is solving the dynamics. Such merged mass points are always exactly coincident no matter how large the forces trying to pull them apart. Merging mass points is useful both in the construction of models and when a character grabs hold of something. Masses may be "unmerged" or disconnected from each other by simply being deleted from the list of merged objects.

Rigid body dynamics may be implemented in the same way. A number of mass points are selected, and their positions relative to the center of mass are recorded. Forces acting on the mass points are applied to the rigid body for the purposes of computing its dynamics and then, at every iteration, the rigid body repositions the mass points relative to its current center and orientation. A point on a rigid body may not be merged with any other mass point, otherwise the constraints would become overly complex or contradictory. (A more elaborate system of constraints involving solving a linear system is a future enhancement to the system.)

3. COLLISION AND CONTACT FORCES

An important element of realism with the system was the need to simulate collision forces between objects. Two approaches were available in the literature. One approach is to split collision processes up into collision and contact events and then handle each separately (Moore and Wilhelms '88, and Baraf '89). Unfortunately this approach can be very complicated for large heterogeneous collections of surface types, especially when they include flexible surfaces. The alternative approach is called the penalty method which involves creating strong collision forces between objects as they come in close proximity to each other. Penalty methods have a number of disadvantages. Firstly, they create very large rapidly varying forces which make the equations of motion hard to solve - leading to small time-steps for an adaptive solver. To produce a convincing animation, it is necessary to make the thickness of the collision boundaries small compared to the size of objects. This raises a problem, however. In a single time step, a mass point may pass completely through a collision boundary.

To prevent missing such a boundary, the system uses the maximum velocity of any particle to determine the time step such that it moves less than a boundary thickness in a single step. (More elaborate schemes have been proposed in the literature for rigid objects with impulse collisions. They involve dividing up space and time adaptively to find when collisions occur. See Von Herzen '89). To prevent a slowly moving point from being pushed through a barrier by a large spring force, the collision force must become infinite for extreme cases of proximity. The force gradient also becomes infinite.

For collision between polygonal meshes in 3-D, it is necessary to consider the following cases - a point against a line, a line against a line, and a point against a triangle.

3.1 A Point Colliding with a Line

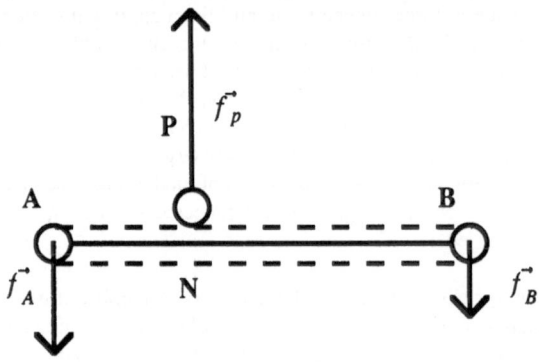

Fig.3. The Collision Forces between a Mass Point and a Line

The collision force for a point against a line is illustrated in Figure 3. It was computed using the following equations:

$$\vec{L} = \vec{B} - \vec{A}$$

$$u = \frac{\vec{L}.[\vec{P} - \vec{A}]}{\vec{L}.\vec{L}}$$

$$\vec{r} = \vec{P} - [\vec{A} + u\vec{L}]$$

$$\vec{N}_v = \vec{A}_v + u[\vec{B}_v - \vec{A}_v]$$

$$\vec{f}_p = -\left[k + D[\vec{P}_v - \vec{N}_v].\vec{r}\right]\frac{\left[1 - \frac{|\vec{r}|}{t}\right]}{\vec{r}.\vec{r}}\vec{r}$$

$$\vec{f}_A = -[1 - u]\vec{f}_p$$

$$\vec{f}_B = -\vec{f}_p$$

where

u is the parameter along the spring.

$\vec{r}$ is the displacement of the mass point from the nearest point on the line.

$\vec{N}_v$ is the velocity of the nearest point on the spring.

$\vec{f}_p$ is the force exerted on the particle by the collision with the spring.

$\vec{f}_A$ is the force exerted on the first mass point on the spring.

155

f_B is the force exerted on the second mass point on the spring.

t is the range of the collision force.

k is the collision stiffness.

D is the collision damping coefficient.

If the particle P was further away than t, the collision force was set to zero. Similarly, if the value of u was greater than 1 or less than zero, the collision force was ramped to zero over a distance t parallel to the line.

3.2 A Line Colliding with a Line

In three dimensions, a line may touch another line part way along their lengths. This geometry is illustrated in Figure 4. The shortest distance between two lines may be found by considering a vector r which is perpendicular to the two line segments.

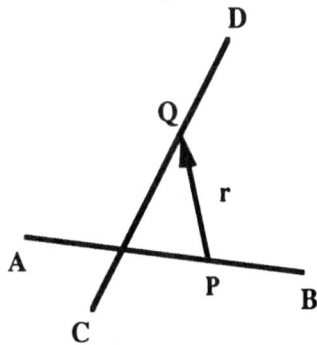

Fig.4. A Line Colliding with another Line

We define the points P and Q on the two lines

$$\vec{P} = \vec{A} + u[\vec{B} - \vec{A}]$$
$$\vec{Q} = \vec{C} + v[\vec{D} - \vec{C}]$$

such that

$$[\vec{P} - \vec{Q}].[\vec{B} - \vec{A}] = 0$$
$$[\vec{P} - \vec{Q}].[\vec{D} - \vec{C}] = 0$$

Substituting for P and Q and then solving the above simultaneous equations for u and v gives:

$$a = [\vec{C} - \vec{A}].[\vec{D} - \vec{C}]$$
$$b = [\vec{B} - \vec{A}].[\vec{D} - \vec{C}]$$
$$c = [\vec{D} - \vec{C}].[\vec{D} - \vec{C}]$$
$$d = [\vec{C} - \vec{A}].[\vec{B} - \vec{A}]$$

$$e = [\vec{B} - \vec{A}].[\vec{B} - \vec{A}]$$
$$f = [\vec{D} - \vec{A}].[\vec{B} - \vec{A}]$$

$$\Delta = ec - bf$$

$$u = \frac{fa - cd}{\Delta}$$

$$v = \frac{ea - bd}{\Delta}$$

where

> a, b, c, d, e, f are intermediate variables for the dot products,
> Δ is the determinant of the simultaneous equations. If this is zero, the lines are parallel.
> u is the parameter along the line from A to B.
> v is the parameter along the line from C to D.

The collision between the lines is valid provided that

$$u >= 0$$
$$u <= 1$$
$$v >= 0$$
$$v <= 1$$

Unfortunately, forces which are discontinuous with position will be virtually impossible to integrate numerically. To avoid this problem, it is necessary to attenuate the forces smoothly as a function of u and for the two lines. A linear ramp for the force is usually adequate, with the ramp extent being comparable in size to the thickness of the collision boundary.

The repulsion force scaling factor for a pair of lines with parameters u and v is given by

$$S_u = 0 \qquad \text{for } u < -t \text{ or } u > 1 + t$$
$$S_u = 1 \qquad \text{for } t < u < 1 - t$$
$$S_u = \frac{[1 + u]}{2t} \qquad \text{for } -t < u < t$$
$$S_u = \frac{[1 - u]}{2t} \qquad \text{for } 1 - t < u < 1 + t$$
$$S_v = 0 \qquad \text{for } v < -t \text{ or } v > 1 + t$$
$$S_v = 1 \qquad \text{for } t < v < 1 - t$$
$$S_v = \frac{[1 + v]}{2t} \qquad \text{for } -t < v < t$$
$$S_v = \frac{[1 - v]}{2t} \qquad \text{for } 1 - t < v < 1 + t$$
$$S = S_u S_v$$

157

where
    S is the repulsion force scaling factor.
    t is the thickness of the end effect for the line segment.

The collision force between the two line segments is given by

$$f_p = - S\left[k + D\left[\vec{P}_v - \vec{N}_v \right] . \vec{r} \right]\dfrac{\left[1 - \dfrac{|\vec{r}|}{t}\right]}{\vec{r} . \vec{r}} \vec{r}$$
$$f_A = - [1 - u]f_p$$
$$f_B = - u\, f_p$$
$$f_C = [1 - v]f_p$$
$$f_D = v\, f_p$$

3.3 A Point Colliding with a Triangle

When colliding a point with a triangle, the first step is to project the position of the point in three space onto the surface of the triangle. This is illustrated in Figure 5.

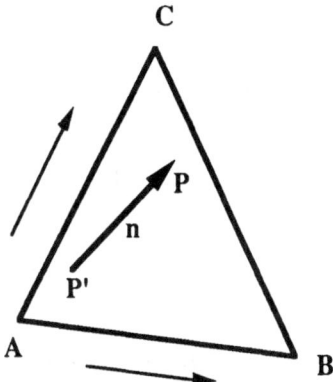

Fig.5. Point Colliding with a Triangle

$$\vec{n} = \dfrac{(\vec{B} - \vec{A}) \times (\vec{C} - \vec{A})}{|\vec{B} - \vec{A}||\vec{C} - \vec{A}|}$$

$$\vec{P}' = \vec{P} - (\vec{n} \cdot (\vec{P} - \vec{A})) \, \vec{n}$$

$$u = \frac{(\vec{B} - \vec{A}) \cdot (\vec{P}' - \vec{A})}{|\vec{B} - \vec{A}||\vec{B} - \vec{A}|}$$

$$v = \frac{(\vec{C} - \vec{A}) \cdot (\vec{P}' - \vec{A})}{|\vec{C} - \vec{A}||\vec{C} - \vec{A}|}$$

where

u is the triangle parameter parallel to the line from A to B.

v is the triangle parameter parallel to the line from A to C.

As with the line against line collision, sudden discontinuities for the triangle repulsion force would be unacceptable. A force scaling factor is found by multiplying values derived from the distance to the three edges.

$$S_u = 0 \qquad \qquad for \ u < -t \ or \ u > 1 + t$$

$$S_u = 1 \qquad \qquad for \ t < u < 1 - t$$

$$S_u = \frac{[1 + u]}{2t} \quad for \ -t < u < t$$

$$S_u = \frac{[1 - u]}{2t} \quad for \ 1 - t < u < 1 + t$$

$$S_v = 0 \qquad \qquad for \ v < -t \ or \ v > 1 + t$$

$$S_v = 1 \qquad \qquad for \ t < v < 1 - t$$

$$S_v = \frac{[1 + v]}{2t} \quad for \ -t < v < t$$

$$S_v = \frac{[1 - v]}{2t} \quad for \ 1 - t < v < 1 + t$$

$$S_{uv} = 0 \qquad \qquad for \ v < -t \ or \ v > 1 + t$$

$$S_{uv} = 1 \qquad \qquad for \ t < v < 1 - t$$

$$S_{uv} = \frac{[1 + u + v]}{2t} \quad for \ -t < u + v < t$$

$$S_{uv} = \frac{[1 - u + v]}{2t} \quad for \ 1 - t < u + v < 1 + t$$

$$S = S_u S_v S_{uv}$$

The repulsion forces for the particle colliding with a triangle are given by

$$\vec{r} = \vec{P} - \vec{P}'$$

$$\vec{f_p} = - S\left[k + D\left[\vec{P_v} - \vec{N_v} \right] . \vec{r} \right] \frac{\left[1 - \frac{|\vec{r}|}{t} \right]}{\vec{r} . \vec{r}} \vec{r}$$

$$\vec{f_A} = - [1 - u][1 - v]\vec{f_p}$$

$$\vec{f_B} = - v \vec{f_p}$$

$$\vec{f_C} = - u \vec{f_p}$$

An important enhancement to the collisions described above is the inclusion of the effects of friction. A static friction model is preferable. Static friction is characterized by the ability to apply a force to objects even when they are stationary. The maximum available frictional force parallel to a constraint is typically a scalar multiple of the collision force normal to the constraint. The spring, torque and collision forces are first computed for all objects in the system. The maximum frictional force is then computed for each collision/contact. If this force is greater than the tangential force acting on the colliding mass point, then it has its net tangential force set to zero and its tangential velocity set to zero. If the frictional force is insufficient to immobilize the mass point, the point has it tangential force reduced by the available amount and the tangential velocity is left unchanged. Static friction has proved to be very useful when doing such tasks as leaning objects against each other and making stacks of blocks.

Collision detection is disabled if two objects are on the same merged list. When mass points are unmerged they are usually coincident. This can lead to infinite collision forces. To overcome this problem, collision forces remain disabled until the separation of the mass points is such that no force will suddenly be turned on when they are enabled. This works well for objects being pulled apart, but is not a general solution for unmerging objects which are being pushed together. This is an area for future research.

4. USER INTERFACE DESIGN

The user interface for an interactive dynamics system is very important. The prototype system was implemented in C++ and a version of InterViews which provides a variety of buttons, menus and graphical primitives (Linton et al. '88). InterViews was modified so that it would run both on a Silicon Graphics Iris Workstation and on an Apple Macintosh II personal computer. A typical interactive display is shown in Figure 6.

Menus are reserved for operations which apply to picked objects, and to global controls which are fixed for the duration of an animation. They are also used to control IO functions such as save and retrieve and record to video. The "edit" menu applies to objects which have already been selected. It allows mass points to be fixed, freed, merged, unmerged and deleted. The "properties" menu is similarly used for setting the scalar properties of objects such as mass and stiffness.

The "solver" menu allows choices to be made between Euler solvers, modified midpoint solvers and a fourth order Runge-Kutta (Press et al '88). The minimum number of steps per iteration may also be set using a dialogue box as well as the threshold value for the adaptive time-step algorithm.

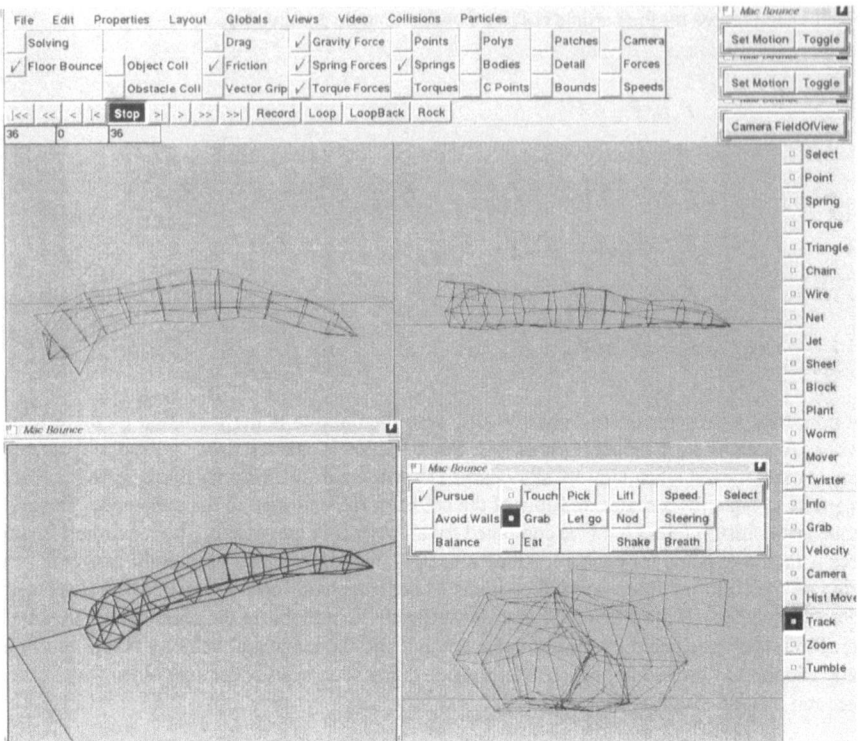

Fig.6. The MacBounce User Interface

Below the menu bar, a set of check boxes allows the user instantaneous control over global dynamic and graphical processes such as the computation of gravity, drag, spring and torque forces as the animation proceeds. Collision forces with other objects and with the walls may be enabled and disabled. The "Solving" check box allows the simulation to proceed without the system keeping a history of the positions of the objects. This is particularly useful during a modeling session when a scene is being assembled.

Below the check boxes is a video cassette recorder type interface for the control of time. Pressing the "Record" command button starts the solver and records the state of the system at each frame time. Pressing "Stop", "I<<" and then ">", plays back the animation which may be stopped at any time and recomputed using changed input from the user. The ">I" button allows a user to single step through an animation.

To the right of the modeling area is a series of radio buttons. These control the action of the cursor when it is in the modeling area. "Select" allows objects to be picked. "Grab" moves the nearest mass point to the cursor position when the mouse button is depressed. A mass point may be created when the "Point" button is active. The down click position is taken as the position of the mass, and the up click position relative to the down position determines the initial particle velocity. When an object is "fixed" its velocity is set to zero. A fixed mass point is shown twice the normal size with a circle of the normal size in the background color in the center. Fixed mass points are useful for objects which are nailed to the screen. They may also be used as hinges.

Springs are created between two existing mass points. A down click draws a rubber line to the nearest mass point. As the mouse moves, the cursor end of the line snaps to the mass point which is nearest provided that it is not the original nearest point. An up click confirms the creation of the spring which is drawn as a thick line. The line thickness indicates the range over which collisions forces occur. Torques are specified as if creating two springs in succession. A chain or a wire are created using the same interaction as for a single spring, joining two existing mass points. A block is created using a rubber rectangle aligned with the coordinate axes.

Key-framed elements called "movers" allow the user to position certain mass-points kinematically over time. However, the interface only allows the mover motion to be changed over future time from the current state of the VCR, otherwise, the recorded history would be inconsistent with the known motion. This must be avoided for the animation to be capable of being recomputed starting at any point. To change an earlier kinematic motion, the VCR must be backed up to the point of the change and then the dynamics must be recomputed from that point. The one exception to this rule is the camera which may be animated after the simulation has been completed. The camera may also have its eye and view point attached to mass points on objects. (This was done for the cannon firing sequence in "The Audition" where the camera tracks the worm as it flies through the air.) "Twisters" are restoring torques where the rest-angle may be key-framed over time.

To allow semi-autonomous complex objects, a facility was included which allows user-programmable objects. When created, they can create masses, springs and torques which are included in the system. At every frame time, the object is called with a method to update the mechanical properties of the objects which it has created. It may also create and delete objects at this time. This class of objects can be very general. Particle systems can be expressed in this way, throwing off new mass points at each iteration. As they do so, they impart momentum to the object from which the particles are being ejected. Such a particle system may even create other particle systems, allowing fire to spread from object to object as is illustrated in Figure 7.

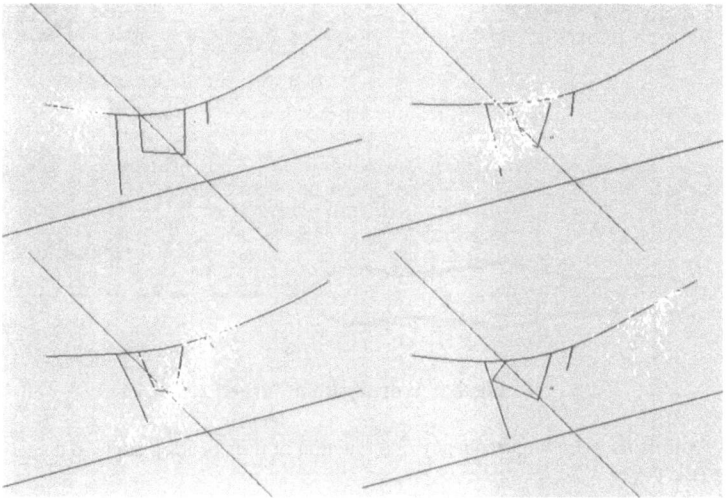

Fig.7. Particle System Fire Spreading

5. CHARACTER ANIMATION

A second use of procedural objects is the creation of characters with behavior. The example chosen was a worm since it is a flexible object with complex behavior and simple topology. A collection of masses, springs and torques is first generated in the rest shape of a worm. The spring rest lengths are animated procedurally every frame time to achieve locomotion. The bulging of the worm as it contracts lifts parts of the worm out of contact with the surface. This effect combined with wriggling produces a net directional force on the worm.

When a worm is created, a new window pops up with control buttons on it. The controls are two-fold. Check boxes are used for binary states of the behavior. Control buttons either invoke an instantaneous action, such as choosing a new target, or they throw up a parameter curve which may be edited to control the variation of a scalar behavior variable over future time. Two such scalar variables control the speed and steering direction of the worm. This allows the worm to be controlled like a radio-controlled car. Unfortunately, it can be quite difficult to control the worm with enough precision to grab a target, especially if the target is moving. To overcome this problem, the worm was given a homing mechanism.

Each worm has a list of mass points which it is interested in. These are called "targets". A mass point becomes a target by being in a selected state when the "Acquire" command button is pressed. At each frame time the worm looks to see which target is closest and uses a bearing vector relative to its head and tail to steer itself towards the target. Steering is achieved by contracting all of the longitudinal springs on one side of the worm and expanding the corresponding springs on the other side of the worm. The determination of the bearing of a target is illustrated in Figure 8.

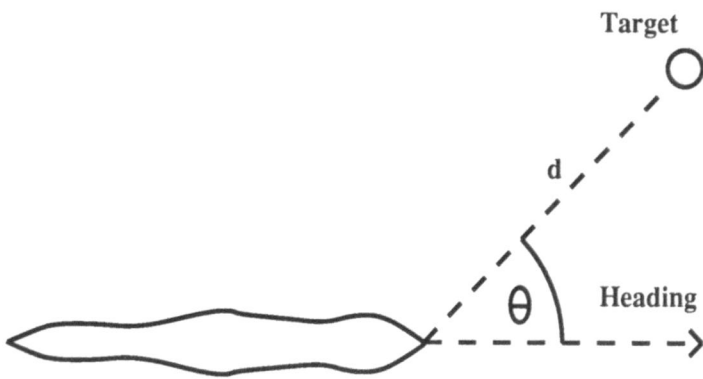

Fig.8. A Worm with a Target

The worm controls its wriggling frequency as a function of if its bearing angle to the target and its proximity to the target.

$$\omega = \omega_0 \left[1 - \frac{e^{-\frac{d}{D}}}{2} \right] \left[1 - \frac{4\theta}{\pi} \right]$$

where

ω is the frequency at which the worm wriggles

ω_0 is the control frequency specified by the user.

d is the distance to the target from the nose of the worm.

D is the "stalking" range.

θ is the angle which the target bears to the line joining the nose of the worm to its tail.

Once the tip of the worm is within a certain distance of the target, the worm may grab the target by merging its nose mass point with the target mass point.

6. THE MAKING OF THE AUDITION

To test the value of MacBounce as an interactive animation system, it was decided to create a somewhat lengthy animation called "The Audition" (Miller et al '90). A worm goes to the circus to try to become a performer, and is put through all sorts of horrible initiations. To enable the creation of the film, some additional procedural objects were created, namely a cannon with motorised wheels, and a seesaw. (These could have been constructed interactively, but due to rather shaky save-and-retrieve code, a procedural definition ensured repeatability.)

The first complex animation segment is illustrated in Figure 9. The worm starts on the ground some distance from the seesaw. The speed control was used to define undulation speed over time to make the worm wriggle forwards. The effects of collision and friction allowed the worm to progress some distance up the ramp at which point it was instructed to stop. The head nodding control was then used to create a single nod which signalled to an unseen hand to drop a weight. This weight, a rigid body which had been previously fixed, was now released. It descended under gravity, collided with the seesaw, which in turn catapulted the worm up into the air. An interesting problem arose with this animation. If the worm crawled too far up the seesaw, it would subsequently be thrown straight up into the air, only to come down on the raised seesaw, causing severe problems for subsequent animation. On the other hand, if the worm was not sufficiently far up the seesaw, it tended to be thrown over backwards but only doing a half somersault, leading to it landing on its top, from which it could not recover. Trial and error on the climbing duration led to the desired result.

The next tricky scene, illustrated in Figure 10, involved the worm grabbing onto a swinging rope. The top end of the rope was key-framed using a "mover". The other end of the rope was made a target for the homing behavior of the worm. It successfully grabbed the end of the rope and was lifted up into the air.

Subsequently, the worm was dropped into the mouth of a cannon. The cannon had torque generators to control the motion of the wheels. It was supposed to accelerate forwards and then come to a halt under the worm. However, if the wheel brakes were applied too rapidly, the cannon fell over, coming to rest with the barrel on the ground. Also, the wheels skidded slightly, making it hard to position the final cannon location exactly underneath the worm. A new feature was used, which allowed an objects current position, plus all of its position history to be moved (The idea was inspired by an informal discussion with Paul Isaacs in 1989). This technique allowed the initial cannon position to be adjusted after the fact to place the final cannon position exactly under the worm (Figure 11). It had to be used with great care, however. If the ground had not been flat, or if there had been obstacles which could collide with the new path, the dynamics constraints would have been violated.

The next complex scene occurred when the worm was grabbed by its tail and lifted up into the air (Figure 12). A rope with an attached grabber, was lowered and swung towards the worm. At the moment when the grabber closed, the rope history was moved to bring the grabber in contact with the tail. The grabber was then attached to the end of the worm by merging the mass points. The steering control of the worm was used to make it "look" at its tail. Simultaneously, the mover at the other end of the rope was raised.

Finally, the worm was dropped onto a swinging trapeze. Moving the position history was again used to bring the nose of the worm in contact with the first bar. The worm was attached to this bar, and then detached at a later point in the swing. This meant that it was thrown forwards until it hit the second bar of the trapeze. Collisions then occurred between the body of the worm and the trapeze (Figure 13). Trial and error was required to get the correct release time for the worm - too soon and the worm fell below the second bar, too late and the worm flew over the top of the second bar without hitting it.

The dynamic simulation time for typical scenes in The Audition varied between one and ten seconds per frame. The duration depended on the scene complexity and the presence or absence of violent collision forces and high velocities. These times were for a single processor 25 MHz Silicon Graphics Iris workstation.

7. CONCLUSIONS

It proved possible to build an interactive dynamics-based animation system with controls for the dynamic and time-dependent aspects of the simulation. Including a feature for moving an object's current and past position proved to be a very valuable tool for producing happy coincidences in the simulation.

The interaction speed for scenes of interesting complexity was below the level usually thought of as real time, and the system needs to experience a speed improvement of an order of magnitude for it to be really spontaneous as an animation medium. However, when procedural and other models had been created for a scene, actually directing the desired motion proved to be both possible and fun.

Compared to a key-frame animation system, the animations had lots of secondary behavior. The physical realism and complexity of some of the motion was produced with very little effort on the part of the animator. However, key-frame systems have a much broader domain of possible animations, and are easier to get to do what you want. A true test of this systems worth will only be possible when it is more complete and more widely available to new users.

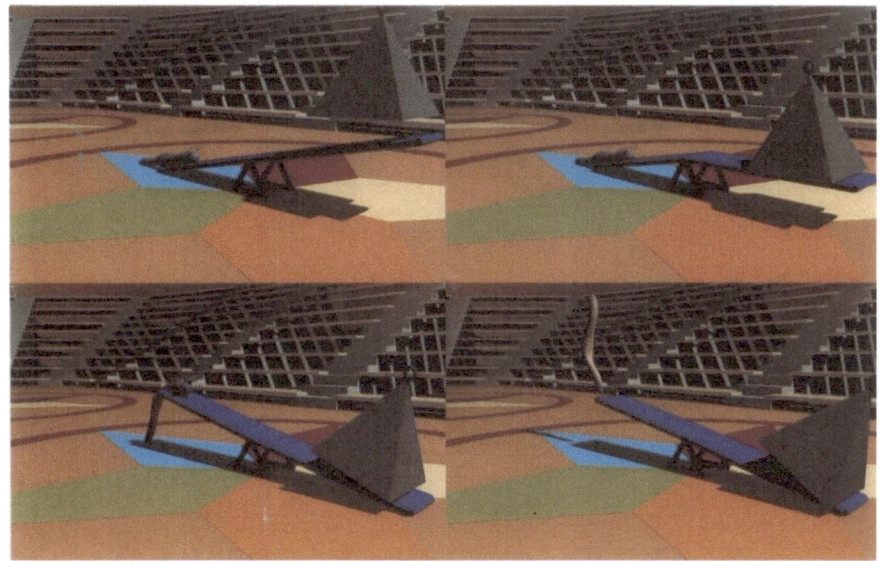

Fig.9. Worm on a Seesaw

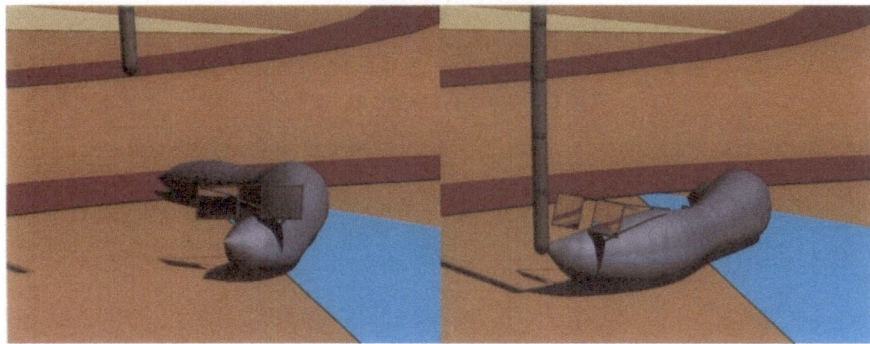

Fig.10. Worm Grabbing a Rope

Fig.11. Worm Falling into a Cannon

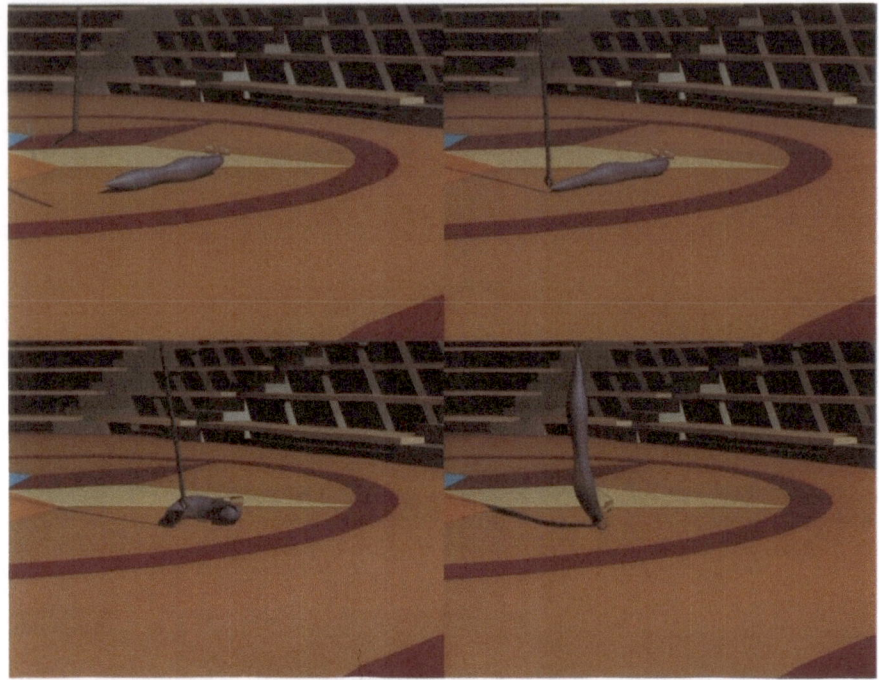

Fig.12. Worm Grabbed by its Tail

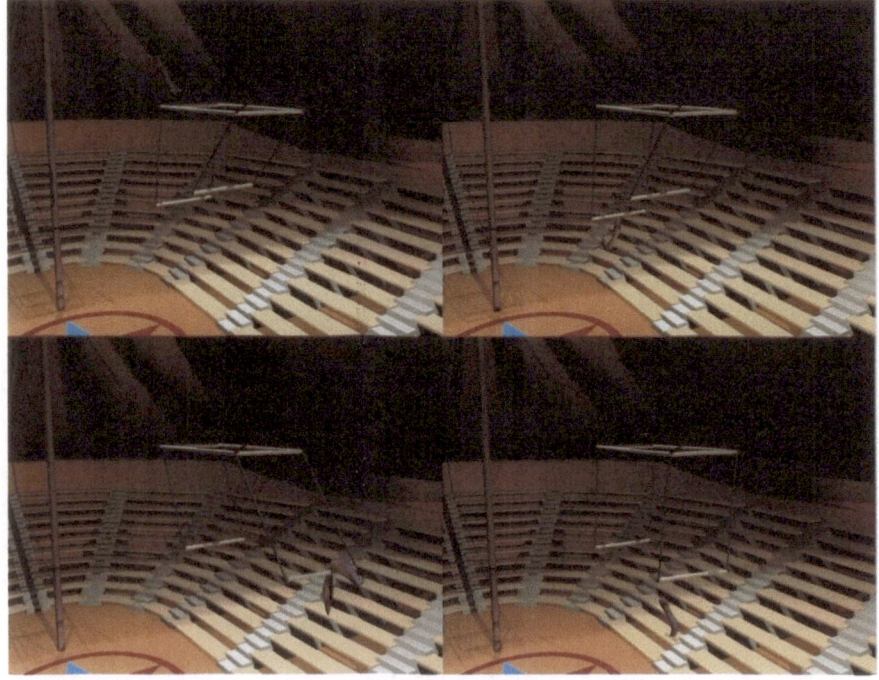

Fig. 13. Worm on a Trapeze

8. AREAS FOR FUTURE WORK

The use of implicit solvers may help with the simulation of much stiffer models, and may improve the performance. A general purpose modeling language may allow users to create procedural models without having to recompile the application.

9. ACKNOWLEDGEMENTS

This experimental system was created at Apple Computer Inc. in the Advanced Technology Group. Thanks are due to Roger Spreen and Peter Litwinowicz for porting and contributing to the version of InterViews used for the user interface. Thanks to Michael Kass for discussions about dynamics in general, and the correct way to deal with friction in particular. Thanks also to Douglass Turner and Eric Chen for the rendering code used to render the images from The Audition, and to Libby Patterson and Steve Rubin for modeling the cannon and tent respectively. Thanks to Mark Cutter for encouraging this work and giving useful advice about the user interface design. And finally, thanks to Eric the Dynamic Worm who continues to suffer through my animations without complaint.

10. REFERENCES

Baraf, David, "Analytic Methods for Non-penetrating Rigid Bodies", Computer Graphics Vol. 23, No. 3, July 1989 pp 223-232.

Isaacs, Paul M., Michael F. Cohen, "Controlling Dynamic Simulation with Kinematic Constraints, Behavior Functions and Inverse Dynamics", Computer Graphics Vol. 21, No. 4, July 1987 pp 215-224.

Linton, Mark A., Paul R. Calder, John M. Vlissides, "InterViews: A C++ Graphical Interface Toolkit", Technical Report CSL-TR-88-358, Stanford University, Stanford, California 94305, July 1988.

Miller, Gavin S. P., "The Motion Dynamics of Snakes and Worms", Computer Graphics, Vol. 22, No. 4, Aug 1988 pp 169-178.

Miller, Gavin S. P., Michael Kass, "Goal-Directed Animation of Tubular Articulated Figures", ACM SIGGRAPH '89 course notes for Course 30, "Topics in Physically-Based Modeling".

Miller, Gavin S. P., et al, "The Audition", SIGGRAPH '90 Electronic Theater reel.

Moore, Matthew, Jane Wilhelms, "Collision Detection and Response for Computer Animation", Computer Graphics Vol. 22, No. 4, Aug 1988 pp 289-298.

Press, William H., Brian P. Flannery, Saul A. Teukolsky, William T. Vetterling, "Numerical Recipies in C', Cambridge University Press 1988. ISBN 0-521-35465-X.

Von Herzen, Brian, "Applications of Surface Networks to Sampling Problems in Computer Graphics", Ph. D. Thesis, Computer Science Department Technical Report Caltech-CS-TR-88-15, California Institute of Technology, Pasadena, California 91125, 1989.

Gavin Miller is currently working as a Senior Research Scientist in the Advanced Technology Group at Apple Computer Inc. Prior to working at Apple, he was Project Leader of Natural Phenomena at Alias Research Inc. in Toronto, Canada. He was born in England and attended Cambridge University where he was awarded a Ph.D. in Computer Aided Design and Manufacture in 1988.

Research Interests

Research interests include the rendering and animation of natural phenomena, the simulation of elastic and fluid materials, the animation of characters using dynamics, and the design of real-time interactive systems for animation and education.

Publications

Miller, Gavin S. P., "The Definition and Rendering of Terrain Maps", Computer Graphics Vol. 20, No. 4, August 1986, pp 39-48.

Miller, Gavin S. P., "The Motion Dynamics of Snakes and Worms", Computer Graphics, Vol. 22., No. 4, August 1988, pp 169-178.

Miller, Gavin S. P., "From Wire-frames to Furry Animals", Proceedings of Graphics Interface '88, Edmonton, Alberta, 6-10 June 1988, pp 138-145.

Miller, Gavin S. P., Andrew Pearce, "Globular Dynamics: A Connected Particle System for Animating Viscous Fluids", Computers and Graphics Vol. 13, No. 3, 1989, pp 305-309.

Miller, Gavin S. P., "An Adaptive Algorithm for the Collision of Flexible Bodies", Proceedings of Western Canadian Computer Graphics Workshop, Sunshine Village, Banff, Alberta, Canada, 4-8 March 1990.

Kass, Michael, Gavin S. P. Miller, "Rapid, Stable Fluid Dynamics for Animation", Computer Graphics Vol. 24, No. 4, Aug 1988, pp 49-58.

Animations

Miller, Gavin S. P., "Natural Phenomena", SIGGRAPH '88 Electronic Theater.

Miller, Gavin S. P., Michael Kass, "Her Majesty's Secret Serpent", SIGGRAPH '89 Electronic Theater.

Kass, Michael, Gavin S. P. Miller, "Splash Dance", SIGGRAPH '90 Electronic Theater.

Miller, Gavin S. P., Douglass Turner, Lance Williams et al., "The Audition", SIGGRAPH '90 Electronic Theater.

Animation Platform:
A Data Management System for Modeling Moving Objects

MYEONG WON LEE and TOSIYASU L. KUNII

ABSTRACT

When we design a moving object, we have to generate an animation sequence as the final output. To make it efficient, a data management system named AnimationPlatform is devised to facilitate the processes of the analysis and control of moving objects as well as displaying them. AnimationPlatform is developed so that the topology and geometry of moving objects can be retrieved and modified at any time instant or at time intervals during animation. A new 4D geometric modeler is defined to provide the topology and geometry of moving objects and drive AnimationPlatform. Algorithms for controlling moving objects are also defined and tested.

Keywords: 4D geometric modeler, data management, topology, geometry, moving objects, boundary representation, nested list

1. INTRODUCTION

In general, animation systems are generated by the following sequence: object definition, motion definition and object display. In such systems, it is difficult and cumbersome to manage data related to the objects to be animated and transformed. In order to visualize the objects and the phenomena in the real world, it is indispensable to generate topologically changing animation besides geometrically changing animation as we can easily see in our previous works on cell growth (Kunii and Takai 1989) and tree growth (Aono and Kunii 1984).

The researches on the generation of topologically changing animation have considered neither the efficiency of data organization nor data management. This is partially due to the fact that it is time consuming even to generate an animation sequence in conventional animation systems and the people engaged in animation making have not been able to sit down to develop a data manager for animation. For controlling or analyzing motion efficiently, it is truly necessary to manage all the data related to the generation of motion.

The data management in animation requires the modeling of moving objects. Although there is a work (Trenish, Foley, Campbell, Haber and Gurwitz 1989) pointing out the importance of data management in animation, it does not present any method to model moving objects. In this paper, we present a method of modeling moving objects as a 4D (four dimensional) geometric modeler and a data management system to analyze and control moving objects.

2. A 4D GEOMETRIC MODELER

We define a 4D geometric modeler in a very general way, and it actually includes all the functions of AnimationPlatform to manage all the topological and geometrical data related to the moving objects during animation. The data is hierarchically organized and hence can handle an object hierarchy, a motion hierarchy and a topology / geometry hierarchy. In this section, we present the 4D geometric modeler which involves the following functions.

* Object modeling:
  The topology and geometry of a moving object at the initial time instant are provided and used to transform it during animation. Differently from the conventional animation systems, the topology including also the partial topology using the topology hierarchy of the moving object can be retrieved and changed during the animation.
* Motion modeling:
  To manage data related to the topology and geometry of the moving object during the animation, the motion of the object is modeled. The model covers all the motion data.
* Motion controlling:
  It is necessary to control the motion after its modeling. To do so, it is indispensable to manage all the data related to the topology and geometry of the object at all the time instants. When we recognize the congruence of the object (Lee, Satoh and Kunii 1989), or motion equality (Lee, Kunii and Dürst 1990) during the animation, all the data related to the moving object must be maintained. As another facility of motion control, there exist collision detection routines. These routines are particularly useful when we have to handle a segmented object because such an object often forms concave polyhedron as well as convex polyhedron. Therefore, the collision detection routine must be involved to check the collision to generate a realistic motion.
* Object and motion retrieval:
  This is the function related to the retrieval and display of moving objects and their motion at a specific time or at time intervals. The topology and geometry of the objects and of the motion can also be retrieved and then displayed.
* Object and motion modification:
  Objects or their motion must be able to be modified without reorganizing the data structure of the objects. In other words, the data structure of moving objects must be managed to see whether the topology of the objects is also changed during animation or not.

Based on the considerations described above, our 4D geometric modeler is developed so that it can efficiently manage all the information required to the generation of animation which can be changing topologically as well as geometrically.

Our 4D geometric modeler is based on a boundary representation which involves the concept of a connected component as a separate geometric entity besides an object, a loop, an edge and a vertex (Lee, Satoh and Kunii 1989) and the concept of a nested relation (Lamersdorf 1989; Linnemann 1989).

(a) logical structure

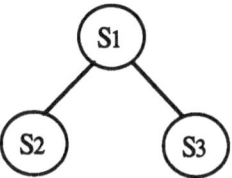

(b) boundary representation

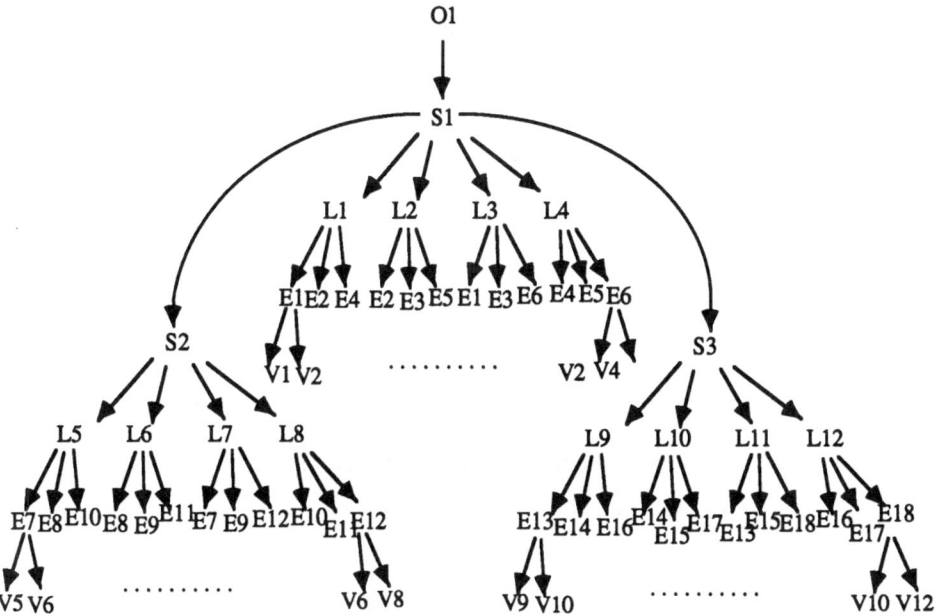

Fig.1 An object with three segments

A segment in an object corresponds to one of the connected components in the boundary representation. Fig. 1 shows the boundary representation of an object which is composed of three segments and two joints. In the 4D geometric modeler, a moving object is defined by the following equation.

$$A \ moving \ object = \sum_t Brep(O_t) \qquad (1)$$

where $Brep(O_t)$ means the boundary representation of an object O at a time instant t as shown in Fig. 1. Using the equation (1), we can easily modify the topology of the object.

A data structure which can be easily modified in relation to the topology and geometry of the objects under consideration is required to manage the boundary representation at all the time instants. Let us first look at topologically invariant cases. The data structure must represent the relationship between different geometric entities which compose each object at a time instant. Given the time interval of object motion, the data structure must also represent the correspondence of the two sets of geometric entities of the object in motion, one at the beginning of the time interval and the other at the end. The relationship makes the generation of topologically changing animation easy. The motion of objects can be controlled or analyzed by checking the correspondence. For example, motion comparison used for the control of motion can be achieved by analyzing the correspondence at all the time instants (Lee, Kunii and Dürst 1990).

In order to manage all the boundary representation at all the time instants, we used the concept of a nested relation (Lamersdorf 1989; Linnemann 1989), since it can represent well the relationships between geometric entities, and the representation can be extended easily to represent the topological entities at each time instant. Then, an object in motion is represented as a nested relation:

$$
\begin{aligned}
&A\ moving\ object(t=t_1,\ t_2...) = \\
&\quad\quad (Object_{t1}(Segment(Loop(Edge(Vertex,Vertex)... \\
&\quad\quad\quad\quad\quad\quad\quad\quad Edge(...)...) \\
&\quad\quad\quad\quad\quad\quad Loop(...)...) \\
&\quad\quad\quad\quad Segment(...)...) \\
&\quad\quad Object_{t2}(...)...)
\end{aligned}
$$

$$(2)$$

In the equation (2), each relationship between geometric entities is represented as follows:

$$A\ moving\ object(t=t_1,t_2...) = \Sigma_{ti}Object_{\ ti} \quad\quad (3)$$

$$Object_{\ t} = \Sigma_i\ Segment_{\ i} \quad\quad (4)$$

$$Segment_{\ i} = \Sigma_j\ Loop_{\ j} \quad\quad (5)$$

$$Loop_{\ j} = \Sigma_k\ Edge_{\ k} \quad\quad (6)$$

$$Edge_{\ k} = \Sigma_l\ Vertex_{\ l} \quad\quad (7)$$

When we design an object using a solid modeler based on a boundary representation, the topology and geometry of the object can be retrieved at any time. In the same manner, our 4D geometric modeler can retrieve the topology and geometry of a moving object at any time, using the nested relation (2) combined with the boundary representation (1). The 4D geometric modeler has the following characteristics which are indispensable when modeling and analyzing moving objects.

• Using the equations (2) - (7), we can establish the correspondence between the nested relation and the geometric entity of the object. For example, if we retrieve a segment in the nested relation, the retrieved segment can be immediately displayed on a window. Fig. 2 shows an example of topological data visualization when an object is created. It represents a polyhedron and its nested relation composed of the geometric entities of the polyhedron. If an object is transformed on a graphics display by an interactive operation, the corresponding nested relation of the object is also changed.

- The 4D geometric modeler can easily generate topologically changing animation as well as geometrically changing animation and, manage the data related to each object without reorganizing the data structure of the object.
- Using a moving object hierarchy, a part of the moving object can also be retrieved and modified easily without restructuring its data structure. Fig. 3 shows the retrieval of a part of a moving object. It represents that the motion of "a pair of ski" is retrieved in the motion of "a skier".
- The topology and geometry of a moving object can be searched and transformed easily.

3. DATA MANAGEMENT OF MOVING OBJECTS

In this section, the data management by the 4D geometric modeler is illustrated when we generate or modify a moving object. For managing the data related to the moving object, the geometric modeler must at least have the following three functions:

- Data definition of moving objects
- Data manipulation of moving objects
- Integrity control of moving objects

In order to generate an animation sequence, the facility to define moving objects is provided. A nested relation is also provided to define a moving object. The facility to manipulate moving objects is provided to control and analyze them. In addition, during the animation, objects are expected to be handled in a semantically correct manner. It means that the integrity of objects is maintained during the animation.

3.1 Data Definition of moving objects

There are two kinds of methods which can define objects in our 4D geometric modeler. One is to define objects using a traditional solid modeler. An interface is needed for the 4D geometric modeler to make use of objects generated by the solid modeler. The relationship between geometric entities is maintained as well as the correspondence of the two sets of geometric entities during the animation. The interface converts the data of the object topology and geometry generated by the solid modeler into the nested list structure which can be used in the 4D geometric modeler (Lee, Kunii and Inaba 1990).

The other method is to define objects by directly using the data structure of the nested lists described in section 2. An object is defined in the following form:

$$(Object(Segment(Loop(Edge(Vertex, Vertex)...)...)...)...) \qquad (8)$$

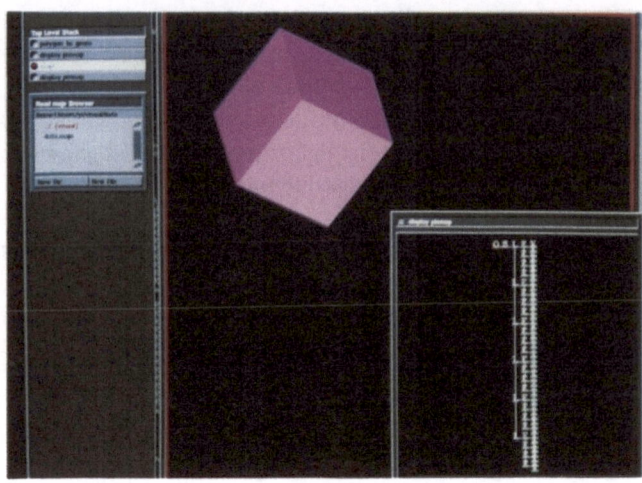

Fig. 2 Topological data visualization of an object

Fig. 3 Retrieval of a part "a pair of ski" of a moving object " a skier"

(a) a cube

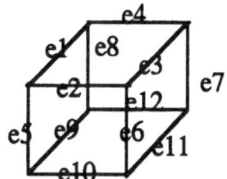

(b) the nested list

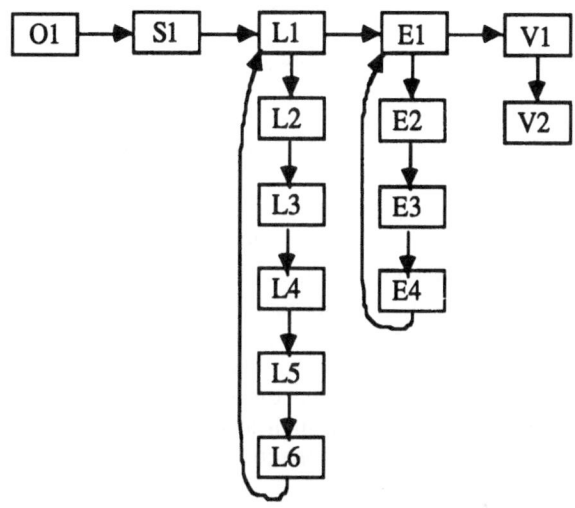

Fig. 4 The nested list of a cube

Then, the following commands are used to generate the object defined above:

> **create object** = *object_id*
>> **where segment** = *segment_id$_1$* , *segment_id$_2$* , ...
> **create segment** = *segment_id*
>> **where loop** = *loop_id$_1$* , *loop_id$_2$* , ...
> **create loop** = *loop_id*
>> **where edge** = *edge_id$_1$* , *edge_id$_2$*, ...
> **create edge** = *edge_id*
>> **where vertex** = *vertex_id$_1$*, *vertex_id$_2$*

The motion of an object can also be created recursively at given time intervals.

> **create motion** = *motion_id*
>> **where object** = *object_id$_{t1}$*, *object_id$_{t2}$*, ..., *object$_{tn}$*

For example, consider the case of generating the motion of a cube at time intervals. The cube at the initial time can be generated as follows:

$$
\begin{aligned}
&\textit{create edge} = e_1, e_2, ..., e_8 \\
&\qquad \textit{where vertex} = (v_1, v_2), (v_3, v_4), ... \\
&\textit{create loop} = l_1, l_2, ..., l_6 \\
&\qquad \textit{where edge} = (e_1, e_2, e_3, e_4), ... \\
&\textit{create segment} = s_1 \\
&\qquad \textit{where loop} = l_1, l_2, ..., l_6 \\
&\textit{create object} = cube \\
&\qquad \textit{where segment} = s_1
\end{aligned}
$$

Then, the nested list of the cube is constructed as shown in Fig. 4. In Fig. 4, the edges in loop L2-L6, and the vertices in edge E2-E4 are not shown for the simplicity of the figure.

3.2 AnimationPlatform for Data Manipulation of Moving Objects

In order to control moving objects during the animation, they must be manipulated interactively at a specific time or time intervals. There are two kinds of manipulations related to the moving objects. One is low-level manipulations which manage the modification of the topological and geometrical data of the moving objects. The deletion, insertion, retrieval, join and projection of moving objects are the examples. The other is high-level manipulations which are used to control and analyze moving objects. The examples are the comparison of objects, the comparison of motion, and collision detection and avoidance. Further types of high-level manipulation on the moving objects can be included. The manipulations of AnimationPlatform are listed below:

- **Retrieve**: The function of retrieval command is to search and display moving objects. Partial motion of objects can also be retrieved at time intervals. The partial motion means the motion of the partial object composed of a subset of the object. The projection and join of moving objects can also be represented. Here, the projection displays the motion of the partial topology of a moving object. The join displays the separate motion of several moving objects. Fig. 5 is an example of the projection of a moving object. It shows the result of the retrieval of the motion of a skier at given time intervals. Fig. 6 is an example of the join of moving objects. It is the join of three skiers at a specified time instant.
- **Insert**: By this function, the motion of an object can be controlled by inserting topology, geometry and any other information to an object at a certain or several time instants. This also makes a topologically changing animation possible.
- **Modify**: The motion of objects can be modified by changing any attributes or objects including the topology and geometry of the objects at a time instant.
- **Delete**: Motion can be corrected by deleting any attributes and objects including geometric and topological entities.
- **Compare Object**: Although object comparison does not change the topology or geometry of objects, they give a very useful function to control the motion. In the same way as conditional statements in programming languages are carried out by comparing the conditions to control the flow of data in an application, animation control is carried

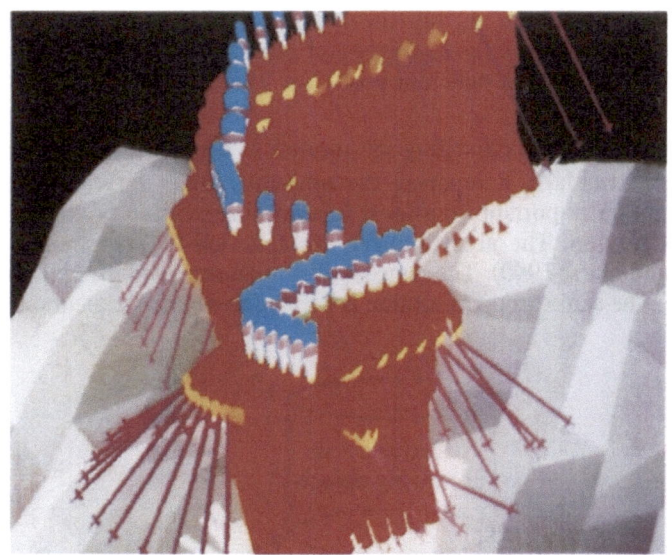

Fig. 5 Projection of a moving object

Fig. 6 Join of moving objects

out by comparing objects during the design of objects. The function of object comparison is used to test if the topology and geometry of the objects generated are the same, although they are in different positions. The algorithm is illustrated in a later section.

- **Compare Motion**: For controlling the motion of objects during animation, motion comparison, particularly comparing the motions having different local coordinate systems is another important high-level function irrespective of their positions or the directions of motion. The algorithm for this function is illustrated in the reference (Lee, Kunii and Dürst 1990). The concept of motion isometry is required to implement this function. The same group of motion is defined to determine the motion isometry.

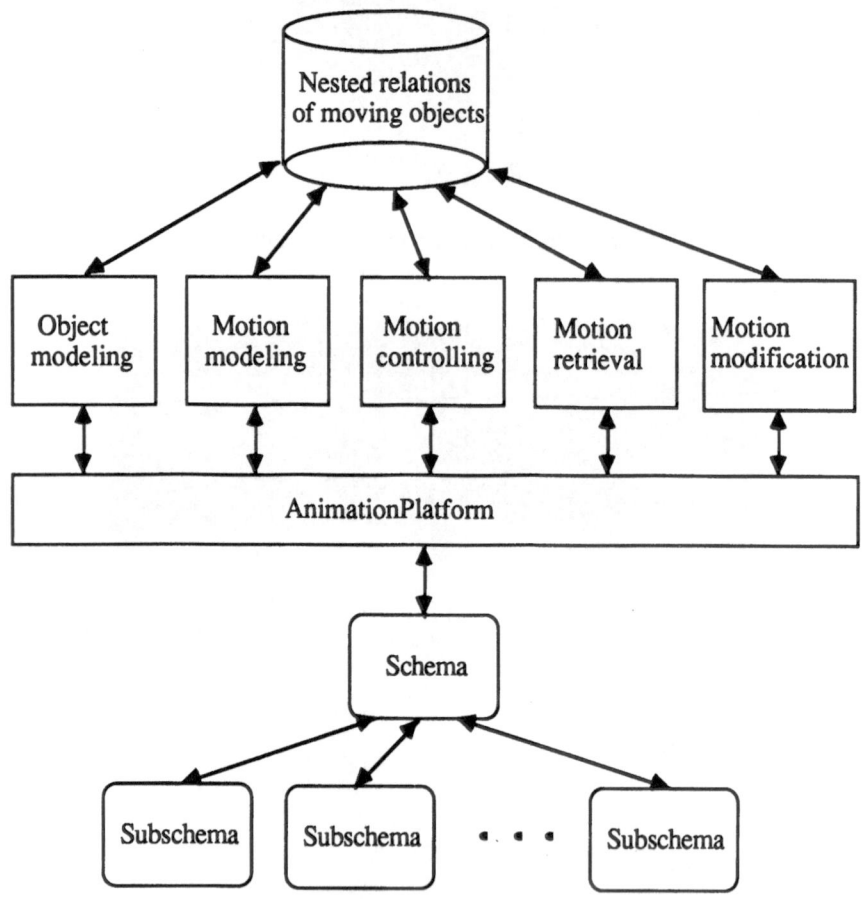

Fig. 7 Organization of a 4D geometric modeler

- **Detect Collision**: In animation systems, collision detection is a very critical factor to generate realistic motion since a segmented object is often transformed in a concave form during animation although it might not be concave at the initial time instant. An efficient algorithm is required to deal with the problem so that the intersection between polyhedra irrespective of the convexity or concavity of the form can be avoided. The 4D geometric modeler can detect collisions by using the information of the topology and geometry of the objects which can be retrieved at any time instant. We propose an algorithm and test it in a later section.

Fig. 7 shows the organization of the 4D geometric modeler including the data management system, AnimationPlatform. Fig. 8 summarizes the syntax of all the manipulations defined in the 4D geometric modeler.

```
SELECT [ALL] {motion | object | segment | loop | edge| vertex }
FROM { motion | object | segment | loop | edge } = identifier
[WHERE predicate]
[[ASCENDING] | [DESCENDING] field(s) ]

INSERT { motion | object | segment | loop | edge | vertex }
        = identifier
INTO { motion | object | segment | loop | edge | vertex }
        = identifier

MODIFY { motion | object | segment | loop | edge | vertex }
        = identifier
[WHERE predicate]

DELETE { motion | object | segment | loop | edge | vertex }
        = identifier
FROM { motion | object | segment | loop | edge }
        = identifier

COMPARE { motion | object | segment | loop | edge } = identifier
[WHERE predicate ] WITH
{ motion | obejct | segment | loop | edge } = identifier
[WHERE predicate]

DETECT COLLISION BETWEEN
{ object | segment | loop | edge | vertex } = identifier AND
{ obejct | segment | loop | edge | vertex } = identifier
```

Fig. 8 The manipulation of moving objects

3.3 Integrity Control of Moving Objects

In order to control the integrity of the moving objects during the animation, two kinds of constraints must be satisfied. The first is topological constraints which should be conserved during animation, particularly in topologically changing animation. For checking the topological constraints, the following integrity formula is used. It is easily derived from Euler's law (Mantyla and Solunen 1982; Mantyla 1984; Williams 1979) by inserting the concept of segments.

$$N_v - N_e + N_l = 2 * N_s \qquad (9)$$
$$N_v - N_e + N_l - N_s + N_o = 1 + N_s \qquad (10)$$

where N_v, N_e, N_l, N_s and N_o represent the number of vertices, edges, loops, segments and objects, respectively. The integrity checking is accomplished whenever the topology of an object is changed.

The other kind of constraints is semantic constraints related to the relationships between segments or to the correspondence of two sets of geometric entities during the animation. Collision detection is one kind of the function to maintain the semantic constraints. Illegal motion can be deleted by checking these constraints.

4. OBJECT COMPARISON

In this section, we illustrate the algorithm for comparing the topology and geometry of moving objects at a time instant. Moving objects can also be compared at separate time instants. This function helps the 4D geometric modeler to control the generation of animation by comparing two moving objects.

The following Definition 4.1, 4.2, 4.3 and 4.4 describe necessary and sufficient conditions to satisfy the equality of moving objects at a specific time instant.

Definition 4.1: conditions of object equality
Given objects O_1 and O_2, it is concluded that they are equal if the following conditions are satisfied.

condition 1:Two objects O_1 and O_2 are graph theoretically equivalent in topology.
condition 2: All corresponding segments of the two objects are equal. They must have the same quantitative and qualitative characteristics.
$$Q(S^1{}_i) \equiv Q(S^2{}_j), \ S^1{}_i \subset O_1, \ S^2{}_j \subset O_2, \text{ for all i and j}, \qquad (11)$$
where Q denotes quantitative and qualitative characteristics of a segment, S denotes a segment.
condition 3: For the two objects, all the corresponding relationships between segments are the same. These are 3D relationships between connected loops.
$$R(S^1{}_i \to S^1{}_k) \equiv R(S^2{}_j \to S^2{}_l), \qquad (12)$$
$$S^1{}_i, S^1{}_k \subset O_1 \text{ for all } k, i \neq k,$$
$$S^2{}_j, S^2{}_l \subset O_2 \text{ for all } j, j \neq l,$$
where $R(A \to B)$ denotes a relationship between A and B, and S denotes a segment in an object. $S^1{}_i$ and $S^2{}_j$ must be equal. $S^1{}_k$ and $S^2{}_l$ must also be equal.

Definition 4.2: conditions of segment equality

Given segments S_1 and S_2, $S_1 \subset O_1$, $S_2 \subset O_2$, it is concluded that two segments are equal if the following conditions are satisfied.

condition 1: They are graph theoretically equivalent in topology.

condition 2: All corresponding loops of the two segments are equal. This includes that all the corresponding loops have the same quantitative and qualitative characteristics.

$$Q(L^1_i) \equiv Q(L^2_j), \quad L^1_i \subset S_1, \ L^2_j \subset S_2, \text{ for all i and j,} \qquad (13)$$

where Q denotes quantitative and qualitative characteristics, and L denotes a loop.

condition 3: For the two segments, all the corresponding relationships between geometric entities composing the segments are the same. There are 2D relationships between connected edges and 3D relationships between loops.

$$R(E^1_i \to E^1_k) \equiv R(E^2_j \to E^2_l), \qquad (14)$$
$$E^1_i, E^1_k \subset O_1 \text{ for all k, i} \neq k,$$
$$E^2_j, E^2_l \subset O_2, \text{ for all l, j} \neq l,$$
$$R(L^1_i \to L^1_k) \equiv R(L^2_j \to L^2_l), \qquad (15)$$
$$L^1_i, L^1_k \subset O_1 \text{ for all k, i} \neq k,$$
$$L^2_j, L^2_l \subset O_2, \text{ for all l, j} \neq l,$$

where $R(A \to B)$ denotes the relationship between A and B. E denotes an edge and L denotes a loop.

Definition 4.3: conditions of loop equality

Given loops L_1 and L_2, $L_1 \subset O_1$, $L_2 \subset O_2$, it is concluded that two loops are equal if the following conditions are satisfied.

condition 1: They are graph theoretically equivalent in topology.

condition 2: For the two loops, all the corresponding edges are equal. This means that corresponding edges composing the loops have the same quantitative and qualitative characteristics.

$$Q(E^1_i) \equiv Q(E^2_j), \quad E^1_i \subset L_1, \ E^2_j \subset L_2, \text{ for all i and j,} \qquad (16)$$

where Q denotes quantitative and qualitative characteristics of an edge in a loop and E denotes an edge in a loop.

condition 3: For the loops, all the corresponding relationships between geometric entities composing the loops are the same. They include the relationships between adjacent edges.

$$R(E^1_i \to E^1_k) \equiv R(E^2_j \to E^2_l), \qquad (17)$$
$$E^1_i, E^1_k \subset L_1, \text{ for all k,i} \neq k,$$
$$E^2_j, E^2_l \subset L_2, \text{ for all l, j} \neq l$$

where $R(A \to B)$ denotes the relationship between A and B, E denotes an edge and L denotes a loop.

The algorithm for determining the equality of objects (Lee, Satoh and Kunii 1989) is summarized as in Fig. 9. In Fig. 9, c-loop denotes an inner loop and p-loop an outer loop when a loop includes a hole.

```
procedure OBJECTCOMP(o1,o2)
       compare number of vertices, edges and segments;
       compare number of straight edges, curved edges and c-loops;
       sort all the edges in the order of length;
       compare the sorted length of edge;
       compare all loops one by one;
       compare 2D relationship between c-loops and their p-loops;
       compare 3D relationship between loops;
       compare 3D relationship between segments;
end OBJECTCOMP
```

Fig. 9 Procedure for determining the congruence of objects

5. COLLISION DETECTION BETWEEN MOVING OBJECTS

Moving objects represented as polyhedra can often become concave due to the movement of joints, and we need an algorithm which can recognize the intersection of objects even in such a situation during animation. There are many works related to this problem (Lee and Preparata 1984; Preparata and Shamos 1985; Shamos 1976). In this section, an algorithm is defined based on the concept of point projection (Turner 1988) and set membership classification (Tilove 1980) for moving objects.

The algorithm to detect the intersection of objects is described as follows:

- For each object, select a vertex and check if the vertex lies inside the other polyhedra. If so, then the two objects intersect. Otherwise, continue to the next step.
- Sort all the vertices of two objects according to the value of one of the coordinates. For example, we can obtain the following ordered vertices sorted by the x-coordinate values in the case of Fig. 10.

$(V_1, V_6, V_5, V_3, V_2, V_4, V_{10}, V_8, V_7, V_{16}, V_{20}, V_9, V_{11}, V_{17}, V_{15}, V_{12}, V_{18}, V_{13}, V_{19}, V_{14})$

- Scan the ordered vertex list and select a vertex pair in which the two vertices belong to different objects. In Fig. 10, the vertex pair <V7, V16> is selected.
- Select the edges adjacent to the second vertex in the vertex pair. In Fig. 10, the edges E_4, E_5, E_6, are selected.
- Prepare the loops adjacent to the first vertex in the vertex pair. In Fig. 10, the loops, L_1, L_2, L_3, are selected.
- Check if the edges intersect the loops. This can be performed by the concept of point projection and set membership classification.
- In the same manner, select the edges connected to the first vertex in the vertex pair. In Fig. 10, the edges, E_1, E_2, E_3, are selected.
- Select the loops adjacent to the second vertex in the vertex pair. The loops, L_4, L_5, L_6, are selected.
- Check if the edges intersect the loops.

- If there exists the intersection between the loops and edges, the two objects intersect with each other.
- Continue to scan the vertex list and to check intersection until all the vertices of the object scanned first are exhausted.

The time complexity is calculated as follows: For sorting all the vertices, $O(nlogn)$ computing time is required. For checking the intersection between edges and loops, in the worst case, $O(N_L*N_E)$ computing time is required when N_L is the number of loops of the object that is scanned first and N_E is the number of edges of the other object.

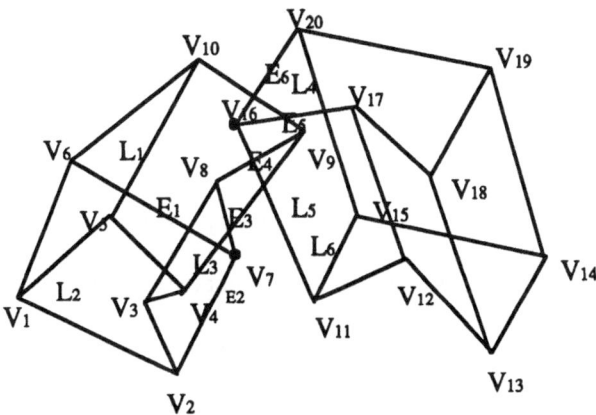

Fig. 10 Object intersection

6. CONCLUSIONS

In this paper, we have presented the organization of a 4D geometric modeler which includes a data management system. Since the 4D geometric modeler can manage all the topological and geometrical data related to moving objects, the motion of objects can be analyzed and controlled. In addition, it can visualize the topological and geometrical data related to the modification of moving objects during animation. It is also easy to retrieve or modify a part of the motion of objects without restructuring their data structure. The data management of moving objects can be well achieved in the case of topologically changing animation as well as geometrically changing animation. Furthermore, algorithms used for controlling moving objects are defined.

ACKNOWLEDGEMENTS

We would like to thank Mr. Yoshinori Kawamura, the director, and Mr. Nobuo Yamada, the manager of Kubota Computer Inc. for their support to this research. In addition, we would like to thank Mr. Tomoo Inaba and Mr. Takashi Sugino, the members of the AVS group of Kubota Computer Inc., for their help in the implementation of the data visualizer in the 4D geometric modeler.

REFERENCES

Aono M, Kunii TL (1984) Botanical Tree Image Generation. IEEE Computer Graphics and Applications 4(5):10-34

Kunii TL, Takai Y (1989) Cellular Self-Reproducing Automata as a Parallel Processing Model for Botanical Colony Growth Pattern Simulation. Proceedings of CG International'89, Springer-Verlag, pp. 7-22

Lee MW, Kunii TL, Dürst MJ (1990) Motion Comparison in Computer Animation. Proceedings of Computer Animation'90, Springer-Verlag, pp191-205

Lee MW, Kunii TL, Inaba T (1990) Interactive Animation Design Using a 4D Geometric Modeler. Proceedings of NICOGRAPH, in Japanese

Lee MW, Satoh T, Kunii TL (1989) Comparative Operations in Solid Modeling. Proceedings of the 1989 IFIP WG 5.10 International Working Conference for Experiments, also in the Technical Report 89-030, Department of Information Science, The University of Tokyo, 1989

Lamersdorf W (1989) Recursively Defined Complex Objects. Lecture Notes in Computer Science 361:176-189

Lee DT, Preparata FP (1984) Computational Geometry - A Survey. IEEE Transaction on Computers c-33(12):1072-1101

Linnemann V (1989) Nested Relations and Recursive Queries. Lecture Notes in Computer Science 361: 205-216

Mantyla M, Solunen R (1982) GWB: A Solid Modeler with Euler Operators. IEEE Computer Graphics and Applications 2(7):17-31

Mantyla M (1984) A Note on the Modeling Space of Euler Operators. Computer Vision, Graphics, and Image Processing 26(1):45-60

Preparata FP, Shamos MI (1985) Computational Geometry. Springer-Verlag, New York Inc.

Shamos MI (1976) Geometric Intersection Problems. Seventeenth Annual IEEE Symposium on Foundations of Computer Science, pp. 208-215

Trenish LA, Foley JD, Campbell WJ, Haber RB, Gurwitz RF (1989) Effective Software Systems for Scientific Data Visualization. SIGGRAPH'89 Panel Proceedings 23(5,):111-136

Tilove RB (1980) Set membership Classification: A Unified Approach to Geometric Intersection Problems. IEEE Transactions on Computers c-29(10):874-883

Turner JU (1988) Accurate Solid Modeling Using Polyhedra Approximations. IEEE Computer Graphics and Applications 8(3):17-28

Williams R (1979) The Geometrical Foundation of Natural Structure. Dover Publications, Inc., New York

Myeong Won Lee is currently working for Kubota Computer Inc. and also a researcher of the Department of Information Science at the University of Tokyo. Her research interests include computer animation, computational geometry, computer graphics, computer aided design and database systems. She received a BS degree in 1981 and an MS degree in computer science in 1984 from Seoul National University, and a Dr.Sc. in computer science from the University of Tokyo in 1990. She is a member of IEEE, ACM SIGGRAPH and Information Processing Society of Japan.

Address: Kubota Computer Inc. 2-8-8 Shinjuku Shinjuku-ku Tokyo 160 Japan, or Department of Information Science, Faculty of Science, the University of Tokyo, 7-3-1 Hongo, Bunkyo-ku, Tokyo,113 Japan.

Tosiyasu L. Kunii is currently Professor of Information and Computer Science, the University of Tokyo. At the University of Tokyo, he started his work in raster computer graphics in 1968 which was let to the Tokyo Raster Technology Project. His research interests include computer graphics, database systems, and software engineering. He authored and edited more than 32 computer science books, and published more than 120 refereed academic/technical papers in computer science and applications areas.

Dr. Kunii is Honorary President and Founder of the Computer Graphics Society, Editor-in-Chief of The Visual Computer: An International Journal of Computer Graphics (Springer-Verlag) Associate Editor-in-Chief of The Journal of Visualization and Computer Animation (John Wiley & Sons) and on the Editorial Board of IEEE Transactions on Knowledge and Data Engineering, VLDB Journal and IEEE Computer Graphics and Applications. He is on the IFIP Modeling and Simulation Working Group, the IFIP Data Base Working Group and the IFIP Computer Graphics Working Group. He organized and was chairing the Technical Committee on Software Engineering of the Information Processing Society of Japan from 1976 to 1981. He also organized and was President of the Japan Computer Graphics Association (JCGA) from 1981 to 1983. He served as General Chairman of the 3rd International Conference on Very Large Data Bases (VLDB) in 1977, Program Chairman of InterGraphics in 1983, Organizing Committee Chairman and Program Chairman of Computer Graphics Tokyo in 1984, Program Chairman of Computer Graphics Tokyo in 1985 and 1986, Organizing Committee Chairperson and Program Chairperson of CG International '87, Program Co-Chairman of IEEE COMPSAC '87, and Honorary Committee Chairperson of CG International '88. He served as Organizing Committee Chairperson and Program Chairperson of IFIP TC-2/WG 2.6 Working Conference on Visual Database Systems in 1989, Program Co-Chairperson of CG International'90 and Program Chairperson of IFIP TC-5/WG 5.10 Working Conference on Modeling in Computer Graphics in 1991 and the member of the Organizing Committee of IEEE COMPSAC'91. He is on the board of directors of Japan Society of Sports Industry and also of Japan Society of Simulation and Gaming.

He received the B.Sc., M.Sc., and D.Sc. degrees in chemistry all from the University of Tokyo in 1962, 1964, and 1967, respectively. He is a fellow of IEEE and a member of ACM, BCS, IPSJ and IEICE.

Address: Department of Information Science, Faculty of Science, the University of Tokyo, 7-3-1 Hongo, Bunkyo-ku, Tokyo,113 Japan.

Tools for Artists

MICHEL BRET

ABSTRACT

Artists seldom have the choice other than to put up with softwares which they did not develop or to build their own tools. The first choice, being by far the most frequent one, has left most of them hopeless. The second one really affects a small amount of creative people.

This paper proposes an in between solution, namely a simultaneously interactive and programmable system offering not only all the synthesis standard techniques but also the power of a programming language : the latter easily obtained , needs a perfect control of the former in order to modify them as well as to make up new ones.

Keywords : art, computer animation, language.

1. INTRODUCTION

Some devicemakers (such as APPLE) stress on their equipment friendliness and their easy-to-use softwares. It is quite true that for simple applications, standard programs based on menus are sufficient. However, when we are faced with complexity and requirement, these systems are limited and other tools have to be drawn up.

Some authors (SELTZER 85), have admitted that programming was the royal path of the synthesis and of animation by computer. On the other hand, a lot of image synthesis producers, besides standard softwares (such as EXPLORE , TDI France, or PIXAR, U.S.A.), conceive complementary programs on request. However, even very sophisticated programming languages do not offer yet the adaptability of analogical tools and discourage most creators. So, ergonomic interfaces have been created allowing a non technician user to manipulate sophisticated graphic systems, but the sole use of the "mouse", excluding writing, limits inevitably the access.

Between the genuine programming, accessible to a minority only and servo-assisted systems, a third possibility must exist : interactive and programmable simultaneously softwares, giving the artists not only the synthesis traditional methods (ray tracing, texture) but also the means to modify them or to conceive other ones.

One should not forget that if the painter's style does not depend on his paint-brushes and color brands, it is not the same as far as the computer is concerned, knowing that implicit aesthetic choices are cabled in the code itself : such an algorithm of the rendering is not accidental but can very well be the reflexion of the program conception on the Universe and the means to represent it.

2. ABOUT TOOLS

Tools from the past are constrained, definite : pliers will not gain anything by changing form. On the other hand, up to date tools are "soft" : they are adaptable, evolve, we can say they are "smart" : a skilled system can considerably increase their knowledge. In this sense, any closed program is an outdated tool, whereas any open system is potentially adaptable to any situation.

If electronics paddles constitute a decisive improvement for traditional tools, they are not fundamentally different from the previous ones, apart from when they become programmable, they make the difference. In the same way, synthesis softwares operating only through manual interface (via the mouse) lose all power pertaining to their own foundation, i.e. the language.

Are ergonomics and user-friendliness supposedly to be the giving up of all thoughfulness and "writing" ?

I will try to demonstrate there is nothing of the kind once I have described some of the tools proposed by ANYFLO software.

3. A LANGUAGE

In order to give the creators immediate access to the synthesis standard methods, without rewriting everything and without being dependent of aesthetic choices made or not, I have designed the ANYFLO software which is an interactive open system built around an interpreter.

Menus, no matter how complexe they are, do proceed only by designation, and finger pointing is not talking yet. And so, a language was necessary. The easiest way of course was to draw inspiration from the most known of them all : the C language. In order to free the user of the burdensome aspects of all programming language, the syntax has been simplified and the compiler has been made tolerant. So, there is no need of declaration (the variables type and dimension are dynamically managed), semicolons, parenthesis can be left out as long as there is no ambiguity.

The graphic vocation of this software has required objects of specific type : polygonal lines, volums, lights, fictitious cameras, fogs etc..., are as many entities the user can name, modify and manipulate through calculation.

Finally, the notion of "actor" has been implemented in local functions and in statistical memory forms which can be assigned to any object. These functions, unknown on the outside, allow to define "behaviors", the static memories playing the role of "knowledge". Messages can be exchanged among objects, and among the latter and the system operating the scene or the animation.

4. EXAMPLES OF PROGRAMMABLE TOOLS

4.1 Mappings

Normally, a classic 2-D mapping (with antialiasing if the mappe is bigger than the facet or extrapolation on the contrary) as well as a reflecting mapping (with spheric modification of a 2-D mapping to avoid deformations) can be allocated to volums or to facets by simple writing as follows :

    mappe vol num = nume, type, parameters
    num = number of the mapping image (illimited number)
    type = reflecting or 2-D mapping
    parameters : indicating the mapping and surface reciprocal
    influence as well as the coefficients allowing to "make a hole in the
    mappe".

The computer user can also write a C function, linked to ANYFLO, which will be used for each pixel : a soft interface which allows the reprocessing of useful parameters is planned for this purpose.

Picture 1 is an example of "auto mapping" (film extract "AUTOMAPPE 89), a technique which consists in taking the image itself as the mappe. After a certain number of iterations, new forms appear. On the other hand, the time-lag between the image and its mapping can produce interesting effects.

4.2 3-D Texture

Besides standard 3-D textures (BLINN 76, PEACHY 85) assigned to volumes, calculating specific parameters, the computer user can also make his own textures. He can do that two ways :

the first one consists in writing functions (in ANYFLO language) which will used for each pixel display. Such a function holds commands which can collect the space point coordinates, the pixel of which is the projection, as well as a set of instructions concerning this point (surface color, normal on this point surface, etc.). A new color can then be calculated according to these values and passed on the display unit. The syntax of such an operation reads :

    texture vol num = func "toto"

which indicates that the function named "toto" will be the function using the texture assigned to the volume number num.

The second way, softer and more effective, consists in writing such a function directly in C and linked it to ANYFLO. A soft interface allows to collect any useful information relative to the database without knowing its internal coding.

Both methods can be applied to a lot of other operations , lights for example (see the following).

4.3 Lighting models

Standard lighting models (BLINN 77) are characterized by the data of parameters (of reflexion, brightness, refective transparency, etc.), and some laws can be specified by the user. For instance, the function W(alpha) which controls the reflecting value according to the angle alpha of the light incidence to the enlightened point can be applied to the volume number num by writing

        law vol num = w

where w is a variable (which can be drawn for instance by means of the mouse or calculated by function).

4.4 Lights

"Light" type objects are normally white sources, punctual, radiating an even constant energy in all directions. The user can build more attractive lights : (FORTIN 85).

* Spots

A spot is defined by :
        - a position P
        - an aimed direction V
        - a variation law W of lighting according to the angle obtained by the ray on the axis PV
        - a variation law of lighting according to the distance to the source
        - a color R,G,B, ...
These informations can be applied to the light number num written as follow :
        poi lum num = P
        fui lum num = V
        loi lum num = W

* Extended sources

They are defined by an emitting surface simulated by a set of luminous points. The latter can be exhaustively characterized (for instance through reproduction of the points of a volume in the light) written as follow
        poi(1,12) lum num1 = poi(1,12) vol num2
or proceeding as statistic distribution in a sphere of a given radius and a given density.

Noisy coefficients can be created between lights and volumes. Certain lights can light up only certain volumes and vice versa. This ability allows the plastic reinterpretation of a realistic scene.

4.5 Constraints

A hierarchy of mechanical constraints can be defined on a set of volumes in order to make it as an articulated structure. Each tree knot correspond to an object, each link represents a constraint . The latter can have two degrees of freedom (link type "ball-and-socket joint"),

Picture 1

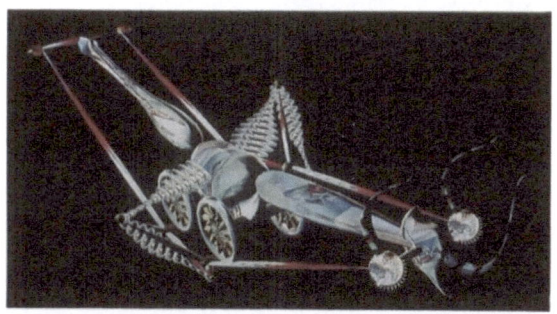

Picture 2

Picture 3

Picture 4

Picture 5

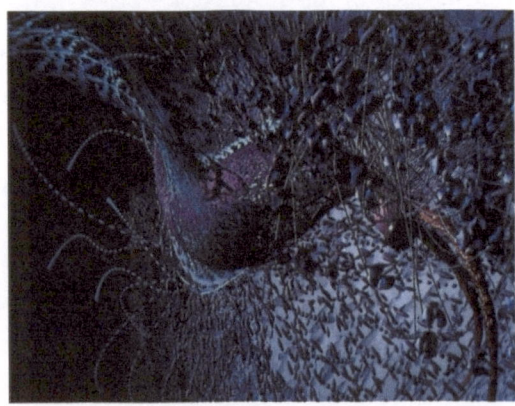

Picture 6

zero degree of freedom (motionless). These links are made independent of the objects on which they are det rmined (elastic links), calculating the positions of anchoring points according to external parameters (angles, forces, amplitude intervals, etc.). (KENNA 90).

Picture 2 shows a mechanical toy all the parts of which are subject to constraints, in order to animate it one needs to act on one of the parts (for instance a wheel) which automatically set in motion all the other parts (film extract "AUTOMAPPE" 1989).

Picture 3 shows a waggon pulled by an individual : all the waggon parts (wheels, subframe, sliding and articulated rods, etc.) are subject to mechanical constraints. The wheels are forced to wheel on the ground pulling along the remaining parts which are automatically animated. The individual himself is operated in the same manner and is linked to the waggon. The waggon cloth roof is subject to dynamical constraints and to the wind strenght.

Picture 4 shows some characters walking in the wind : their hair as well as their clothings undergo forces (wind, body straps), and are automatically managed by the resolution of these constraints (film extract "TOCCATA" 1990).

These methods have been developed for the need of realistic animation, but it is interesting to use them for plastic purposes. And so, picture 5 shows a bird the structure of which is generated by a hierarchy of the preceeding type, but its flight influences its environment. Picture 6 shows the fictious links which have been established between the positions of the points of the bird body and those of the landscape. This programmed interaction leads to reconsider the relations of content and form in terms other than basic physics and agree with the painters questionnings on the subject.

4.6 Collision detections (HERZEN, 1990)

A function :
        internal vol num 1, num2
turns over the list of volumes vertices number num 1 internal to the volume number num2 : if this list is empty, there is no intersection between the two volumes, if not, this list can be used to determine the normals to the surfaces at the impact point and to calculate a reaction force according to the distance and the velocity of penetration.

Some other functions allow one volume to adhere to another one, to block one volume (or just specific points) by another one, to control the volumes movements (or just some points of these volumes) when they have been affected with masses and placed in a force field (ZELTZER, 85), etc.

4.7 Adaptable perspective

The same method has been applied to the perspective implementation by interfacing its calculation with a user function. More precisely, this calculation is no longer a processus isolated from its context, but can, on the contrary, adapt itself to whatever it deals with : just like real vision or the eye, during the multiple steps it takes to analyse its environment, fits itself with what it is "looking at" ; this function will have the ability to modify the parameters defining the fictious camera according to what is seen. The famous painting of Sandro BOTTICELLI " Portrait of a stanger", (Florence, Musée des Offices, around 1474) is a good illustration of this processus. One can see a man presenting a medal, but the main interest of this painting lies in the form of the river banks, situated in the background which, oddly enough, follows the portrait shape instead of converging on a point of the horizon as expected according to traditional perspective rules. In the same way, if we take certain paintings of the italian "quatrocento", a perspective (with a vanishing point to the left) is attached to left panel, whereas another perspective (with a vanishing point to the right) is attached to the right panel. Such pictorial effects can be easily obtained through the writing of an adequate function which will be used for each calculation of a perspective point.

The same procedure goes for all ANYFLO objects which can be controled by local functions which role consists in adapting them to their environment : such the virgin Mary portrayed taller than the donor (not because she is nearby, but because she is more important), or such part of the painting more luminous than others (not because it is better lit up, but because the artist wants to particularly attract the spectator's attention on this spot).

4.8 Actors

All ANYFLO objects (volumes, lights, views fogs, trajectories, motion law, etc) can be provided with a set of "local functions" and with static memories. The former allow to simulate a "behavior", the latter playing the role of "knowledge".

These functions, unknown outside the objects where they are defined, can be specifically used inside of a same object, or again, from a user function. Thus, a volume placed in a given environment (constituted of other volumes, of force fields, of contact conditions, etc.), can fit itself to it (by decoding the received messages), take decisions (with regards to these informations and according to knowledge a priori stocked in static memories). It can also transmit messages and modify the state of its memories.

Thus, the animator sees his role of puppet manipulator changing to the one of producer which can control situations having a certain autonomy.

For instance, we can write :
          local(1) vol num = func "toto"
which takes the text of function "toto" as first local function of the volume number num (this function will have a compliled coding proper to this volume)

        exec local("shift") fac(5) vol(2) var("move") var(10,20,30)
calls the local function named "shift" corresponding to the facet number 5 of the volume number 2 by giving the string "move" and the vector (10,20,30).

5. CONCLUSION

In a certain way, synthesis has enabled the automatic making of images, but, just like photography, it has not solved the aesthetic problem.

The coming out of a ray tracing software has no reason, no more than a camera, for producing attractive images. The latter only take up a plastic dimension through the creator 's touch who, beyond the simple use of tools, will be able to make them show more, and use them other than for what they have been created for.

REFERENCES

(BLINN 76) BLINN J.F., NEWELL M.E."(1976)Texture and reflection in computer Generated images " Communications of the ACM, Vol 19, Num 10, pp. 542-547.

(BLINN 77) BLINN J.F. (1977) "Models of Light Reflection for Computer Synthesized Pictures" SIGGRAPH Proc., Computer Graphics, Vol 11, Num 2, pp. 192-198.

(BLINN 78) BLINN J.F. (1978) "Simulation of Wrinkled Surfaces", SIGGRAPH Proc., Vol 12, Num 3, pp. 286-292.

(FORTIN 85) FORTIN M., LEONARD N., MAGNENAT-THALMANN N., THALMANN D. (1985) "Animating Lights and Shadows" M., ZELTZER D. in Computer Generated Images". Editors Nadia Magnenat-Thalmann and Daniel Thalmann pp 45-55.

(HERZEN 90) Von HERZEN B., BARR A.H., ZATZ H.R. (1990)"Geometric Collisions for Time-Dependent Parametric Surfaces" Computer Graphics, Vol 24, Num 4, pp 39-48.

(KENNA 90) Mc KENNA M., ZELTZER D.(1990) "Dynamic Simulation of Autonomous Legged Legged Locomotion"Computer Graphics, Vol 24, Num 4, pp 29-38.

(PEACHY 85) PEACHY D.R. (1985) "Solid Texturing of Complex Surfaces" Computer Graphics, Vol 19, Num 3, pp 279-286, Juillet.

(ZELTZER 85) ZELTZER D. (1985)"Towards an Integrated View of 3-D Computer Animation" in "Computer-Generated Images". Editors Nadia Magnenat-Thalmann and Daniel Thalmann, pp. 230-248.

Michel BRET is Assistant Professor of A.T.I. (Arts andTechnologies of the Image) at the University of Paris 8. He works in the field of "Computer Animation" since 1976. Author of several technical books, he has also written some animation and synthesis softwares (used for different systems). He has produced a large number of animation films some of which have obtained International Prizes (IMAGINA 89, PARIGRAPH 89, IMAGE DU FUTUR 89).

Address : A.T.I. University of Paris 8, 2 rue de la Liberté, 93526 Saint-Denis Cedex 02

Part IV
Rendering Techniques for Animation

Forest: An Interacting Tree Model for Visualizing Forest Formation Processes by Algorithmic Computer Animation — A Case Study of a Tropical Rain Forest

Tosiyasu L. Kunii and Hirohisa Enomoto

ABSTRACT

An interacting tree model is developed to visualize the dynamics of forest formation processes by algorithmic animation. For the dynamic model to work properly, the model includes a parallel algorithmic model of individual tree growth which considers both the differences among the species and the time dependent interactions among the trees through mutual shading to incorporate a part of the ecologically interacting system of a forest. A tropical rain forest in the equatorial zone is chosen as a typical case because the other types of forests can be derived from it by imposing a set of constraints on it in terms of the less rain falls and the lower temperatures which slow down the speed of forest growth. The results of visualization by algorithmically animating a few hundred years of forest growing processes by our model validate the model against the data obtained at an experimental observation site in Pasoh of peninsular Malaysia.

Key words: forest growth model, forest succession, interacting tree model, ecological model, parallel algorithmic animation

1. INTRODUCTION

1.1 A Forest as an Ecological System: A Forest Succession Model in Forestry

Let us clarify the fundamental processes of forest formation by briefly reviewing the related works in forestry to the extent necessary for our purpose of visualization by animation. There are many kinds of trees in a forest. Trees in a forest are interacting with the other trees of the same or different species, the environment including the other vegetation and animals from the time of its start as a seed through the growth and maturity periods until the time of its death. In forestry, the process that vegetation invades a large and bare area and grows into a stable state, is called the *primary succession*. Clements (1916) called the stable state the *climax*. The process that trees cannot live their lifetime by the accidents such as diseases and insects causing damages is called the *secondary succession*. Forestry considers the succession as the main feature of a forest (see, for example, Shugart 1984). In a forest, many trees, the other life and the environment interacting with each other form an ecological system, or a *ecosystem*. Then, modeling a forest ecosystem means modeling the *forest succession*.

In modeling the forest succession, two approaches exist: A top-down approach and a bottom-up approach. The top-down models are called the forest models and the bottom-up models the tree models. The *forest models* view a forest as a whole with its attributes such as biomass, numbers of trees, indices of diversity, and timber volume. As a top-down approach, the forest models is based on an implicit assumption that the important determining factors for predicting stand dynamics are factors that emerge at the forest-stand level of organization. In contrast, as a bottom-up approach, the *tree models* are based on the assumption that the dynamics of forests is the consequence of the changes and interactions of individual trees in the forest. The simplest tree model takes the form of a simple tabulation of the probabilities of individual trees of one species being replaced by those of another species. The most complex and detailed tree model is built on the *four dimensional (4D) modeling* of many species of trees incorporating the interactions among individual trees as seen in this paper.

The general models of forests as dynamic systems can be further classified into two categories in forestry: one focusing on the states taken by the systems and the other focusing on the *processes* performed by the systems. In forestry, a particular state the climax proposed by Clements (1916) as a stable state is emphasized as explained before and the word processes often means the sequences of ways through which forests reach the climax dynamically and then decline. To animate the growth processes of the forests, we look at the prominent features in the ecological succeeding processes of forests, particularly of the rain forests in the equatorial zone.

1.2 Rain Forests as a Typical Model of Forests

We now explain the reason why we choose rain forests as a typical model of forests in general. It is the generic characteristics of rain forests. Enough resources for plants exist in the equatorial zone. A favorable climate with warm temperature, abundant rainfall and flooding sunlight promotes plant growth to make trees taller in a shorter time period throughout the year. A tropical rain forest ecosystem exhibits the maximum possible performance of the plant community among so many varieties of forests on the earth, and is one of the most complex ecosystems on the earth. And hence, the other types of forests in the areas ranging from the northern to desert through temperate zones are assume to be derived from it by imposing constraints on it in terms of less rain falls and lower temperatures which slow down the speed of forest growth. We expect that understanding a tropical rain forest and its ecosystem leads us naturally to the understanding of the other types of forests and their ecosystems. Fortunately, a large amount of data on the rain forest ecosystem in Pasoh of peninsular Malaysia, were gathered by a Japanese team during the period of 1970-1974 (Kira 1987). We can evaluate our ecological model and verify it against the observed data by comparing the data with the results of the visualization of the tropical rain forest formation processes by computer animation.

2. An Interacting Tree Model of a Forest

The top-down and bottom-up models are just two different forms of views of the same reality called a forest. In this chapter, we present a model which can integrate the two forms into a single model capable of representing the ecological succession of a tropical rain forest as a set of interacting trees in a given environment.

2.1 Tree Models for Computer Graphics

Let us examine now what kind of model of trees is appropriate for our purpose. It is known that, among the internal properties of trees, the *sunlight-photosynthesis relation* is dominating the production rate of trees. Then, mutual shading is the dominating interactions among trees to control the forest growth. It means that the model appropriate for representing forest formation processes should be able to control the growth of trees by utilizing the sunlight-photosynthesis relation and then by automatically computing the amount of sunshine received after mutual shading. However, to the best of authors' knowledge, the tree models used in computer graphics so far have no such capability except the model we published in May, 1984 under the name of the A-system (Aono and Kunii 1984). Before going into the details of the A- system and extending it to better meet our new requirements, let us briefly survey the other tree models for computer graphics.

In modeling trees for computer graphics, two approaches exist: *algorithmic* (also called *procedural* ; see, for example, Smith 1984) and texture mapping approaches (see, for example, Bloomenthal 1985). The algorithmic approach includes *formal language-based* (Prusinkiewicz, Lindenmayer and Hanan 1988; Reffye, Edelin, Francon, Jaeger and Puech 1988; Green and Sun 1988), *fractal-based* (Mandelbrot 1983; Demko 1985; Norton 1982; Barnsley, Jacquin, Malassenet, Reuter and Sloan 1988) and *particle-based* (Reeves 1983) models. The research results based on these models and published so far, all lack the type of modeling capability described above and cannot be used "as they are" as the foundation of our research. Usefulness of each approach and model for our purpose is rather straightforward. The algorithmic approach, particularly a formal language-based model, is most versatile and flexible, and if we carefully design a language grounded on appropriate data structures and algorithms, it will become the most promising candidate. Fractals are appropriate only where recursive structures are observed in the objects or phenomena to be modeled. Particles behave concurrently based on the rules given to the particles, and useful only where the particles are appropriate elements of the objects to be modeled. Texture mapping should be considered rather as a convenient method than an independent approach to or model of trees, to paste any set of selected textures on a given image.

2.2 The KEA-System as an Enhanced Algorithmic Tree Model for Visualizing Forest Formation Processes

In the previous work we developed a botanical tree image generation system named the A-system (Aono and Kunii 1984). As a matter of fact, it belongs to the algorithmic approach, and is a parallel formal language-based tree model. It allows interactive tree image generation, and produces the three-dimensional geometric model of the most kinds of higher order trees from a few parameters (see Figs. 1 and 2):
(1) A divergence angle(d),
(2) Branching angles($h1$, $h2$) and
(3) Contraction ratios($r1$, $r2$).
The A-system has enough facilities for tree image generation. It also has the capabilities to compute the total area of the all the leaves of a tree, the effective total leaf area to receive sunlight, and the production rate of the tree by the *sunlight-photosynthesis relation*. To efficiently compute the effective total leaf area of a tree to receive sunlight, a scan-line incremental method was developed as explained in the next section. The disadvantages of the A-system are as follows: (1) The aim of the A-system is the generation of final tree shapes, and the rendering processes of the A-system do not correspond to the processes of tree growth, particularly the branching process(see Fig. 3). (2) The shape of the seedlings is not appropriately represented. For the use in gardening and city planing, the A-system has the basic capability. Unfortunately, the A-system does not satisfy our requirements necessary for visualizing and animating the dynamics of forest formation processes.

Enhancements are made to take the other internal properties of a tree into consideration such as modeling the *branching sequence,* the *growth and death* of the branches and the trunk, the *rate of the foliage active in photosynthesis,* all depending on the species and age of the tree. The enhanced system is named the KEA-system.

2.3 A Scan-Line Incremental Method

In the previous work of us (Aono and Kunii, 1984), we developed and used a *scan-line incremental method* to quickly calculate the sunlight which bathes each leaf of a tree. In this method, a leaf is modeled as a circle of the radius which depends on the given species of the tree, and is assumed to be parallel to the ground. Honda (1978) called the net total area of overlapped leaves the *Dirichlet domain* (see Fig. 4) which approximates the leaves as overlapping circles spread over a plane. The sunlight is modeled vertical to the earth, and the total sum of the sunlight received by a tree is proportional to the Dirichlet domain of the tree.

A brief explanation of the algorithm of the scan-line incremental method is as follows:
(1) First, each circle (referred to as the structure type "disk" defined below) is initialized. It includes the center coordinates (cx, cy), the y value (y) which is decremented for each scan line, and the pointers to the adjacent circles, *back and *next.
(2) Next, Y-bucket sorting together with X-insertion sorting is performed (see Figs. 4 and 5). That is, sort the given circles, first along the y-axis (scan-line) and then along the x-axis.
(3) After sorting all the circles, the Y-bucket is scanned from the top to the bottom. During this sorting, the "A-list" (active list) is maintained, which keeps track of the circles currently intersecting the scan-line.

The basic information each circle contains is illustrated by the following structure type "disk":

```
typedef struct disk {
    int y; /* the remaining y value intersecting the scan-line */
    int cx; /* the x coordinate of the disk center */
    int cy; /* the y coordinate of the disk center */
    struct disk *back;
    struct disk *next;
}
```

The overlaps of the two adjacent circles in the entries of the A-list fall into three cases (see Fig. 6).
(4) For each case, the line segment is added until the scan-line reaches the bottom or the top of the screen.

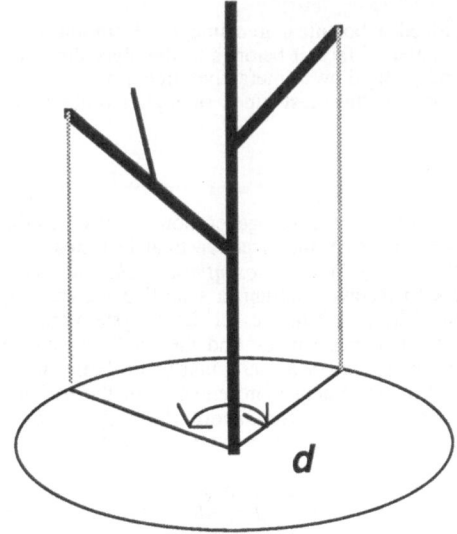

Fig. 1. A divergence angle *d*

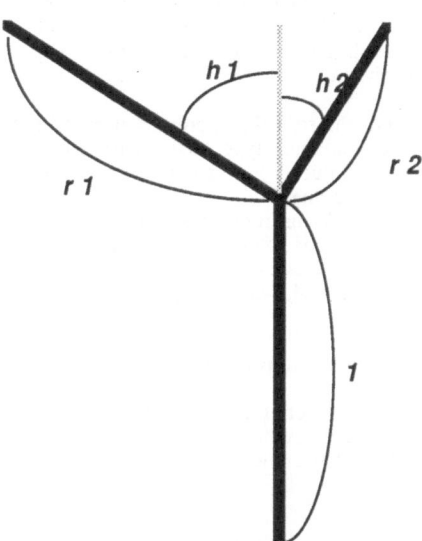

Fig. 2. Branching angles *h1, h2*
and contraction ratios *r1, r2*

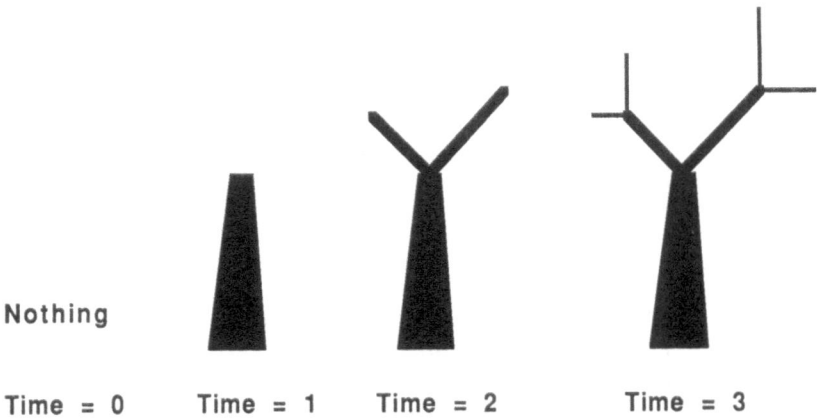

Fig. 3. Time in the A-system

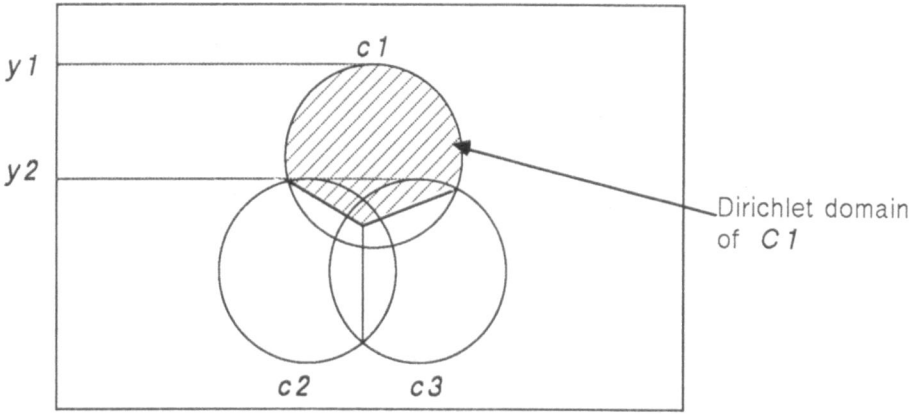

Fig. 4. Shadowed area shows the Dirichlet domain of the circle *c1*

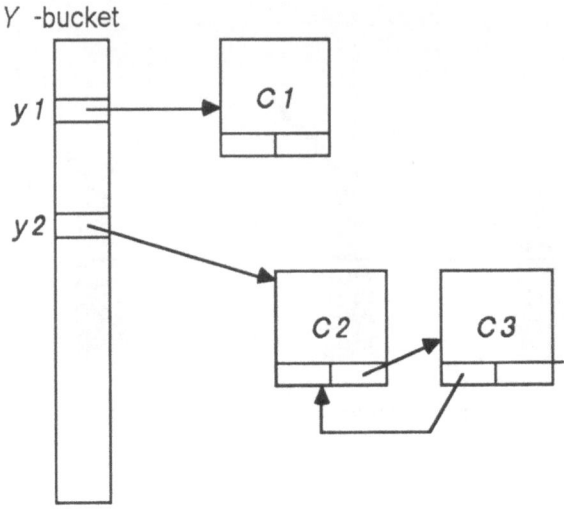

Fig. 5. Structure information of circles
c1, c2, and *c3*

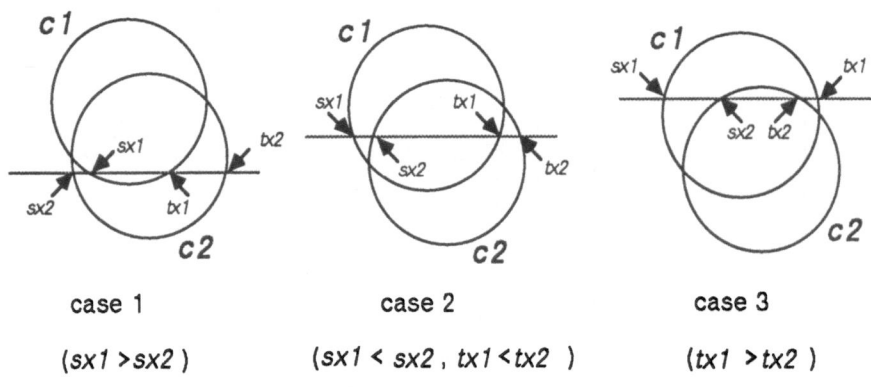

case 1	case 2	case 3
(*sx1* > *sx2*)	(*sx1* < *sx2* , *tx1* < *tx2*)	(*tx1* > *tx2*)

Fig. 6. 3 cases of 2 circles *c1* and *c2* intersecting with a scan line

2.4 A Circle model of a Tree

To model a forest, many species of trees must be considered. So far, if we use the scan-line incremental method, the unit of processing to calculate the sunlight has been a leaf. There are too many leaves in a rain forest, and it is a waste of time to calculate the amount of sunlight each leaf is bathed in. It is advantageous if we can change the processing unit into a larger one without the loss of generality. Here, let us examine what happens if we choose a tree as the processing unit. To simplify a model of a single tree, the top view of a tree is assumed to be a circle (see Fig. 7). From the scan-line algorithm, the amount of sunlight received by each tree is given by the formula:

Sum = $K*R*R*\pi$ (0.6 < K < 0.7)

where R is the radius of the circle of a tree, and K is a constant obtained from the algorithm. The ground under the tree is not fully shaded, and there is some light streaming through the leaves. By the scan-line algorithm, the amount of the sunlight falling through the leaves is calculated. The physical mutual exclusion rule is taken into account so that no two trees can physically occupy the same place. (see Fig. 8). To show the differences in the intensity of sunlight at the different parts of a tree, we define the light consumption function (see Fig. 9). The above formula is modified assuming that the light intensity over the tree is I_{ovr}, as:

$$
L_{consume} = \begin{cases} I_{ovr} & \text{if } \frac{D}{R} < \frac{1}{\sqrt{2}} \\ I_{ovr}*(aD^2+bD+c) & \text{if } \frac{1}{\sqrt{2}} \le \frac{D}{R} < 1 \\ 0 & \text{if } \frac{D}{R} \ge 1 \end{cases}
$$

where D is the distance from the tree root, R is the radius of the circle of the tree (see Fig. 7), and a, b, and c are the constants for adjusting the sum of the sunlight to make it equal in the above two formulae. The sunlight bathing a lower tree is obstructed by the neighboring taller trees. The amount of the sunlight received by the lower tree (see Fig. 10) is calculated by the same method with that for the taller tree, by representing the sunlight through the taller trees as the reduced absorption rate of the light consumption function (Fig. 9).

2.5 Modeling the Differences among the Species

The sheer species richness features in tropical rain forests. For example, any one hectare of the forest in Pasoh of peninsular Malaysia hardly has two trees of the same species. It is too complex to model all the species separately. However, the outer appearances of the trees in a forest can usually be categorized into a far smaller number of classes than the number of species, and fortunately this is also true for a tropical rain forest. It means only a limited number of parameter sets can do well to model trees even in a tropical rain forest. A tropical rain forest ordinarily has three layers of trees in their heights. The internal properties of trees vary significantly depending on the species. We distinguish only three kinds of internal properties of trees which affect the appearances of trees. The three properties are: the rate of the light-photosynthesis relation, the death rate of the branches, and the rate of the foliage active in photosynthesis. We hypothesize that the difference in the height and shape among the three layers of a tropical rain forest originates from the difference in these internal properties of the trees, and test the hypothesis through numerical simulation and visualization by algorithmic computer animation against the observation.

3. Numerical Simulation of the Tropical Rain Forest Formation Processes

By the method introduced in the previous chapter, the sunlight intensity for each tree is calculated, and from these results, the production of each tree is calculated. To change the tree shape by the production, we assume that the weight of trees are proportional to $R*R*H$, where R is the circle radius of the tree based on the circle model of a tree (see Section 2.4), and H is the height of the tree. We also assume the seeds germinate randomly, and its count is determined by the amount of sunlight that reaches the ground. The trees in the highest layer are sparse, although with the rise of the average temperature they become denser. The species of trees in the highest layer require plenty of sunlight to grow, at least after reaching the height of the layer, and keep their distance from each other to avoid the mutual shading.

206

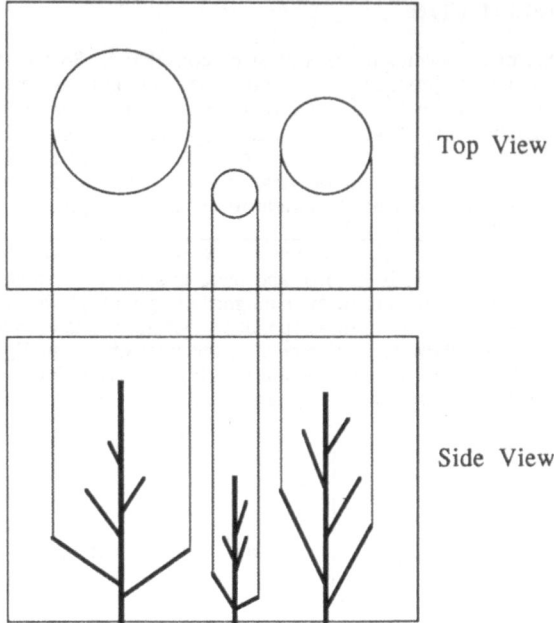

Fig. 7. A Circle Model of Trees

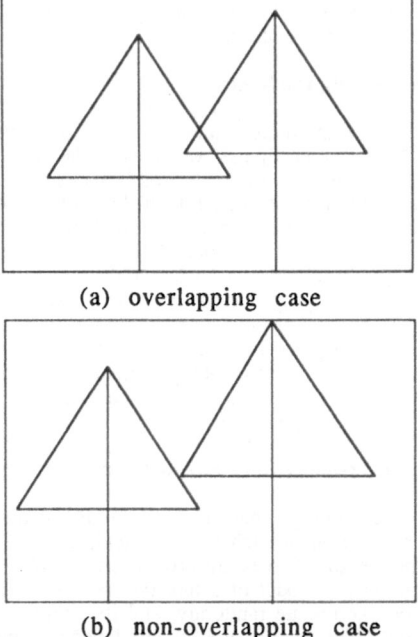

(a) overlapping case

(b) non-overlapping case

Fig. 8. Overlapping trees are excluded

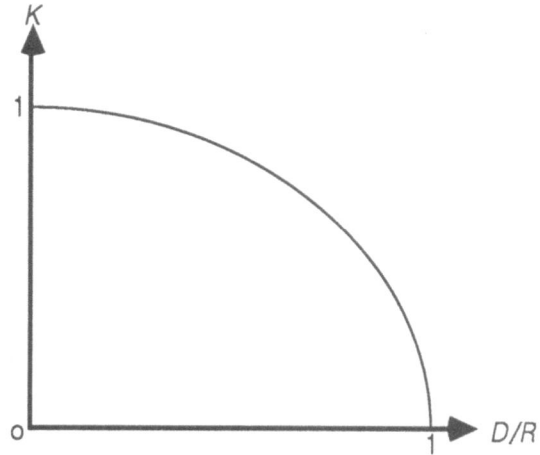

K is the absorption rate and D is the distance
from the center of a tree of radius R

Fig. 9. A light consumption function

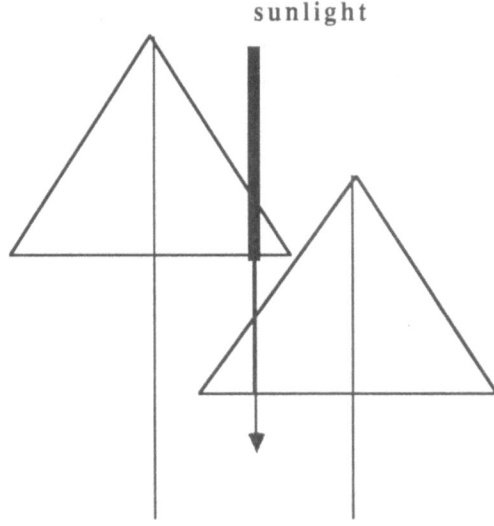

Fig. 10. Modeling the overapping tree

(a) at age 3

Height	No. of Trees
0– 3	132
3– 6	0
6– 9	0
9–12	0
12–15	0
15–18	0
18–21	0
21–24	0
24–27	0
27–30	0
30–33	0
33–36	0
36–39	0
39–42	0
Total	132

(b) at age 30

Height	No. of Trees
0– 3	159
3– 6	0
6– 9	0
9–12	0
12–15	0
15–18	0
18–21	0
21–24	0
24–27	0
27–30	0
30–33	0
33–36	0
36–39	0
39–42	0
Total	159

(c) at age 60

Height	No. of Trees
0– 3	47
3– 6	12
6– 9	0
9–12	0
12–15	0
15–18	0
18–21	0
21–24	0
24–27	0
27–30	0
30–33	0
33–36	0
36–39	0
39–42	0
Total	59

(d) at age 100

Height	No. of Trees
0– 3	71
3– 6	9
6– 9	1
9–12	4
12–15	0
15–18	0
18–21	0
21–24	0
24–27	0
27–30	0
30–33	0
33–36	0
36–39	0
39–42	0
Total	85

(e) at age 150

Height	No. of Trees
0– 3	98
3– 6	11
6– 9	2
9–12	5
12–15	2
15–18	1
18–21	4
21–24	0
24–27	0
27–30	0
30–33	0
33–36	0
36–39	0
39–42	0
Total	123

(f) at age 200

Height	No. of Trees
0– 3	103
3– 6	14
6– 9	5
9–12	3
12–15	3
15–18	2
18–21	8
21–24	1
24–27	0
27–30	3
30–33	0
33–36	0
36–39	0
39–42	0
Total	142

(g) at age 250

Height	No. of Trees
0– 3	89
3– 6	33
6– 9	1
9–12	2
12–15	3
15–18	2
18–21	16
21–24	0
24–27	0
27–30	1
30–33	4
33–36	0
36–39	0
39–42	0
Total	151

Table 1. The result of numerical simulation of tropical rain forest growth

To verify our interacting tree model of forests against the observed forest formation processes in Pasoh of peninsular Malaysia as described in Oikawa (1985, 1986) and Kira (1987), we conducted a numerical experiment to see whether the model can simulate the real processes by heuristically changing the parameter values of the tree model and then letting the modeled trees interact with each other. To simulate the secondary succession, we considered the phenomenon such that one of the trees of the highest layer is blown down by a surrounding tree accidentally or after its death to create a large hole called a gap in the forest . The simulation was done by randomly choosing a tree in the highest layer and removing the trees in the circle, the center of the which is at the root of the falling tree and the radius of which is decided by the height of the tree.

The whole numerical experiment and simulation were conducted on a graphics mini supercomputer, Stellar GS1000. The trees were tabulated by the heights in a five meter unit. The highest tree was sixty meters tall. The following tables, Table 1 (a) - (g), show the result. In the tables, the word age means the number of cycles of simulation, one cycle corresponding to the yearly growth of the forest under simulation. The tables show the results of up to 250 cycles.

4. Visualization by Algorithmic Animation

By using the KEA-system as an enhanced tree model which is formal language-based and algorithmic, each tree in the forest was drawn. For rendering numerous numbers of tree leaves, they were substituted by the tips of the branches painted in the color of the leaves. By performing the *algorithmic animation* of the tree growth at a year interval, the tropical rain forest formation processes were visualized (regarding the extended explanation of algorithmic animation, see Thalmann and Thalmann 1990). The animation system was constructed on a graphic workstation, Personal IRIS.

Figs. 11 and 12 show the results of the visualization. Figs. 11 (a) through (g) are the side views of the forest, (a) at age 3, (b) at age 30, (c) at age 60, (d) at age 100, (e) at age 150, (f) at age 200 and (g) at age 250,respectively. Here, (a) through (c) up to the age of 60, visualize the early stage of the forest formation at which the trees have almost the same heights and are short. The following figures from (d) through (g) clearly visualizes the highest layer formation process started at age 60 and completed at around age 200 − 250, during the *primary succession* of the forest. Figures 12 (a) and (b) show the top and upper left views of an example of a gap in the forest created by a tree of the highest layer falling down accidentally or after its death at age 250 after the forest is turning into the *secondary succession*.

5. CONCLUSIONS

A simple interacting tree model FOREST is shown to be reasonably valid to visualize the global features of tropical rain forest formation processes during the primary and secondary successions by computer animation. It is a simplified model of the ecological interactions of trees through mutual shading, spatial mutual exclusion and gap creation at the death or accident of old trees blowing down the neighbors. The model of individual trees, the KEA-system, considers the internal properties of trees such as the rate of the light-photosynthesis relation, the death rate of the branches, and the rate of the foliage active in photosynthesis. It is a 4D tree model based on a parallel algorithm, and the algorithm is capable to be driven by the values of the internal properties to visualize the real processes of tree growth including the shapes of seedlings, the real branching sequence and the death of old branches.

From the ecological point of view, the work reported here represents the first-order approximation model in which only sunlight and physical mutual exclusion are considered as the factors of tree interactions and as the environmental factor. The higher-order approximations are those which take the other factors into account such as the effects of the other vegetation in the forests than the trees, the interactions with the animals living in the forests and the global factors. The global factors include the atmospheric change, particularly the change in the carbon dioxide density caused by the forests being modeled , the other forests and the other sources as well as the effects of ocean and soil. There is the environmental importance of forests and it is worth a brief mention here as the background motivation for our common interest in them. They heavily influence the density of carbon dioxide in the atmosphere. It used to be believed that the main reason for the atmospheric increase of carbon dioxide was consumption of oil and coal. Then, as Woodwell (1978) reported,

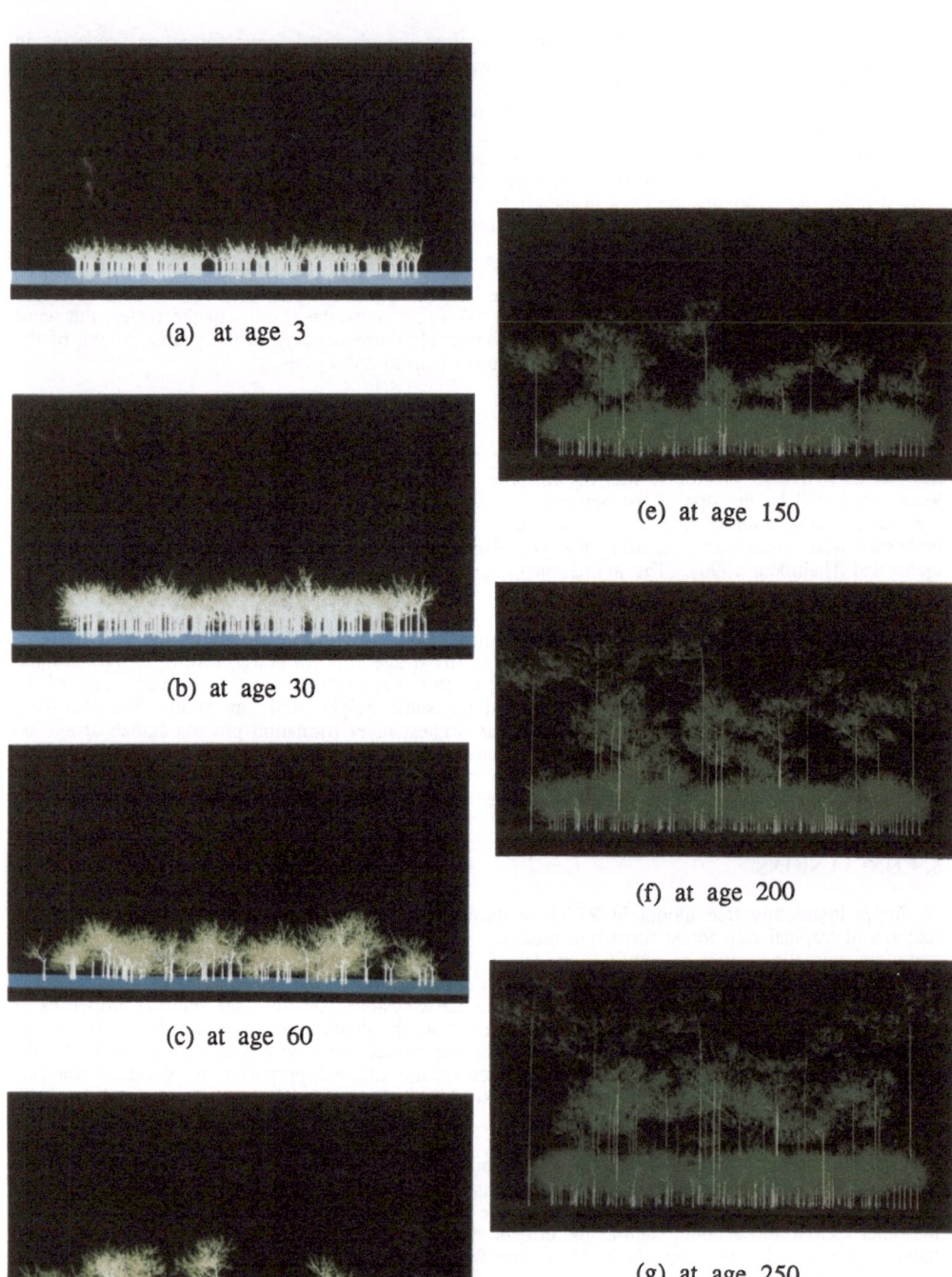

(a) at age 3

(b) at age 30

(c) at age 60

(d) at age 100

(e) at age 150

(f) at age 200

(g) at age 250

Fig.11   Side views of tropical rain forest growth

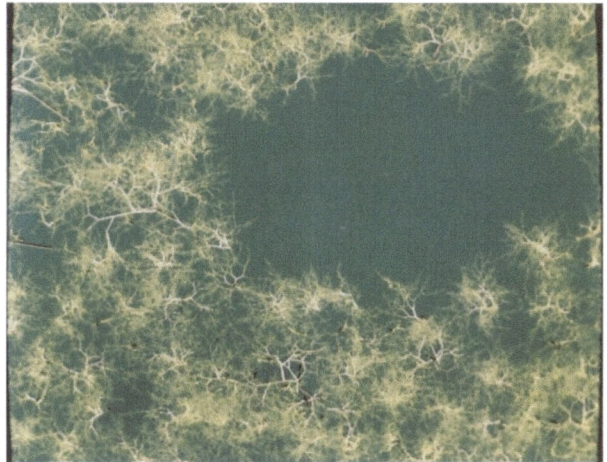

(a) top view

(b) upper left view

Fig.12 A forest with a gap at age 250

the destruction of forests, particularly tropical rain forests, is the more important reason of the increase of carbon dioxide. Including this report, the SCOPE Report series is an excellent source of information on the carbon cycle of the earth, and it indicates that the density of the atmospheric carbon dioxide is increasing, and consequently, the average temperature of the earth is rising. The warmer the earth becomes, the larger the total area of the deserts becomes. To rescue our planet the earth, the true knowledge on the nature of rain forests is now essential.

Thus, forests are the universe with unlimited importance, challenge and attraction for us, and this research represents only the initial effort of us to test the effectiveness of algorithmic computer animation to visualize the forest formation processes based on our previous research on a parallel algorithmic approach to tree shape modeling.

ACKNOWLEDGEMENTS

We are grateful to Professor Takehisa Oikawa of the University of Tsukuba, Professor Fusato Ogawa of Osaka City University and Mr. Nobuo Ikeda of NHK Osaka Station for valuable information on the structure of tropical rain forests. Particularly, Mr. Ikeda supplied us with necessary data on the tropical rain forests in Pasoh of peninsular Malaysia. Thanks are due to Asahi Chemical for providing us with Stellar GS1000 and to Nippon Silicon Graphics for Personal Iris.

REFERENCES

Aono M, Kunii TL (1984) Botanical tree image generation. IEEE Computer Graphics & Applications 4(5): 10-34

Barnsley MF, Jacquin A, Malassenet F, Reuter L, Sloan AD (1988) Harnessing chaos for image synthesis. Computer Graphics 22(4): 131-140

Bloomenthal J (1985) Modeling the mighty maple. Computer Graphics 19(3): 305-311

Clements FE (1916) Plant succession: An analysis of the development of vegetation. Carnegie Institute Pub. 242, Washington, D.C

Demko S (1985) Construction of fractal objects with iterated function systems. Computer Graphics 19(3): 271-278

Green M, Sun H (1988) A language and system for procedural modeling and motion. IEEE Computer Graphics & Applications 8(6): 52-64

Honda H (1978) Description of cellular patterns by Dirichlet domains: The two- dimensional case. J. Theor. Biol. 72: 523-543

Kira T (1987) Primary production and carbon cycling in a primeval lowland rainforest of peninsular Malaysia. Tree Crop Physiology. Elsevier, Amsterdam, pp 99-199

Mandelbrot B (1983) The fractal geometry of nature W. H. Freeman and Co., San Francisco

Norton A (1982) Generation and display of geometric fractals in 3-D. Computer Graphics 16(3): 61-67

Oikawa T (1985) Simulation of forest carbon dynamics based on a dry-matter production model. I. Fundamental model structure of a tropical rainforest ecosystem. Botany Magazine Tokyo 98: 225-238

Oikawa T (1986) Simulation of forest carbon dynamics based on a dry-matter production model. II. Effects of dry season upon a tropical rainforest ecosystem. Botany Magazine Tokyo 99: 213-223

Oikawa T (1986) Simulation of forest carbon dynamics based on a dry-matter production model. III. Effects of increasing CO_2 upon a tropical rainforest ecosystem. Botany Magazine Tokyo 99: 419-430

Prusinkiewicz P, Lindenmayer A, Hanan J (1988) Developmental models of herbaceous plants for computer imagery purpose. Computer Graphics 22(4): 141-150

Reeves WT (1983) Particle system - A technique for modeling a class of fuzzy objects. Computer Graphics 17(3): 359-376

Reffye P, Edelin C, Francon J, Jaeger M, Puech C (1988) Plant models faithful to botanical structure and development. Computer Graphics 22(4): 151-158

Shugart HH (1984) A theory of forest dynamics. Springer-Verlag, New York

Smith AR (1984) Plants, fractals, and formal languages. Computer Graphics 18(3):1-10

Thalmann NM, Thalmann D (1990) Synthetic actors. Springer-Verlag, Heidelberg

Woodwell GM (1978) The carbon dioxide questions. Scientific American 238: 34-43

Tosiyasu L. Kunii is currently Professor of Information and Computer Science, the University of Tokyo. At the University of Tokyo, he started his work in raster computer graphics in 1968 which was let to the Tokyo Raster Technology Project. His research interests include computer graphics, database systems, and software engineering. He authored and edited more than 32 computer science books, and published more than 120 refereed academic/technical papers in computer science and applications areas.

Dr. Kunii is Honorary President and Founder of the Computer Graphics Society, Fellow of IEEE, Editor-in-Chief of *The Visual Computer: An International Journal of Computer Graphics* (Springer-Verlag), Associate Editor-in-Chief of *The Journal of Visualization and Computer Animation* (John Wiley & Sons) and on the Editorial Board of *IEEE Transactions on Knowledge and Data Engineering, VLDB Journal* and *IEEE Computer Graphics and Applications*. He is on the IFIP Modeling and Simulation Working Group, the IFIP Data Base Working Group and the IFIP Computer Graphics Working Group. He organized and was chairing the Technical Committee on Software Engineering of the Information Processing Society of Japan from 1976 to 1981. He also organized and was President of the Japan Computer Graphics Association(JCGA) from 1981 to 1983. He served as General Chairman of the 3rd International Conference on Very Large Data Bases(VLDB) in 1977, Program Chairman of InterGraphics in 1983, Organizing Committee Chairman and Program Chairman of Computer Graphics Tokyo in 1984, Program Chairman of Computer Graphics Tokyo in 1985 and 1986, Organizing Committee Chairperson and Program Chairperson of CG International '87, Program Co-Chairman of IEEE COMPSAC '87, and Honorary Committee Chairperson of CG International '88. He served as Organizing Committee Chairperson and Program Chairperson of IFIP TC-2/WG 2.6 Working Conference on Visual Database Systems in 1989, Program Co-Chairperson of CG International '90 and Program Chairperson of IFIP TC-5/WG 5.10 Working Conference on Modeling in Computer Graphics in 1991 and the member of the Organizing Committee of IEEE COMPSAC '91. He is on the board of directors of Japan Society of Sports Industry and also of Japan Society of Simulation and Gaming.

He received the B.Sc., M.Sc., and D.Sc. degrees in chemistry all from the University of Tokyo in 1962, 1964, and 1967, respectively. He is a fellow of IEEE and a member of ACM, BCS, IPSJ and IEICE.

Address: Department of Information Science, Faculty of Science, the University of Tokyo, 7-3-1 Hongo, Bunkyo-Ku,Tokyo, 113 Japan

Hirohisa Enomoto is currently a doctoral graduate student of information science at the University of Tokyo. His research interests include computer graphics and parallel processing. He received the B.Sc. and M.Sc. degrees in information science from the University of Tokyo in 1988 and 1990 respectively.
Address: Department of Information Science, Faculty of Science, the University of Tokyo, 7-3-1 Hongo, Bunkyo-Ku,Tokyo, 113 Japan

Dynamic Scenes Management for Animation with Ray-Tracing Rendering

H. Maurel, B. Moisan, J.P. Jessel, Y. Duthen, and R. Caubet

ABSTRACT :

In this paper, we present an animation method based on a dynamic management of the scene. These works have been developed within the framework of the VOXAR (VOXel ARchitecture) project which initial purpose was to build a real time parallel machine to compute image synthesis by the ray-tracing method. We describe the space repartition on the hardware topology by rolling up the space around the processor network. We explain the data connexity needed for ray tracing. Then, we present the capabilities of handling object using the same partition of space. This approach allows us to compute animation of complex scene without prohibitive time in front of rendering time. We show the animation kernel and the automatic mechanism used to control motions and variations of the components (objects, lights, camera) in a 3D scene.

Key Words : ray-tracing, voxel, space management, animation, mobile.

1. OVERVIEW

The initial purpose of the VOXAR (**VOX**el **AR**chitecture) project (Gaildrat 1988, Pitot 1989a) is to build a real time massive parallel machine to compute image synthesis by the ray-tracing method (Whitted, 1980). The cost of this rendering method is one of the most expensive because, in a basic implementation of the algorithm, the computation time increases like an exponential function of the objects' number, but on contrary, it seems to be one of the most attractive because of the high quality of produced images inclosing reflecting, refracting and shading effects.

Two approaches appear to speed up the rendering time, when increasing the computational power by using a parallel machine : either duplicating the scene in each processor and sharing out the pixels of the screen (Brusq, 1986), or sharing out the scene among the processors and using a regular (Fujimoto, 1986) (Amanatides, 1987) or an adaptative (Glassner, 1984) (Dippe, 1984) (Kobayachi, 1988) (Bouatouch, 1988) spatial subdivision method. We have chosen to implement an incremental integer logic algorithm into a regular space partition.

The roots of the VOXAR project are in the real world observance : the smallest physical item is an actor of the world (Gaildrat et al , 1988). It is able to send and receive requests such as light energy, sound .... Each quanta of matter can analyze and respond to a message coming from its environment with its own knowledge and its own physical features. More over, we can note that this information exchanges are between neighbouring items. So, we divide space into voxels which are small cubic elements used as spatial increment unit for objects' storage and light propagation. So we join an active space location (a voxel) with a processor, communicating with its neighbours, like the natural item, using links on the six adjoining processors (the six faces of a voxel). But for a common 1000x1000x1000 voxels scene, it means a giga-processors network, this is not credible. Then we introduce the metavoxel, which is a cubic matrix of contiguous voxels, to reduce the processors number.

In the first part, we describe the data distribution method on the hardware topology (Hypertorus) by rolling up the metavoxels on the processors network (like a rope around a ring), then we present the cutting up of the application into a set of tasks duplicated on each cell. In a second part, we study the capabilities to handle and to animate objects in the VOXAR system. In this paper, we show the capabilities of our system to produce movies. The implementation of the ray-tracing in Voxar has been presented in the following publications (Pitot 1989a, 1989d, 1990a).

In the image synthesis world, different modeling methods exist (CSG, polygons, free form surfaces, ...). Our special feature is to use the atom mesh model, an unified representation that has been introduced in (Jessel et al 1989c, 1989e), which allows to use the same rendering algorithm in the VOXAR machine for objects of a scene built with non equivalent primitives. This representation makes the rendering time independent of the objects' complexity because it associates the whole information of an object (color, texture, ...) with an atom. So, it permits to store a local knowledge in atoms and then, in voxels (Cipres et al 1989b, Pitot et al 1990b). As for the mesh concept, a topologic link is used to implement an interpolation mechanism. We explain why and wherefore we place the meshes into the voxels and why "voxelised" objects are not continually used.

For many handling operations, the minimal internal representation model can be used, in which meshes are only known in the metavoxels. So we deduce the different abstraction levels in the objects' processing, belonging to the hierarchical set of the objects' states implemented in the software. We decompose each possible transformation with a state transition graph, to apply it on the suitable internal form of the object. This allows a complete dynamic handling of the scene. This approach has been used to implement a first animation kernel. From the software development, we introduce the "mobile" notion and the timing structure. We present the advantages of this method to implement an error handling mechanism : the capability of recovering the computation anywhere in a sequence.

2. GENERAL WORKING DESCRIPTION

The VOXAR machine is composed of two processor sets : cells and devices. The first set is the computation network. Organized in an HYPERTORUS (a tri-dimensional cyclical matrix (see fig. 1), cells are working in an asynchronous way, by achieving the same program with a distributed data set. The second one is a set of particular processors added like grafts on the computation network. In a basic configuration, this set is reduced to the Host, which permits communications with a conventional host machine.

The model nowadays used consists in a network composed of 36 Transputers T800c by INMOS, with each 4 Mb, set up in a 4 x 3 x 3 HYPERTORUS. The network is managed via a T800c communication board connected on the PC-bus of a DOMAIN 4000 Apollo workstation.

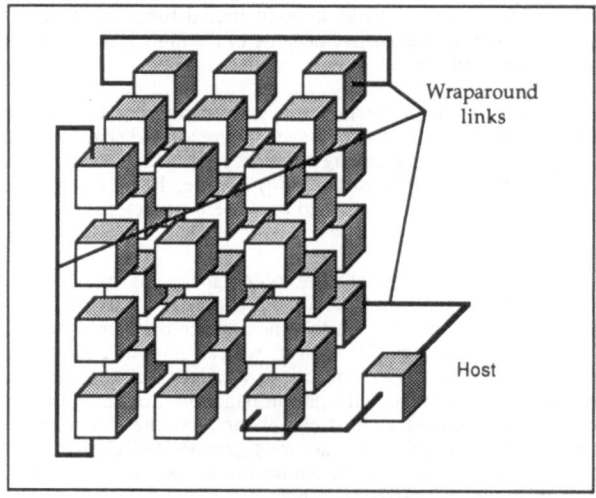

fig. 1 : an example of HYPERTORUS

The Transputer is designed to multi-tasks, then the context permutation is a basic operation. These characteristics have led us to a conceptual cutting for the application where a treatment is affected to a task. A task starts a local treatment when it receives a message, and may emit itself messages to other tasks. To support this conception, we have developed a communication layer, allowing two tasks on any two processors in the network to converse in a transparent way. The control and the driving of the application are ensured by a set of specialized tasks grouped on the Host. This allows, for instance, the data distribution or the computed image gathering.

3. MODELING AND DATA DISTRIBUTION

There are two main characteristics of the implanted modeling. The first one is the capability to unify many classical models such as CSG, polygons, free form surfaces, particles, fractals... The second one is the ability to store objects' features (color, texture, light...) locally.

To satisfy these criteria, the sampling of objects' surface has been chosen to represent objects. These samples are called atoms and contain object's characteristics at the sampled point. Atoms are linked together by topological links, allowing to simulate the sampled surface. Elementary items on which intersections are computed are meshes of tree atoms (see fig. 2). Optical features at the intersection point are interpolated according to its relative position into the mesh. Each mesh may be seen as a simple face with the assumption that the surface between the samples is plane.

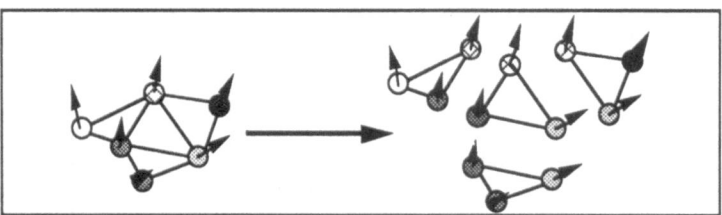

fig. 2: a net and atoms meshes

Objects handled by VOXAR are described by meshes nets. They are initially loaded on the Host, then distributed on the network. This scattering is based on space rolling around the processors matrix, because wraparound links allow space continuity. So, a mesh is attributed to the processor handling the space part, actually a Metavoxel (a cubic set of contiguous voxels) in which it is physically located, as shown in fig. 3.

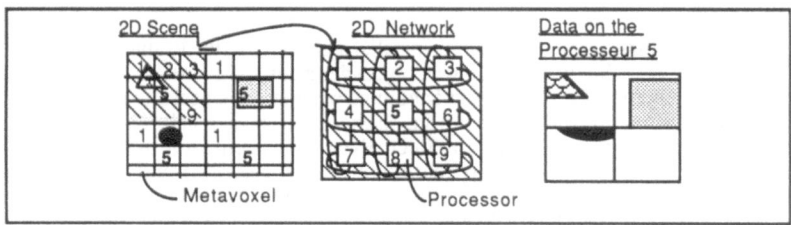

fig. 3 : data distribution in a 2D space

This distribution method ensures a statistical load balance between cells, but points out a problem: a mesh must be represented only once in the machine. A mesh may belong to several volumes handled by several processors. In order to avoid this, a mesh is asserted to have only one reference point, and it is stored in the cell owning the vertex (atom) with the smallest coordinates. The total order in the coordinates space is given by :

$$(x1, y1, z1) < (x2, y2, z2) <=> x1 < x2 \text{ or } (x1 = x2 \text{ et } y1 < y2) \text{ or } (x1 = x2 \text{ et } y1 = y2 \text{ et } z1 < z2)$$

4. LOADING OBJECTS

According to the data distribution, the loading process may be resumed by : the creation request is sent to every cell, then each one creates an object descriptor and a storage structure for associated meshes. After this, each mesh is received by the target processor determined by the Host.

Meshes are stored in a list associated to their object, see fig. 4. Because the loaded meshes may have common atoms, without any control, these atoms would be duplicated and the maximum modeling data quantity would be reduced. To solve this problem, atoms are created in a structure avoiding duplication. Objects' meshes refer to atoms in this structure. This knowledge state is the minimal objects representation in VOXAR.

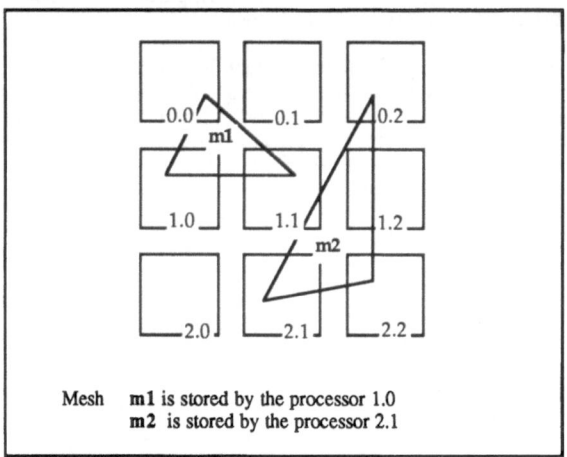

Mesh **m1** is stored by the processor 1.0
      m2 is stored by the processor 2.1

fig. 4 : cells state after loading (in a 2D space)

We can note that the object meshes list may be empty in a cell, if the corresponding processor does not handle any volume crossed by an object part.

5. OBJECTS HANDLING

In many ray-tracing algorithm implementations on parallel architectures, the loading time of complex scenes can be greater than the rendering time. Moving an object demands sometimes the complete loading of the scene. Our representation model allows object handlings without comebacks to the modeling or loading steps. To apply a transformation on an object leads to execute it in each cell. The Host distributes to the cells an object number and the operation to effect. Every transformation that does not affect atoms coordinates may be implanted in such a way (changing texture, color, ...). In case of modification, two steps are needed, as shown in fig. 5. The first one is the coordinates and normal vector transformation itself, the second one is the meshes re-affectation according to the mesh location assumption.

These operations are applied using homogeneous coordinates matrices. An atom can be stored in different cells. As the same determinist treatment is done everywhere in the same step, the distributed database is always coherent. After the transformation of objects' meshes geometry, meshes are scanned in each cell. Those that do not belong anymore to the space associated with the cell are removed and sent to the appropriate cell to be stored. This is shown in fig. 5 : the Host sends to every cell the message that specify the operation and the concerned object (see bold arrow), then each cell, once the transformation effected, sends meshes removed by itself, one after one, to their respective storage processors (see simple arrow).

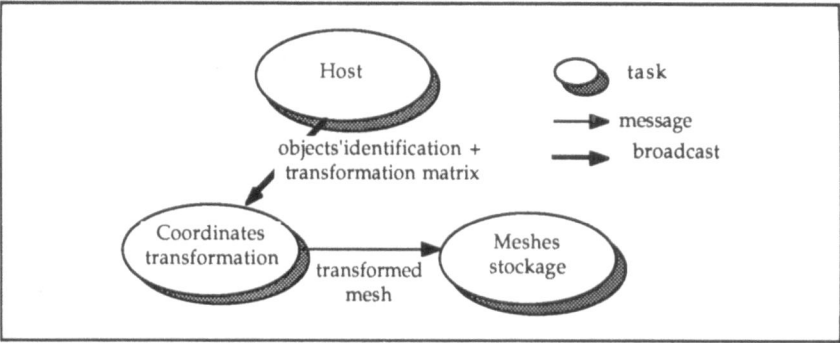

fig. 5 : object 3D transformation tasks and data

We can notice that these operations may act on several objects in parallel. Elements treated by these operations (meshes) know the object they are belonging to. To replace meshes, the task which manages the mesh location into a cell acts according to the object's number read into the mesh and with respect to the location rule. So, receiving a mesh relative to an object then another one for another object does not present any problem.

6. THE RAY-TRACING IN VOXAR

The ray-tracing algorithm in VOXAR is based on following up the light path from voxels to voxels. So, it is obvious that voxels must know meshes crossing their space. But it is also clearly impossible to create all the voxels into the scene space : a great deal of voxels would not refer to any mesh. So, grouping voxels into metavoxels has been introduced to avoid empty voxels generation, and to allow rays to cross empty spaces faster.

Since the loading step, objects are assumed to be known by cells as lists of meshes. As voxels and metavoxels must know which meshes cross their space, a mechanism to merge meshes into the two structures of voxels and metavoxels is needed to compute images. This new knowledge representation is the maximal objects representation state supported by the application: objects are "voxelized".

With respect to the meshes distribution on processors shown in fig. 4, for this new state, **m1** is stored by processors 0.0, 1.0, 1.1, and **m2** is stored by processors 0.2, 1.1, 1.2, 2.1, 2.2.

To allow minimal to maximal representation changing, there are two successive cuttings for objects' meshes. The first one, according to the metavoxel structure, which leads to metavoxel identification and points out processors which have to memorize the mesh. The second cutting is to select voxels involved in each metavoxel. In every voxel cut by a mesh, the knowledge of the whole mesh is needed in order to interpolate feature linked to the intersection point (see fig. 6). The use of topological links is very useful for this.

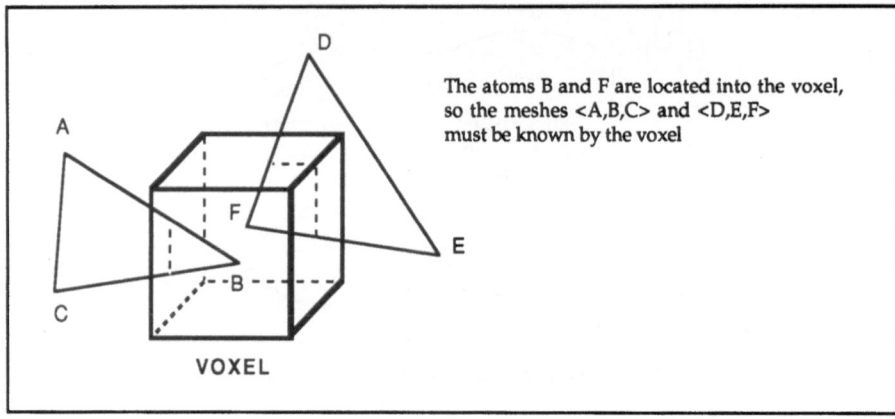

fig. 5 : meshes-voxel association

7. TWO REPRESENTATIONS

These two states of representation for objects define two accesses to the objects' modeling data : a global access by objects' meshes lists, and a local access by voxels which allows to identify matter samples (from one or several objects) present in that voxel. From the "voxelized" representation , it is easy to come back to natural representation. To find voxels to be modified, in each cell, meshes are cut in voxels (not in metavovels). If the treated mesh does not agree the location rule, it is removed from this cell, and this operation is locally executed in each cell. At every time, an object loaded in the machine is characterized by his state, which is a subset of the following set of states : {"voxelized"= present in voxels, "un-voxelized"= access by cells lists only, "located"= location rule respected, "un-located"= location rule transgressed}.

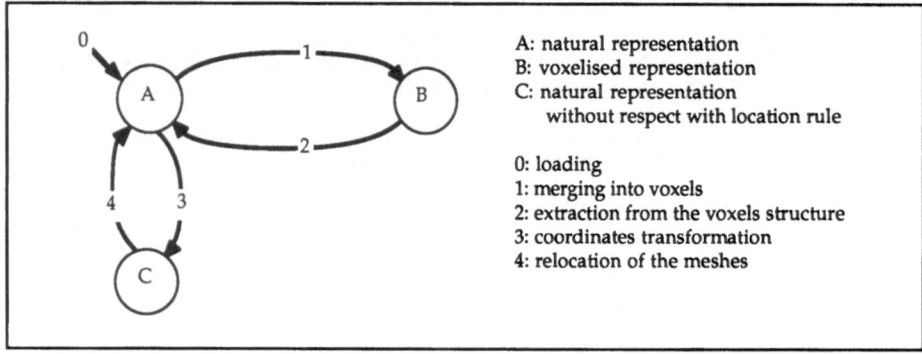

fig. 6 : state changes automaton

The combination of these different states associated to the dynamic mechanism of transformations application have allowed us to build a set of functions to handle objects:
- translations, rotations in the objet or the scene basis
- scaling (homogeneous or not)
- color, texture and optical properties changes
- creation (loading), removal
- hiding (object is present but not visible for the ray-tracing)

To define a state automaton allows us to determine automatically which state changes to execute before handling an object or computing images.

8. ANIMATING OBJECTS.

A lot of ray-tracing implementations compute images sequences in which only the observer is moving, and so, a scene re-organization is not needed, as it is viewer independent. On the other hand, creating, moving, removing objects lead to change the scene organization. This is a very expensive treatment, and almost, often equivalent to load and create the whole scene, as before the first image computation.

In this case, our approach is very economical : we dispose of basic functions to modify the scene between two images. A software layer involved to animation, based on the dynamic scene management allows to take into account the following tools for scenography :

> 1 - image parameters
>   rays tree depth
>   image size
>   background color
> 2 - view characteristics
>   viewer location
>   aimed point location
>   viewport orientation and aperture
> 3 - object staging and objects' characteristics changing
>   as described in §7
> 4 - light staging
>   creation and removal
>   intensity changes
>   moving

Each of these functions group is fitted with a list of entry points into the interface, allowing either an interactive use, or an automatic treatment driven by a script (text file interpreted by the machine).

The above decomposition, materialized in the software by an abstract data type hierarchy, points out the capability to handle fundamental objects involved in the animation: objects, lights, and the observer, which is selected into a set of potentially activated cameras. To allow an uniform management for all these actors, we introduce the notion of "mobile", that is the active component in a sequence, based on a couple actor-role. The role is, until now, reduced to the description of the actor's evolution in the scene according to the time : that is its trajectory in the space-time. The main interest of this approach is the ability to assign the same role (trajectory) to several actors : for example, if we have to follow a plane flying in a given direction with the camera, it is sufficient to link the aimed point for the camera and the plane reference point to the same physical trajectory.

A trajectory is defined as the linear interpolation of a set of continuous Bezier's curves. The duration and rotation angles around the three axes are linked to each segment. Furthermore, when the mobile is defined, we may restrain the course from a starting date to an end date. For complex motion with object rotations, we must associate a local basis to the object. In a simple way, we don't change the object in its local basis because it is more advisable for the user to choose the rotation axis and the angle when the object keeps the same orientation in its basis. In fact, to define the rotations of an object the user gives a rotation angle on each axis of the local basis.

The animation kernel is based on a scheduler. It ensures the script to be executed step by step, with or without associated image computation. This is allowed by giving a starting date available for all the sequence shooting. The sequence is defined by its duration in seconds and the number of images to be shot in a second. The general structure of the scheduler is given by the following algorithm:

```
Begin
For t = 0 to t_end step delta_t
        Begin
        For_each mobile m
                pre-location of m using trajectory(m,t)
        If t >= t_beg Then
                Begin
                freeze the scene
                compute image(t)
                End
        End
End
```

The mobile pre-location step consists in the evaluation the treatment to apply on the mobile between the date t and the date t + delta_t. For sources and cameras, this step is reduced to the change of one or several characteristics. For objects, this step is made of two distinct operations. First of them is the automaton evaluation, as shown in fig. 6, to deduce state changes needed to apply modifications to the mobile (translation and rotations according to the trajectory). After this, it is necessary to react modifications on atoms coordinates using transformation matrices built using parameters from the trajectory (location, angles). The process to freeze the scene leads visible objects set in the state allowing images computation (see fig. 6) : it ensures relocation of meshes belonging to modified objects and the associated voxel creation.

The interest of this approach is that expensive treatments are used only before computing an image. First, these operations are made only on modified objects, and then, computation time needed for them are negligible in front of image computation time, that minimizes the time required for the animation (Maiocchi, 1990). According to the time used to compute a sequence, the failure probability for a parallel machine running a software still in development step is quite important. Technics used for our animation allow back-up mechanisms to work. As seen before, while introducing the scheduler, time to start the shot is different to time to start script interpretation. If we want to restart a sequence from image n, images from 0 to n-1 do not cost anything, as there is no image computation, no meshes relocation, and no merge into the voxels structure. The resumption time is linear with respect to number and complexity of objects, and also it is always less important than time used to load the scene. This point is linked to the two following observations : the first one is that the loading operation from the modeling file is the most expensive work, and the second one is that the relocation is executed after the end of the resumption only, before computing the first image.

9. RESULTS, LIMITS AND PERSPECTIVES

These developments allowed the realization of several animated sequences, for a total time of more than 30 seconds. The computation of more than 500 images has been necessary. The images size is 576x768 pixels (NTSC standard), with an average computation time of 20 minutes, for tree depths from 5 to 8. These sequences are included in "Grimoire", a videotape produced by the I.R.I.T. and regional partners.

The figure 7 is a quite simple example that shows some typical ray-tracing effects such as shadows, reflects and transparency. The mirror is made of a transparent glass behind a perfect reflector. The figure 8 presents an animation of 25 images (128x128 pixels). The scene takes place into a children bedroom. The bedside lamp flies through the room to the window, producing shadows and enlightened parts changes. The lamp is composed of a transparent sphere around a spotlight. Both of them are linked to the same trajectory.

In our application, un-voxelized objects are not treated by the ray-tracing. In a complex 3D scene, each object is not necessary visible. So, it would be interesting to look for objects effectively reached by a ray, and then, to put them into the voxels structure. G. Hégron proposed in 1987 an algorithm for the dynamical management of 3D scenes based on a binary space partition in which a sensor, or a viewer, moves. The database modifications needed according to the viewer's displacement are computed using a sub-area adjacency graph. This approach is not directly suitable to the ray-tracing. Objects involved in rendering a scene including specular objects are not easy to find, and surely not if the viewer's perception field is restricted to a close space.

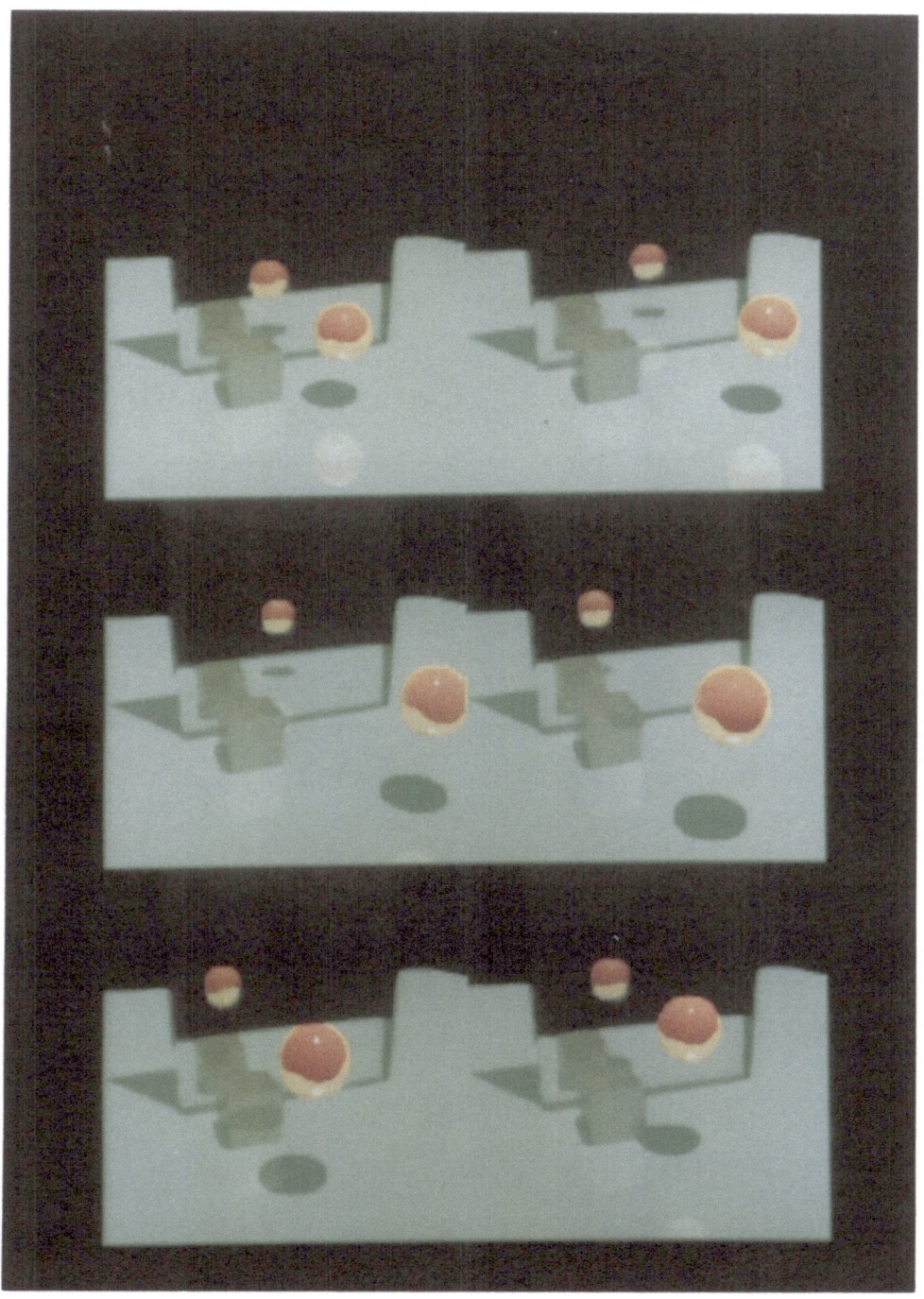

fig. 7

fig. 8

Until now, all the animation work is handmade by the system user. The introduction of hierarchical levels to manage groups of objects will relieve him of the burden of animate a group of characters with the same global motion. The modeling elements location into voxels allows to consider the implementation of an inter-object collisions detection algorithm (Moore et al 1988) using the parallelism induced by the space partition on the network. Even if our approach allows animation process automation with ray-tracing rendering, it does not include neither "intelligent animation" concepts (Boulic R, Thalmann , 1990) to describe sophisticated motions, nor behavorial simulation paradigms (Rainjonneau 1988, 1989, 1990a, 1990b) to simulate flocks animations. This aspect is one of our main orientations for future works.

10. BIBLIOGRAPHY

Amanatides J, Woo A (1987) "A Fast Voxel Traversal Algorithm for Ray Tracing"
  Proceedings of EUROGRAPHICS '87

Bouatouch K, Priol T (1988) "Parallel Space Tracing: An Experience on an IPSC Hypercube"
  Proceedings of CGI, May 88, page 170.

Boulic R,Magnenat-Thalmann N and Thalmann D (1990) "Human Free-Walking Model for Real-Time Interactive Design of Gaits" Proceedings of Computer Animation'90 (Springer - Verlag)

Brusq R (1986) "Synthèse d'image par lancer de rayon: la machine CRISTAL; Résultats et Perspectives."
  Cesta, Nice 1986.

Cipres P, Jessel J. P, Caubet R, Duthen Y, Martin V (1989b)
  "Intégration des textures solides à la modélisation des objets." MICAD Février 1989.

Dippe M, Swensen J (1984) "An adaptative subdivision algorithm and parallel architecture for realistic image synthesis"
  SIGRAPH ACM vol 18, n° 3, 1984.

Fujimoto A, Tanaka T, Iwata K (1986) "ARTS: Accelerated Ray-Tracing System"
  IEEE Computer Graphics & Application 04/86.

Gaildrat-Inguimbert V, Caubet R, Duthen Y (1988)
  "A tridimentional architecture for fast realistic image synthesis." Proceedings of COMPUTER GRAPHICS INTERNATIONAL, Mai 1988.

Glassner A.S (1984) "Space subdivision for fast ray tracing".
  IEEE Computer Graphic & Application, April 1984.

Hégron G (1987) " Dynamic management of 3D scenes" In the acts of *proc* EUROGRAPHICS'87, Amsterdam,
  EUROGRAPHICS, AUGUST 1987.

Jessel J.P, Cipres P, Pitot P, Caubet R, Duthen Y (1989c)
  "Une modélisation unifiée intégrant des informations locales: La discrétisation en atomes." PIXIM Septembre 1989.

Jessel J.P, Pitot P, Caubet R, Duthen Y (1989e)
  "Deformations d'objets modélisés par réseaux d'atomes" Journées AFCET-GROPLAN, Strasbourg, Décembre 1989, Actes: Revue BIGRE n° 67, Janvier 1990.

Jessel J.P , Caubet R, Duthen Y (1990b)
  "A progressive radiosity including specularity: a parallel approach" Computer Graphics 90, conference proceedings.

Kobayachi H, Nakamura T, Shigei Y (1988) "A strategy for mapping parallel Ray-tracing into a hypercube multiprocessor System" Proceedings of CGI, Mai 88, page 160

Maiocchi R, Pernicci B (1990) "Directing an animated scene with autonomous actors"
  Proceedings of Computer Animation'90 (Springer - Verlag)

Moore M, Wilhelms J (1988) "Collision detection and Response for Computer Animation".
  Computer Graphics, Volume22, Number 4, August 1988

Pitot P, Caubet R, Duthen Y, Gaildrat V (1989a)
  "Le suivi analytique de rayons: Un algorithme incrémental rapide pour la machine VOXAR." MICAD Février 1989.

Pitot P, Caubet R, Duthen Y (1989d)
"A parallel Architecture for the ray tracing" Proceedings of CG89, October 1989.

Pitot P, Moisan B, Caubet R, Duthen Y (1990a)
"A Transputer based implementation of the VOXAR project" Euromicro 90.

Rainjonneau S, Caubet R, Duthen Y (1988) "Synthèse d'image: Une approche par objet pour l'implantation d'un nouveau modèle d'éclairage et la simulation comportementale d'objets animés."
Journées AFCET GROPLAN novembre 1988.

Rainjonneau S, Caubet R, Duthen Y (1989) "Synthèse d'image: La simulation comportementale d'objets animés, une approche
orientée objets couplée à un moteur d'inférence." JTEA 1989.

Rainjonneau S, Caubet R, Duthen Y (1990a) "Object oriented technology for implementation of a behavorial simulation model" Firth international Eiffel user group conference, Paris june 1990

Rainjonneau S, Prouvost O, Caubet R, Duthen Y (1990b) "A behavorial simulation model for computer animation" Computer Graphics 90, conference proceedings

Whitted T (1980) "An improved illumination model for shaded display."
Comm ACM vol 29, n° 6, June 1980, pp. 343-349.

Hervé Maurel is PhD student since september 90. His interest is in animation and motion control.
Address: I.R.I.T, université Paul Sabatier 118 rte de Narbonne
        31062 Toulouse cedex
        E-mail address : herve@fermat.irit.fr

Bruno Moisan is also PhD student since september 90. He feels an interest in communication systems involved to parallel architectures.
Address: I.R.I.T, université Paul Sabatier 118 rte de Narbonne
        31062 Toulouse cedex
        E-mail address : moisan@fermat.irit.fr

Jean Pierre Jessel will be PhD graduate in 1991. He takes interest in modeling and rendering, he brought out the atom mesh model.
Address: I.R.I.T, université Paul Sabatier 118 rte de Narbonne
        31062 Toulouse cedex FRANCE
        E-mail address : jessel@fermat.irit.fr

They are both at Paul Sabatier University of Toulouse and they belong to the IRIT computer graphics team directed by Professor René Caubet assisted by Yves Duthen.

Utilizing Parallel Processing in Computer Animation

F. Van Reeth and E. Flerackers

ABSTRACT

When designing and developing a 3D computer animation system, numerous interrelated issues and concepts have to be taken into account. Given our limiting factors of a low starting budget and the knowledge that current and future animation systems require huge amounts of processing power, we came to the development of a 3D computer animation system using a transputer platform. A description is given of how we combined traditional animation techniques with the facilities of our Computer Animation Environment Language, yielding a powerful 3D animation system in which animations can be produced that previously could take a considerable amount of time.

Keywords : computer animation, programming environments, 3D modelling, transputers

1. INTRODUCTION

During 1987, our research group at the Applied Computer Science Laboratory in the Limburg University Center set out a goal to develop a computer animation system that could satisfy the always increasing demands of three-dimensional computer animation productions. Given the limiting conditions of a relatively low starting budget, our former inability to develop special purpose hardware, and the knowledge that the ultimate system would require a large processing capacity, it turned out that a parallel processing approach was the one we had to follow.

On the one hand this allowed us to start designing and implementing the basic algorithms on a modest three processor platform, while on the other hand we could be able to satisfy the processing power need in fullfledged systems by gradually increasing the number of working processors in the system. The processors at issue are of the transputer family. These are fast 32-bit micro processors with built-in features for parallel processing. In the early stage of the project, the OCCAM language (INMOS Ltd. 1988) turned out to be the most suitable and almost only available programming language. OCCAM is based on Hoare's parallel programming model of communicating sequential processes (Hoare 1985). Currently we are gradually transfering our implementation towards a parallel version of the C programming language. The availability of high-level data structures, recursion, a more suitable programming infrastructure and a larger potential of people that efficiently can program in C (as opposed to OCCAM) are the main reasons for this.

In (Magnenat-Thalmann 1985) one can find a classification of computer animation systems that distinguishes between *computer-assisted* and *modelled* animation. The former is closely related to traditional animation and merely aims at using a computer for supporting and improving the (mostly two-dimensional) animation production : the support delivered by the machine involves mainly automated coloring and/or inbetweening. In the latter, the computer is not just used for assisting the animation process, it is the central instrument by which complete three-dimensional productions are built.

Modelled animation involves, from a designers point of view, (1) the creation of objects, (2) the specification of motion and (3) the rendering of images (the development of a storyboard, video recording and post production techniques are not treated in this paper). Recent research on modelled animation has resulted in numerous techniques and systems for developing complex animation. Aside interactive and scripting systems, methods for goal-directed motion, kinetics-, (inverse) kinematics- and/or dynamics-based animation have been developed (Krömker 1989; Magnenat-Thalmann 1985, 1989).

The system we have developed (and still continue to develop) basically is a hybrid between an interactive and a scripting system (Feiner 1982; Gomez 1984; Reynolds 1982; Stern 1983). On the interactive side, the animator has an environment at his/her disposal for positioning 3D object models, lights and camera's in the virtual world at key-frames. After the specification of the key-frames, suitable interpolation is applied for defining 3D data between the key-frames. On the scripting side, a specialized programming language is provided for definition of 3D object data, as well as 3D motion data. Both approaches have their advantages and limitations: Movements that exhibit algorithmic behaviour and objects that can be defined mathematically, can easily be handled by scripting systems. Not every refined motion, however, can comfortably be specified by them. In interactive systems, animators have the ability of freely controlling every aspect of the animation. Their major disadvantage, however, is that they induce the specification of substantial amounts of input data by the animator. By using powerful parametrization mechanisms, some systems (Ostby 1989) tend to overcome this problem.

By providing a hybrid animation environment between an interactive and scripting system, we try to get the best of both worlds. The utilization of interactively manipulatable curves and CAEL, our computer animation environment language, play an important role in this approach, as will be shown in subsequent sections.

Section 2 gives an overview of our parallel hardware platform and stipulates the main characteristics of transputers. Section 3 and 4 subsequently elucidate the object and motion modeling aspects of our system, whereas Section 5 focuses on the rendering. Conclusions and possible future research are given in Section 6.

229

2. SYSTEM OVERVIEW

In the design and development of a 3D computer animation system, numerous interrelated factors have to be taken into account, influencing software decisions as well as hardware decisions : Does one opt to use existing workstations and/or architectures or does one choose to develop special purpose architectures... Can one use existing software packages or does one decide to develop a fully integrated software system with in-house software... We took the challenge to create a 3D animation system from scratch, so we could tune the system in any direction we wanted and explore ideas that otherwise would be difficult (if not impossible) to realize.

As stated in the introduction, several limiting conditions forced us to look for a parallel processing solution. Concretely, processors of the transputer family turned out to be well-suited for the job. Transputers are 20 MIPS / 1.5 MFlops 32-bit micro-processors that are specifically designed to work in parallel (Fig. 1). Indeed, the four serial link interfaces enable the processor to communicate at 20 Mbit / sec with other members of the transputer family (and this without bothering the CPU too much). The communication is synchronized : i.e., if a process wishes to communicate with another process, it has to wait until the other is also ready to communicate. Hardware logic for rapid context switching during scheduling and descheduling of different parallel processes on one specific processor is also foreseen. We will come back to utilization of buffering techniques and parallelism on one processor later on. Together with the parallel processing features, the traditional logic for system services, memory interfacing logic and the CPU, the transputer also has 4K of very fast on-chip Static RAM. Moreover, the processor type we use (T800) has an on-chip 64 bit floating point unit.

Figure 2 gives an overview of the entire hardware platform. At the top left of the figure one can see we use a PC as our host system. This PC boots our transputer network and it acts as a platform for the I/O equipment. Currently, the I/O equipment consists of a graphical tablet (or mouse) for input purposes (e.g. 2D digitizing), an optical disk storage device (WORM) for storing a digital back-up of our images and a video recorder for single framing our images. A 3D digitizer is under development and some other non-standard input/output media (e.g. speech and speech recognition) are under investigation. Depending on the functionality of the processor in the system, a different amount of memory is available to the processor. For the workers, a capacity of 2 Mbyte is foreseen, while the host boards could have any capacity (influencing the maximum size of the object- & texture data base) from 4 Mbyte up to 32 Mbyte. The graphics boards also have a graphical coprocessor at their disposal.

As transputers are relatively simple to interface at the hardware level, a gateway is left open for incorporating other processors (e.g., the Intel i860 or DSP chips) or special purpose hardware (e.g., large memory banks) in our system. Currently, however, these gateways have not yet left the design stage.

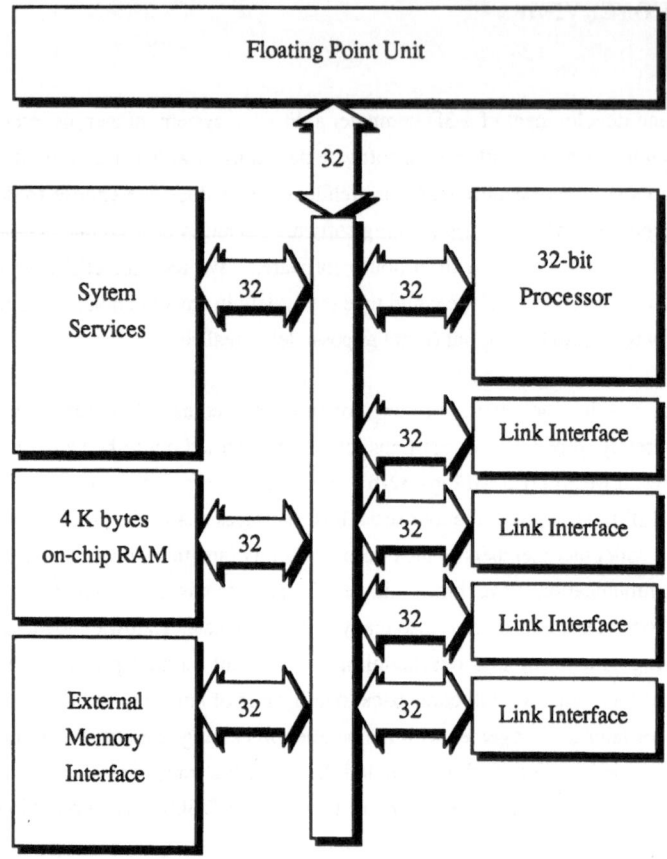

Fig. 1 . Transputer Functional Diagram

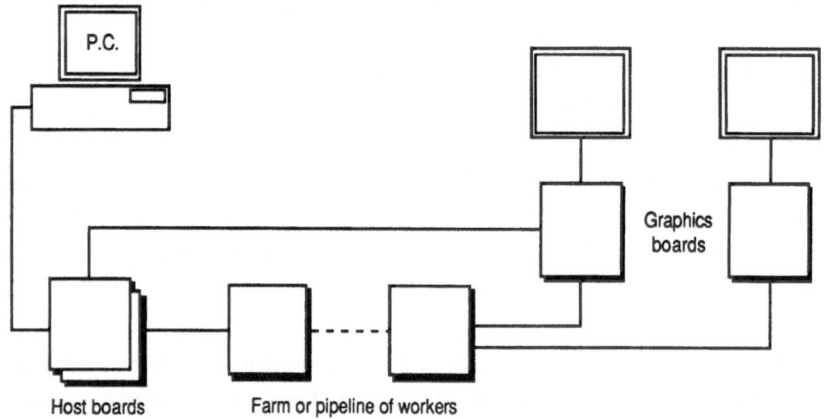

Fig. 2. System Overview

3. OBJECT MODELLING

When developing a 3D object modeller in a Computer Animation system, several important issues have to be tackled relating to object creation, object animation and object rendering respectively. Of course, the ultimate goal of the animation severely influences the representation of objects : e.g., when the animation has structural analysis purposes, a polygonal approximation of objects often will not suffice, while animations for the "fun industry" rarely require exact mathematical representations via higher order curved surfaces.

Objects should be represented in such a way that they can be easily created and manipulated by animators. Appropriate tools have to be offered, enabling animators and designers to define and shape objects according to their specific wishes. These tools should maintain a consistent internal representation as much as possible (i.e., no zero area polygons, reversed normals, broken smoothness, unforeseen holes, etc. should be introduced) as data anomalies can cause serious problems in the rendering stage of an animation project with deadlines looking around the corner. A good user interface is very important in order to satisfy the above statements. On the one hand, the available tools should be accessible to a novice animator/user of the system via a graphical interface, while they also should be accessible to an experienced user through a fast command line alike interface. On the other hand, a continuous visual feedback has to be available alerting the user in case something should have gone wrong. Hence, the shading and rendering technique ultimately used in the rendering stage and data integrity checks are required in the modelling stage.

In our system we utilize several techniques for representing 3D objects, depending on the rendering algorithm at issue. Two popular methods are boundary representations (B-reps) and procedural representations. In the former method objects are approximated by a set of planar polygons or higher order surfaces (patches), while in the latter objects are represented by means of Abstract Data Types and procedures. Objects in our system are structured as a hierarchical composition of more elementary objects, enabling advanced possibilities during the motion specification. Each of these elementary objects has a reference to its parent object, and consists of a number of groups, being sets of polygons (or patches) with identical coloring, shading and/or texturing attributes.

At the user interface level, we developed a modeller in which hierarchical objects can be created, deleted, repositioned, shaped, etc. in an interactive fashion. Starting from 2D primitives (polygons, splines, ...) simple 3D objects can be created, e.g., by transformational sweeps. Two examples of elementary transformational sweep methods, are those in which objects are created by rotating and linking primitive surfaces around an axis or by translating and linking primitives in a certain direction. Through parameterization and combination of these primitive transformations (e.g., scaling and/or translating the 2D primitive while rotating around an axis), more sophisticated objects can be created, e.g., accordions and the like. Other modelling tools enable the animator to construct 3D objects starting from two perpendicular 2D object sections; useful, e.g., while approximating the body and the wings of an airplane. More advanced tools, of which polygonal CSG operations (Laidlaw 1986) are the most important, are under development.

Supplementary to the interactive modeller, we incorporated an integrated programming environment. This environment is a descendant of our IGIP environment (Van Reeth 1988, 1989) and incorporates a language called CAEL - Computer Animation Environment Language - which has the power of a large subset of the Pascal programming language. We use the term "environment language" since the border between language and environment becomes fuzzy in CAEL. The environment makes it possible to visually write (and interprete) syntax-directed programs in order to model objects that are not easily (if not, time consumingly) created "by hand". Examples of such objects are fractal objects (e.g., trees and mountains) or objects consisting of many regularly placed sub-objects (e.g., tiled floors, bridges, sphereflakes (Fig. 3), ...) or objects that change in shape over time.

A simple worked-out example is the construction of a grid consisting of hundreds of tiles which are positioned according to the specifications of the curves "Xtrans" and "Ytrans" (we come back to the curve paradigm in the next section). Figure 4 gives a snapshot of a CAEL program that creates this object. Firstly, a new empty group *grid* -which becomes the current group- is created with a call to *creategroup*. Consequently, object *tile* is made currentobject with an assigment statement. After this, the grid is constructed by repeatedly copying and translating an object "tile" within two nested loops. The routine *copyobjecttogroup* takes the currentobject and copies it into the currentgroup. The routines *tx* and *ty* translate the currentobject (in the currentgroup) by offsets given in previously specified curves *xtrans* and *ytrans* respectively. If an animator should only be capable of specifying the inner loop, then he/she can always use the interactive facilities for repositioning the current object *tile* in order to initialize the next copy iteration in the X direction. (We also have a representation that resembles more to a Pascal alike notation; it just narrows down to invoking another unparser for our internal program representation.)

Other more complicated object modelling programs may, of course, need the intervention of a more experienced programmer. By utilizing curves as parameters, however, the animator can still have control over the shape of the object at issue. Botanical growth models and our sphere mass of Fig. 5 (which is, in fact, a metamorphosis of a colored object) are examples of this.

4. MOTION MODELLING

Three-dimensional computer animation is, in general terms, concerned with manipulating graphical data over time. Hence, an appropriate representation and user interface have to be foreseen that enable the specification of 3D data changement over time. The specification of motion for objects, light sources and virtual cameras in three-dimensional animations, however, is a far from trivial task. In order to enable an animator to perform this task, we developed an animator-oriented graphical motion specification system, incorporating four important aspects : (1) parentizing, (2) curve manipulation, (3) programmings facilities of CAEL, and (4) real time preview.

Fig. 3. A sphereflake, easily created in CAEL

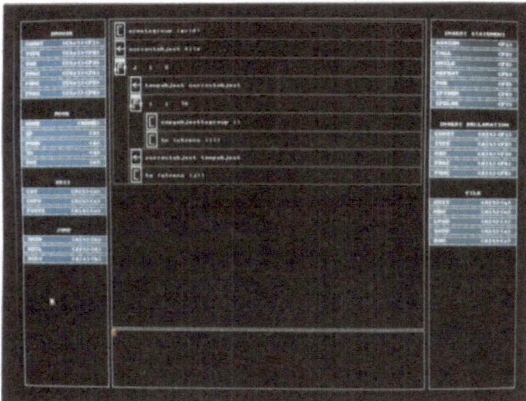

Fig. 4. CAEL program for producing a grid of tiles, according to specifications in the curves "xtrans" and "ytrans"

Fig. 5. Frame of a metamorphosis sequence

Parentizing signifies that objects are defined in a hierarchical structure, implying easy local motion specifiaction (many existing systems have hierarchy in one way or another). By giving a local coordinate axis to each object that moves, animation within objects can easily be performed. As an example, a robot can be taken in which fingers are parentized to a hand, hands are parentized to an arm and arms are parentized to a body : by moving (translating, rotating, skewing, etc. ...) the body, everything parentized to it will move automatically with it, while rotating a finger only requires a rotation relative to its local coordinate axis (as opposed to some global reference point, requiring appropriate additional transformations).

By representing each motion degree of freedom by an *interactively shapable curve*, animators can easily specify choreography of objects without having to write a program. Curves are 2D piecewise cubic splines with a selectable degree of continuity at the joint points, drawn on an axial grid by means of a pointing device (mouse or stylograph). They are manipulated by inserting and repositioning control points. The effect of a changement of a curve on a control point is automatically displayed on the screen. An example of some curve is shown on the screen snapshot in Fig. 6. "Time" is represented on the horizontal axis as a sequence of frame numbers, while on the vertical axis a function XVolume (representing a degree of freedom in volume changement) within a specified range is given.

The ideas behind the curve metaphor are closely related to the ones in (John 1989). An extra potential is available in our metaphor, however, as we can utilize the curve values as parameters in our integrated CAEL progamming environment; cfr. next paragraph. This approach turned out to be well suited for defining local hierarchical motion of objects. We found out the hard way, however, that working with separate 2D curves (e.g., in x-, y-, z- translation and/or rotation) for specifying smooth 3D paths simply doesn't work comfortably. Hence, for objects, lights and cameras that follow certain 3D paths in an animation, 3D splines with editable control points (explicitly represented as objects in the scene) are foreseen. Figure 7 shows a screen snapshot of a 3D path modelling session. By interactively repositioning the 3D curve in the scene, every desired 3D path can be obtained. We currently are finishing an implementation of 4D splines (Spencer-Smith 1989), enabling specification of smooth object movements with accurate control in the time domain.

If a motion nevertheless should be too complex (or have too many parameters) to be specified by curves, one always can take resort to the integrated *programming facilities of CAEL*. By writing a program that calculates consecutive positions of animated objects at issue, one can specify sophisticated motion. Conceptually, the animation features of CAEL narrow down to the ones described in (Ostby 1989). Aside the utilization of traditional functional values and variable values, however, we can also utilize curve values in the environment language. This implies that animators can provide parameter data for fine tuning the animated data - which can be a definition of (or change in) an object's shape, colour, orientation, density, transparency, position or whatever - just by drawing appropriate curves. It turned out that the utilization of curve values is also very handy for experienced programmers, as graphical curves are far more intuitive than encoded functions. We

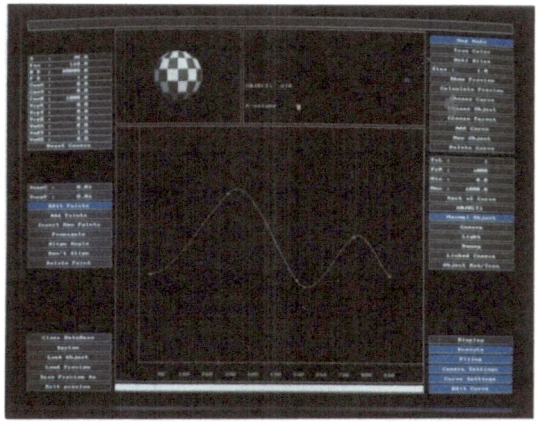

Fig. 6. An example of a curve

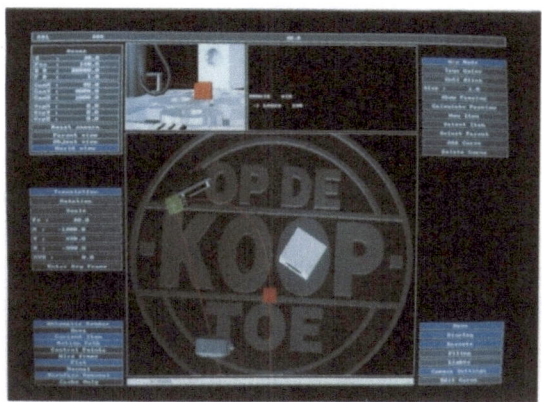

Fig. 7. 3D motion path editing

Fig. 9. Frame from a pinball animation

refer back to Fig. 5 for an example frame from an animation metamorphosis sequence that would require a frustrating amount of data specification if we wouldn't have been able to take recourse to the CAEL facilities.

Last but not least, we implemented the facility to display in real time (25 frames/s) a part of the animation on the screen in any desired rendering technique. This so-called *real time preview* is very important in an animation environment, as it offers the opportunity to get an exact impression of the animation movements without having to make a video recording. The cycle between animation specification and verification can be much faster and more precise in this way. The preview is realized by (i) calculating rapidly a number of frames at lower resolution (one third of the resolution), (ii) storing the frames in the memory of the worker boards, and (iii) finally dumping them in real time to the video RAM via the transputer links. In Fig. 6, a chess-patterned sphere is displayed in the lower resolution preview screen.

5. RENDERING

Image synthesis algorithms can generally be divided in three classes : scan-line algorithms, Z-buffer algorithms and ray tracing algorithms. In the scan-line approach, it is possible to generate images very fastly, given a not too complex scene and a relatively low degree of realism (for fairly complex scenes, rendering times tend to grow drastically). A Z-buffer algorithm can process very complex scenes, implying that an average application takes more time. Because of the potentially higher complexity, images of higher quality can be rendered. The most superior images, however, are created with the ray tracing technique, as (opposed to the previous approaches) reflection-, refraction- and shadow-effects are taken into account. On classic workstations, the rendering timings per frame for complex scenes can be several hours or even days.

In our rendering system a parallel Z-buffer algorithm as well as a parallel ray tracer are implemented. Conceptually, these algorithms are akin to the ones in INMOS technical notes 37 and 7 (Atkin 1987; Packer 1987). In the ray tracer as well as in the Z-buffer, parallelism is introduced by dividing the overall screen into screen regions and by distributing the pixel values to be calculated among the available processors. Each of these regions can be looked upon as being the screen of virtual region cameras, which are subcameras of the overall virtual camera. The m x n resolution of the screen region depends on the rendering algorithm at issue. For ray tracing, this resolution is about 16 x 16, whereas in scan conversion algorithms the horizontal screen region resolution equals the overall resolution. The exploitation of coherence is one of the main factors in the resolution determination.

The amount of work - opposed to the amount of communications - to be done at the pixel level, is crucial for maintaining a linear ratio "perfomance / number of processors". The load balance in the ray tracer can be kept optimal relatively easily, as (1) rays are fired in the scene independently of one another, and (2) the number and the complexity of the calculations to be performed per pixel are rather large. The more simple the processing per pixel becomes, the more complicated it becomes to keep the procesors usefully busy. Hence, the optimizing of parallelization of a Z-buffer algorithm is already a bit more difficult. Through introduction of some buffering processes (Fig. 8) and a good distribution of the rendering pipeline (transformation - clipping - perspective division - shading - scan conversion - image storage) over the available processors, it is possible to maintain an almost linear expandability. The buffer processes are an example of useful parallelization on one specific processor.

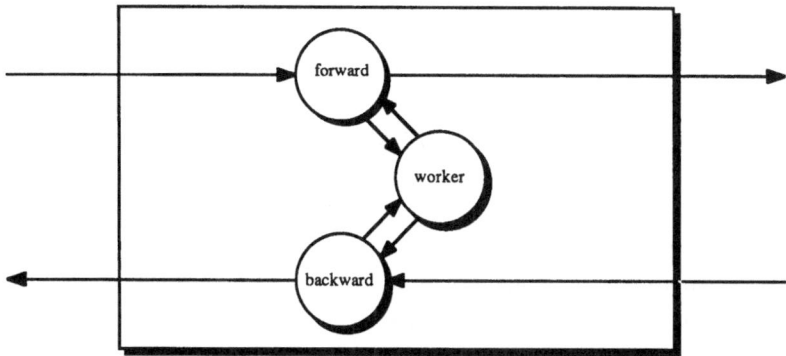

Processes on the raytracer

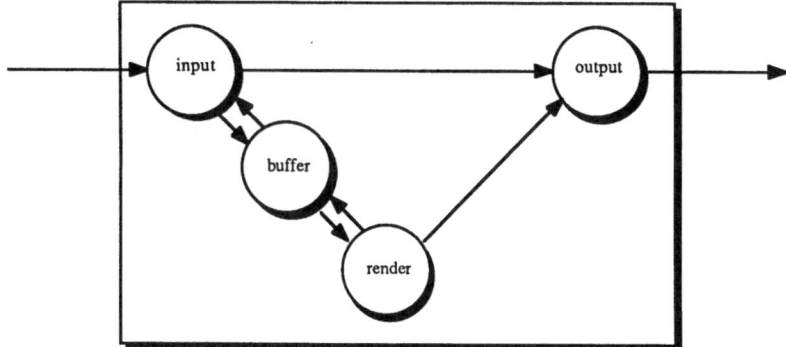

Processes on the polygon renderer

Fig. 8. Buffering processes

Within the basic rendering algorithms, some other facilities are integrated also. First of all, parallel algorithms to conquer anti-aliasing (Crow 1981; Van Reeth 1990) are incorporated. Figure 9 gives a snapshot of one frame from a one minute ray traced pinball animation. It took 6 minutes to render the anti-aliased 768 x 576 frame on 13 processors.

Additional optimizations, of which the exploitation of coherence (Kaplan 1987) is the most important, have been incorporated in the ray tracer. (Indeed, the parallelization of an efficient algorithm is always preferable above parallelizing a less efficient one). Aside the anti-aliasing algorithms, a number of parallelized methods are available to enhance the surface structure of 3D objects via texture mapping techniques (Heckbert 1986). Appropriate illumination models (Hall 1989) are foreseen in the shading process, enabling the simulation of several lighting effects. We finish this section by stating that considerable effort has been put in efficiently parallel ray tracing curved surfaces (Lamotte 1991).

6. CONCLUSIONS AND FUTURE RESEARCH

This paper gave an overview of the design and implementation of our parallel computer animation system. We described how transputers can be utilized in order to realize a powerful, extensible animation platform. It is shown how we combined traditional object- and motion modelling techniques with more sophisticated facilities of our Computer Animation Environment Language CAEL.

Future research can be done in several directions. Firstly, it can be very interesting to investigate what the advantages to computer animation can be of utilizing an order of magnitude more processors (i.e. going from our current number of 32 transputers to a tenfold of this). Secondly, it might be useful to see how special purpose hardware can be incorporated in a transputer based architecture (given the fact that they can easily be interfaced at the hardware level). Finally, it can be beneficial to further investigate what the effects of CAEL alike systems in (i) the modelling of particle systems (Reeves 1983) are in parallel architectures (given the fact that particle systems can take hours to render), and in (ii) the modelling of promising motion specification approaches (Van Overveld 1990).

7 ACKNOWLEDGEMENTS

We would like to thank all our colleagues at the Applied Computer Science Lab for providing the plesant surroundings that enabled the realization of our computer animation system. Our special expression of thanks goes to Johan Claes, Koen Elens, Wim Lamotte, Raf Van Ham, Erwin Vanhees and Rudi Welter for their tremendous help at the implementational level.

REFERENCES

Atkin P, Packer J (1987) High Performance Graphics with the IMS T800. INMOS Technical Note 37

Crow F (1981) A Comparison of Antialiasing Techniques. IEEE CG&A 1 (1) : 40-48

Feiner S, Salesin D, Banchoff T (1982) Dial: A diagrammatic animation language. IEEE CG &A 2 (7) : 43-54.

Gomez JE (1984) Twixt: a 3D Animation System. Proc. Eurographics'84, pp. 121-133.

Hall R (1989) Illumination and Color in Computer Generated Imagery. Springer Verlag, Tokio Berlin Heidelberg New York London Paris

Heckbert PS (1986) Survey of Texture Mapping. IEEE CG&A 6 (11) : 56-57

Hoare CAR (1985) Communicating Sequential Processes. Prentice-Hall, U.K.

INMOS Limited (1988) OCCAM2 Reference Manual. Prentice-Hall, New York London Toronto Sydney Tokyo

John NW, Willis PJ (1989) Some Methods to Choreograph and Implement Motion in Computer Animation. In: Magnenat-Thalmann N, Thalmann D (eds.), State-of-the-art in Computer Animation. Proc. of Computer Animation'89, pp. 125-140.

Kaplan MR (1987) The Use of Spatial Coherence in Ray Tracing. In: Rogers DF, Earnshaw RA (eds.) Techniques for Computer Graphics. Springer Verlag, Tokio Berlin Heidelberg New York London Paris

Krömker D, Hofmann GR (1989) Computer Animation. Tutorial Notes 13 of Eurographics'89

Laidlow DH, Trumbore WB, Hughes JF (1986) Constructive Solid Geometry for Polyhedral Objects. Computer Graphics (Proc. SIGGRAPH'86) 20 (4) : 161-170

Lamotte W, Elens K, Flerackers E (1991) Surface Tree Caching for Rendering Patches in a Parallel Ray Tracing System. accpeted for publication in Proc. Computer Graphics International '91.

Magnenat-Thalmann N, Thalmann D (1985) Computer Animation, Theory and Practice", Springer-Verlag, Tokio Berlin Heidelberg New York

Magnenat-Thalmann N, Thalmann D (1985) An indexed Bibliogaphy on Computer Animation. IEEE CG&A 5 (7) : 76-86

Magnenat-Thalmann N, Thalmann D (1989) (eds.) State-of-the-art in Computer Animation. Proc. of Computer Animation'89, Springer-Verlag, Tokio Berlin Heidelberg New York London Paris

Ostby EF (1989) Simplified Control of Complex Animation. In: Magnenat-Thalmann N, Thalmann D (eds.), State-of-the-art in Computer Animation. Proc. of Computer Animation'89, pp. 59-67.

Packer J (1987) Exploiting Concurrency : A Ray Tracing Example. INMOS Technical Note 7

Reeves WT (1983) Particle Sytems - A Technique for Modelling a Class of Fuzzy Objects. Computer Graphics (Proc. SIGGRAPH '83) 17 (3) : 263-269.

Reynolds CW (1982) Computer Animation with Scripts and Actors. Computer Graphics (Proc. SIGGRAPH '82) 16 (3): 289-296

Spencer-Smith T, Wyvill G (1989) Four Dimensional Splines for Motion Control in Computer Animation. In: Magnenat-Thalmann N, Thalmann D (eds.), State-of-the-art in Computer Animation. Proc. of Computer Animation'89, pp. 153-167

Stern G (1983) Bboop: A System for 3D- Key Frame Figure Animation. Tutorial Notes of SIGGRAPH'83 pp. 240-243

Van Overveld CWAM (1990) A Technique for Motion Specification in Computer Animation. The Visual Computer 6 (2) : 106-116

Van Reeth F, Flerackers E, D'Hondt T (1988) IGIP: A Framework Towards Open-Ended Visual Programming. Proc. 4th IEEE CS Workshop on Visual Languages, pp. 239-247.

Van Reeth F, Flerackers E (1989) Visual (Meta-) Porgramming in a CASE Context. Proc. CASE'89, suppl. vol., pp. 101-114.

Van Reeth F, Welter R, Flerackers E (1990) Virtual Camera Oversampling : A New Parallel Anti-Aliasing Method for Z-Buffer Algorithms. Proc. Computer Graphics International '90, pp. 241-254.

Frank Van Reeth is a research assistant at the Limburg University Center and a member of the research staff at the Applied Computer Science Laboratory in the same university. He obtained his Master's Degree in Computer Science in 1987 at the Free University of Brussels, Belgium. His current research interests include 3D rendering, animation, parallel processing and visual programming environments. He is member of CGS.

Address: Applied Computer Science Laboratory, Limburg University Center, B3590 Diepenbeek, Belgium

Eddy Flerackers is currently full Professor of Computer Science at the Limburg University Center, Belgium. He studied Physics at the University of Louvain, Belgium. He received his PhD in Physics in 1980 at the Free University of Brussels with a thesis on nuclear structure calculations. Since 1987 he is Director of the Applied Computer Science Laboratory at the Limburg University Center. He is also promotor of a Governmental project for the introduction of computers and computer science in education. His research interests include computer graphics, 3D computer animation, scientific visualisation, simulation and programming environments.

Address: Applied Computer Science Laboratory, Limburg University Center, B3590 Diepenbeek, Belgium

Extensions of the Color-Cell-Compression-Algorithm

MARKUS PINS

ABSTRACT

A non information preserving technique for compression of images and image sequences is presented. The algorithm can be applied to color images and colored image sequences, which are created with synthetic image generation methods or digitized by a video scanner.
The method is based upon the color-cell-compression-algorithm (CCC) described by CAMPBELL ET AL. Using the extended CCC-algorithm for image sequences, a reduction in storage space to 0.6% to 3% of the original data size can be achieved. Implementation on todays workstation is easily done, real-time decompression and displaying on bitmap-screens is possible with conventional hardware.

Keywords: data compression, block-truncation-coding, quantization

1 INTRODUCTION

Compression algorithms can be distinguished in information preserving methods, which eliminate redundancy, and information loss algorithms, which do not preserve the original but perform well with respect to some fidelity criteria.
Information loss methods achieve better compression ratios than information preserving methods. They are suitable for images and image sequences when bigger changes in luminance are avoided. Because the human eye is sensitive to luminance faults but insensitive to changes in chrominance, small deviations have only minor effects on image quality.
This paper uses as a starting point the CCC-algorithm which is described in section 2. The Extended CCC-algorithm (ECCC) with a dynamic subdivision scheme is presented in section 3. How the ECCC-algorithm is applied to image sequences is shown in section 4. A summary of the paper is given in section 5.

2 THE CCC-ALGORITHM

Raster images, occurring in computer graphics, typically require 24 bit/pixel. Every raster element (i, j), called pixel, is a combination of three channels, red, green and blue.
The CCC-algorithm for the compression of color images bases upon block truncation coding, developed by DELP and MITCHELL (1979,1980). The CCC-algorithm, published in CAMPBELL ET AL.(1986), is described in three refinement levels. The last refinement, achieving a compression ratio of approximately 2 bit/pixel is explained in this section.

In a first step, the RGB-image is extended by a luminance channel Y, known from the *NTSC*-TV standard. The luminance value Y can be computed to

$$Y(i,j) = 0.30 * R(i,j) + 0.59 * G(i,j) + 0.11 * B(i,j). \tag{1}$$

In a second step, the input image is decomposed in non-overlapping cells of size 4×4. For every cell, the average luminance $\overline{Y}$ is computed with (1).

To explain the algorithm, an example cell is shown in fig. 1.

$(182, 121, 242)$	$(142, 129, 138)$	$(230, 9, 162)$	$(190, 17, 58)$
$(22, 153, 82)$	$(238, 161, 234)$	$(70, 41, 2)$	$(30, 49, 154)$
$(118, 185, 178)$	$(78, 193, 74)$	$(166, 73, 98)$	$(126, 81, 250)$
$(214, 217, 18)$	$(174, 225, 170)$	$(6, 105, 194)$	$(222, 113, 90)$

Figure 1: A 4×4 color cell E

Figure 2 contains the additional luminance channel, computed for example cell E.

152	133	92	73
105	192	45	54
164	145	103	113
194	203	85	143

Figure 2: Luminance channel of example cell E

The mean luminance $\overline{Y}$, (in our example $\overline{Y} = 125.17$). is used to partition each cell into two areas, one with higher luminance than $\overline{Y}$, one with lower or equal luminance. Both areas are represented in a bitmap B. A binary 1 means, that the luminance is higher than $\overline{Y}$. The resulting bitmap B, computed for cell E, is shown in fig. 3.

1	1	0	0
0	1	0	0
1	1	0	0
1	1	0	1

Figure 3: Bitmap B of example cell E

The bitmap b is used to partition the pixels of the corresponding RGB-cell. An average color is chosen for both partitions of the bitmap and stored in a temporary file. Having collected all values of the temporary file, a color lookup table of 256 colors is chosen by HECKBERTS median-cut-algorithm (1982). Now every 4×4 cell can be represented by a 4×4 bitmap and two lookup table entries. At this point, the cell has been compressed to $4 * 4 * 1$ bit $+$ 2 byte $= 4$ byte, requiring $4 * 4 * 3$ byte $= 48$ byte without compression.

Additionaly, the 256 color lookup table, needing $256 * 3$ byte $= 768$ byte, must be stored. If large images are stored, the additional lookup table has only small influence to the compression results. Choosing a smaller color table yields only minor improvements of the compression results, but increases run-time, because additional bit-access-operations are needed.

When compressing with information loss, we are not only interested in the achieved compression result. We also need a measure for the visual performance of the compression algorithm. Commonly used image fidelity measures are the *mean-square-error* (MSE) and the *signal-to-noise-ratio* (SNR), compare PRATT(1978) and CHANG (1989).

Definition MSE:

Let A denote the original data and B the compressed and then decompressed data. The size of an image is given by $N \times M$ pixel. The number of images in a sequence is denoted by T. The MSE between A and B is then defined as

$$MSE_{(2)} = \frac{1}{M \cdot N} \sum_{i=1}^{N} \sum_{j=1}^{M} (A(i,j) - B(i,j))^2$$

$$MSE_{(3)} = \frac{1}{T \cdot M \cdot N} \sum_{s=1}^{T} \sum_{i=1}^{N} \sum_{j=1}^{M} (A(i,j,t) - B(i,j,s))^2$$

Definition SNR:

The SNR is defined as

$$SNR_{(2)} = \frac{\displaystyle\sum_{i=1}^{N} \sum_{j=1}^{M} A(i,j)^2}{\displaystyle\sum_{i=1}^{N} \sum_{j=1}^{M} (A(i,j) - B(i,j))^2}$$

$$SNR_{(3)} = \frac{\displaystyle\sum_{s=1}^{S} \sum_{i=1}^{N} \sum_{j=1}^{M} A(i,j,s)^2}{\displaystyle\sum_{t=1}^{T} \sum_{i=1}^{N} \sum_{j=1}^{M} (A(i,j,t) - B(i,j,t))^2}$$

If A and B are identical, the value of SNR is infinite.

Both measures are easy to compute; therefore they are often used for compression system design and tuning.

To compare compression ratios and image fidelity of the CCC-algorithm and the ECCC-algorithm, nine test images with size 512×512 pixel = 786432 byte were chosen. The first three pictures (**O1, O2, O3**) are generated by raytracing, using no texture mapping. The next three pictures are created by raytracing, using texture mapping. The last three pictures (**K1, K2, K3**) are digitized by a video-scanner.

The CCC-algorithm was applied to all test images, using cell-sizes from 2×2 to 8×8. Figure 4 shows the size of a compressed image, giving absolute and relative values.

(2×2)	(4×4)	(6×6)	(8×8)
164598 Byte	66294 Byte	48090 Byte	41718 Byte
20.76 %	8.36 %	6.06 %	5.26 %

Figure 4: CCC-algorithms compression ratios, using different cell-sizes

The visual performance of the CCC-algorithm, applied to the test images, is shown in fig. 5.

Image	(2 × 2)		(4 × 4)		(6 × 6)		(8 × 8)	
	MSE	SNR	MSE	SNR	MSE	SNR	MSE	SNR
O1	179.821	112.536	200.267	100.895	291.611	67.708	323.307	60.649
O2	431.412	20.937	402.357	21.636	523.567	15.986	557.845	14.679
O3	811.982	10.431	862.472	8.896	1112.827	6.3395	1233.387	5.418
M1	85.964	69.181	72.753	78.646	148.330	36.460	174.724	29.969
M2	368.753	39.907	482.892	29.151	650.2185	20.755	714.594	18.400
M3	157.056	109.729	185.125	90.683	279.479	58.499	325.4092	49.393
K1	59.205	196.965	76.737	149.315	121.029	93.088	153.501	72.512
K2	15.140	230.732	21.802	157.829	27.345	123.975	31.276	107.372
K3	59.876	176.649	78.229	132.129	130.164	77.577	158.199	62.869

Figure 5: CCC-algorithms information loss, using different cell-sizes

3   THE EXTENDED CCC-ALGORITHM FOR SINGLE IMAGES (ECCC)

The CCC-algorithm guarantees that the compression ratio will not change with image complexity. This may be regarded as a disadvantage, because this inflexibility spends as much information on complex parts of the image as on simple background.

Using a dynamic subdivision scheme, this deficit may be circumvented by chosing a varying number of colors per cell and different cell sizes, depending on the complexity of the image. Allowing one, two or four colors per cell, none, one or two bit per pixel are needed to partition the cell in areas of differing luminance.

Selecting the colors for each cell proceeds similar to the CCC-algorithm. The mean luminance $\overline{Y}$ is computed for each cell. If four colors are wanted, the average luminances for both resulting areas from the first step (one with higher, one with lower luminance) are computed once more again.

A simpler method is to divide the minimal, average and maximal luminance into four intervals

$$[Y_{min}, \frac{Y_{min} + \overline{Y}}{2}) \quad ; \quad [\frac{Y_{min} + \overline{Y}}{2}, \overline{Y}) \quad ; \quad [\overline{Y}, \frac{\overline{Y} + Y_{max}}{2}) \quad ; \quad [\frac{\overline{Y} + Y_{max}}{2}, Y_{max}) \tag{2}$$

The computation of the four color values is done by averaging all color values, whose luminance is contained in one interval.

Another strategy to adapt the algorithm to image complexity is to vary the sizes of the cells. The algorithm starts with a predefined maximal cell size of 32 × 32 pixel. If the estimated deviation between the original values and the compressed version of a cell exceeds a preset threshold, the cell is subdivided into four subcells and the algorithm is applied to each subcell. Subdivision is repeated until the deviation is smaller than the preset threshold or a minimal cellsize is reached. The deviation is measured as mean-square-error (MSE) of the original image cell and the compressed and decompressed cell. Experience has shown that the value for the average deviation should be approximately 10 to 15 units. Subdivision is terminated whenever the cellsize reaches 8 × 8 pixel.

To decide wether a cell is divided into four subcells or wether it can be coded with two or four colors, the mean-square-error needs to be computed for two and four colors. If the mean-square-error for two colors is smaller than the preset threshold, no subdivision is needed and the cell can be coded with two colors. If the mean-square-error exceeds the preset limit, coding with four colors is tested. Exceeding the threshold again, the cell must be subdivided into four subcells. These extensions result in better image quality and better compression results, compared with the simple CCC-algorithm. The biggest part of the compressed image consists of the bitmaps, therefore attention should be payed to them. Executing a foreground/background analysis, which can be done with edge detection for example, the parts of the image needing exact reproduction can be estimated. For other parts like the background, exact reproduction is not necessary, because the human eye is nearly unable to distinguish minor changes in uniformly colored and unmoved areas of the image.

Therefore, the computed bitmap can be replaced by a reference to a similar bitmap, occurring in the picture. Without this modification, the ECCC-algorithm achieves a compression to approximately 7 − 8% of the original size. Using the reference method, approximately 6 − 7% can be achieved.

If a bitmap attached to the background is nearly uniform (less than 5% ones respectively zeros), it can be substituted by a uniform bitmap of zeros or ones. Because the color lookup table entries are identical for uniform bitmaps, it is not necessary to store the bitmap.

Similar to the representation of bitmaps by references, color lookup table entries can be replaced by references too. But this modification is not profitable, because there are minor improvements only.

Better compression results (approximately up to 4 − 5%) can be achieved, if the output created by the ECCC-Algorithm is compressed with other information preserving methods.

If the compression results are more important than image quality, another improvement is to reduce the vertical resolution. Approximately 2 − 3% can be reached when only every second line is compressed. During decompressing the unconsidered lines are reconstructed by doubling the last line or interpolating between two successive lines.

Figure 6 shows the compression results of the ECCC-algorithm, compared with the CCC-algorithm. The original image size is 512×512 pixel = 786432 byte. The threshold for subdivision was chosen in a way to achieve really good image quality. Column one shows the image names, column two, three and four the relative resulting size ρ of the compressed image, the MSE and the SNR for the CCC-algorithm. The results of the ECCC-algorithm are shown in columns five, six and seven.

Name	CCC-algorithm (4×4)			ECCC-algorithm		
	ρ	MSE	SNR	ρ	MSE	SNR
O1	8.36%	200.267	100.895	5.99%	35.389	568.272
O2	8.36%	402.357	21.636	7.29%	65.151	140.171
O3	8.36%	862.472	8.896	7.47%	272.489	31.474
M1	8.36%	72.753	78.646	8.31%	40.336	150.886
M2	8.36%	482.892	29.151	7.31%	47.009	318.634
M3	8.36%	185.125	90.683	7.91%	69.519	249.983
K1	8.36%	76.737	149.315	5.69%	50.097	234.314
K2	8.36%	21.802	157.829	5.08%	20.479	171.252
K3	8.36%	78.229	132.129	6.83%	51.996	205.266

Figure 6: ECCC-algorithm with small information loss

By allowing more deviation between original data and compressed and then decompressed image the rate of compression can be improved. Figure 7 shows the compression results of the ECCC-algorithm with moderate information loss.

Name	CCC-algorithm (4×4)			ECCC-algorithm		
	ρ	MSE	SNR	ρ	MSE	SNR
O1	8.36%	200.267	100.895	4.68%	45.214	443.835
O2	8.36%	402.357	21.636	6.52%	91.409	99.687
O3	8.36%	862.472	8.896	7.51%	296.375	28.675
M1	8.36%	72.753	78.646	6.09%	72.793	83.576
M2	8.36%	482.892	29.151	6.50%	69.910	213.286
M3	8.36%	185.125	90.683	6.88%	92.709	186.859
K1	8.36%	76.737	149.315	4.42%	63.090	186.099
K2	8.36%	21.802	157.829	3.41%	31.068	112.958
K3	8.36%	78.229	132.129	6.29%	67.249	158.625

Figure 7: ECCC-algorithm with moderate information loss

4 THE EXTENDED CCC-ALGORITHM FOR IMAGE SEQUENCES (ECCCS)

The advantages of dynamic subdivision described in the last section can be used for image sequences, too. Instead of using cells of size ($n \times m$), cubes of size ($n \times m \times t$) are considered. Experience has shown that both the width n and the length m should adopt values of eight pixels each. Dynamic subdivision is achieved by varying depth t, with legal values of one, two or four. Every cube is now represented by two or four color lookup table entries and the bitmap. If the two colortable entries in a cell are identical, no bitmap is needed. The bitmap has only depth one. If the cube has depth two or four, the bitmap of size $n \times m$ is repeated implicitly for the planes two to four.

The algorithm works in two steps. In the first step, a color lookup table is computed for each image. We have to consider two major points:

- We are interested in only small deviations between successive lookup tables.

- The labels of a particular color in two successive lookup tables should be equal, in order to achieve better compression results.

An algorithm which incorporates these ideas is the FAMM-algorithm (Frame Adaptive Migration Mean), described by GOLDBERG and SUN (1988). It is an iterative clustering algorithm, working in three steps. The first step includes the quantisation of the next image, using the last lookup table. In the second step, the average of all colors, quantized to a label in the lookup table, is computed and the lookup table is updated. This process is repeated, until the distortion between input image and quantized image can not be further reduced. Now, the third step takes place. Each color of the previous and the present lookup table is compared. If the difference is greater than a preset threshold, the previous lookup table entry is replaced by the new value.

It can be shown that the FAMM-algorithm converges only to a local optimum, depending upon the initial lookup table. Therefore it is very important, to chose a high quality initial lookup table. Algorithms having this property are described in HECKBERT (1982) or HILD and PINS (1989).

In the second step of the ECCCS-algorithms, four images are considered simultaneous. By making a foreground/background analysis, which can be done with edge detection for example, the parts of the image needing exact reproduction can be estimated. The background is coded with cubes of depth four, complex or motioned parts are coded in cubes of depth two or one, depending on the contents of the cube. The algorithm, described up to now, can be improved:

Figure 8: Original image with 24 bits per pixel

Figure 9: Same image reduced to 2.89% of the original size

Figure 10: Same image reduced to 1.81% of the original size

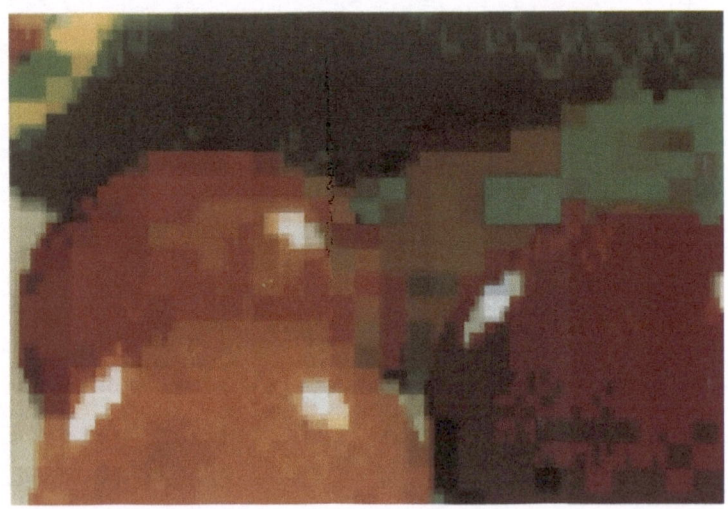

Figure 11: Zoomed up region from fig. 10

- If two colors which describe one cube are very similar, only one is used and the bitmap needs not to be stored. This strategy is only allowed, if the cell to be coded is very dark or very bright, because the human eye is insensitive to luminance in this range, compare MURCH (1986) or DURETT (1987).

- If a bitmap attached to the background is nearly uniform (less than 5% ones respectively zeros), it can be substituted by a uniform bitmap of zeros or ones. Because the color lookup table entries are identical for uniform bitmaps, it is not necessary to store the bitmap.

- When the minimal cube depth is preset to the value two, better compression ratios can be achieved. A drawback is the reduced image quality.

- Despite reducing resolution in depth, the horizontal or vertical resolution can be reduced, too. Experience has shown, that bisection of vertical resolution increase alias effects. De-compression is done by doubling of lines or linear interpolation between two successive lines.

- Because there are a lot of parts in most image sequences with no or only minor changes, up to 50% of the image can be maintained. Cubes with no or minor changes will be replaced by a special command, reducing information to be stored from two colortable entries and one bitmap to one special command.

Three test sequences were used, to examine the ECCCS-algorithm. Sequence one and two were generated synthetically by raytracing, the third sequence was digitized by a video-scanner.
The first column of the tree following tabulars contains the options, used by the algorithm. No option means, that image-resolution is not reduced. Option 1 allows only cubes of depth two or four. With Option 2, vertical resolution is bisected. The second column displays the compression result, columns three and four shows the visual performance of the algorithm.

Options	ECCCS-algorithm	MSE	SNR
No option	1.826%	153.205	168.291
Option 1	1.236%	166.099	153.625
Option 2	0.989%	348.572	73.193
Option 1 + 2	0.657%	355.786	71.586

Application of ECCCS-algorithm on sequence 1

Options	ECCCS-algorithm	MSE	SNR
No option	2.893%	130.2713	61.603
Option 1	1.805%	170.019	46.883
Option 2	1.719%	258.886	30.806
Option 1 + 2	1.001%	303.242	26.104

Application of ECCCS-algorithm on sequence 2

Options	ECCCS-algorithm	MSE	SNR
No option	3.121%	366.122	76.527
Option 1	1.986%	376.218	73.879
Option 2	1.645%	447.233	61.837
Option 1 + 2	1.019%	461.106	59.836

Application of ECCCS-algorithm on sequence 3

To visualize the properties of the ECCCS-algorithm, an image out of sequence 2 is shown in fig. 8. Figure 9 shows the same image using the ECCCS-algorithm with no additional options. The result using the ECCCS-algorithm with option 1 is presented in fig. 10. A zoomed up region is given in fig. 11 to show edge aliasing and other artifacts in detail. The brown region is the position of a moving sphere occuring in the next frame. This temporal aliasing has no effect on visual performance, because display time is too short to recognize these artifacts.

5   CONCLUSIONS

In this paper, the Extended Color Cell Compression algorithm (ECCC) has been described. It is useful for lossy compression of color images and colored image sequences, which are created with synthetic image generation methods or digitized by a video scanner.
The savings in space are superior to the CCC-algorithm and receive a better image quality also at the same time. Using the ECCC-algorithm for image sequences, compression ratios from 0.6% to 3% can be achieved.
Implementation on todays workstations is easily done, real-time decompression and displaying on bitmap-screens is possible with conventional hardware.

ACKNOWLEDGEMENTS

The author would like to express his appreciation to Prof. Heinrich Müller and Hermann Hild for reviewing this manuscript, and to Achim Stößer, who has designed the pictorial examples.

REFERENCES

G. Campbell, T.A. DeFanti, J. Frederiksen, S.A. Joyce, A.L. Lawrence, J.A. Lindberg, D.J. Sandin (1986). *Two Bit/Pixel Full Color Encoding. Computer Graphics*, 20(4):215–223.

S.K. Chang (1989). *Principles of Pictorial information systems design*. Prentice-Hall.

E.J. Delp, O.R. Mitchell (1979). *Image Compression using Block Truncation Coding. IEEE Transactions on Communications*, 27(9):1335–1342.

J.H. Durrett, editor (1987). *Color and the Computer*. Academic Press.

M. Goldberg, H. Sun (1988). *Frame Adaptive Vector Quantization for Image Sequence Coding. IEEE Transactions on Communications*, 36(5):629–635.

P.S. Heckbert (1982). *Color Image Quantization for Frame Buffer Display. Computer Graphics*, 16(3):297–305.

H. Hild, M. Pins (1989). *Variations on a Dither Algorithm*. In *EUROGRAPHICS'89*, pp. 381–392. North-Holland.

O.R. Mitchell, E.J. Delp (1980). *Multilevel Graphics Representation using Block Truncation Coding. Proceedings of the IEEE*, 68(7):868–873.

G.M. Murch (1986). *Human Factors of Color Displays. Eurographic Seminars*, Advances in Computer Graphics II:1–27.

W.K. Pratt (1978). *Digital Image Processing*. John Wiley and Sons.

Markus Pins is currently a research and teaching assistant in Computer Science at the University of Karlsruhe (Germany). He received his diploma in 1987 and the doctoral degree in computer science from the University of Karlsruhe in 1990. His research interests include computer games, computer graphics, computer aided design, image reproduction techniques and data compression.
Adress: Universität Karlsruhe, Institut für Betriebs- und Dialogsysteme, Fasanengarten 5, 7500 Karlsruhe, Deutschland
E-mail: mp@ira.uka.de

Author Index

Keyword Index